UNIVERSITY WRITING: SELVES AND TEXTS IN ACADEMIC SOCIETIES

STUDIES IN WRITING
Series Editor: Gert Rijlaarsdam

Recent titles in this series:

VAN WAES, LEIJTEN AND NEUWIRTH
Writing and Digital Media

SULLIVAN AND LINDGREN
Computer Key-Stroke Logging and Writing

HIDI AND BOSCOLO
Writing and Motivation

TORRANCE, VAN WAES AND GALBRAITH
Writing and Cognition

ALAMARGOT, TERRIER AND CELLIER
Written Documents in the Workplace

HA AND BAURAIN
Voices, Identities, Negotiations, and Conflicts: Writing Academic English Across Cultures

L'ABATE and SWEENEY
Research on Writing Approaches in Mental Health

Related journals:

Journal of Writing Research
Written Communication
L1 - Educational Studies in Language and Literature
Learning and Instruction
Educational Research Review
Assessing Writing
Computers and Composition
Journal of Second Language Writing

UNIVERSITY WRITING: SELVES AND TEXTS IN ACADEMIC SOCIETIES

EDITED BY

MONTSERRAT CASTELLÓ

Department of Psychology, Ramon Llull University, Barcelona, Spain

CHRISTIANE DONAHUE

Institute for Writing and Rhetoric, Dartmouth College, Hanover, NH, USA

United Kingdom • North America • Japan
India • Malaysia • China

Emerald Group Publishing Limited
Howard House, Wagon Lane, Bingley BD16 1WA, UK

First edition 2012

British Library Cataloguing in Publication Data
A catalogue record for this book is available from the British Library

ISBN: 978-1-78052-386-6
ISSN: 1572-6304 (Series)

ISOQAR certified
Management Systems,
awarded to Emerald for
adherence to Quality
and Environmental
standards ISO 9001:2008
and 14001:2004,
respectively

Certificate Number 1985
ISO 9001
ISO 14001

INVESTOR IN PEOPLE

Contents

List of Contributors

Charles Bazerman

Education Department, University of California, Santa Barbara, CA, USA.
E-mail: bazerman@education.ucsb.edu

Rebecca Bilbro

Office of Communications, Occupational Safety and Health Administration, U.S. Department of Labor, 200 Constitution Avenue, Washington, D.C. 20210.
E-mail: bilbro@gmail.com

Françoise Boch

Laboratoire Lidilem, EA609, Université Grenoble 3, France.
E-mail: francoise.boch@u-grenoble3.fr

Paula Carlino

CONICET (National Council of Scientific and Technical Research)/University of Buenos Aires, Miguel Cane 2046, Villa Adelina (C. P. 1607), Buenos Aires, Argentina.
E-mail: paulacarlino@yahoo.com

Montserrat Castelló

Department of Psychology, Graduate School of Psychology, Blanquerna, Císter, 34, 08022; Ramon Llull University, Barcelona, Spain.
E-mail: Montserratcb@blanquerna.url.edu

Madalina Chitez

Department of Applied Linguistics, Zurich University of Applied Sciences, Theaterstrasse 17, Winterthur, 8401 Zurich, Switzerland.
E-mail: madalina.chitez@zhaw.ch

Viviana Cortes

Georgia State University, 34 Peachtree St. Suite 1200, One Park Tower Building, Atlanta, 30303 GA, USA.
E-mail: eslvsc@langate.gsu.edu

Isabelle Delcambre

Education Sciences, Théodile-Cirel (Ea 4354)-UFR des Sciences de l'education, Université de Lille III, Villeneuve D'ASCQ, France.
E-mail: isabelle.delcambre-derville@univ-lille3.fr

Christiane Donahue   Institute for Writing and Rhetoric, Dartmouth
College (USA) and Théodile-CIREL (Ea 4354),
208 Baker HB 6250, IWR, Hanover NH 03755, USA.
E-mail: Christiane.Donahue@Dartmouth.Edu

Olga Dysthe   Department of Education, University of
Bergen, Norway.
E-mail: Olga.Dysthe@iuh.uib.no

Anna Iñesta   Department of People Management and
Organization, ESADE Business School, Universitat
Ramon Llull, Av. Torre Blanca, 59, Sant Cugat,
08172 Barcelona, Spain.
E-mail: ana.inesta@esade.edu

Nancy Keranen   Facultad de Lenguas, Benemérita Universidad
Autónoma de Puebla, 24 Norte #2003
Colonia Humbold, Mexico.
E-mail: Lajoya108@yahoo.com

Otto Kruse   Department of Applied Linguistics,
Centre for Professional Writing, Zurich University of
Applied Sciences, Theaterstrasse 17, Winterthur,
8401 Zurich, Switzerland.
E-mail: otto.kruse@zhaw.ch

Mary R. Lea   Institute of Educational Technology,
Open University, Walton Hall, Milton Keynes, UK.
E-mail: m.r.lea@open.ac.uk

Theresa Lillis   The Open University, Milton Keynes, UK.
E-mail: T.M.Lillis@open.ac.uk

Mar Mateos   Universidad Autónoma de Madrid, Campus de
Cantoblanco, Facultad de Psicología, 28049
Madrid, Spain.
E-mail: mar.mateos@uam.es

Nancy Nelson   College of Education, University of North Texas,
1155 Union Circle #3100740, Denton,
TX 76203-5017 USA.
E-mail: Nancy.Nelson@unt.edu

Paul Prior   Department of English; Center for Writing Studies,
275 English Building, 608 S. Wright Street,
University of Illinois at Urbana-Champaign,
Urbana, IL 61801, USA.
E-mail: pprior@illinois.edu

Fátima Encinas Prudencio Facultad de Lenguas, Benemérita Universidad
Autónoma de Puebla, 24 Norte #2003
Colonia Humbold, Mexico.
E-mail: fatimaencinas@gmail.com

Fanny Rinck Laboratoire Modyco UMR7114, CNRS/Université
Paris Ouest Nanterre La Défense, France.
E-mail: fanny.rinck@u-paris10.fr

Anna Robinson-Pant Centre for Applied Research in Education (CARE),
School of Education and Lifelong Learning,
University of East Anglia, Norwich, NR4 7TJ, UK.
E-mail: A.Robinson-Pant@uea.ac.uk

David R. Russell Iowa State University, 251 Ross Hall, Ames,
50011 IA, USA.
E-mail: Drrussel@iastate.edu

Isabel Solé Universitat de Barcelona, Facultat de Psicologia,
Campus Mundet, Pg.Vall d'Hebron 171, Edifici de
Ponent, 08035 Barcelona, Spain.
E-mail: isoleg@ub.edu

Brian Street Kings' College London, Flat 4, 111 Marine Parade,
Brighton BN2 1AT, UK.
E-mail: bvstreet@gmail.com; brian.street@kcl.ac.uk;
brian.street@btinternet.com

Preface

Writing in universities around the world is ubiquitous: students write, teachers write, scholars write — all for a multiplicity of purposes, the most visible ones being assessment, learning and publication. Yet exactly what is understood by 'writing' and exactly how, where and why writing sits in different academies around the world vary enormously. Furthermore, understandings, ideologies and theories about 'academic' or 'scientific' writing (contested terms debated within this volume) often remain resolutely localised, that is, within the confines of local institutionalised practice and local frames of scholarly production. This volume seeks to challenge such localism by bringing together researchers from some nine countries to articulate their specific frames of reference and to thus encourage transnational debate about the nature of writing in the university landscape of the 21st century.

This book brings together in one volume contributions from around the world to open a window on to a number of traditions of writing research and pedagogy, which is an important accomplishment in itself; we cannot begin to have meaningful transnational conversations without learning much more about how writing is conceptualised, theorised and construed as a pedagogic and research object in different institutional, cultural and linguistic contexts, particularly those contexts with whose scholarly traditions we may be least familiar. The descriptive content of the contributions in the book will serve to challenge any straightforward (and often mistaken) assumptions about where writing figures in curriculum and institutional spaces, while the diversity of theoretical and analytical tools on offer illustrates the richness of the resources available for exploring 'university writing' — of students, faculty publishing scholars — once we conceptualise university writing as a necessarily transnational concern. What we might think of as the critical informative dimension of the book — to inform readers about the range of traditions in existence — is therefore clearly successful. So too is the comparative or contrastive dimension of the book. By juxtaposing interests, frames of reference and objects of inquiry — sometimes explicitly within the same chapter and sometimes implicitly through the sequencing of chapters — our attention is drawn towards identifying the precise nature of differences and similarities, an activity that, once again, encourages the kind of active engagement that is key to efforts towards developing a dialogue between differently situated communities (theoretically, historically, linguistically and geographically). In inviting us to notice and listen/look out for such similarities and differences, the book serves not only to direct our attention to 'others' but rather (and indeed in an effort to avoid 'othering') encourages us as readers to reflect critically on some of our assumptions about the approaches we have come to adopt in what can be our often very localised (too easily routinised perhaps?) understandings. Indeed, the book reminds us that what each of us (in/from our specific geodisciplinary locations) may have come to understand as 'the' field of academic, scientific, scholarly or university writing is inevitably partial, often built out of very specific traditions and approaches and indeed from only those to which we have more easily (or regularly) sought access to. For many scholars in the Anglophone centre who routinely access research and traditions published in the medium of English only, the collection provides access — albeit via English — to theories, policies and institutional practices shaping understandings about writing which they may not have encountered before. Monolingualist assumptions and practices underpinning any scholarly endeavour are necessarily limiting, and in this book are challenged by the many contributors who bring to bear a number of linguistic and culturally diverse scholarly traditions, evident in discussions and citations, on the key concern of this collection, that is, university writing construed in terms of objects, writers and practices.

'University writing' of scholars and students is — and will continue to be — an important object of transnational inquiry because such writing is highly consequential; most obviously students can pass or fail, scholars can get published or not, depending not only on what they/we produce but on how our writings are looked at, read and evaluated. And given the increasing mobility globally — of people and all types of writings — there is an urgent need to consider not only what we understand by writing but to scrutinise how these understandings feed into the many routine evaluative practices in which we engage alongside our research activity — activities of pedagogy and assessment, peer review and editing. And here I think is where the book makes a further significant contribution, by encouraging us to think carefully and critically not only about our research and analytic practices but our evaluative working practices around academic writing more generally.

This collection, brought together by Montserrat Castelló and Christiane Donahue, is an exciting contribution to contemporary debates about university writing and is an invitation to us all to continue to engage in transnational conversation and debate.

Theresa Lillis
The Open University, Milton Keynes, UK

Introduction

This volume focuses on new trends in different theoretical perspectives (social, cultural, and cognitive) and derived practices, as relevant to the situated nature of the activity of writing in higher education. These perspectives are analyzed here on the basis of their conceptualization of the *object*, which is scholarly writing; of the *writers*, particularly their identities, attitudes, and perspectives, be it students, teachers, or researchers; and of the instructional *practices*, especially the ways in which the teaching–learning situations may be organized taking the former into account.

In order to draw on some of the best available research in these three domains, the contributions analyze writing using research approaches from various traditions and perspectives, both in Europe and in North, Central, and South America, working on their situated nature and avoiding easy or superficial comparisons in order to broaden our understanding of common problems and of emergent possibilities or affordances that might address them. Each contribution builds from well-established previous work in the domain of teaching and learning academic or scientific writing as situated and discipline-dependent, to move our collective conversation forward in terms of new trends. The final aim is to promote a dialogue among these perspectives and traditions and, by addressing the identified needs and unsolved questions, to bridge gaps and move forward in our knowledge regarding academic writing activities in various higher education settings.

In this introduction we do not aim to characterize the traditions mentioned above, nor to present an overview of their many contributions and specificities. This has already been done in several previous works, some of them integrating both European and the US perspectives (e.g., Russell, Lea, Parker, Street, & Donahue, 2008), and others focused on one or the other. Rather, we have a twofold aim. First we would like to highlight a few relevant turning points in academic writing research in the last decade, and second, we plan to reflect on some notions that can be considered key when trying to identify research needs and unsolved questions in the field of academic writing in higher education settings. These notions include "academic" and "scientific" writing, genre, and academic text types. All of these, with different emphasis and level of explicitness, are addressed by all the contributions of the volume. We will also focus on how voices are intertwined, as well as how dialogues and conversations are developed in and through the chapters, trying to make visible the networking of the field in relation to these. We are aware that mapping the different conversations that are going on in the field and consequently identifying the networking of voices is a complex issue and, since the analysis of all the existing approaches cannot be fully accomplished in the limited scope of this introduction, our reflection will be restricted to those perspectives represented by the different contributions of this volume. Our aim in this introduction is thus to focus on their similarities and differences, as well as to point out the concerns this comparison raises and the educational implications of different contributions in conversation with each other.

A Sampling of Points from Higher Education Writing Research in the Last Decade

This volume builds on existing traditions in writing research that have not always been in communication with each other. We offer here representative samples of the work preceding this volume in several of the institutional and national contexts that are the horizon for the work of this volume's individual chapters, which are designed to foster the exchange and dialogue we hope to create here. Each chapter provides its own more detailed review of parts of the traditions.

Publications, research initiatives, and knowledge have increased exponentially in Europe since 2003 when the volume *Teaching Academic Writing in European Higher Education* was published. This publication represented the first attempt of the Series in Writing volumes to describe the state of the art of teaching and research about higher education academic writing in Europe, and it was possible only because increasing and persistent work around writing at different European universities had developed at least from 1993. In English we should acknowledge the seminal work of Ivanic (1998) and Lea and Stierer (2000), Lea and Street (1998) or Lillis (1997, 2001) among others in the UK, as well as in some countries of the North of Europe (Dysthe, 2007; Gustafsson, 2011; Björk & Räisänen, 1996). It is much more difficult to find out what has been done in other European languages because of the diversity of national languages, journals and research traditions (to know more about these difficulties and about recent advances, see e.g., Chitez & Kruse, this volume). For example, Jacqueline van Kruiningen, Kees de Glopper, and Thea Mepschen at Groningen University in the Netherlands have worked extensively on researching the effectiveness of writing tutoring. Or, if we take as another example the work being done in France and Belgium, we see great attention to, for example, students' use of sources in their university writing, their positioning as student writer-author, their difficulties with university reading and note-taking, and so on (the bibliographies, this volume, for Rinck and Boch and for Delcambre and Donahue offer specific references). In Spanish language the field has developed differently in Central and South America in which some aspects of North American research and practices on academic writing have had a more visible impact than in Spain. This can be seen for instance in the development of a first-year reading and writing courses in some South American Universities which are inexistent in Spain as well as in most European countries. Germany develops in yet another way, with publications such as Zeitschrift Schreiben, and German language conferences on writing and disciplinarity. In any case, while there is a broad body of research, it is still not easy to draw on the changes in the field of academic writing in Europe in recent years because of the expansion of research and its own historical, geographical, and linguistically grounded nature.

The context of European higher education is one of the variables that has changed significantly from the beginning of the 21st century. Since the Bologna Declaration, which was signed on June 19, 1999 and called explicitly for structural and methodological changes in higher education to enhance students' active learning of transversal and disciplinary competences and mobility around European universities, the need to converge in what has been called the European Higher Education Area has involved many changes in most of the European universities (47 countries are formally involved in the process in 2011), although those changes are different and have had different impact on university structures, methodologies, and practices in each of those countries. Briefly, some of the methodological aspects of the required changes, such as the need to assure students' learning of complex competences (and not simple skills) and consequently to modify the instructional practices and activities in classrooms in order to promote a more active and constructive learning, are confronting university teachers with the need to promote students' awareness of and reflection upon their learning process. These then will provoke the need to develop the necessary teaching strategies to help them construct new knowledge. When adequately addressed, these new demands are frequently met by means of increasing students' writing, which is used as a way for them to show their learning process during the courses, as has been pointed out by some authors in this volume (for instance Castelló & Iñesta; Dysthe; Chitez & Kruse). Unfortunately, in many cases this not has lead to a more clear understanding of the need to teach students how to address the new writing demands nor how to give meaning to the new writing practices. Nevertheless, we can see change in terms of awareness of writing problems and needs in some countries, related in different ways to a great increase of research interests and practices. This translates not only into more European publications devoted to academic writing in higher education but also into a greater convergence of some theoretical assumptions among those authors working in the field in Europe. In the introduction of the 2003 volume cited above, authors noted that only a few references were shared all throughout the different chapters, Bereiter and Scardamalia's seminal work on writing processes (1987) being the most shared one. This is radically different to what happens in this volume, as we will explain in much more detail in subsequent sections. Not only have references to general writing processes almost disappeared, with those specifically devoted to explaining the nature of writing practices, conditions, genres, and other writing characteristics in higher education favored instead, but a higher level of agreement regarding some theoretical assumptions, such as the social nature of writing in university contexts, has been reached by an important number of researchers in the European field of writing in higher education, some of them gathered in this volume.

Another variable that has contributed to the evolution or at least to the visibility of European studies in higher education writing has to do with the increase of conferences and arenas to discuss and share studies and worries. Among those, we can mention associations such the European Academic Teaching of Academic Writing (EATAW), which from 2001 has provided a fruitful space to discuss and share advances in teaching academic writing at European universities. The volume edited by Björk, Bräuer, Rienecker, and Jørgensen (2003), is a clear example of these advances and one of the milestones when analyzing the evolution and the growth of attention to higher education academic writing in Europe both from an applied and a research perspective. As Russell pointed out in the preface, the volume brought fresh approaches which were grounded in specific needs and European traditions. This volume, and some other related publications from EATAW (Perrin, Böttcher, Kruse, & Wrobel, 2002), facilitated interesting discussions of issues such as genres used and taught in the European universities, writing in the disciplines, and the role of university faculty in this teaching, transitions between school, university, and professional writing, or institutional proposals adopted in some of the European countries to address teaching academic writing in different European languages and contexts, without necessarily adopting some of the formulae broadly developed in the United States. The products and discussions of other associations and conferences such as the European Writing Centers Association (EWCA), Writing development in Higher Education (WDHE), or the SIG-Writing of EARLI, not to mention the dozens of associations working within particular languages and national contexts, have also been contributing greatly to the knowledge and networking in Europe. Excellent publications such as *L1 Educational Studies in Language and Literature* or the recently developed *Journal of Writing Research* have been key in disseminating knowledge and research. Recently, the COST project "European Research Network on Learning to Write Effectively" (http://www.cost lwe.eu/) has gathered researchers of most of the European countries with the aim to create networks and disseminate scientific knowledge regarding different research areas on writing. Due to its nature and objectives the COST project was specifically devoted to promote European networking and had a specific subgroup devoted to genre and academic writing.

Despite the great difficulties those initiatives have to confront, they also contribute, no doubt, to starting the dialogue and the discussion around shared problems and interests among European countries and traditions that in some cases, specially those with different languages than English, have remained historically isolated and dispersed.

The developments represented by U.S. authors in this volume are set on a stage built by what came before them, in the latter half of the 20th century. Briefly, a field focused on issues of "composition" and rhetoric developed early in the U.S., in response to a curricular and structural presence shared by most U.S. universities: that of first-year writing courses required of most students in most institutions of higher education since as early as the 1800s. That field and its various stages and practices is not the direct object of our work in this volume, but it contributed to years of attention in particular to the kind of writing students might do as they enter college, how it might be taught, and how it might be learned. In particular, it affected the construction of the term "academic writing." One of the later developments in this field was its attention to writing beyond that initial entry phase — writing done in more advanced courses, writing as part of different disciplinary configurations, and writing as a mode of learning the subject matter of those disciplines. These interests came to be known as Writing in the Disciplines (WiD) and Writing across the Curriculum (WAC); they engendered a new set of discussions about theories, pedagogies, and practices (see references, Russell & Cortes, this volume), in many ways more closely aligned with those of European countries in which university studies are located early on within disciplines rather than in a more generic first-year curriculum as we see most often in the U.S.

At the same time, the curious evolution of the field of composition and the particular pattern of stages it went through created years of alienation from certain kinds of research, in particular "RAD" research ("replicable, aggregable data-driven") (Haswell, 2005; Anson, 2009). While these broad research categories might be explored in a variety of complex and intriguing ways, and while we do not seek to take a stand here about this kind of research, its marginalization for some time in U.S. post-secondary writing research by members of the field of composition has created a particular scholarly landscape that now benefits from interaction with other research traditions — such as those we often find in European contexts — while bringing to that dialogue years of discussion about some large specific populations and the institutional and ideological forces that shape our work with them. That is, we all stand to gain a great deal from the dialogue that is growing rapidly between North, Central, and South America and Europe.

Unfortunately, that dialogue has often been hampered by obvious language barriers and less obvious but related cultural and disciplinary barriers. Because U.S. scholars have not tended to seek out and cite work written in other languages (Horner, Necamp, and Donahue, in press), or even in English from anglophone regions (Lillis & Curry, 2006), they haven't known what is available. It hasn't occurred to many U.S. scholars to ask, because they have believed for so long that no one else does the work they do. This is partly true because of the specific contexts mentioned above, but it is also partly an issue of using U.S. frames to try to know what is happening elsewhere and thus missing key practices and traditions that might have unfamiliar shapes.

Examples of the kind of European work that hasn't been widely known include broad curricular initiatives to introduce first-year students to college writing and reading, deep attention to student writing in the later undergraduate and graduate years, often in research methods courses, and extensive research on questions of intertextuality, sentence control, or disciplinary discourse in students' college work.

More recently in the U.S., attention turned to deep attention to genre studies and to notions of communities of practice; most recently, attention has turned to the value of translingual and transdiscursive approaches to writing and writing studies. While the use of English in publications around the world is increasing, so is U.S. scholars' willingness to stumble through work in other languages, to try to connect. Technological advances have supported this shift, via both increased global interaction and access, and crude but encouraging translation mechanisms. Even the terminological discussion about "composition" versus "writing studies" has raised awareness and has enabled discussions with European scholars to thrive.

The growing development of shared methodologies or the need to compare methods and contexts is evident.

In the last five years, dialogue between United States' and Europe's traditions on writing research has fruitfully advanced and some publications have appeared with this aim (for instance, Reuter & Donahue, 2007 or Russell, Lea, Parker, Street, & Donahue, 2009, among others). In addition, some initiatives such the international conference on writing research "Writing Research Across Borders" which has already had two editions, are the most visible evidence of the existence of will and channels to dialogue and construct shared knowledge. We see these evolutions directly in this volume, as part IV of the introduction will highlight.

Cross-Chapter Themes: Academic Writing, Scientific Writing, Genre, and Text Type

As soon as scholars work across domains, institutions, contexts, and national frames, they encounter differences; these can be surface or deep. For example, some chapters in this volume use the term "tutor" while others designate "faculty," both meaning higher education instructors. At a deeper level, all chapters evoke "academic" and/or "scientific" writing, but these terms take on different shapes. For some, "academic" writing is what students do; for others it is what academic scholars do as they contribute to communal knowledge in their disciplines; for yet others, the term refers to both; and for still others, "academic" has negative connotations. For some, "scientific" writing is produced only by scientists in the fields of, say, chemistry or zoology; for others, it is systematic inquiry by expert members of any discipline. Delcambre and Donahue use "scientific" for all writing by Masters students and beyond, thus including expert writing in publications and advanced studies, while "university" writing rather than "academic" writing is considered more expressive. Nelson and Castelló, on the other hand, are clearly comfortable with "academic" writing precisely because of its scope and all the term might include, while Rinck and Boch specify the distinction between research writing — published scientific works across disciplines — and writing for university research training, the "the very diverse pieces of writing that accompany students' paths through university," with doctoral writing at a bridge point between these poles. The scientific writing they evoke is explicitly defined as figuring in sciences, social sciences, and humanities, similarly as proposed by Castelló and Iñesta, but in contrast to Prior and Bilbro's use of "scientific" for texts and practices in the hard sciences, a use shared by Bazerman, Keranen, and Prudencio. Authors drawing on academic literacies models, including Lea and Robinson-Pant and Street, use "academic" to point to a broad range of literate practices, and suggest that "professional" writing and "academic" writing might be another way to slice the domains. Mateos and Solé posit still another kind of opposition, between the scientific (broadly, the research community) and the teaching community, suggesting that the former sees writing as complex and situated while the latter focuses on communication. In Carlino's treatment of doctoral candidates in Education, clearly the work in this field is considered scientific (science writing, science presentations), in relation to "reflective" writing, while "academic" processes align with broader university community concerns, although Dysthe does not mention scientific writing at all as she treats science doctoral students' work. These differences are part of the productive challenge of exchange; the underlying point remains, across the chapters, to understand the work of writing among various constituencies across the institutions studied, in part by taking on these different constructions of writing.

As for genre, all the contributions included in this volume rely on the broad consideration of genres as social and cultural products rather than convention-driven text typologies. Nevertheless, under the general umbrella of this agreement, some particular interpretations and emphasis on some elements can be observed which, together with some historical and cultural traditions, can account for some differences on authors' stance regarding genres and how this impacts research and educational decisions. We have differentiated these interpretations in three subgroups, largely based on the theoretical frames and scholarly work upon which each draws. Although there is not a clear division line among them, due to the importance of shared assumptions, we hope this will help us to clarify some of the nuances of common and different elements in the theoretical underpinnings of the notion of genre in this volume, which surprisingly has not explicitly defined by almost none of the chapters (this is not the case of Chitez & Kruse, this volume, who offer an explicit analysis of the notion of genre).

The first group is broadest and includes most of the shared assumptions also by the two others. It is shaped by those contributions that primarily rely on the pioneering contribution of Miller and her concept of genre as social action (Miller, 1984) and its later development quite close to sociological theory (Miller, 1994). In these chapters, the emphasis is first placed on genres as actions, and specifically on those actions that particular forms of discourse use to accomplish. This first acknowledgment is expanded with the complementary assumptions of the socio-cultural and historical Vygotskian approach, Bakhtin's theory of genre, and systems genres as proposed by activity theory (AT) (see Russell, this volume). The result of the integration of these perspectives — which is to some extent common to all contributions — with the former consideration of genre as action, has led gradually to a conceptualization of genre as patterns of functional actions, culturally and historically situated, through which writers' participation in different systems of activity is mediated (see for instance Bazerman, Keranen, and Prudencio).

In a second group, major sources and references are similar and although almost all the contributions explicitly rely on Bakhtin's conceptualization of genres as relatively stable sets of utterances in particular spheres of activity, some contributions make their interpretation of this conceptualization explicit, and this makes the difference. This interpretation is shaped by the following related aspects. First, an explicit emphasis on the dialogical nature of genres as well as a clear distinction of the practical issues of this dialogue, namely the interaction between individuals, texts, and communities (see Dysthe, this volume). Second, a growing interest in identifying and studying the characteristics of new emergent genres, probably due to the evidence of great changes in the patterns of interaction and systems of activity displayed in higher education contexts, which in turn lead to new practices and genres which are emerging in these new scenario (see Lea or Robinson-Pant & Street, this volume.) Third, in this group of contributions a clear link between the writers' expectations, emotions, or identity and their use of genres is established (see, among others, Carlino, or Castelló & Iñesta, this volume). This link accounts for some specific conceptual questions and authors' focused methodological approaches, both in research and in educational settings that are grounded in dialogic perspectives.

Finally, it is still possible to identify a third group shaped by those contributions, closely related to the previous ones but which explicitly advocate for the articulation between the linguistic, textual, and socio-historic dimensions of writing (see Rinck & Boch, this volume). These contributions, when talking about genres and their analysis, make clear their claim for taking into account the interrelated nature of the challenges of discourse organization, linguistic choices, and conceptualization or mastery of content when teaching genres in higher education or analyzing writing difficulties (see also Delcambre & Donahue, this volume).

Despite the differences we have identified here, the foundation the authors in this volume share is that of genres as social and cultural, as flexible and dynamic, shaping and shaped by interactions in particular communities.

Finally, another shared-different category is text type. The ranges of texts considered implicitly and explicitly by different contributions are mostly linked to research genres such as research papers or articles, written by students or teachers-researchers, as well as undergraduate, Masters, or Doctoral theses in different stages (this is the case of Bazerman, Keranen, & Encinas; Carlino; Castelló & Iñesta; Rinck & Boch, this volume). But other texts analyzed here are linked to "new genres" such as meeting notes in doctoral supervision or administrative writing associated with research (see Robinson-Pant & Street, this volume), and professional reflective writing in courses for university professors (see Lea, this volume). Finally, texts used to learn and think about disciplinary content such as summaries, synthesis, portfolios, or essays are also represented (see Dysthe; Mateos & Solé; Delcambre & Donahue, this volume).

The picture is, of course, not so simple. Labeling texts is not enough to understand their meaning and their associated practices and products in the different contexts and countries (as Chitez & Kruse point out, this volume). Each text label needs to be accompanied by additional information about the context, the practices, the actors, the disciplines, the language, the discursive mechanisms, and the genre families, in order to build its specific meaning in a particular time and place and, in some cases, to differentiate it from other "similar" texts. Only this detailed description will help us to avoid partial comprehension and to promote a deeper dialogue around the commonalities and specificities of texts and genres through these contexts.

One example is the research paper or academic research paper (ARP) that appears in some of the contributions. In U.S. contexts, a "research paper" at the undergraduate level can be anything from a 5- or 10-page review of sources about a particular topic or argument to an extensive synthetic review of key sources that support a particular interpretation or argument, as Russell also point out (this volume). In graduate studies this term, and text type, appear less frequently. In Europe and especially in Spain and France (as it is exemplified by Castelló & Iñesta or Rinck & Boch contributions, this volume), it is both an advanced text type and quite complex. In some cases, it is very similar to scientific articles — following the IMRD structure — while in other cases, especially at the undergraduate level it can be closer to a reduced version of a Masters thesis (in some contexts of Italy and Spain it is also called *tesina*, which literally means "little thesis", as Chitez & Kruse also mention, this volume). Additionally in Europe, practices around writing a thesis deserve a careful analysis depending on whether we are talking about a Masters thesis or a Doctoral thesis (and in some contexts also undergraduate theses); only this analysis can help us to begin the discussion about the characteristics of the expected texts in each case.

New texts and practices associated with the process of receiving feedback and supervision when writing these theses should also be taken into account in this analysis. In this sense, some supervision practices, and their associated texts, reported by some chapters seem to be quite different to those developed in other countries (see for instance Robinson-Pant & Street versus Dysthe or Castelló & Iñesta, this volume). Although changes promoted by the Bologna process in Europe have the final aim of making higher education structures and university systems comparable, countries and universities differ in history, traditions, expectations, values and practices and common terminology might hide enormous differences that should be investigate, as some authors also argue in their contribution.

Emerging genres such as those analyzed by Lea or Robinson-Pant and Street, which may also be classified as internal genres produced in academic settings by teachers and researchers according to Russell and Cortes' proposal, are generating new texts whose presence in formal higher education contexts is increasing in most of the different European countries, although at different paces. This increasing presence is already modifying the practices of both professors and students and this global phenomenon adds complexity to our study of texts and literacy practices in higher education.

Finally, a deep analysis regarding the common and the differential characteristics in different countries of what Kruse (this volume) has called *educational genres* is needed (see also Russell's "classroom genres" (1997) and Donahue's "genres of academic apprentissage" (2008)). These can include portfolios or seminar papers, but also other many texts that seem *a priori* totally different. Actually, in some countries (like Spain, France, or Portugal among others) synthesis or general argumentative writing assignments based on read sources — such as "*analyze the author's approach and compare it with the perspective discussed in class*" — are much more frequent and representative of the writing activities required to accomplish a similar educational function than, for example, portfolios or essays. One of the challenges of future research from an international perspective has to do with the analysis of the functions and the *practices* (a frame that is equally extensively developed across countries with different emphases and grounding) associated with different texts in each context more than in their linguistic or structural characteristics — which will be necessarily situation-dependent — if we want to improve our knowledge of the students' meaning-making processes on these practices and of their impact on learning and identities. We might begin to consider these different types of writing as functioning along a continuum; they appear in many contexts and they play many different roles. This aspect can also be very fruitfully studied through research on the actual assignments given in different national writing contexts.

Voices, Dialogues, and Conversations in and through Texts

"Academic writing," in whatever form or frame it is taken up across the chapters here, implies being able to dialogue with other voices and texts, establishing a conversation in which each voice is individual and collective at time, as Bakhtin has suggested. The analysis of how these voices are intertwined could help us to draw a more accurate picture of the conversations that are going on at a given moment in the field. To comment on the references on which different authors draw is the objective of this section in which we will look for the dialogue between countries and specially between the United States and Europe, as well as for the nature of those more common references and their relationship with the topics of the volume.

The first finding is that authors participating in this volume are fully aware of this dialogic and intertextual dimension of academic writing. Bakhtin is the most frequent reference among all the chapters and sections (he appears in ten of the thirteen chapters). In fact, when we look at chapters and sections, this is especially true for some chapters of the first part, those focused on the nature of the academic and scientific texts and writers' voice, and those of the third part focused on practices, the ways in which the teaching-learning situations may be organized. Nevertheless, it should be noted that emphasis on dialogical aspects of genres are especially evident on those chapters dealing with practices, mostly located in the third part of the volume. This is coherent with the conceptualization of genre that we have discussed above. The second part of the volume is devoted to the analysis of the writers — their identities, attitudes, and perspectives, be it students, teachers, or researchers — and here other aspects besides dialogue and intertextuality seem to be more relevant. This is the case of identity, with references to Ivanic as the most frequent ones followed by some of her collaborators.

The second finding situates the references. Forty-seven percent of them are from U.S. authors while 52% come from Europe. This equilibrium, which is not typical of many of the publications on academic writing, seems to indicate that in this case the dialogue and discussion is already well underway, maybe because of the balance between authors' origins and the aim of the volume, which could have stimulated mutual knowledge and an active search for connections between different geographic, historical, and linguistic traditions. Except in few cases, this balance can be observed within each chapter. We also see an important presence of sources in other languages different from English, specially French but also Spanish, German, Italian, or Romanian.

Finally, it is also rich testament that some of the most referenced authors of this volume (Bazerman, Russell, or Dysthe) were respectively cited by ten, eight, and seven out of the thirteen chapters of the volume, while all the other authors were cited at least by two other chapters other than their own, prior to the peer exchange of chapters carried out as part of the publication process. This implies that 10% out of the total of references belong to the authors' voices of the volume and we have the hope that this could be the basis from which to built a fruitful dialogue of international scope between varied traditions and perspectives.

Seeds of Dialogue

In this final part, we will launch preliminary interchanges and threads across chapters and sections, in order to facilitate the beginning of a dialogue we hope readers will hear and join. The first section, *Academic writing and writers: Frames in conversation* establishes what can — and cannot — be considered as academic writing, what the delimitations and the relationships between academic writing and scientific writing are, and, at the same time, how these different notions can be imagined as literacy practices. This reflection cannot be appropriately addressed without analyzing theoretical approaches and situating the debate in current advances in research, themselves diverse in their grounding and framing. Frames of communit(ies), of voice, and of social and cognitive relationships alternately question and inform each other. "Academic writing" as an object is thus questioned in this first part, both questioning of its nature and questioning whether it can be considered an "object," taking into account the diverse traditions and research trends in European countries and the Americas.

Thus, Russell and Cortes, in their framing chapter "Academic and scientific texts: the same or different communities?" unpack layers of terminology, such as "research paper," "scientific writing," or "science," in order to set the stage for the volume's exploration of academic writing's sense, shapes, and roles. For Russell and Cortes, the question of what it means to "write scientifically" or "academically" opens us to broader questions about the nature and purpose of research. As they suggest, "both academic and scientific discourse and practice [are] functioning parts of wider networks of communication, political, social, etc." They consider several different research traditions that speak to important aspects of this functioning, using the categories (academic and scientific) as generative for discussing the purposes of research about writing and its many disciplinary homes. Most of the research traditions they evoke are found throughout the volume, and their chapter thus offers a key starting-point for the work of the volume.

A different kind of starting point is offered by Prior and Bilbro's chapter on academic enculturation. They explore the underlying ongoing process (or processes, as they suggest) experienced by writers. Explicitly, they ask what knowledge and/or practices are being learned and developed, where is this learning happening, and how does it occur? These questions help scholars to understand the interactive dynamism of social spaces such as disciplines and the "open-ended, sociohistorical processes that produce, represent, and contest disciplinary practices and identities." While resisting the commonly accepted version of enculturation as progressive integration of an individual into a stable (disciplinary or academic) community, Prior and Bilbro ld work across disciplines, languages, and national contexts.

The question of "voice" is key to studying and understanding students' authorship. And yet, as Nelson and Castelló's chapter highlights, what we mean by "voice" has developed in different strands over the decades, in part because of the range of disciplinary interests in exploring voice and writing. For academic writing in particular, the point is that this voice evolves with a writer's work, defining and creating that identity which is always situated in a social and historical context. "When readers *know* (in some sense) a particular author, they *hear* his or her voice," suggest Nelson and Castelló. This implies that voice appears when readers interpret it and when authors discuss and dialogue with others in their community of practice; this social nature of voice is also related to the way an individual author might both join and resist a dominant academic discourse.

Additional factors in the work of academic communities grow out of students' perceptions about the writing they do and their cognitive frames. These conceptions influence how they participate, how they learn to write, how they represent writing. Mateos and Solé distinguish students' personal conceptions from the social conceptions that shape them, while highlighting their interrelationships. The social aspects, they remind us, attribute levels of value to different kinds of writing and to different writers; these levels of value are not negligible.

In the second part, *Writers' knowledge and practices in evolving academic contexts*, the focus shifts to the nature and development of identities in discursive communities broadly conceived (i.e., without endorsing a particular framework among those in use — communities of practice, enculturation, or discourse community for example). Each contribution here undertakes an analysis of different writers' variables, such as knowledge, practices, beliefs, conceptions and attitudes, in relationship with various social and literate practices in institutional contexts, including comparative national and cultural contexts.

Dominant discourses and their development are targeted as well by Street and Robinson-Pant's treatment of "new" academic literacy practices. In their study, both students' and teachers' perspectives matter, in relation to institutionally imposed expectations and requests for accountability. The same kind of possibilities for negotiation evoked by Nelson and Castelló are posited here as restrained or limited in some ways by new UK institutional practices of documenting student and teacher interactions around work together. The attention is to the complexities and nuances of the new practices and the ways they control integration into academic discursive community conversations.

For Lea, as for Street and Robinson-Pant, the academic literacies frame allows an exploration of this diversity and complexities in very productive ways, resisting the "individual cognition" and "individual transfer of knowledge" approaches in favor of complex, layered understandings of students' interactions with the literate environments of higher education and their attendant power structures. "Literacies," Lea highlights, as a plural, "signals a concern with literacy as a range of social and cultural practices around reading and writing in particular contexts, rather than individual cognitive activities." This perspective encourages us to understand new genres in the academy as locus of meaning making; studying these at the micro level while understanding them in the broader institutional practices in which they operate illuminates these genres. She focuses on examining changing contexts as a starting point in interrogating a very specific space, when university lecturers themselves become student writers, and studies how emergent genres of writing articulate diverse literacy practices and academic identities.

At the same time, students' understandings of what disciplines expect of them, specifically, in their writing also shape their sense of what is possible and valued. Rinck and Boch's textual analyses over years of research have pinpointed the ways in which writers manage point of view, source use (in the deep way it calls on subject positioning), and voice in their texts. They identify novice and expert strategies in this management, in order to propose possible ways of intervening in students' learning. For Rinck and Boch the question of voice goes well beyond conventional markers, leading to questions of the stakes in research writing: "above and beyond, academic demands such as citing sources or using quotation marks, how and why is it important to document oneself, to take on board previous knowledge and to define one's position in a field?" This chapter considers some specific features that might give us insight into broader processes; if we are to teach students, they muse, how might we balance passing on a history of conventions and genres with opening up the possibilities for thinking through writing? And, as Russell also suggests in chapter 1, what kind of writing is it, really, that novice researchers produce?

For Delcambre and Donahue, university literacies are explored through students' eyes. What is "writing" to students? What kinds do they do, and how challenging are the demands for them? Through two studies, one from France and the other from the U.S., students' descriptions of writing genres, of their values and priorities as compared to those they perceive among their professors and of their sense of growth through writing in their coursework are highlighted. We see that the "academic" or "scientific" writing treated by Russell and Cortes takes on different layers of meaning from the students' perspective. Because the students in each study come from a variety of disciplines, we also see their relationship to knowledge, know-how, and epistemology as tightly tied to their writing, as it moves from earlier academic studies to later integration into scientific work. The diversity of disciplinary or other demands students encounter is a shared object of attention across several chapters, most notably Lea, and Robinson-Pant and Street.

And finally, Chitez and Kruse, through a comparative analysis of writing cultures in European higher education, draw out the features of university literacy that evolve in different institutional and cultural contexts. They suggest that the genres of writing we might include in "university literacy" have histories, evolved practices, and purposes linked to the way disciplines are understood, the structure of institutions, and the linguistic effects of different languages. As they suggest, "each educational system creates its unique mix of educational genres, writing practices, assessment procedures, instructional materials, expectations, and learning opportunities. Writing cultures are characterized not only by the particular genres used but more so by the embedding of genres in learning arrangements, as Russell and Foster (2002) have pointed out." For the various subsequent contributions in the volume, these comments are essential to understanding the ground out of which a particular focus comes.

The chapters in this section thus help us to build a complex picture of writers as authors looking to establish their academic voices in situated academic contexts.

In the final section, *Research about writing from a teaching and learning perspective: Fostering the development of identities and attitudes,* the authors focus on new trends in research focused on teaching and learning about writing in higher education. This meant focusing on new proposals designed with the clear aim of fostering the development of literacy, practices, attitudes, voices, and identities in situated environments both in the American and in European countries.

The first chapter in this section thus develops a detailed description of an educational intervention in Psychology, and analyzes the impact of this intervention on student writing and identity. Based on the consideration, proposed by Activity Theory, that tensions and contradictions are the engine of constructive and transformative learning, Castelló and Iñesta analyze whether these contradictions could be interpreted as conflicts by the participants and which actions were developed to solve or to deal with these conflicts. Their work highlights the ways in which students struggle, in terms of authorial identity in the disciplinary environment. In particular, and this thread weaves through much of the work presented in this volume, suggesting that interaction with sources is one of the indices of intellectual work in higher education. They note the use of discursive resources and the ways students interact with each other as a subset of the disciplinary community overall — perhaps even as a distinct though overlapping community. The unique perspective of this chapter is grounded in the disciplines of the authors, Psychology. That introduction of a new disciplinary frame affords particularly strong insights because they see academic writing — and student writers — from this double frame. One of the chapter's key conclusions is that "shifting between communities and adjusting participation," something students, teachers, and researchers all must do, is a complex activity at the heart of negotiation of identity through writing.

Here as well, student-writers' identities and emotions are central — and plural. Plurality can also be considered as multivoicedness, heteroglossia in the Bakhtinian sense. Dysthe's contribution focuses on this multivoicing in students' writing as something to foster and facilitate in higher education. Using a lens from Bakhtin and Rommetveit, she explores the dialogic heart of the intersubjective interactions between peer writers, located in what Rommeveit calls a "temporarily shared social reality" that makes this intersubjectivity possible. While the chapter focuses on rich case study examples of how peer feedback work functions dialogically, Dysthe also calls for us to "find new ways of synthesizing qualitative studies" in order to enable deep understanding of such functioning and its relationship to critical thinking and writing.

This challenge appears in a different frame in Carlino's treatment of graduate students' difficulties completing dissertations. The dispositions needed, she suggests, are less often taken into account than more obvious factors of literate ability, cognitive processing, or enculturation per se. Carlino's description of a particular doctoral seminar offers insights into the diversity of types of writing that can help

PhD candidates to successfully write, the connections between emotion and cognitive processing, and gives a path for developing the field of teaching writing beyond the social-acculturating approach. Writing serves to both explore and focus different identities and different writing purposes and this implies a stressful activity that can be accompanied in order to help students to manage it.

And finally, Bazerman, Keranen, and Prudencio explore in depth the essential and inextricable relationship between language, science, and thinking that leads to fragile positioning for NNS scientists working to join the global dialogue. The specific struggles and fraught moments they describe, ranging from the disruption of expression, formulation, and recognition of thinking, to confronting anxiety in terms of participation and lack of regular opportunity to participate, lead to an understanding of deep linguistic-scientific relationships. For Bazerman, Keranen, and Prudencio, engagement in a full participation with the communities of practice in question will come about only through "situated practice in significant, immersive, accountable and consequential activities [that lead] to motivated problem-solving and habituated use that advances fluency and accuracy." These activities are not strange to the learning of all scientists and writers but rather support "conscious control of the immersion process" in ways that fully engage. They suggest, "We can in fact describe the fundamental problem as one of gaining immersion in the rich and motivated language experiences that would lead to further specialized L2 language learning that would then support further immersion and engagement. NNES scientists seem to have high practical, experiential, and emotional barriers keeping them from those bootstrapping interactions that would lead to communicative fluency and publications, and they need to find ways to overcome those barriers." Forming networks that enable full engagement is crucial to successful engagement, but far from obvious. Bazerman, Keranen, and Prudencio describe a workshop that opens up possibilities for Mexican scientists; the underpinnings of this workshop are powerfully relevant to the general issues raised across several chapters.

The dialogue among the perspectives and traditions presented here addresses identified needs and unsolved questions, bridges gaps, and moves us collectively forward in our knowledge regarding academic writing activities in higher education settings. We are pleased to offer this comprehensive framework for designing educational practices that take into account the challenges of writing as a member of scientific and academic communities in different national contexts.

Montserrat Castelló
Christiane Donahue

SECTION I

ACADEMIC WRITING AND WRITERS: FRAMES IN CONVERSATION

Chapter 1

Academic and Scientific Texts: The Same or Different Communities?

David R. Russell and Viviana Cortes

The question our title poses has neither a single answer nor a simple answer. The purpose of this chapter — and in large measure this book — is in large part is to explore its complexity.

The question is at one level terminological, a question of particular usage. The authors of this collection agree that "academic" means having to do with higher education (though in France the term carries such negative connotations ("formal, conventional, even pretentious") that researchers prefer the term "university literacies" (Delcambre & Donahue, this volume). The term "scientific" is a bit more difficult. In Anglo-American countries, it refers to the natural sciences and much of the social sciences, but not the humanities. In much of continental Europe, "scientific" refers to all disciplines, including the humanities — any discipline that systematically studies something. It is in this continental sense that this chapter uses the term "scientific," in order to distinguish the writing of students from that of professionals, though we realize this is ambiguous and that other authors (e.g., Nelson & Castello, this volume) specifically use the term "academic" for both. Still others (e.g., Rinck & Boch, this volume) use the term "academic and research writing" to distinguish the two.

But at a deeper level, our title question is also institutional and systemic, and here is where distinctions are more than terminological, because they may indicate fundamental differences in the way writing, learning, and research are conceived and practiced inside and outside formal higher education — and the way the identities of students, teachers, and scientists (broadly) are constructed. We have tried to capture the complexity in Figure 1.1, which shows the relationships between, on one axis, scientific and nonscientific texts, and on the other axis, academic and nonacademic communities.

University Writing: Selves and Texts in Academic Societies
Studies in Writing, Volume 24, 3–17
Copyright © 2012 by Emerald Group Publishing Limited
All rights of reproduction in any form reserved
ISSN: 1572-6304/doi:10.1108/S1572-6304(2012)0000024005

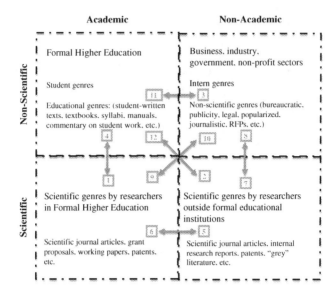

Figure 1.1: Some relationships among texts/genres and communities, academic and nonacademic, and scientific and nonscientific.

Obviously at some levels and at some times, those categories interpenetrate in terms of intellectual and psychological development as well as in terms of institutional categories. And for students (arrows 1–3), such penetrating into the world of professional work is the goal of higher education and their goal. For example, a thesis is published in a scientific journal and becomes and article. Indeed, from one perspective — perhaps the dominant one — the goal of writing academic texts is to prepare students to write scientific texts, to reproduce the professoriate (arrow 1) or to do scientific research in nonacademic institutions (arrow 2).

But this is not the whole story, of course, because most students do not go on to become scientists in this sense, to do research and make new knowledge (and write scientific articles or books). In most disciplines, most all of them become professionals in nonacademic institutions doing writing that is not scientific by any strict definition (arrow 3). They go on to do myriad other things in myriad genres (Ivanič, Edwards, & Barton, 2009). Teacher-researchers prepare (form) practitioners in many fields who do not do scientific research for publication but who nevertheless carry out systematic inquiry, whether a therapist looking into a client's neurosis or a veterinarian looking into a horse's mouth. And again, they write myriad kinds of texts, myriad genres (to use another term we will take up later). This becomes most evident in research into the writing practices of certain groups such as teachers-in-training (Daunay, Hassan, Lepez, & Morisse, 2006), where practitioners must learn the discursive practices of the field. There they write genres that, though not research in the strict sense, at least require them to think scientifically. They re-present their discipline/profession in what they write (to "discipline" their thinking and their activity). However, these workplace genres are almost never required of or taught to students in Higher education (HE), though they can be.

Although we are considering academic those texts written by students and scientific those written by scientists, we must not ignore the simple fact that in higher education in most countries, researchers are also teachers. The current French hyphenated phrase sums it up neatly: enseignant-chercheur, teacher-researcher. Both students and teachers are part of the same institution. Scientists working in higher education as teachers do not write only scientific texts. They often write "academic" texts for students such as teaching materials, syllabi, textbooks, manuals, and so on, as well as occluded genres (Swales' 2004 term) such as feedback on student writing, e-mails to students, and so on (arrow 4). They also write a wide range of bureaucratic texts within the "academic" institution: committee reports, curriculums, and so on (Lea & Stierer, 2009; see also Lea, this volume).

Disciplines and their researchers within higher education are linked to researchers outside higher education through their shared goals, methods, ethos, professional organizations, journals, meetings, and so on (arrows 5 and 6), though there may be a tension between "pure" and "applied" research. In most countries, there are institutions (institutes) devoted exclusively (or almost) to scientific research, without any formal relationship to institutions of higher education, though researchers often move back and forth between the two.

These "nonacademic" researchers certainly work at the service of business, government, and so on through their research and texts (arrow 7) or attempt to influence those institutions (arrow 8). These sites of nonacademic research may be government funded or private. Indeed, the majority of scientific research goes on in corporations and other for-profit institutions, though their findings are often not shared, as they are proprietary. And much research also goes on in nonprofit, nongovernmental "research and advocacy" organizations (e.g., NGOs). And these produce a research that is termed "grey literature," because it attempts to influence public policy and is not typically published in scientific journals (Lindeman, 2007). Of course relationships among scientists in all these institutions are often close, at times too close for some. It may be that linguistically they might be considered all part of one "community" of discourse or register, that of science (in various disciplines/professions). But this would gloss over the differences in their motives, values, practices, genres, and the many linguistic manifestations of these differences in different scientific disciplines and subdisciplines. (See Bazerman, Keranan, & Prudencio, this volume, on the particularly strong impact of these differences for nonnative English-speaking scientists.)

Disciplines, professions, and their researchers in higher education are often deeply influenced by institutions beyond those of higher education, most obviously through funded research, from governments, corporations, NGOs, and so on (arrow 9). And here, tensions are often great between interested and disinterested research, so-called. But academic researchers also often attempt to influence government (and other) policy and may write genres such as white papers, reports, popularizations, and so on (arrow 10). Finally, to come full circle, business, government, NGOs, and so on also influence or attempt to influence the teaching of students in higher education, which also often produces tensions (arrow 11). And scientific researchers outside formal educational institutions rely on formal higher education for future scientists/ employees and attempt to maintain quality through gatekeeping and other means, such as accreditation (arrow 12).

The diagram and its analysis do not consider two other factors that profoundly influence the question in our title. First, each nation and culture has different attitudes toward these differences. In the United States, for example, the term "professional" is associated with middle class or "white collar" work; in France, by contrast, "professional" work is associated with people from all walks of life, the *métiers*, and as Delcambre and Donahue point out, there was until recently a "clean split between vocational training and 'academic' education." Second, each national education system has different institutions, with different expectations for writing and literacy. (See also, this volume, Castelló & Iñesta; Dysthe; Delcambre & Donahue.) With these, *distinctions* (as the sociologist Pierre Bourdieu has long argued) come different communities, values, attitudes, even physical postures (*hexis*) — and of course different writing and textual practices. These have been the objects of research on writing (e.g., CDA below, and see, this volume, Chitez & Kruse; Delcambre & Donahue).

For the study of student writing, these questions are important, because they influence deeper questions: What sorts (genres) of text will be admitted in higher education? What sorts of people will be produced (identity) and what kinds of people will be admitted as teachers (e.g., will practitioners from these other domains and institutions be allowed to teach, as in engineering or creative arts)?

In this chapter, we will take a broad view, seeing both academic and scientific discourse and practice as functioning parts of wider networks of communication, political, social, and so on. We will consider several different research traditions that speak to important aspects of this functioning. This will allow us to see the relation between academic and scientific texts as a problem (or problematic, in the continental tradition) involving a wide range of disciplines: linguistics and applied linguistics, rhetoric, rhetoric of science, sociology, sociology of science, psychology, social psychology, "writing studies," technical communication, business communication, and so on. These traditions of research on texts and writing also grow out of different regional, national, and institutional/system contexts and address different intellectual problems and practical issues. For example, some research traditions focus on the thesis, or second language writers, or writing across the undergraduate (first cycle) curriculums. Indeed, one of the goals of this volume is to make researchers in some traditions aware of research in other traditions and the reasons for those differences as well as the commonalties in the practices.

Obviously, this chapter will not be a comprehensive literature review. All we can hope to do is provide an informal theoretical perspective, an overview from a high-flying airplane. But we will point readers to different literature reviews and seminal work in each one of the areas we mention. We also do not venture much into research in languages other than English. This is not because of a paucity of research there, but because of our ignorance of it. Where we do know some of that research we mention it, and we invite here for not being competent to include more and invite reviews of those writing research literatures to be disseminated. We also do not mention here the large literature from cognitive psychology on writing in higher education, again not only because of our lack of knowledge of it but also because it does not, in the research traditions we the authors of this chapter are familiar with, bear directly on the problem of the relation between the two communities and their texts. Other traditions, such as those of Mateos and Solé in this volume, look at students' perspectives on academic and scientific texts from a cognitive perspective.

We organize this overview by research traditions, first of all, and for each tradition, we discuss how they approach the two major problems the title raises. The first problem is describing the academic communities and their texts — and the relation between the two (formal schooling and its associated institutions), as well as the scientific communities and their texts — and the relation between those two (scientific inquiry and its associated institutions). The second problem is that of describing the relationship between the two communities through their texts.

Applied Linguistics Traditions

In most applied linguistics traditions, the focus is on analyzing the needs of students (or novices more generally) through analysis of scientific texts, and, to a lesser extent, the texts that students produce in moving toward writing those target texts, what we are calling here academic writing. The term Language for Specific Purposes (LSP) describes this effort broadly, which is mainly at the service of language teaching in second or foreign language learning settings in higher education. Although there have been important studies of nonacademic texts (e.g., English for hotel maids, brewers, and air traffic controllers), the great majority of studies have been on what is called Language for Academic Purposes (LAP) and the great majority of these on English for Academic Purposes (EAP) (Johns, 1981). EAP is further classified into English for Science and Technology (EST), the oldest and by far the largest, English for Medical Purposes, English for Legal Purposes or English for Management, Finance, and Economics, and so on (Dudley-Evans & St. John, 1998). For the applied linguistics traditions, we are discussing (mainly Anglophone) the expression *academic writing* includes both novice and expert writing, often referred to as *student writing* and *published writing*, and involves not only professors writing as researchers but also brochures, syllabuses, recommendations, reviews, and so on. The assumption is, as Biber (2006) explains, that one needs to provide full linguistic descriptions of those registers in order to help students in higher education learn to use language in new ways and for new purposes. The four main research traditions below have addressed the problem our chapter takes up. These traditions in general answer the question about academic and scientific texts posed in our title in the affirmative, by distinguishing the two as a matter degree of expertise in some field, some disciplinary community.

Swalesian Approaches

In a seminal study, John Swales (1981) investigated what was "really going on in the composition of" (p. 13) the introduction sections of experimental articles in scientific journals. His goal was to inform the design of teaching materials for nonnative university students in science. This dominant genre in natural sciences (and many social sciences) has a set structure: Introduction, Methods, Results, and Discussion (IMRD or *em-rad*). For further discussion of the IMRD structure, see Robinson-Pant and Street; Carlino, this volume.

Swales and others (1990, 2004) found that almost all introductions to experimental articles in almost all disciplines have three common "moves": Move 1, Establishing a territory; Move 2, Establishing a niche; and Move 3, Occupying a niche. But each move can be realized in a variety of ways. "A move in genre analysis is a discoursal or rhetorical unit that performs a coherent communicative function in a written or spoken discourse" (Swales, 2004, p. 229). Moves are identified not strictly by the presence or absence of certain words or syntax, but by analyzing the meaning in context and making judgments about the communicative purpose of each stretch of discourse. Given that moves are genre-bound, they can be considered building blocks to be taught to novice writers to successfully compose texts in that genre (Dudley-Evans, 1995).

Even though move schema are primarily used in the analysis of the different sections of the IMRD research article (see, e.g., Crookes, 1986; Kanoksilapatham, 2005; Thompson, 1993; Williams, 1999; Wood, 1982), this methodology has been extended to other research genres (Swales, 2004) such as book reviews (Motta-Roth, 1998) or review articles (Myers, 1991; Noguchi, 2001). Swalesian analysis shows that scientific texts are in genres that have certain regularities that nonscientific texts do not. And academic (student) texts can be taught and evaluated in terms of those genre regularities.

Corpus Approaches

Computer analysis has extended knowledge of the relation between texts and communities by allowing more subtle and more reliable distinctions to be made — thus both illuminating and complicating the question posed in our title. Computers now make it possible to quickly do quantitative analysis of the language of not just a few texts but thousands of texts, leading to more informed qualitative analysis. In the last three decades, applied linguists have assembled for analysis *language corpora*: large numbers of texts collected according to strict principles of size, sampling, and representativeness closely related to the purpose of that collection (e.g., experimental reports in nuclear medicine journals in the last three decades).

In the last 10 years, corpus-based methodologies have been favored in applied linguistics to investigate writing in many different communities, but the bulk of the studies conducted using this approach have been in LAP. Some studies look for grammatical features that researchers suspected occur more frequently in academic/ scientific prose, such as passive voice, or tense and aspect combinations like present perfect verb phrases (they do) (Biber, Johansson, Leech, Conrad, & Finegan, 1999) Or researchers do "bottom-up" searches to see what patterns emerge. For example, *lexical bundles*, groups of three (or four or five etc.) words that frequently recur in a corpus reveal differences between disciplines and between novice and expert writing within disciplines.

Some corpus studies have specifically looked at the differences between scientific (expert) and academic (novice) texts written by students in several fields. For example, Conrad's (1996) study of history and biology students found that writing becomes increasingly more informationally dense as students advance in level. Cortes's (2004) study of lexical bundles in student and published writing showed that while published authors made frequent use of certain recurrent expressions (e.g., *as a result of*, *on the other hand*, and *the fact that the*), students rarely used them, and in the few occasions they did, the function the expressions performed was slightly different from those they conveyed when used by published authors. (See Rinck & Boch, this volume, for analysis these sorts of linguistic features using different methods.)

Corpus analysis has been applied not only to experimental research articles in different disciplines but also to book and article reviews, course syllabi, university admissions materials, master's theses and doctoral dissertations (Hyland, 2008a, 2008b), or the use of particular linguistic features such as evaluative *that* (Hyland & Tse, 2005) or conditional sentences (Ferguson, 2002).

It is undeniable that corpus-based methodologies have brought about important advancements in the research of academic writing. The findings of these studies provide invaluable information for the better description of the discourse of academia that can be directly applied to the teaching of these registers to L1 and L2 writers. And they add to and complicate our understanding of the relationship between academic and scientific, student and expert writing in a range of disciplines and across disciplines.

Systemic Functional Approaches

Systemic Functional Linguistics (SFL) has made an important contribution to academic writing research and pedagogy, particularly in Australia (Jones, 2004). Drawing on M.A.K. Halliday's views of language, genre in SFL has its origins in the work of Martin (1989) and Christie (1991). SFL approaches describe texts in terms of the functions they perform and the way in which the elements that constitute those texts are organized to perform those functions. Martin (1984) defines genre as "a staged, goal-oriented purposeful activity in which speakers engage as members of our culture" (p. 25). SFL views texts in relation not to communities, per se, but to registers, linguistic manifestations of communities, analyzed in terms of the ideational, interpersonal, and textual functions of meaning-making. The register is the context. That is, text is analyzed in terms of the surrounding texts; context is constituted by texts.

SFL has extensively analyzed important registers of scientific writing, particularly those of the natural sciences and certain of the humanities, especially history.

Halliday and Martin (1993) analyze various features of scientific English such as interlocking definitions, special expressions, lexical density, syntactic ambiguity, and grammatical metaphor, among others, providing examples extracted from scientific writing of many genres and many historical periods, beginning with the origins of modern science in the 17th century.

Martin's notion of genre has been extensively used in the teaching of academic writing in the Sydney School of genre studies (Hyon, 1996). Christie (2000) analyzes teaching and learning as "staged and purposeful" social activities, "leading to the creation of classroom genres" (p. 315). Using systemic functional grammar, the analyst can trace patterns of language and literacy in progress over time and in differences in discourse across school subjects. Most SFL research has been on academic writing at the elementary and secondary school level and L2 university work, but there is a considerable literature on L1 postsecondary education. Especially notable are attempts to integrate literacy skills into particular disciplinary courses or curricula, such as accounting (Webb, Dury, & English, 1995), pharmacy (Jones, Turner, & Street, 2000), geography (Purser, Skillen, Donohue, & Peake, 2008), and a range of disciplines at Wollongong University (Skillen, Merten, Trivett, & Percy, 1998).

Critical Discourse Analysis

Critical Discourse Analysis (CDA) finds its origins in Critical Linguistics, which started at the University of East Anglia in the 1970s (Flowerdew, 2008a), and was powerfully influenced by SFL. This movement was led by Fowler (1991) and Fowler and Fowler (1996) and included names such as Kress and Hodge. These scholars focused on the development of a social approach to linguistics with a theoretical core in power relationships and the text as its unit of analysis. For CDA, "language use is always social" and "discourse both reflects and constructs the social world" (Rogers, 2004, p. 5). CDA focuses, for example, on issues of gender, ideology, and identity and on how these issues are reflected in particular texts (Paltridge, 2006). It is difficult to define CDA, but Fairclough and Wodak (1997) present a number of principles that have been used as a rationale for many studies in the field:

- discourse constructs and reflects social and political issues,
- discourse helps negotiate and perform power relations,
- social relations are reflected and reproduced by discourse, and
- the uses of discourse produce and reflect ideologies.

For Van Dijk (2001), CDA studies "the way social power abuse, dominance, and inequality are enacted, reproduced, and resisted by text and talk in the social and political context" (p. 352), and the task of critical discourse analysts is to take a position and try to comprehend, describe, and resist social inequalities.

Although power and dominance are associated with specific domains such as education, studies on academic writing in higher education that employ CDA are rare. CDA has very much influenced ACLITS approaches, however (see below).

An important exception are critical studies of the bureaucratic discourse of higher education, such as Fairclough's (1993) famous analysis of a page from the 1990 undergraduate prospectus of Lancaster University, in which he shows the closeness of university discourse to consumerism in late capitalism. In this and other respects, CDA helps to answer our question by pointing out the relations between texts of all sorts and communities of all sorts, within and beyond academe. And it sees the question in political terms.

CDA has been strongly criticized for relying too much on theory and global contextualization, that is, concentrating too much on the power relations that take place in the context in which the texts occur and not linking those generalizations about ideology to the text itself (Toolan, 2002). It has also, like SFL, been criticized for reading off sociological or ideological contexts from texts without support of other sorts of evidence beyond the text/s analyzed (Slembrouck, 2005). The next group of traditions addresses that concern.

Linguistic Anthropology and Sociolinguistics Traditions

Research on writing has also approached the problem of scientific and academic texts and communities from the perspectives of linguistic anthropology and socio-linguistics, in the tradition of Dell Hymes (1974) in the United States and Basil Bernstein (2000) in the United Kingdom. The focus is on understanding the *practices* of the *communities* around language use. Indeed, the term "practice" (evoking sociologist Max Weber's notion of social action and the Marxist concept of praxis) and the term "community" (evoking the sociolinguistic concept of "speech community" and later "discourse community") suggest the importance for these traditions of going beyond language *per se* or even the functions of language to observe people using language, with the methods of the anthropologist or sociologist.

Classroom Ethnography and Writing

The first important research on writing in higher education out of the Hymes tradition comes from research in the United States. The Writing Across the Curriculum Movement is an educational reform whose goal is to help teachers in the disciplines improve their students' academic writing and their learning through writing. A student of Hymes, Lucille McCarthy, wrote "A stranger in strange lands: A college student writing across the curriculum" (1987), a study of one first-year U.S. student's struggles to write in courses in different disciplines. Her participant, Dave, experienced great difficulty when asked to write in radically different genres in biology, poetry, and English composition classes, with little sense of the scholarly and research activities of the disciplines that motivated those genres. And the theme of misunderstandings of students and university teachers is central to later work in the United States, France, and England (see, this volume, Lea; Delcambre & Donahue; Robinson-Pant & Street).

Later work by Fishman and McCarthy (2002) takes up issues of class and race in university classroom discourse and writing, and takes up an even older tradition of analyzing the relation between school and society in communication in communities, that of Fishman and McCarthy (2007). Much other work in other countries came out of Writing across the Curriculum (WAC) as researchers trained in U.S. methods returned to do work on other countries, such as Olga Dysthe in Norway, included in this volume.

Academic Literacies (ACLITS)

The ACLITS tradition began in the mid-1990s in England and emphasized studies of the practices of higher education students and teachers, focusing, as did McCarthy, on their differing perceptions of writing. It shares with CDA an emphasis on the critical analysis of identity and power relationships, but it gets its data primarily from interviews and, to a lesser extent, classroom observations and student texts. Research by Lea and Street (1998) introduced new theoretical frames to research on writing, which was, at the time in the United Kingdom, still predominantly influenced by psychological accounts of student learning (e.g., Gibbs, 1994). Rather than frame their work in terms of "good" and "poor" writing, Lea and Street suggested that any explanation needed to examine faculty and student expectations around writing without making any judgments about which practices were appropriate. Drawing on the findings from an empirical research project conducted in two very different universities, they examined student writing against a background of institutional practices, power relations, and identities, with meanings being contested between faculty and students, and an emphasis on the different understandings and in-terpretations of the writing task. Findings from their research suggested fundamental gaps between students' and faculty understandings of the requirements of student writing, providing evidence at the level of epistemology, authority, and contestation over knowledge, rather than at the level of technical skill, surface linguistic competence, and cultural assimilation.

Based on their analysis of their research data, they explicated three models of student writing. These they termed study skills, socialization, and academic literacies. The study skills model is based on the assumption that mastery of the correct rules of grammar and syntax, coupled with attention to punctuation and spelling, will ensure student competence in academic writing; it is, therefore, primarily concerned with the surface features of text. In contrast, the academic socialization model assumes students' need to be acculturated into the discourses and genres of particular disciplines and that making the features and requirements of these explicit to students will result in their becoming successful writers. In some respects, the third model, academic literacies, subsumes many of the features of the other two; Lea and Street (1998) point out that the models are not presented as mutually exclusive. Nevertheless, they argue that it is the academic literacies model that is best able to take account of the nature of student writing in relation to institutional practices, power relations, and identities, in short to consider the complexity of meaning–making, which the other two models fail to provide (see Lea; Robinson-Pant & Street, this volume, for additional brief overviews of ACLITS). Theresa Lillis' (2001) critical ethnographic study of working class and L2 students entering higher education is a particularly important example of this work, combining qualitative and discourse analysis.

There has been little study of writing among scientists or other professionals in ACLITS. But recently, Lea and Stierer (2009) (and Lea, this volume) have studied university lecturers' everyday writing as professional practice in the university as workplace, though not their scientific writing *per se*. Perhaps, the most thorough study of the relation between writing in higher education and professions is Ivanic et al.'s (2009) *Improving Learning in College: Rethinking Literacies across the Curriculum*, which is a multiyear ethnographic study of students and teachers in what is called "further education," courses in catering, child care, and so on, and their struggles to make the transition across academic and scientific communities is highlighted. Lillis and Curry (2010) provide insight into academic and scientific intersections in their study of researchers in non-English-speaking countries attempting to publish in English language scientific journals, as do Bazerman, Keranen, and Encinas in this volume.

Rhetorical Traditions

In rhetorical traditions, mainly the North American ones with which we are most familiar, the focus is on what writing *does* (in and among communities) and how it does it (Bazerman & Prior, 2004). In one sense, both academic and scientific (or, more broadly, professional) writing are viewed as persuasive. The writers and their texts make arguments in order to have an effect on readers, but texts recently have been viewed as means of coordinating human activity more broadly. Academic and scientific texts are viewed as tools that people use — within and across communities — to carry on a host of different kinds of work, including constructing new knowledge and institutions, and maintaining, expanding, and contesting the old. In this view, texts and communities are dynamic, shifting, always only stabilized for now (Schryer, 1993).

Stylistic Analysis and Beyond

Rhetoric has often been identified with style, but rhetorical studies of scientific writing from the 1980s and beyond have looked not only at style but also at content, or rather the invention of arguments, and the topoi, or places where writers go to find arguments. For example, Fahnestock and Secor (1991) identified the specialized topoi of Anglo-American literary criticism, such as *contemptus mundi*. Or researchers look at the rhetorical construction of scientific facts in the stylistic choices of scientists and popularizers as knowledge circulates in different genres (Fahnestock, 1986). Other studies look at style as an index of the epistemology and social organization of disciplines. MacDonald's seminal study of grammatical subjects in three subdisciplines (1994) shows how different the activity of knowledge building is in each field and how their motives, methods, and social organizations differ. This early work led to a wider field of study called the Rhetoric of Science (Gross, 1990), which forms the background for much study of students' writing in reference to scientific writing.

Technical and Business Communication Research

Another tradition of research on scientific and academic texts grew out of the teaching of business writing and technical writing courses in the United States, courses required of many students in their last year of university (first cycle). Before the 1980s, these courses had focused on static forms and conventions (e.g., memos and technical descriptions). But a new rhetorical approach to its teaching led to ethnographic and case study research on *Writing in Nonacademic Settings*, as the seminal study was called (Goswami & Odell, 1985). Researchers examined ways writing is used in workplaces of various types; particularly the ways documents circulate to coordinate the activity of people across time and space. One of the workplaces they studied was that of scientific research, drawing on Bruno Latour and Stephen Woolgar's seminal study *Laboratory Life* (1979) to examine scientific communication as workplace communication. Professional organizations and journals grew up in the late 1980s to support this research, which now has an international dimension as well.

Activity and Genre Analysis (North American Writing-in-the-Disciplines Tradition)

In the late 1980s, theorists and researchers in a range of disciplines began to investigate the ways that intellectual, professional, and cultural forms of work are mediated by writing — the *Textual Dynamics of the Professions*, as an important early collection is titled (Bazerman & Paradis, 1991). These studies grow out of the writing-in-the-disciplines movement in the United States, which attempted to help students learn to write for specialized fields and "write to learn" their fields, though this research tradition has studied writing in all levels of schooling and professional training, professional and workplace writing, writing within play and leisure activities, writing mediating various spheres of public and private activity, and writing in all media of production and dissemination, especially including electronic environments. Activity approaches use a variety of research methods, qualitative and quantitative — though all empirical, including surveys, text-based interviews, protocols analysis, and ethnographic observations, as well as discourse and linguistic analysis of texts (though the latter plays a much smaller role than in applied linguistics traditions).

Bazerman (1988) began the tradition of cultural-historical activity research into scientific writing because he wanted to understand the origins and functions of student writing, the humble undergraduate (first cycle) "research paper," taught in

U.S. first-year university writing courses for almost a century. He asked what kinds of writing go on among researchers in various disciplines and how writing helps disciplines work. He focused first on the most important scientific genre, the experimental article (IMRD), from its beginnings in the 17th-century Royal Society through the 20th century, to see how communities of science evolve textual genres and how students' writing participates (or not) in that activity.

The concept of genre as social action (Miller, 1984) provided the theoretical genesis, which Miller (1994) has developed in relation to sociological theory, particularly Schutz's concept of typification and Giddens's structuration theory (Schutz & Luckmann, 1989). This tradition focuses "not on the substance or the form of discourse but on the action it is used to accomplish" (Miller, 1984, p. 151). Bazerman developed the notion of genre further with speech act theory into his theory of genre systems (1994), which traces how people and institutions use "stabilized-for-now" (Schryer, 1993) patterns of communication to accomplish coordination of action and thought.

A second theoretical framework, Vygotskian activity theory from cultural-historical psychology, furnished a theory of the relation between writing and activity, particularly learning. Bazerman's work was extended by a number of researchers who have examined student texts in academic communities in relation to scientific texts and communities, in various social practices. They found, for example (Russell, 1997), how student's identities are shaped by genre systems linking higher education to research and other domains beyond formal schooling. In a series of case studies, he and others traced the ways students' texts form developmental pathways, full of resistances often, however, and always conditioned by and conditioning institutional forms, and the texts outside schooling (Russell & Yañez, 2003; Yañez & Russell, 2009).

Drawing not only on Bazerman's work but also on Bakhtin's theory of speech genres, Paul Prior's studies of graduate students' development in applied linguistics, sociology, geography, and American studies extends Bazerman's genre systems analysis to "the ways historical activity is constituted by and lays down sediments in functional systems that coordinate with various media with different properties" (1997, p. 36) — the messy flow of graduate students' literate activity over time in multiple "streams of activity." See, this volume, Prior and Bilbro's related discussion of literate practices and disciplinary identities.

The most extended research in the North American rhetorical tradition on the similarities and differences between the writing of students and that of scientists comes from a Canadian group. In a series of case studies from the early 1990s to the present, these researchers explore the transition from university education in the workplace: the world of finance, industry, banking, law, and in social work, as well as among engineers and architects and other professionals. They use North American genre theory, situated learning, distributed cognition, and a version of activity systems to delineate the profound differences between writing at school and writing in the workplace — and ways in which student-writers become professionals who write.

The Canadian group has found significant continuities between university writing and professional writing. But they are quite obvious: grammar, spelling, personal discipline, facility with writing, and so on. But they found enormous differences, even in texts that looked very similar in terms of structure, lexicon, and grammar, because they come from two different activity systems. The most notable difference is in motivation. Students write for epistemic motives (to learn, or earn a mark), whereas professionals, including scientists, write for instrumental motives (write to get work done) (Dias, Pare, Freedman, & Medway, 1999). The outcome for students is a mark, a credential, for professionals a product or service (even if that produce is an "article"). Student writing processes are primarily individual whereas professionals (including scientists) are collective. The audience for students is primarily the professor, for professionals primarily colleagues, who have a complex system of circulation of texts (for scientists academic journals, peer review, citation, commentary, and so on).

Further work on thesis writing and writers (Paré, Starke-Meyerrin, & McAlpine, 2009) used large-scale interviews to understand the thesis as a "multi-genre," which addresses multiple requirements, which operates under multiple systems, and addresses multiple readers. Because of the Bologna process, and the consequent increase in the number of Masters and PhDs, thesis writing is a critical problem in Europe and an object for European research (Rinck, 2006a). And this is a theme in many of the chapters in this volume (Dysthe; Chitez & Kruse; Castelló & Iñesta; Rinck & Boch).

Finally, there have been many critiques of teaching scientific discourse to undergraduates as limiting their creativity and knowledge-making capacity (Thaiss & Zawacki, 2006) and a critical analysis of writing as initiation or apprenticeship at the expense of personal development and interdisciplinary prospects.

Conclusion

We end not with an insight but with a truism: The ways researchers understand academic and scientific communities and their texts as similar and different are shaped by the object, motives, and conditions of the research program undertaken.

If the goal is purely to develop linguistic analysis and theory or to provide linguistic resources to students to pursue work in a linguistically specialized and relatively stable context of activity that the researchers understand well and teachers can control (e.g., air traffic control and secondary school history exams), then fine-grained linguistic analysis is useful. If students are highly motivated and homogeneous, then perhaps little more than a logical pedagogical sequence is necessary to arrive at target proficiency. One can use only the linguistic context (the other words), perhaps supplemented by a few brief interviews (Hyland, 2000).

If the goal of research is to provide critical perspective on the writing that teachers and students in higher education do, to make generalizations about the social and cultural situation broadly, then one can also read context from texts without systematic inquiry into context using paralinguistic or nonlinguistic methods. As Slembrouck (2005, p. 622) puts it, "CDA's pivotal and privileged moment is that of the social–theoretical interpretation and explanation, and its projected unit of reference is 'societal,' broadly speaking, the stage of Late Modern/Advanced capitalist societies."

However, if the goal of research is to understand the situation of learning in relation to texts and their production in order to create or evaluate pedagogical and other institutional interventions — programs — then the researcher must move beyond linguistic context to social context, understood in anthropological or sociological or other terms. And that is what much of the North American and UK research with which we are familiar has done as well as much research on the continent under the rubric of didactics.

Finally, if the goal of research is to design and evaluate interventions to improve learning and writing — at a very deep level, both students and scientists are not only writing to communicate but also writing to learn — then one must look at the social psychological processes, the developmental trajectory of students/scientists as well as the linguistic targets, a social critique of schooling, or even ethnographic description of practices. The ways writing works beyond — and in interaction with — formal schooling and scientific research become important. And that has been the task of activity and genre approaches and the reason this chapter began with a wide view of texts and communities.

Thus, the answer to our title question depends very much on the objects studied and the motives for studying them. The heterodoxy of approaches to the question posed in the title does not mean at all that they are mutually exclusive. Learning from each other across disciplinary and geographic boundaries can produce useful cross-fertilization.

Chapter 2

Academic Enculturation: Developing Literate Practices and Disciplinary Identities

Paul Prior and Rebecca Bilbro

Introduction

Over the past 40 years, researchers and theorists have worked in varied ways to understand and document the place of writing, and literate practices more broadly, in academic enculturation. This work has increasingly taken on board a keen re-cognition of the great diversity of genres and practices displayed among the varied disciplines and professions of the academy. Not only are physics articles different from the texts that represent dance choreography, an aerospace engineering proposal, or a literary-cultural analysis, but the literate practices and ideologies associated with such work varies, sometimes radically. Recognition of such layered diversity has led to movements in two directions. The first aims to drill down into specific contexts and identify the often tacit forms and practices of academic enculturation. The second move is to look up at the trajectories people, texts, and other objects trace across contexts, to consider how students and professionals become able to navigate and negotiate the complex, multiple academic spaces of their lives. From both these perspectives, the relationships between writing and academic enculturation, whether in terms of deepening theoretical understanding or improving practical activity (including teaching/learning activity), have proven to be neither trivial nor simple.

As we undertake to represent in this chapter research from a wide range of cultural and linguistic contexts, we should first locate some of the sociocultural, disciplinary, and institutional contexts of our work. Situated in a large, public, research university in the United States and in a cross-disciplinary Writing Studies program with deep roots in both an English department and a campus

University Writing: Selves and Texts in Academic Societies
Studies in Writing, Volume 24, 19–31
Copyright © 2012 by Emerald Group Publishing Limited
ISSN: 1572-6304/doi:10.1108/S1572-6304(2012)0000024006

writing-across-the-curriculum program, our contexts orient us not only to the diversity of writing in the university but also to the complex practices of writing found before and beyond the university (in homes, schools, workplaces, and communities). In our theoretical interests, we engage with scholars who identify with the humanities, the social sciences, education, and various blends of these, while our work focuses especially on sociocultural theories and research that highlight dialogic semiotic practices, disciplinarity, and culturally-situated and embodied activity. Our research methodologies are mainly qualitative, ethnographic, and textual.

In this chapter, we suggest that research on academic enculturation has been taken up through different perspectives on three basic questions:

1) What is the content of academic enculturation? In other words, what knowledge and/or practices are being learned and developed?,
2) Where (in what spaces or what kinds of spaces) is academic enculturation happening?, and
3) How does academic enculturation (learning/development) happen?

First, we should clarify our understanding of some of the key terms. *Academic enculturation* has often been taken up as the one-way transmission of relatively stable cultural knowledge from experts to novices. Although some of the work we consider here does seem to take this position, we do not ascribe to that view. Instead, we understand enculturation to refer to the totality of processes that are involved in the ongoing production of cultural forms of life. As Lave and Wenger (1991) argued, situated learning involves processes of social (re)production that occur as relative newcomers to a social practice come to engage more intensely with that practice (and are changed by that encounter) while relative old-timers and the social practice itself encounter (and are to some extent remade) by the participation of relative newcomers. In other words, we see academic enculturation from this perspective as nothing less than the dialogic formation of academic disciplines and professions within dynamic cultural-historical fields. We take academic enculturation to be a fundamentally semiotic process, to involve semiotic (re)mediation (see Prior & Hengst, 2010) at every level, from how learning happens in situated contexts to how disciplinary knowledge circulates and is represented across different media. However, we approach this semiotic process with a special interest in writing, or more precisely in the *literate practices* (see also Robinson-Pant & Street and Lea, this volume) that weave together writing, reading, talk, observation, and action to achieve what we typically and metonymically call writing.

As the question on spaces of enculturation hints, a key issue for research on — and teaching and learning of — academic enculturation has been how disciplines and professions are imagined or conceptualized. In some cases, researchers seem to take an emic approach, accepting self-contained, culturally-named entities as the given space for inquiry (history is history, biology is biology). In other cases, such cultural categories are not taken as the final word; instead the social spaces of enculturation are theorized (e.g., as discourse communities, activity systems, or actor-networks). Finally, although some approaches continue to view spaces of enculturation as relatively discrete and self-contained (a kind of model of disciplines as separate stovepipes, conically shaped with wide entrance points leading to pinnacles of expertise), we and others view spaces of enculturation as open systems in constant interaction with other social spaces. It is this shift from thinking of disciplines as enclosed spaces to thinking of ongoing negotiations of disciplinary practice, that led one of us (Prior, 1998) to critique notions of discourse communities and suggest a focus instead on *disciplinarity*, on the open-ended, sociohistorical processes that produce, represent, and contest disciplinary practices and identities.

Answers to any one of the three questions above might succeed in abstracting patterns in certain elements of academic enculturation (e.g., in textual artifacts or genres, learning and teaching practices, disciplinary values, institutional spaces and materialities, or alignments between "disciplinary" and "non-disciplinary" spaces and activities), but also routinely raise new questions about interrelationships amongst such elements. Our examination of these three questions in this chapter is a necessarily (perhaps painfully) partial sampling of the work on academic writing and enculturation. Our goal in this chapter is the modest one of presenting a framework for understanding academic enculturation and writing, offering examples of the way that framework might organize international writing research and theory interested in writing in higher education, and concluding with some reflections on future directions the framework might recommend.

The Content of Enculturation

A great deal of writing research on enculturation focuses on identifying the content of disciplinarity. In other words, studies often focus on *whatever* it is that is seen to be developing in the course of academic enculturation. Answers to the what-question vary widely, shaped by researchers' disciplinary traditions, institutional positions, and sociocultural identities. One common object of inquiry (as seen, e.g., in Rinck & Boch, this volume) involves varieties of language, registers, textual genres, rhetorical features, and/or semiotic forms (language plus visual and other semiotics) that are associated with disciplines and professions. Research then may offer quantitative and/or qualitative analysis of the target artifacts (the texts and other forms of communication, including transcripts of conversations) displayed by experts in the disciplines or students in the process of pursuing expertise. A second approach (as seen, e.g., in Delcambre & Donahue, this volume) conceptualizes the content of academic enculturation as practices, what people (again recognized experts or students) *do* as they engage in disciplinary work. Research then may attend to phenomena such as writing processes, the negotiation of authorship and knowledge, engagement in learning as practice, and discourse or rhetorical practices (as doings rather than as artifacts). Such work tends to rely on interviews of various kinds and on observational data as well as (or sometimes in place of) texts and other artifacts. Here too we are most likely to find pedagogy or interventions in pedagogy as an object of inquiry. A third approach (as seen, e.g., in Castelló & Iñesta,

Robinson-Pant & Street, and Dysthe, this volume) sees the content as identities and social formations, taking up enculturation as the remaking of the person (i.e., not simply adding some skill set to a person, but altering the person's personality or identity as such), the remaking of the discipline (i.e., as the ongoing historical working out of what that discipline might be), and/or the renegotiation of broader social identities and power in the specific settings of academic work. Research in this approach is generally ethnographic and sociocultural. As we consider these three approaches to the content of enculturation (describing artifacts, practices, or persons and social formations), it should be clear that artifacts might be considered in examining practices and both might be considered in examining the development of social identities.

Studies of *language varieties* of the academy and the disciplines typically use techniques such as linguistic analysis (recently including corpus linguistics) and discourse analysis to investigate student and scholarly writing. Such analyses often focus on named genres, although a large and complex literature exists around academic genres (e.g., Bawarshi & Reiff, 2010; Bazerman, 1988, 2004b; Devitt, 2004; Swales, 1990, 2004), with different genre theories defining genres in different ways and many researchers drawing on multiple traditions (e.g., see Russell and Chitez & Kruse, this volume). Recent work has begun to shift from studies of individual written genres to multimodal genre systems (Bazerman, 2004b; Molle & Prior, 2008; Swales, 2004). In general, a prominent research strategy is to relate language (and sometimes other semiotic) patterns to rhetorical functions and textual organization in named genres.

Linguistic-rhetorical studies have taken varied objects of inquiry. Rowley-Jolivet and Carter-Thomas (2005) compare the syntactic patterns of information structuring displayed in native-speaking (NS) and non-native-speaking (NNS) physicists' oral and visual conference presentations and written articles. Their analysis found differences between NS and NNS physicists and between the oral and written modes. For example, NNS physicists used more passive voice in talk than NSs, fewer inversions of subject and predicate (which NSs often used to introduce new visuals), and fewer cleft structures (e.g., "What we did was..."), which were often used as a way to highlight information. Drawing on Swales' (1990) work on linguistic-rhetorical moves in research articles and analyzing two articles in microbiology (one in English, one in French), Negroni and Humbley (2004) identify linguistic markers of argument and terminology, which they suggest could be useful for LSP (language for specific purposes) courses. Drawing on analytical frameworks developed by MacDonald (1994), Samraj (2004) compares academic research papers in graduate seminars of two related disciplines (wildlife behavior and conservation biology), finding not a common genre but quite different types of texts in terms of such features as rhetorical organization, author persona, intertextual links, and focus on epistemic or phenomenal themes.

A number of studies have analyzed general and specialized text corpora. Henderson and Barr (2010) present a comparative corpus analysis of texts by French psychology students, texts by British psychology students, and published articles in psychology to examine how authorial stance was signaled through personal pronouns, adjective and adverb use, and lexical selection. Hyland (2004a) analyzes five genres (research articles, book reviews, scientific letters, abstracts, and textbook chapters) from eight disciplines, using discourse analysis and corpus linguistics to identify linguistic patterns writers use to achieve such rhetorical ends as persuasion, achieving credibility, and marking disciplinary membership. Hyland also broaches the subject of discipline-specific literacy pedagogies. Biber (2006) presents an interesting corpus linguistic analysis of spoken and written registers of "university language." The corpus includes classroom talk, textbooks, pamphlets, service encounters, administrative documents, promotional materials, and so on, but not scholarly academic books and articles. Aimed at capturing the language that undergraduates encounter in the institution, the analysis found a great variety of linguistic patterns, with complex disciplinary variations in classroom talk and textbooks as well as marked overall variation between spoken and written language.

Studies of the practices of academic enculturation move beyond consideration of the discourse of texts alone. Various in-depth studies, drawing on ethnographic methods, have looked at the processes and contexts of academic enculturation from the perspective of students and scholars (e.g., Beaufort, 2007; Canagarajah, 2002; Casanave, 2002; Chiseri-Strater, 1991; Ivanič, 1998; Lillis, 2001; Lillis & Curry, 2010; Prior, 1998; Tardy, 2009). Illustrating that attention to practice can also be realized in historical research, Bazerman (1988) examined the co-evolution of scientific research reports and scientific practice, analyzing information on the activities of writers, their rhetorical goals and contexts, as well as tracking changes in the content and language of scientific texts.

Studies of literate practices and disciplines have frequently examined work in scientific fields. Myers (1990), for example, offered insights, drawn from extended case studies, into how biologists produced both technical and popular articles, considering the intersections of authors' positionality in their fields, their rhetorical goals, and specific language and visual choices. Berkenkotter and Huckin (1995) analyzed a biologist, June Davis, in the process of negotiating publication of an article, detailing how she worked to claim novelty in response to reviewers' comments by revising the text, by conducting additional analyses, and by how she communicated with journal editors. Blakeslee (2001) represented the ongoing apprenticeship of an advanced graduate student (and then post-doctoral fellow) learning through repeated cycles of writing and response how to present scientific arguments in solid-state physics. Work in science studies (e.g., Knorr-Cetina, 1981; Latour & Woolgar, 1979) has also provided detailed accounts of literate activity in laboratories, and Latour (1999) offers an insightful case study of the way writing and other material and semiotic practices translated from field work on soil processes in the Amazon to publication of a scientific article in France.

Some studies have focused on student practices with an interest in characterizing trajectories of academic enculturation. Delcambre, Donahue, and Lahanier-Reuter (2010) (see also Delcambre & Donahue, this volume) present a cross-national, cross-language study of writing in multiple disciplines, using analysis of discourse, questionnaire responses, and interviews to examine ruptures and continuities in the experience of academic enculturation. Morton (2009) investigated the architectural presentations of students, analyzing how contextualizations, narratives, and metaphors in the presentations seemed to distinguish better received presentations from those judged less successful. Gentil (2005) presented longitudinal case studies of three francophone Quebec students to explore how they went about becoming biliterate (i.e., what kinds of practices they reported). Of interest was that friendship and social relations with anglophones emerged as one key strategy/factor in these accounts of academic enculturation. Like Lillis and Curry (2010), Gentil highlights the roles of language and of cultural brokers for students in this multilingual academic environment.

Castelló, Bañales, and Vega (2010) review different approaches to understanding regulation (control, directivity) in academic writing; they describe a movement from seeing regulation as an internal cognitive process to, as in their own work, recognizing it as dimension woven into socially-situated, dialogic, co-regulated activity. That approach is also reflected in Castelló and Iñesta's research (in this volume) on the development of academic voice and identity in academic research paper writing. Prior and Shipka (2003), using a drawing protocol and document collection for interviews about writing processes, discuss distributed regulation in the writing processes of undergraduate students, graduate students, and professors, arguing that writers display ESSPs (environment-selecting and -structuring practices) as they seek to optimize themselves and their environments for writing by selecting and structuring certain places and paces, activities and ambient environment (e.g., music), food and drink, and chains of specific social interactions.

The third view on the content of enculturation focuses on changes in identity and social formation. Lea and Street (1998) proposed the notion of academic literacies rather than academic skills or socialization (i.e., in its one-way transmission version). Seeing academic literacies as culturally and institutionally embedded and noting the ways that academic literacies implicate broader social identities and ideologies, they stress the fairly tacit, dispositional nature of academic literacies, as tutors for example could often not describe in detail the terms (e.g., "critical analysis") that they used. Students for their part emphasized the difficulty of moving from class to class and finding different, even conflicting, expectations. Extending this approach, Lea (this volume) considers the ongoing academic socialization of instructors studying to develop their teaching and Robinson-Pant and Street (this volume) consider how administrative genres (reports on meetings with students and regulation of research ethics in research on human participants) are reshaping academic practices. In studies of non-traditional students, Ivanič (1998) and Lillis (2001) provide close analyses of complex negotiations around social and academic identity, reflected in students' stances, even on specific words, and enacted in instructors' uptake of their writing.

Units of analysis for research on academic enculturation may focus on social formations rather than people. Kruse (2006a), for example, traced the historical development of the German seminar (cf. Hoskin, 1993; Prior, 1998). Historical studies of scientific and technical practice (e.g., Bazerman, 1988, 1999) focus on the ways literacy has shaped those social formations as much as how the social formations have led to particular literate practices. For instance, Bazerman (1997) examines the disciplinarity of science in relation to western, primarily American, institutions, as well as other evolving disciplines, national politics, and shifting communities of practitioners. Russell (2002) reflects on how what counts as an academic or disciplinary literacy evolves and changes as a function of institutional and national forces.

In sum, research on the content of enculturation is in many cases becoming an effort to divine relationships between meaning-making, discipline-making, and people-making. Such studies of the content of enculturation point as well to the second question of how we imagine the contexts of academic enculturation.

Spaces of Academic Enculturation

Spaces of academic enculturation have been conceptualized and imagined in quite varied ways. Taking named disciplines (physics, biology, history) as emic contexts without further specification or discussion is common throughout the literature. Various theoretical concepts (including discourse communities, communities of practice, discourses, nexus of practice, institutions, and actor-networks) have also been used to theorize the social character of academic enculturation.[1] However, in many cases, these notions mainly seem to re-designate the already given emic boundaries of disciplines (which are neither altered nor interrogated empirically) or perhaps to re-characterize the nature of the given space (e.g., as more or less homogeneous or hierarchical). The question of space also raises issues of the relationship of the academy, disciplinarity, and other social formations, of whether inquiry into academic enculturation should be focused solely on higher education and culturally-marked knowledge enterprises (e.g., laboratories, think-tanks, analytic/research units within corporate and public institutions) or should be seen as a dispersed, rhizomatic phenomenon that extends to a wide range of public and private spaces not culturally-marked as academic or disciplinary.

Theoretical representations of the spaces of academic enculturation vary in terms of their territoriality, openness, heterogeneity, and social organization. Becher (1989) offers a particularly explicit instance of the use of spatializing metaphors (conceptualizing disciplines as territories) linked to a particular kind of social hierarchy (a tribe). Hierarchical ownership and control of disciplinary spaces (cf. Swales' 1990, accounts of discourse communities) locates disciplinary enculturation in particular groups of individuals who serve as the arbiters of disciplinarity. Viewed as spaces owned and organized by a core of central experts, discourse

---

[1] For key literature on different approaches to spaces and practices of enculturation, see the following for: community of practice (Lave & Wenger, 1991; Barton & Tusting, 2005), nexus of practice (Scollon 2001; Norris & Jones, 2005), discourse (Gee, 1990), activity systems (Engeström, 1993; Russell, 1997), and actor-networks (Latour, 2005). For current formulations of the notion of discourse communities, see Swales (2004) and Beaufort (2007). For a new rhetorical model that combines several traditions of cultural-historical activity theory, see Prior et al. (2007).

communities have been defined (e.g., Beaufort, 2007; Swales, 1990, 2004) as entities that establish norms of communication, thinking, inquiry, and argument. This notion has been critiqued as underspecified, over-idealized, and over-homogeneous (e.g., Prior, 1998). Less territorial, more theorized, and more open-ended accounts of the social have been sought in notions of communities of practices, activity systems, and actor networks. These notions, and other imaginings of the social, have begun to re-map academic enculturation.

One line of work has focused on unpacking the presumed links between academic and workplace practices, challenging the assumption that enculturation offers a smooth trajectory from novice to expert (cf. Delcambre & Donahue's discussion, this volume, of the complications in transitions between levels of schooling). Dias et al. (1999) offer an in-depth, richly detailed ethnographic exploration of relations between school and workplace in several disciplines, but insist on stark differences between these two "worlds." On the contrary, Barajas (2007), Scollon and Scollon (1981), and Ochs, Taylor, Rudolph, and Smith (1992) all suggest strong relations between even the most mundane everyday discourses and academic discourses. Deyrich (2004) argues, following Lave and Wenger (1991), that the notion of professional domains (*milieu*) is too simple and static, proposing instead a notion of professional landscapes (*paysage professionnel*) that emphasizes the dual tensions between the plural material and subjective, production and reception dimensions of such landscapes. Deyrich then considers how to implement this perspective in LSP pedagogy for the field of public administration. There is, in fact, interesting evidence (e.g., Winsor, 1996) of a reverse trajectory, as research attributes disciplinary literacy learning to workplace experiences that then shape formal coursework.

In addition to illuminating processes of enculturation, such studies draw attention to the dissonances and synchronies between academic discourses and non-academic, counter-institutional, and private discourses. Lillis (2001) draws attention to the often discordant relationship experienced by multilingual, multicultural students between everyday spaces, such as the home, and institutional spaces of higher education. For example, she reports an instance where one of her participants, Nadia (a 22-year women from Yemen who was studying to be a bilingual support teacher in England), deletes a personal observation from a paper, a sentence where she observed that she had "slip[ped] through the [educational] system" and not gotten support for her bilingualism. When Lillis asked why she had cut it, Nadia reported that another tutor had told her she should not "offend anybody," though the paper Nadia was writing was intended to be read only by Lillis, the other tutor, and Nadia herself. Like Casanave's (2002) case study of the struggles of Virginia, a Latina women who receives alienating responses from professors and ends up exiting a traditional sociology program, this small but explicit regulation of Nadia's expression of her perspective exposes the micropolitics of social identity and power as well as of academic enculturation.

Locating academic enculturation in national and global spaces represents another expansion of the traditional mapping. For example, Laffont's (2006) investigations of what it means to be an engineer show that the discipline does not mean the same thing in France, America, and England. Chitez and Kruse (this volume) consider how national writing cultures (and regional cross-national institutions) shape the genre systems of education. Likewise, Dysthe (this volume) discusses how national traditions and cross-national institutional reforms play out in complex ways in terms of practices, like teacher response. Foster (2006) traces differences in the structuring of time, writing processes, and texts in a cross-national (Germany and US) comparison of writing in several disciplines. Canagarajah (2002) examines the challenges of scholars working on the periphery of the global system. Focusing on his experiences writing and submitting articles for publication while he was in Sri Lanka, he notes how lack of current journals, lack of paper and technologies of production (which the government was banning for political reasons during the civil war), and the need to cover unusual contingencies for contact information in letters to the editor, all marked his place and his texts in problematic ways.

Taking trajectories of academic enculturation to be rooted in and connected to processes of development in other social arenas also alters conceptions of academic enculturation significantly. Hawisher, Selfe, Kisa, and Ahmed (2009) explore how transnational lives and new digital spaces are woven into the development of students' literacies. Prior's (1998) chronotopic case study of Lilah and Prior and Shipka's (2003) drawing protocol studies examine complex ways that academic writers structure their lives, recruiting, for example, their families as collaborators as they engage in academic writing tasks. In a fascinating case study of Kate, an MA student in English, Roozen (2009) traces how Kate's fan fiction practices (writing and drawing) move from her home life to high school to college. Kate composes a graphic (drawings and text) version of *Spy vs. Spy* (a black and white comic strip), doing a kind of self-directed writing- and drawing-to-learn activity to understand the "agent" in Kenneth Burke's pentad for a graduate course on rhetoric. Roozen's analysis suggests the unexpected, but very consequential nature of such links between the everyday and the academic.

Current inquiry then is increasingly focused not only on higher education and culturally-marked knowledge enterprises, but on the social and personal trajectories that students and professionals trace through multiple worlds. Studies of academic enculturation from this perspective have begun to reveal the extent to which academic enculturation must be theorized as a dispersed, rhizomatic phenomenon that extends to public and private spaces not marked as academic or disciplinary. Implications of such re-mapping of enculturation call attention to the third question, how learning — and teaching — happen across these settings.

Enculturation as Learning

Academic enculturation involves not only what is learned but also *how learning occurs*. Theoretically, learning is widely understood as some kind of appropriation of practices from, or through interaction with, other people, cultural artifacts and (natural or made) environments (see Lave & Wenger, 1991; Valsiner & Rosa, 2007; Wertsch, 1991). Practically, how to effectively structure learning (whether through direct instruction or relatively implicit apprenticeship) remains a challenge. Accounts of how writers learn across settings (as in Roozen, 2009) and of the challenges writers face to adopting new practices and identities (as in Lillis, 2001) suggest the complexity of learning when understood as systems of practice rather than isolated focal events of instructional transmission and directed task activity.

The past decade has witnessed a growing recognition of the complexity of learning to write and communicate in a disciplined way (or of teaching others to do so) and an increasing rejection of simple transmission models of writing development in favor of greater emphasis on complex relationships between language and disciplinarity (Reuter & Donahue, 2007). In Cooke's (2002) study, for example, we see not only how different disciplinary spaces can come together in a language center, but also how the practices of non-scientists (like English editors and writing coaches) come into play in the scientific enculturation of scientists and the reproduction of scientific disciplines. Mitchell and Andrews' (2001) collection of essays on learning to argue in higher education suggests how certain learning contexts emphasize explicit pedagogy, while others demonstrate a telling absence.

Much of the work on academic enculturation has been either silent on how such learning happens or seems to presume that learning is transparent, that transmission (e.g., awareness-raising) of, say, language patterns in a genre will suffice to promote learning. Consider how, informed by interviews and text analysis, Dressen (2002, also Dressen-Hammouda, 2008) examines textual and intertextual moves in the field reports, conference papers, and eventually published articles of a doctoral student in geology. She suggests that the student was learning to manage complex semiotic frameworks grounded in field experience through certain textual practices (including explicit and disguised representations of research activity in the field) as well as developing increasing mastery of specialized lexical and thematic markers of the discipline. Working from a novice-to-expert, text-centered approach, Dressen-Hammouda's impressive analysis, however, offers no insight into *how* the student developed these practices in the course of multiple years of enculturation. In contrast, Goodwin (1994, 2000) examines a similar case, the activity of archeologists in the field, tracing moment-to-moment sequential acts in short episodes where relative novices seem to be learning "professional vision" through embodied and situated apprenticeship, but he then pays little to no attention to texts, literate practices in this setting, or the chains of situated activity over time that must constitute a trajectory of enculturation. Likewise, Mateos and Sole (2009) offer a rich study (using think-aloud protocols in an educationally-sensitive source synthesis task with writers at four levels of education) that documents interesting practices and textual patterns in a cross-section of academic writers. As the task complexity increased for more advanced students, they found the students often failing on key elements of the topic synthesis. However, their study again is silent on *how* students changed and *why* some did not seem to be achieving the mastery of such tasks that might be expected; their pedagogical conclusion is grounded in a model of simple transmission, that is, that students should be taught more (or better) how to undertake these tasks. If some studies attend to texts but not learning, other research, as Castelló, Bañales, and Vega (2010) note, that *does* attend to questions of learning practices may be less attentive to genres and texts.

Research has also looked at the power of particular learning/teaching practices or structures for academic enculturation. Qualitative research has examined learning practices, such as instructional trajectories, study activities, response to writing, and organizations of instruction (Leki, 1995, 2002; Thaiss & Zawacki, 2006; Zamel & Spack, 1998). Response to writing has received considerable research attention. Ferris (2003) offers a detailed review of theory, research and pedagogical approaches to response and how such response shapes students' texts, learning, practices and disciplinarity (see also Prior, 1998). The role of mentoring in academic enculturation is another interesting object of inquiry in graduate education. Belcher (1994) documents some of the different kinds of relationships that mentors forge with students and some of the positive and negative consequences of those relationships. Dysthe's (2002) ethnographic studies of teachers and advisors suggest that these actors sometimes identify themselves as arbiters and other times as collaborators, and that these identifications are somewhat dependent on disciplinary location. Some longitudinal studies of writing have considered the structuring of students' writing development at specific universities over the college years (see, e.g., Bartholomae & Matway, 2010; Fishman, Lunsford, McGregor, & Otuteye, 2005; Haswell, 1991; Sommers & Saltz, 2004). Dysthe's (1996) observations of writing-to-learn pedagogies in two countries demonstrate how such programs can encourage students to learn academic discourse by writing and speaking in their own languages, dialects, and discourses. Investigations have also considered how national forces exert influence over educational initiatives such as writing-across-the-curriculum and academic literacies approaches in England, France, and the United States (Russell, Lea, Parker, Street, & Donahue, 2008).

Social conceptions of learning trajectories (Castelló et al., 2010) based on sociocultural psychology (Valsiner & Rosa, 2007) tend to envision more relationships between learning contexts and communication contexts (Camps, 2003), and the subsequent construction of informed pedagogies (Carlino, 2005a, this volume). One active line of sociocultural research on learning theories and processes is exploring the ways that self-regulation theory applies to writing (Castelló, Iñesta, & Monereo, 2009; Castelló & Iñesta, this volume). For instance, Vazquez, Pelizza, Jakob, and Rosales (2007) report on a study of writing regulation instruction to undergraduate psychology students, analyzing the extent to which such instruction produces better writing and more autonomous writers. While such studies underscore the socially shared processes of disciplinary enculturation, they may not attend to broader spaces of enculturation, to learners' discursive and material relationships with extra- and non-disciplinary actors (such as faculty from other departments, mentors from outside the academy, generalized institutional requirements, and previous and concurrent learning experiences in other classes and spaces). Broadly, developing rich and convincing accounts of the learning and teaching activity that shapes academic enculturation represents a critical need for future work in this area.

Conclusion

Work on academic enculturation has varied radically in terms of theoretical frameworks, methodologies, and units of analysis. On the one hand, a number of studies have focused on the nature of academic texts or genres, generally assuming (1) that a variety of language is the content of enculturation, (2) that culturally-given (emic) spaces of enculturation are unproblematic, and (3) that the question of how such genres are learned is relatively transparent. In terms of our introduction, such studies tend to drill down (looking at particular sets of texts), although some (Biber, 2006; Henderson & Barr, 2010) take more comparative and open-ended stances. At the other extreme is work (e.g., Casanave, 2002; Castelló & Iñesta, this volume; Ivanič, 1998; Lillis, 2001; Prior, 1998; Robinson-Pant & Street, this volume; Roozen, 2009) that takes academic enculturation to be a matter of remaking the person with a disciplined identity, remaking the discipline as it engages new participants, and remaking society through these processes; that sees the spaces of enculturation to be open-ended dynamic, and contested (neither autonomous nor stable); and that attends closely to questions of learning practices in relation to what might be regarded as relatively successful, unsuccessful, or even conflictful enculturation. Such studies are more likely to look up (seeking connections among contexts), though they may selectively drill down into certain key practices.

In the middle ground between these extremes, complex patterns obtain. For example, Rowley-Jolivet and Carter-Thomas's (2005) study of NS and NNS physicists, noted earlier, illustrates the complexity of these patterns. On the one hand, their research works to move beyond the privileging of written texts (as seen in Swales' 1990 focus on linguistic-rhetorical practices in research articles), not only taking up conference presentations (as Swales, 2004 did) but also considering their multimodal character (both by examining the relations of language to visuals and comparing conference talk to written articles). On the other hand, they seem to assume that the appropriate linguistic-rhetorical forms are those of the NS physicists and recommend that EAP instruction work through consciousness-raising to call attention to the patterns they found in spoken registers. The privileging of national languages, particularly English and its role in international scholarship, is also coming under greater scrutiny as seen in work by scholars like Casanave (2002), Canagarajah (2002), and Lillis and Curry (2010).

Our sense is that the broadest framework for understanding academic enculturation is one that sees it as situated, historical, evolving dialogic activity, as sites where students, professionals, and societies are being remade in practice. In the fullest sense of the term, enculturation not only includes specific discursive forms but also practices that migrate and are recontextualized across settings, practices that implicate ideologies and changes in participant identities. Increasing theorization and interrogation (both theoretical and empirical) of culturally-given academic and disciplinary categories is a promising development, as is the widening array of pedagogical innovations designed to make academic content and practices more visible, whether for critical inspection and reform or for enhancing learning and adoption.

Given the complexity of the phenomena, we believe it is critical for research to orient to some broad framework that links textual forms, literate and semiotic practices, identities, and social formations in dynamic and historical trajectories. Within such a framework, we are not suggesting the impossible — that individual researchers become expert at everything or that studies can only proceed by studying the expansive, spatial-temporal, open-ended whole of academic enculturation. Strategically, drilling down and paying very close attention to the linguistic and other visual features of disciplinary texts can provide a richly detailed portrait of language and semiotic patterns in such texts. Likewise, drilling down into the interactional practices (oral, written, gestural) of participants around a single disciplinary site (classroom, laboratory, research group) may be very productive. Alternately, it is critical to trace how people move among across multiple genres (in modes that may be spoken, written, other, or mixed) and across multiple contexts (e.g., a student moving from one class to another to a research site, a professor moving from undergraduate instruction, to highly specialized disciplinary journal publication, to a conference paper at an interdisciplinary conference or a popular publication, or a student moving from writing in a religious or community organization to writing in the academy). Tracing people, artifacts, practices, and identities across settings blurs boundaries between academic and non-academic settings, suggesting the need to interrogate sociohistoric developments, social practices and social identities, to understand how they shape, and are shaped by, academic enculturation. Any inquiry then should keep in mind this kind of expansive framework for academic enculturation (rather than imagining that whatever has been brought into focus actually constitutes the whole phenomenon), and the field should support occasions to bring together data from different studies under such encompassing frameworks. Such an approach also suggests that multidisciplinary, multilingual, multinational teams might effectively study disciplinary enculturation by linking attention to different elements and dimensions in single cases, making the integration of knowledge about academic enculturation a key goal of the research enterprise itself.

Chapter 3

Academic Writing and Authorial Voice

Nancy Nelson and Montserrat Castelló

Shifts in discourse theory have often been accompanied by changed conceptions of *voice*. One shift occurred when this term, which had been used only for oral language, came to be used for written language too. *Voice* began referring to distinctive ways of writing associated with particular authors and thus became a near synonym for *style*. Not only did literary scholars examine the aesthetic qualities of particular authors' language, but composition educators in the expressivist tradition of the 1960s and early 1970s called for novice writers to discover, and to write in, their own individual voices. Elbow (1973) put it this way, "In your natural way of producing words there is a sound, a texture, a rhythm–a voice–which is the main source of power in your writing. … [T]his voice is the force that will make a reader listen to you, the energy that drives the meaning" (p. 7).

This individualistic notion of voice is being questioned, and the concept of voice has become more complex in the past four decades. Today, attention is going to the multiplicity of voices associated with writing as well as to voice as a manifestation of writers' discursive and relational identities (cf. Ivanič, 1998, 2005). The French poststructuralists made academics aware of the polyphony of written language, and Bakhtin's (1981) notions of heteroglossia — the multiple, competing, and often conflicting voices that comprise a text — came to Western European as well as North American theory. Research into the social nature of writing has emphasized the various kinds of collaboration that are involved in writing, not only coauthorship but also response from those whom Reither and Vipond (1989) called "trusted advisors." These activities have implications for a conceptualization of authorial voice. Also providing complications has been research into the use and appropriation of textual "sources" that is customary in academic writing (e.g., Nelson, 2001a; Spivey, 1990) and the changes that translators make when they transform a text for another linguistic community. Any analysis of the concept of voice must consider complexities

University Writing: Selves and Texts in Academic Societies
Studies in Writing, Volume 24, 33–51
Copyright © 2012 by Emerald Group Publishing Limited
All rights of reproduction in any form reserved
ISSN: 1572-6304/doi:10.1108/S1572-6304(2012)0000024007

resulting from appropriation and transformation of other writers' texts in the writing of a "new" text.

In this chapter, we consider the question of voice/s in light of research that we and others have conducted into social processes and cultural practices. Our purpose is to interrogate the concept of voice and to consider its complications, particularly as the construct relates to academic writing. We use the term *academic writing* to refer to writing produced in and for "the *academy*." The concept thus encompasses the writing that scholars in academe produce as they engage in the knowledge-making practices of their disciplinary communities. It also refers to the writing of students who, as disciplinary neophytes, are learning — and are beginning to adopt — the forms and conventions of scholarly communication in their fields. Our attention is first on the nature of voice as it is projected and interpreted in written communication, particularly the complexities associated with authority and authenticity in academic writing. That leads to a focus on particular discourse markers, including metadiscourse and self-mention, which seem to communicate an authoritative and authentic voice but which vary across disciplines, languages, and cultures. That section is followed by a consideration of the complex challenges student writers face as they seek to adopt such features. After these discussions, attention goes to the complexity resulting from the mixing of voices and insertion of voices in other voices as academic writers engage in discourse practices. The conclusion draws from the previous sections to consider the matter of individual identity as well as social identity as these two constructs relate to voice.

Voice Projected and Interpreted

The complex and often elusive concept of voice refers to attributes associated with the writing of a single or collective writer. In referring to an individual, we might say, for instance, that a writer has an authoritative voice, a deferential voice, or a strident voice. Although written language signals voice for its author, it is important to note that voice is not somehow *in* the language of the text. Instead, a writer's voice is inferred from textual cues by those who read the text; it is manifested in the social relation between writer and reader in a particular context. A writer may seek to project a certain kind of voice and make choices for writing that seem associated with that kind of voice, but voice is not realized until perceived by a reader.

Readers' Inferences

This point about the role of readers was made by Matsuda (2001) when he defined voice as "the amalgamative *effect* of the use of discursive and non-discursive features that language users [appropriate], deliberately or otherwise, from socially available yet ever-changing repertoires" (p. 40, italics ours). In a subsequent article, Tardy and Matsuda (2009) described voice as a writer-reader negotiation "motivated" by the text, and they pointed out that differences can be expected across readers in terms of the effect. Castelló and Iñesta (this volume) argue for a dynamic conception of the *voicing* that writers do in the process of crafting a text. This dynamic activity includes writers' choosing discursive and nondiscursive features based not only on their knowledge but also their intentions relative to the discourse community. It is important also to note the dynamic nature of a reader's interpretation of voice — an interpretation that may change as the text is read and also when it is discussed or simply remembered.

Concepts related to voice include *persona* and *ethos*, which also refer to perception of the writer's character and subjectivity. Cherry (1988) has researched the distinction between the two interrelated terms. The concept of *ethos*, which dates back to classical Greek rhetoric, is one of three traditional means of persuasion, which also include *pathos* and *logos*. *Ethos* refers to "a set of characteristics that, if attributed to a writer on the basis of textual evidence, will enhance the writer's credibility" (p. 268). *Persona*, which has developed within a literary tradition, refers to "roles authors create for themselves in written discourse given their representation of audience, subject matter, and other elements of context" (pp. 268–269). In establishing an ethos appropriate for a text one is writing, the writer must analyze the audience and consider the persona he or she is projecting. For instance, Booth (1963) described the need for a writer to establish "a rhetorical stance" — balancing, for a particular situation, elements related to the topic, the audience, and "the voice, the implied character, of the speaker" (p. 27). Other items that collocate with voice in that they also draw attention to the writer's "self" are *agency*, *presence*, and *ownership*.

Readers derive, or rather they *construct*, a sense of an author when they infer human characteristics from the text. Writers' choices in terms of textual features as well as content do much to communicate these characteristics, which may be attributed to that particular individual. But these choices in terms of textual features and content may also be associated with the subject positions of particular groups, and so, such phrases are heard as "a feminist voice," "an ethnographer's voice," "a bureaucratic voice," or "a graduate student voice." In this chapter, we focus on features associated with academic writing, particularly on the part of scholars who publish in their fields and also postgraduate students preparing for academic careers. So our attention is now on writing that is considered to have some degree of authority and is seen as authentic by members of academic discourse communities.

Authority and Authenticity in Academic Writing

In academic discourse practices, writers are generally expected to conform to certain norms, which include the conventions of academe in general as well as more specific conventions associated with their own disciplinary specialization. Through adopting and employing these conventions, writers are more likely to be seen as having a voice that is *authentic* for the practices in which they engage. These features extend well beyond guidelines that journals provide for those seeking publication and also specifications faculty give to postgraduate students, such as following a sanctioned style manual, such as the *APA Publication Manual*. We are speaking here of what often falls in the realm of tacit knowledge, since it is often unarticulated but is developed by practitioners through engaging in disciplinary activities.

With respect to academic writing, one may speak of *authority* as well as *authenticity*. As pointed out elsewhere (Nelson, 2001b), even though their etymologies differ, the two concepts have been linked together in considerations of academic writing. The goal of much formal and informal instruction in academic writing is for students to write with some authority in a way that is authentic for academe and for their disciplines and specializations. Like *author*, the term *authority* came from *auctor* (Latin for "originator," which was derived from *augere* "to increase"). Although the Bakhtinian conception of voice/s has informed this piece, we should note that we are not using the term *authoritative* as Bakhtin (1981) did when he described "authoritative discourse" as discourse that does not enter into dialogue. We use *authority* as it is frequently used in writing studies as "capacity to convince others" and "credibility," and our use of *authoritative* accords with commonplace uses in writing studies as "of "having or arising from authority." We assume that a text can be authoritative in this sense and still enter into dialogue with others. The other concept, *authenticity* (from *authentes* (Greek for "doer of the deed")), is also critical to academic writing because it is not enough just to have the authority that accompanies knowledge of one's topic. The writer must write in a way that is appropriate for the audience, context, and community; the writing must be authentic in the sense of being consistent with the practices in which the writer is engaging. This can be challenging for students as they often lack understanding of how, when, and why some discursive resources are useful and appropriate. As Castelló, Iñesta, Pardo, Liesa, and Martinez-Fernández (2011) have pointed out, students must learn communal expectations but must also learn how to adapt conventions so that their texts fulfill their own goals.

Tardy and Matsuda, cited earlier, conducted a study addressing these twin themes of authority and authenticity. They interviewed journal article reviewers regarding the thoughts they had about writers' voices when they made decisions on submitted articles. Interestingly, it was the negative responses that seemed to provide the clearest insights into what was desired in terms of rhetorical features. Consider the following comments regarding lack of authority and/or lack of authenticity:

> The only times I start thinking about the author come when (1) sh/e seems more like a graduate student than an established researcher (needs to adopt a more authoritative tone), (2) the language errors suggest that English is not the writer's first language (more help is needed with final editing), or (3) there's a lack of careful copy-editing (which creates an impression of the writer as rather

slip-shod, which doesn't help the writer's overall credibility all that much.) (p. 40)

My speculation is not something that I intend from the start. Usually it is triggered by anomalies in the text: strange use of in-discipline jargon that suggests the writer may be trained in another discipline, self-reference to the author's sex or previous work, stylistic features that suggest the piece is a graduate seminar paper, etc. (p. 43)

The most 'telling' type of author self-reveal is the tentative-voiced author with a manuscript that appears to be a paper prepared for a graduate class by someone new to the field and not very certain of how to prepare a research paper. Often such manuscripts further self-reveal as being written by a non-native speaker based on an accumulation of language errors. I have rarely if ever recommended publication of those pieces that are written by novices who should not have been encouraged to submit them in the first place. (p. 43)

These reviewers responded negatively to writing that seemed to come from a novice rather than someone more grounded in the field (sounding like a graduate student, sounding tentative), from someone who was an outsider (sounding like someone who is not in the field), or from someone who did not have command of academic English (sounding like a nonnative speaker). The importance of the conventions of writing was underscored in this study, showing the extent to which reviewers were influenced negatively by deviations from norms. Tardy and Matsuda concluded, "Although readers may find certain breaks from convention to be refreshing and thus rhetorically effective, those rupture still have to occur within particular parameters" (p. 45). These researchers also pointed out how closely language is interrelated with content in impressions regarding a writer's voice and concluded that knowledge and style overlap in discursive identity. This connection between content and language presents challenges to researchers who struggle to identify the linguistic resources that are tied to those concepts that are now considered authorial voice and discursive identity (e.g., Rinck & Boch, this volume).

Discursive Resources that Communicate Authorial Voice

Voice in writing is cued, of course, through language — lexical items, word order, clusters of words, syntax, text organization, markers such as italics, and much more. In this section, we focus attention on features that have been shown to be especially important for academic writers with respect to that construct labeled *voice*. As such, they can be considered discursive resources for projecting an authorial academic voice to one's readers.

Metadiscourse Relative to Discourse Norms

Much of the research relevant to voice in academic writing addresses what is called *metadiscourse*. Credit for the notion often goes to Crismore (1983), who spoke of its elements as both informational and attitudinal. She and her colleagues (Crismore, Markkanen, & Steffensen, 1993) defined metadiscourse as linguistic material that does not add to the propositional content of the text but "is intended to help the listener or reader organize, interpret, and evaluate the information given" (p. 40). Also important in conceptualizing metadiscourse has been Vande Kopple (1985), who explained that metadiscourse helps readers "organize, classify, interpret, evaluate, and react" (p. 83). Today, much of the work in metadiscourse is associated with Hyland, who has conducted extensive research through corpus analyses. In 2004, he linked metadiscourse and voice by claiming that metadiscourse in academic writing contributes to communication of "a 'voice' consistent with disciplinary norms," and this is done "by revealing a suitable relationship to [one's] data, arguments, and audience" (p. 136). In Hyland (2005b), he defined metadiscourse as "a cover term for the self-reflective expressions used to negotiate interactional meanings in a text, assisting the writer ... to express a viewpoint and engage with readers as members of a particular discourse community" (p. 37).

Many researchers have adopted a conception of metadiscourse that has the two major components mentioned above: *textual*, those devices that signal the organization of the writing, and *interpersonal*, those devices that suggest the writer's attitude toward the content. However, Hyland and Tse (2004) argued for a renaming of the two types, using the label *interactive* to replace *textual* and *interactional* to replace *interpersonal*, since all metadiscourse is really "interpersonal" in that it is a means for writers to relate to readers. Interactive metadiscourse includes frame markers ("first," "in conclusion"), transitions ("therefore," "moreover"), endophoric markers ("as discussed below"), evidentials ("according to"), and code glosses ("that is to say"). Interactional metadiscourse include boosters ("certainly," "without doubt"), hedges ("possibly," "might"), attitude markers ("correctly," "arguably"), self-mentions (I, me, my, we, us, our), and engagement markers ("consider," "note").

The features collectively labeled metadiscourse seem to contribute to both authenticity and authority in terms of voice in academic writing. Their use in a way that is conventional for the disciplinary group helps a writer show that he or she *belongs* and also helps the writer be more convincing in presenting the claim. Metadiscourse is said to encompass various linguistic devices that writers use to shape their writing for their audience — helping readers interpret the text in the way intended by the writer. It has become an umbrella concept encompassing various aspects of writing, including some aspects of writing that have been associated with stance or evaluation and also self-mention. Kuhi and Behnam (2011) have argued that its use is necessary for scholars as they engage in the following practices associated with academic life:

securing acceptance for academic arguments, constructing an intelligent and engaging self firmly established in the norms of the discipline, and reflecting an appropriate degree of confidence that is needed for producing symbolic capital in [the] academy, marketing the research, underscoring its novelty, and showing that the work deserves to be taken seriously. (pp. 123–124)

Although metadiscourse is common in academic writing, there are, however, significant differences across disciplines and across national, linguistic, and cultural traditions — too many differences to review in this brief article. General claims regarding metadiscourse are few in number, such as those from corpus studies showing that articles from the natural sciences tend to include fewer metadiscourse markers than those from social sciences and humanities (Hyland, 2008b) and that more advanced practitioners of a discipline employ metadiscourse to a greater extent than the less advanced (Hyland, 2004b; cf. Boch & Rinck, 2010). Nevertheless, research in metadiscourse is accumulating and can be used as a basis for educational reflection. Some studies point rather specifically to particular features that tend to mark writing as either expert or novice in particular disciplines. For instance, Koutsantoni (2006) found differences in the density and function of hedges when he compared students' theses with published research articles in engineering. Students had more hedges and used them as a means of avoiding responsibility for claims, whereas the published engineers had fewer hedges and those tended to be personally attributed. To have a full understanding of metadiscourse, attention must also go to intentional and strategic use of the features that are so labeled. The ability to choose particular features is likely related to what Walker (2007) has called "academic regulation" — a term that refers to co-regulation by the writer and also by the academic community in which the writer sees acceptance.

Much of what is known about metadiscourse relative to writing in higher education comes from studies of one particular discourse form, the research report, which for students often takes the form of the academic research paper. It is important to emphasize that there can be important differences across genres and that it would be a mistake to try to generalize to all kinds of scholarly writing. Moreover, along with disciplinary differences, genre differences, and differences associated with position in the community, there are also differences associated with language and with culture. (See discussion in Bazerman, Keranen, and Encinas's chapter, this volume.) Back in 1993, Mao argued that the features included in metadiscourse tend to be Western in nature. He claimed that undergirding the metadiscourse of Western rhetoric are assumptions that the writer is separate from the discourse and that there is a need to lead, even "control," the reader. A Chinese rhetoric, Mao pointed out, would not share such assumptions. In Chinese discourse, there is a privileging of harmony of the writer and the community and also a unity of the writer with the discourse. Much of the authority associated with the writing would come not from the writer but from citing authorities or referring to ancient practices.

First Person Pronouns and Self-Mention

Especially in the North American English tradition but increasingly in research associated with other places and languages, attention in studies of "voice" has been devoted to one particular metadiscursive element: use of the first-person pronoun. This is understandable, as self-mentioning would seem to make readers conscious of the subjectivity of the author. For instance, Ivanič (1998) has said that use of first person plays a role in writers' presentations of "discoursal selves." First-person pronouns seem to be so strongly related to authorial voice that some educators have attempted to put "voice" into "voiceless" learning materials by incorporating these pronouns (e.g., Beck, McKeown, & Worthy, 1995). Through the years, though, much debate has surrounded use of first person in U.S. academic writing, as shown in Donahue's (2007) review of this issue. It is clear that use of first person has tended to increase in disciplinary writing through the years, and many of the former stylistic sanctions against it are gone. Nevertheless, students' problems in using first-person pronouns often reveal lack of clarity within academic disciplines regarding the issue. Consequently, students often use it tentatively, wondering if it is appropriate for academic writing. They ask, Will using *I* make my writing seem less academic?

First person is used by publishing academic authors, but there is much variability in the extent to which it is used as well as the functions that it can fill in a particular text. Disciplines differ in terms of first-person pronouns, as shown in Hyland's (2001) corpus analysis of articles from eight disciplines. Writers in the humanities and social sciences tended to use first person — and thus personal reference — to a much greater extent than writers in science. In another corpus analysis of research articles, Harwood (2005) found that writers are able to promote themselves and their own work while ostensibly using these pronouns for other purposes, such as creating a space for the research, providing organization for the article, explaining procedures, and reporting findings. Most studies of personal pronouns have focused on written research reports, but there are differences across genres. For example, according to Rowley-Jolivet and Carter-Thomas (2005), use of first person tends to increase when a written research paper is presented orally at a conference. Moreover, different uses can be observed that relate to theoretical approaches or specific purposes for the writing.

It seems clear that, along with the disciplinary differences, there are also complex national, linguistic, and cultural differences. These were shown, for instance, when Fløttum (2003) examined single-authored articles in French, English, and Norwegian in three disciplines. Overall, when singular and plural were combined, Norwegian had the most frequent use, and French had least frequent. But these results were not consistent across disciplines; nor were they consistent when first-person singular and first-person plural were considered separately. In speaking of academic writing in China, Mao (1993), who was cited previously, pointed out that the first-person pronoun *wo* does not communicate the same individualism that *I* does in English, and its possessive form can refer to plural as well as singular. He stated, "Any conclusion that generalizes our characterization of metadiscourse beyond its own parochial boundary is to deny a rich tradition of rhetorical practices in other non-Western cultures" (p. 284).

What is the answer to the student's question regarding first person that was asked at the beginning of this section? There is no easy answer because much depends on context, not only the cultural context but also the context in which the work is written and the context in which it is read. In an academic setting, a student who is not yet positioned as a contributor to the disciplinary discourse cannot refer to himself or herself in the same way that a publishing scholar can — which is a point made by Vergaro (2011). Needless to say, self-mentioning as it relates to authorial voice is a complex matter.

Issues Regarding the "English Voice"

With globalization of English, one questions the extent to which "alien norms" are being adopted throughout the world's cultures and also the extent to which cultures maintain their distinctive ways of writing following conventions that are often known tacitly rather than explicitly (cf. Bennett, 2007). The issue arises as to what extent an authoritative voice in academic writing is an "English voice," or even, more particularly, an American English voice, since British and other Anglophone traditions differ in some respects.

Particular features, as noted above, tend to be associated with writing in English, and one of those is directness. Ulla Connor (1999), who came to the United States from Finland, has provided an account of her own experience in acquiring what she called the "Anglo-American direct manner," which provides strong guidance for the reader. Learning to write in this way took some time, but eventually she realized that her writing had become Americanized. This happened when she returned to Finland for a sabbatical and was very much aware of rhetorical differences across the two languages. Among other differences, she noted that, in contrast to leading their readers, Finnish writers "let the facts speak for themselves" (p. 34). In an article on struggles for voice, Canagarajah (2004) discussed the accommodation that was made by Connor and also pointed to other approaches to appropriating English. In his book on the geopolitics of academic writing, Canagarajah (2002) described his own experience in revising his writing to make it acceptable for publication in an American journal but then being criticized by his colleagues in Bangladesh for doing so. In related work, French scholars (e.g., Hidden, 2011) have pointed out differences between French and English with respect to providing explicit guidance for the reader. Thus, there are challenges with respect to this directness feature for second-language writers attempting to publish their studies in international English. Among researchers in this line of work is Iñesta (2009), who discovered that Spanish writers had difficulties in communicating this "direct manner" in English when their attention had to go to such low-level matters as spelling (cf. Roca, Manchon, & Murphy, 2006).

We should note variability and should emphasize that there is no singular academic English voice. Instead, there is variability yet to be examined — different scholarly voices associated with different groups and contexts. For instance, code-switching (English/Spanish) and sometimes genre-mixing tend to characterize a scholarly Latino/a or Chicano/a voice in American scholarly discourse. Encompassing many theoretical essays and even research reports (e.g., Garcia, 1997; Hurtado & Gurin, 2004), it is a hybrid counter discourse in which the mixing is often for rhetorical effect and for positioning oneself.

Students' Perspectives on Voice

Interesting insights into authorial voice have come from individuals who are learning to be academic writers. In the 1980s, students' encounters with disciplinary discourses and subsequent changes in their writing were often viewed in terms of initiation or enculturation into a particular discourse. Increasingly, over time, there has been more attention to the complexity and nonlinearity of discourse change through attention to the varying practices in which students engage with other participants. This work illustrates a point that Reynolds (1993) made, "Authoritative discourse grows out of pieces, tidbits, leftovers, and scraps — just as authoritative writers become agents of change through moments of struggle, glimpses of conflict, and in-between stages" (p. 209). Here, we review findings from a small number of these studies that relate to the concept of voice.

The well-known "Nate Study," conducted by Berkenkotter, Huckin, and Ackerman (1988), can be considered an investigation of "voice." Focused on a single doctoral student over the course of his first year in a U.S. rhetoric program, this was a study of his enculturation — his initiation — into a particular discourse community. This student, who was actually a coresearcher and the third author of the published article, began his program with a strength in expressive writing, which was at odds with the discourse expected by a faculty member with whom he studied. According to the three authors, when he began his program, "Nate held the writer's voice to be as individual as a thumbprint. He was therefore taken aback early in his first semester at a professor's suggestion that his (and other graduate students') prose would come to reflect their thinking 'as research scientists'" (p. 18). As he received instruction and response to his papers, he began incorporating changes that made his writing for that professor accord more closely with the writing style of the texts he was reading. His use of first-person pronouns diminished; he discontinued some use of "off-register" items, including highly figurative language, and he produced longer sentences. However, within the reflective pieces he also produced for the study, he continued to employ expressive features and figurative language, and, as he noted in a postscript to the study (Ackerman, 1995), the study focused on only a small part of the discourse practices in which he engaged that year and did not include all mentors with whom he interacted.

Whereas Berkenkotter, Huckin, and Ackerman approached their study as enculturation, a contrasting perspective was taken by Prior (1998), who framed his study, also conducted in the United States, as participation of graduate students, their mentors, and other individuals in activity systems. These systems were, as he explained, "situated, mediated, and dispersed," and students' education occurred through "laminated processes" in "spaces for (re)socialization of discursive practices" (p. 32). Throughout his work, Prior (e.g., 1995, 1998, 2001) has related student writing to networks of disciplinary dialogue and to the reproduction and transformation of social practices. Some of his 1998 cases were presented as microhistories, showing how a piece of writing often had a history that began before its articulation for a particular seminar. Although the study did not focus specifically on voice, two issues that emerged regarding voice are particularly relevant to this chapter. One issue came in the writing of a student called Mai, who was limited in her command of academic English and was also ineffective in incorporating others' voices — those of her sources — into the paper. She appropriated material in their voices but did not credit them in a conventional way. The other issue came from the writing of the student called Moira, whose faculty mentor did such detailed editing that the student did not recognize her own voice when she read her revised writing. Whose voice was it? This finding relates to our focus in a subsequent section on writers' incorporation of others' "voices," not only of those individuals with whom they interact directly but those whose texts they read and whose writing they transform. Of more relevance at this point in the chapter is the attention that Moira's question draws to the awareness that a student can have of the expropriation performed on her own discourse as she is expected to appropriate another. Other researchers (Castelló, Corcelles, Iñesta, Bañales, & Vega, 2011a; Castelló et al., 2009; Rinck, 2006b) have also pointed to the difficulties that students experience when reconciling discourse differences in developing their authoring identities.

In her study of writing identity, Ivanič (1998) had eight doctoral students in England as her coresearchers when investigating how these students reproduced or challenged hegemonic discourses associated with academe. Thus, through this focus on critical appropriation of language, the study was also an examination of authorial voice. Students could often recall when they acquired particular language from their reading or from lectures. For instance, John used the term "opportune infections," which he had picked up from material he encountered, but he intentionally used no quotation marks. He explained that it had "filtered into" his own discourse; it was his to use. This matter of when and how to credit was a major issue for most of these writers. At another time, John critiqued a piece of his own writing, which included the following phrases: "On first consideration this may seem ... ," "This idea immediately begins to run into problems because ... ," and " ... great implications." He explained: "It's not me ... it's academic waffle, it really is. I've learned it by reading books, being lectured at, getting comments back, writing essays" (p. 210). This study thus showed that, when appropriating the new discourse, this student had some awareness of the nature of the "filtering" process and of his own appropriation of discourses. It was not an automatic enculturation; instead, this appropriation entailed activity and choice on the student's part. Ivanič summed up what this example and others illustrated: "The sources of the threads with which they weave their discourses are extremely heterogeneous" (p. 211). In subsequent work, Ivanič (2005) has continued to relate students' voices to their identities — their subject positionings that are constructed relationally and discursively.

Like Prior and Ivanič, Casanave (2002) positioned her cases in situated practices. She described students' disciplinary participation as "experiences that are necessarily partial, diverse, conflicted, and fragmentary" and influences on their writing as "personal and local factors that may not be anchored by more stable genre practices: (p. xiii). Among her multiple cases from various U.S. universities are illustrations of students who hold different kinds of expectations, goals, and interactions. One was a student who sought to develop the kind of authority in her writing that her professors encouraged, and another was a student who, after making unsuccessful attempts at appropriation, rejected what she perceived to be the disciplinary discourse of the department in which she studied. The first was Karine, a master's student in ESL who had been educated in Russia and had been a teacher there. She sought an authoritative voice for her writing and wanted it to be "academic enough." Particularly valuable to her was the extensive feedback, especially criticism, she received from faculty, which focused mainly on the logic of her arguments. She described the style she sought in one of her interviews: "You have to know how to present your argument and write with a certain level of detachedness. Not say, well, I think that such and such, you have to say it like you're not there" (p. 104). The second student was Virginia, a doctoral student in sociology who withdrew after deciding that the language expected for sociological theory differed too greatly from the everyday language she wanted to use in communication with people who were not sociologists. This study, like Ivanic's, illustrates students' agency, but this study provides a dramatic contrast between one student who sought to adopt the hegemonic discourse and one who rejected it.

The final study summarized here is Erling and Bartlett's (2008) investigation, conducted in Germany, that examined seven postgraduate students' perceptions of voice relative to their writing in English. These students, for whom English was not their first language, recognized the need to write and publish in the global language of academe. Their comments relate to the issue discussed above, the English voice. Some mentioned a nonnative disadvantage, questioning whether they would be able to develop an authoritative voice in a language for which they did not have full fluency. Aleksander, one of the students, made a point that is relevant to this chapter:

> The problem with English seems to be that there are not just rules, but also ways of saying something. Sometimes all rules which I know are OK, but still something is wrong. I just try to keep eyes wide open when reading hoping that those "ways of saying something" will be memorized somewhere and will activate while I need them. (p. 182)

Aleksander made an important point that has also been made by researchers — the discourses of academe have expectations that are not all articulated as "rules." The latter "ways of saying something" likely include some of those discourse markers that researchers are studying under the label *metadiscourse* as well as the "direct style" to which Connor (1999) referred in describing her own experience. Another student asked an interesting question about voice and identity: Would he, in his academic writing, be able to incorporate features that are not conventional in

English in order to emphasize his own identity? The latter question is a big one and is one that we consider in the conclusion of this chapter: To what extent can a writer be unique and still produce writing that is considered authentic in terms of discourse conventions?

Appropriation of Multiple Voices in Writing

In writing about the multivocality of language, Bakhtin (1981) argued that language is "populated–overpopulated–with the intentions of others" (p. 294). In scholarly writing, which is very much a social process, academics must appropriate the voices of others even as they generate writing presented as their own. Dialogue can thus be put at the center of writing activity, since utterances are produced as answers to other utterances in the chain of communication. Based on such assumptions, educators have emphasized multiplicity of voices in their teaching of writing. Among them is Dysthe (1996, this volume), who has focused on what she called "the multivoiced classroom." Our attention in this section is on the merging of others' voices as writers convey their own in their writing. We focus on four ways in which voices can converge: use of other writers' texts, collaborative writing, response to writing, and translation from one language to another.

Voices of Authors of Prior Texts

In their own texts, academic authors incorporate the writing — the voices — of others. Much of this use is tied to social identity, which is developed, in part, through reading, discussing, and drawing on the work of particular scholars (cf. Nelson, 2001a; Spivey, 1997). This facet of writing was addressed by Ken Gale, a doctoral candidate, when he responded in the following way to an examiner at his dissertation defense:

> So my thinking, feeling, and writing in this dissertation has been charged by the writing of Marx, of Foucault, and now, most recently, by Deleuze. These are my ancestors! But ... there have been many others. Without effort I think of Satre and De Beauvoir, Kerouac and Ginsberg, and Irigaray and Butler. (Gale, Speedy, & Wyatt, 2010, p. 27)

This matter of appropriation is certainly relevant to our consideration of voice: What happens to authorial voice when voices of other writers are appropriated?

Writers use other authors' work to support their own claims, to show how their own work builds on what has come before but makes a novel contribution, and to indicate their own social alliances in the field. The averral/attribution distinction discussed by Groom (2000; cf. Tadros, 1993) is one way of thinking about this matter. Averral is the author's acceptance of responsibility for the words, whereas attribution is giving credit to the other author. In the latter, as pointed out by Groom, there is an "intertextual marker to acknowledge the presence of an antecedent authorial voice" (p. 15); however, as also pointed out by Groom, "every attribution is embedded within an averral" (p. 179). A particularly useful way to think about the relation of the writer's voice to those other voices is Bakhtin's notion of *double-voicing*. Vološinov (1986), Bakhtin's colleague, explained,

> An author may utilize the speech act of another in pursuit of his [or her] own aims and in such a way as to impose a new intention on the utterance, which nevertheless retains its own proper referential intention. Under these circumstances and in keeping with the author's purpose, such an utterance must be recognized as originating from another addresser. Thus, within a single utterance, there may occur two intentions, two voices. (p. 197)

In discussing double-voicing, Baynham (1999) explained, "To qualify a statement positively or negatively is precisely to take up a speaking/writing position in relationship to that statement, to bring into play the authorial voice, the scholarly 'I'" (p. 489). For instance, after quoting someone, the writer might take a positive position on the other writer's claim ("Smith's distinction is a useful one") or might take a negative position ("What Smith's distinction misses is"). Evaluative messages are intended to lead readers to take similar positions on other authors' work.

Writers report on what other scholars have said or have discovered. In doing so, they recontextualize that content as they establish their own scholarly credentials and carve out a place for their own work. There are various ways in which a writer can report, including quoting directly or indirectly, paraphrasing, and summarizing. In performing any of these, a writer can suggest a particular attitude toward the work being cited. It may come through the particular reporting verb that is used. Consider, for example, the difference between "Jones's study suggested" and "Jones's study demonstrated." Some of the features discussed earlier under "metadiscourse" also suggest the writer's viewpoint regarding the cited author's work, particularly those that have an evaluative component. These include the elements of boosters, hedges, and attitude markers that Hyland and Tse (2004) include in interactional metadiscourse. Farmer (1995), in discussing the Bakhtinian conception of voice, pointed to the "reaccentuation" of others' voices that writers do when they position themselves relative to those voices. This reaccentuation that comes through presenting one's viewpoint as a way to *novelize* what is said when incorporating other's words into one's own. Students develop strategies for working with the texts written by others that may or may not accord with those of publishing academic writers. In her cross-cultural study of university students in the United States and France, Donahue (2008) found a common "reprise-modification" approach taken by students in both countries. They tended to employ the same strategies of appropriation, resistance, and negotiation as they used — but modified — available resources.

When must credit be given? How should credit be given? This matter of attribution presents challenges to many academic writers, including Mai in Prior's (1998) study and some of the students in Ivanič's (1998) study, discussed above. It also presents challenges to writers from cultures that do not share Western conventions for acknowledging prior work but seek to publish in Western forums. Studies in other context have also shown some difficulties that students have in handling quoted material and citations. For example, Castelló Inésta, Pardo, Liesa, and Martinez-Fernández (2011b) found Spanish undergraduate students making more use of direct quotations and lesser use of indirect quotations than more experienced writers, and Rinck and Boch (this volume) noted in their study that French doctoral students' limited themselves to references that were of direct use to their argument but did not link them to a more general context. With respect to the latter finding, these authors suggested that students do not yet feel legitimated to take a stance in the field. Persistent issues surround writers' use of other writers' work and the degree of transformation that is required before the "words" become one's own (Nelson, 2008).

Voice in Collaborative Writing

At this point, the focus moves to the matter of voice in collaborative writing when there are multiple writers of a single text. We should acknowledge that, at this point, more is known about the structural arrangements that collaborators establish than about the ways in which two or more voices are blended to become a singular voice. For instance, Sharples et al. (1993) identified some recurring patterns: collaborators taking different sections to write and then combining those parts; one collaborator writing a section and then passing it along to someone else to write the next part; and the collaborators actually writing together. The latter is sometimes called "side-by-side," since the pair sit together at the computer with one member at the keyboard. In addition to these three forms, there is also the arrangement in which one person writes for the pair or team — is lead author for that manuscript.

When different people write portions of a text, there are likely to be disconnects between sections of the text that need to be linked, and some editing is necessary to reconcile differences in style — so that readers perceive a singular voice. When interviewing collaborative writers in Sweden, Kim and Eklundh (2001) collected descriptions of how writers managed their collaborations and learned that much attention seemed to go to such reconciliation in revising. One participant explained that, in producing a collaboratively-written manuscript, his team devoted almost a whole day to revising, sentence by sentence: "We sat down together. It was a very slow process. But I thought the product was actually better because we thought every single line all the way through" (p. 251). When collaborators write together (side-by-side), there would likely be a blending of voices as the text is generated. In writing produced solely by the lead author, there may be reviewing and possibly editing by team members when a draft or sections of a draft are completed, but the lead author's voice predominates.

Collaborative writing is facilitated by electronic technology, which provides shared spaces for writing and also an easy means of exchanging drafts. Tracking programs allow collaborators to see how others have revised — "written over" — previous writing and inserted their own language. Voices come together as consensus is built. However, with e-mail exchange, there can still be problems when some collaborators work on something other than the most recent version.

In recent years, with increasing incidence of collaborative writing in academe, some universities have opened the door to coauthored papers by students, including theses and dissertations. When permitted for doctoral dissertations, coauthorship occurs most often when a set of three or so articles are accepted in lieu of the typical monographic dissertation. In such cases, university programs typically specify whether or not some of the articles may be coauthored and, if they are, require that the student indicate those portions for which he or she was responsible. It is still a rarity in academe for two doctoral students to coauthor a single monographic dissertation. Within that small group of students who have done so are Kenneth Gale and Jonathan Wyatt, who have published accounts of the collaborative process in which they engaged for their dissertation (2008). In a 2006 article, based on e-mail correspondence over a three-month period, they considered their writing styles — how their writing had changed as they wrote together. Their blended voices, according to Wyatt, were becoming a "discourse of resistance" challenging formalism and singularity of meaning. In a subsequent article, written after their dissertation defense, the coauthors along with their dissertation chair reflected on the challenges all had faced in going against convention (Gale et al., 2010). One challenge was a requirement by the "guardians of tradition" at their UK university that individual authorship be clearly evident with respect to portions of the text.

From an educational perspective, collaborative writing can be seen as a tool for helping students to understand the social nature of writing practices, to become more aware of different voices and other writers' contribution to the final text, and to learn to negotiate between those voices that accord with their text and those that do not (Camps & Milian, 2000). Dialogic activities have been shown to assist in developing students' academic identity and awareness of authorial voice as well as improving the quality of their texts (e.g., Castelló et al., 2011b; Dysthe, 1996, this volume; Read & Francis, 2001).

Voices of Respondents

Voices also converge when writers receive response to their writing from other individuals. Respondents put themselves in the writer's role — considering how the text might be developed or changed to be more effective for the audience and situation. In doing so, they often incorporate their own voices with the voice of the writer, adding words and phrases, changing a sentence or combining sentences, replacing whole sections, as well as making suggestions, small or large, for adding or deleting content. In an academic context, students receive response on drafts from their instructors in conferences or from fellow students when they work in response groups. Academic scholars also solicit response quite frequently from their colleagues, as Hunt and Vipond did in the study reported by Reither and Vipond (1989). Connor (1999) also solicited response when she was beginning her career that required publishing in English. In the autobiographical account cited above, she emphasized the value of her work with other authors who served as peer respondents. For students and for publishing scholars, response from others helps move the writing toward a community's discourse expectations. This is one way in which writing is collaborative and is multivoiced even if there is only one named author.

Insights into respondents' re-voicing come from Prior's (1998) study, cited earlier, particularly with respect to the experience of the doctoral student called Moira. Moira had indicated in an interview that, because of the rewriting of her advisor, who was also her research director, she felt a dissonance at times between the voice of her completed papers and her "own" voice. Her advisor, Professor West, explained that she did the rewriting to make Moira and other students see how to make the writing "clearer." She would cross things out and rewrite them because she felt this was a better approach than simply saying that something was wrong. In his intertextual analyses, Prior traced various modifications made by the advisor and by the student, and at times, it was questionable as to who was speaking at a particular time in a text. He stated that "West's words came to populate Moira's texts, altering not only their style, but also their content, their motives, what they indexed socially, and what disciplinary discourses they referred to intertextually" (p. 241). This study had symmetry in that it documented not only changes in Moira and her texts but also the influence that Moira and her texts had on West as well as their role in the activity system of the project.

Authorial Voice in Translation

This last matter to be mentioned before we conclude is translation — an issue that also raises issues about multivocality but is not often discussed by writing researchers. It too is often a major factor relevant to voice in academic writing, and it deserves much attention as globalization removes many barriers across languages, nations, and communities in academic communication. A treatment of voice in academic writing must acknowledge the revoicing that occurs when a text is translated from one language to another. Hermans (1996) asked the questions that are relevant to our discussion: "Can translators usurp the original voices and in the same move evacuate their own enunciating space? Exactly whose voice comes to us when we read translated discourse?" (p. 26). Although it is the translator's voice that is read and is associated with the named author, all too often the translator's name is not even included in a citation. Yet that translator has interpreted the text, has considered the rhetorical situation, and has made choices in the language that is used. He or she has command of two languages and, to a greater or lesser extent, has knowledge of both cultures. Translators play a role, often hidden, in the discourse practices of academe. They translate texts when authors seek to present or publish those texts in another language, and many of the academic texts that scholars read, cite, and transform for their own writing have been translated. There is thus another voice that intervenes when writers make use of other writers' translated texts in their own writing. To see how much a translator contributes to the writing and the meaning, one has only to read two different translations of the same text and make comparisons. For student writing, translators are sometimes called on to transform students' essays, as, for instance, when they apply to study in other countries.

Translation of another's writing requires some decisions regarding authorial voice in terms of the original language and the target language into which it is to be translated. For more than a century, attention has gone to the issue of *foreignizing* versus *domesticating* of a text through translation (cf. Schleiermacher, 2004/1813; Venuti, 1993). The translator can prepare the language so that it accords with the culture of the targeted readers, which is domesticating, or can retain its "foreignness" for the intended readers, which is foreignizing. Thus, the voice may sound familiar to the targeted readers or may sound strange — or something in between. Here in translation, as in other forms of academic writing, one can see the tension between conflicting discourses. In this case, the conflict comes when attempting either to reproduce the voice suggested by the text or to replace it with another voice.

Conclusion

We began this chapter with a quotation from Elbow (1973) that affirmed an individualistic conception of voice. What do we do with this long-standing idea that each individual has a unique voice that should be fostered and developed? In this chapter, our emphasis has been on the social and communal rather than individual aspects of writing. We have considered a number of complexities related to the notion of voice in writing: (1) voice as an interpretation by readers from textual cues in social, cultural, and historical contexts; (2) the socially adopted conventions of writing, such as metadiscourse and first-person pronouns, that help make readers aware of the author guiding them through the text; (3) the practices through which students learn to write in a way that is acceptable for others in their social community; and (4) the ways in which writers appropriate the writing (and voices) of others through using extant texts, writing collaboratively, receiving and providing response, and translating from one language to another.

How, then, does voice relate not only to social identity but also to personal identity in academic writing? We can respond to this question by focusing on the role of readers who discern a sameness in an individual's writing — and thus interpret a voice. *Sameness* is the key word here, and even the term *identity* (from the Greek term *idem*) signals sameness. Writers become identified by their readers with certain groups whose members address similar topics and sound similar or write in similar ways, following shared discourse conventions. This is the social, communal aspect of voice — and of identity. We pointed to this kind of sameness when we discussed authenticity in writing for a particular community.

Responding to the second part of the question presents challenges, since for much academic writing, particularly the forms considered here, writers adopt and follow shared discourse conventions and write similarly to others. Bakhtin (1981) himself stated that the word "exists in other people's mouths, in other people's contexts, serving other people's intentions." However, to that statement he added, "It is from there that one must take the word, and make it one's own" (p. 294). It is important to note that *identity* can apply not only to a commonality with others but also to a commonality that readers can discern within a particular individual's writing (cf. Castelló et al., 2011b; Spivey, 1997). In academic writing, authors develop a recognizable and individual sameness with respect to their body of work, which contributes to inferences regarding their voices. They become associated with particular kinds of texts, particular topics, and citations of particular others, and cues to their identity come through those commonalities as well as the language that they use. When readers *know* (in some sense) a particular author, they seem to *hear* his or her voice. And then there is also the possibility of some degree of resistance to norms; we all know academics who have succeeded in a minor "rebellion." Canagarajah (2004) made this point:

> Discourses cannot be totally deterministic. There is always room to negotiate, modify, and reconfigure — if not resist — dominant discourses. ... [However,] one cannot write without any relevance to the established discourses. The dominant conventions have to be taken seriously and reworked sensitively in order to find acceptance. (pp. 268–269)

Chapter 4

Undergraduate Students' Conceptions and Beliefs about Academic Writing

Mar Mateos and Isabel Solé

The study of conceptions or beliefs about writing has a relatively recent history in Europe, especially as far as the study of personal conceptions is concerned. However, the analysis of the ways in which this technology has been, and is, conceived of socially has tended to attract greater attention (Olson, 1994; Olson & Torrance, 2009; see Lea or Robinson-Pant & Street, among others, this volume) than ways of conceiving of it cognitively. Although it is not here a matter of establishing a parallel between both types of representations, it seems logical to suppose that the social ways of conceiving of writing — or any other aspect of culture — influence the ways in which individuals represent it. The social representations of writing are not manifested only in neutral definitions; they also involve attributing a certain value to writing, establishing the criteria in regard to what being able to write involves, who is and who is not a writer, and the provision of the means and the distribution of responsibilities to ensure its appropriation by students. Students' participation in social practices shaped according to certain conceptions of writing will contribute to how they learn to write and to a personal way of conceiving of writing, representing it to themselves and seeing themselves as writers. Thus, the personal conceptions are constructed within the framework of scientific and popular conceptions about writing as well as within the writing practices promoted by these conceptions.

We focus on those aspects in the first two sections of the chapter, whilst in the third one our objective is to offer a comprehensive review of cognitive studies that analyze how students conceive academic writing, understood as those texts they write in the academic context (see Russell & Cortes, in this volume), how these conceptions develop, and how they relate to academic writing practices.

University Writing: Selves and Texts in Academic Societies
Studies in Writing, Volume 24, 53–67
Copyright © 2012 by Emerald Group Publishing Limited
All rights of reproduction in any form reserved
ISSN: 1572-6304/doi:10.1108/S1572-6304(2012)0000024008

Among the different approaches on academic writing research (see Russell & Cortes, this volume; Prior & Bilbro, this volume), our focus on the personal conceptions about writing can be situated in the tradition of cognitive psychological research about the processes involved in writing. In particular, we analyze some approaches from which the personal conceptions about writing have been studied — metacognition, phenomenography, implicit models and epistemological beliefs. For each of these perspectives, the most relevant work and its contributions to the field are identified. Many are grounded in research focusing on pre-university writing, but we feel the points made and framing thus provided contribute to the discussion and help us to better understand university students' writing conceptions. The chapter finishes with a brief agenda regarding the conceptualisation of and research on writing conceptions for the coming years.

It is important to notice that the scope of our analysis is limited to the contributions of the research regarding perceptions and writing representations from the approaches already mentioned, and therefore, we have not reviewed studies developed from other social and cultural approaches such as 'academic literacies' framework, or from other disciplines such as linguistics, didactics, ethnography or anthropology, which are represented by other chapters of this book (see, for instance, Carlino; Castelló & Iñesta; Lea; Delcambre & Donahue; Russell & Cortes or Prior & Bilbro, this volume).

Popular and Scientific Conceptions of Writing

Various popular and scientific conceptions of writing have existed and probably still coexist. Faced with the impossibility of reviewing them all, we shall put forward a brief characterisation based on three major dimensions: First, we'll reflect on the characterisation of writing representations related to orality and thought. Second, we'll focus on the conceptualisation of writing as a social construction *versus* an individual competence, and finally we'll analyze its situated nature, meaning the consideration of writing as an ability that is reconstructed in different contexts *versus* writing as a general procedure.

What Writing Does and Doesn't Represent: Orality, Writing and Thought

One traditional view has regarded writing as a transcription of speech, that is, that writing systems represent what speakers of a particular language say. From this perspective, writing is simply a way of recording speech; writing systems evolved until they reached suitable ways of explicitly representing oral language. Although this tradition has had supporters from Aristotle to Saussure, its foundations have been strongly challenged by various scholars (Olson, 1994; Ong, 1982, among others).

Olson holds — and adduces compelling arguments to back up his contention — that it is wrong to conceive of writing as a mere transcription of speech and its development as an attempt to represent language structures (words, phrases, sentences, etc.), as these concepts do not precede writing, but are generated — as is all awareness of the structure of language — by writing itself. Olson, like many others — see, for example, Chartier and Hébrard (1994), Tusón (1997) — places the appearance of writing systems in the context of the need to relieve the burden on human memory and to communicate. These purposes were already able to be attained from the time of visual systems, which employed 'emblematic' forms of writing that enabled certain meanings to be recovered from them: the inscribed shapes represented both the 'thing' and its name, and the 'reading' of them was not much different from the description of an image. But when writing becomes syntactic, when the signs represent words, and not things, then it can be taken as a model for analysing language, for thinking about its constituents — words, phrases, etc. — and making them the object of reflection. In addition to its original communicative function, writing can begin to fulfill a representational or ideational function, making it possible to express feelings, ideas, emotions and, in general terms, to represent thought, revise it and reflect on it. The *epistemic* function of writing, as a specific function within the representational function, refers to the possibility of using it as a tool for acquiring awareness, self-regulation and the development of one's own thought (Miras, 2000).

We have here, then, a clear distinction between different ways of understanding writing. In one interpretation, writing is regarded as a means for *transcribing* — for saying through writing — thought codified in oral language, with an eminently communicative intention. In a different interpretation, writing, without losing this intention, is conceived of as a conceptual tool that makes it possible to represent thought, requires certain processes that order thought and offers a model for oral speech. The effort of making things explicit required by writing — so that not only 'what one wants to say' but also the way in which 'it should be interpreted' is understood — helps the writer to think intensely about meanings, gives rise to the use of new words and concepts, requires self-regulation and leads one to become conscious of one's own ideas. In this interpretation we can say writing is a means of *transforming* thought. The roots of this idea can be traced back to Vygotsky's explanation (1978) of, first, the dynamics of condensation and expansion in the passage from internalised language to written language; and second, the functional distinction he establishes between dialogue and monologue, highlighting the greater degree of control, involvement and responsibility we exercise in the case of what is written, which is monological, even though, along with Dysthe (this volume), we acknowledge that academic writing implies dialogue with other texts and authors.

Writing as Individual Competence/Writing as Social Construction

Flower and Hayes (1981) characterise writing as *ill-defined problem-solving* for which the writer must construct a representation, a rhetorical problem with parameters approachable by means of recurrent planning, textualisation and revision strategies. Expert writers, who are able to construct an appropriate representation of the task, can make competent use of these strategies, which will allow them to successfully solve the problem of writing. Bereiter and Scardamalia's (1987) well-known distinction between the 'knowledge-telling' model and the 'knowledge-transforming' model also explains writing as problem-solving, albeit in a different way. In this model, in representing the task to themselves simultaneously in terms of the problem of what they want to say and the problem of finding the most suitable way to say it, writers enter a dynamic that may lead them to modify both their initial knowledge about the topic and their discursive knowledge. Writing's epistemic function appears here quite clearly. These models of writing have been constructed as a result of the growth of cognitivism in some research communities and the gradual shift of researchers' interests to the processes and role of writing in learning and thought. In both models, 'the essential characteristic of expertise in writing is a matter of mastering problem-solving strategies' (Tynjälä, Mason, & Lonka, 2001, p. 11). The emphasis on cognitive processes has been attenuated in research pointing out the importance of aspects such as the person's interest in writing, or their beliefs about their own efficacy as a writer, although these motivational variables are also approached from a basically individual perspective.

To this conception of writing as a cognitive problem-solving process favouring learning has been added a view stemming from socio-constructivism which holds that writing — like learning — is both an individual and a social activity (Tynjälä, Mason, & Lonka, *op. cit.*). The internalisation of the construction and transformation processes involved in writing requires participation in significant cultural practices, in 'textual communities' (Olson, 2009) that share specific ways of creating and interpreting texts (see also, Dysthe; Rinck & Boch among others, this volume). As noted by Kozulin (2000), the practices and uses in which literacy intervenes are essential to explain the impact of writing and reading on cognition and learning. At the same time, stress is laid on the fact that the impact of these cultural practices on the way writing is approached may be mediated by the representation or meaning the task has for the writer (see, for example, Delcambre & Donahue this volume). The socio-constructivist perspective about writers' representations helps to introduce into the conception of writing aspects such as the social value given to it, the expectations generated in relation to it, and the social practices in which it intervenes. Also, this perspective helps to delimit the criteria according to which it can be established whether societies and individuals attain what we might call literacy. This conception of writing has important consequences in relation to a new dimension, which we shall now discuss.

Writing as a General Procedure/Writing as an Ability that is Reconstructed in Different Contexts

From certain theoretical perspectives, such as some specific formalist cognitivist approaches and their derived instructional methods, and also from the standpoint of what may be regarded as 'common sense', writing is conceived of as a technique which, once it has been mastered, can be applied in diverse contexts and situations to achieve different ends. Despite the substantial differences between considering that the mastery of this technique involves essentially the learning of the relevant codification, graphomotor and formal aspects, and considering that it involves the learning of more complex procedures, this view accepts that once a person has learned to write, the development of his or her skill as a writer follows an essentially quantitative course (writing texts of different kinds, about more subjects, for more audiences) in which basically the same skill is employed.

However, from perspectives linked for the most part to socio-constructivism, writing is viewed as an ability that is reconstructed and whose development must be seen in eminently qualitative terms. Authors such as Wells (1988), who describe various levels in achieving complete literacy — executive, functional, instrumental, epistemic — have stressed the qualitative differences between the different forms of writing. Olson (2009) points out the difference between a restrictive definition, which regards a literate person as one who 'possesses the ability to read and write', and a broad definition, which regards being literate as being *'learned, acquainted with literature'*. According to the first definition, literacy is a personal competence that enables someone to read and write at a basic level. In the second definition, which is more in keeping with the type of literacy required by our society, literacy implies the ability to deal with the written materials typical of 'textual communities', each of which has its own conventions of composition, interpretation and use of texts: *'This is what makes reading* [and we can add writing] *a social practice rather than strictly an individual skill'* (*op.cit.*, p. 145). The competences necessary in this case, frequently described as 'linguistic or academic literacy' go beyond the strategies involved in the basic ability to read and write, and in oral language; mastery of these competences is an essential component of learning any discipline.

So the comfortable belief according to which writing is a single procedure — more simple or more complex — that the writer learns at a certain period and can use in a diversity of situations to achieve different objectives, is challenged by positions holding that more sophisticated uses of writing (such as for learning, for thinking) are possible only in the context of significant social situations that lead the person to reconstruct this ability and make it more complex and difficult (on these distinctions, see also, Russell & Cortes; Prior & Bilbro; Nelson & Castelló, this volume).

(Teaching) Writing Practices in Spain

From the characterisation given in the previous section, it follows that there exist various conceptions of writing that have taken root differently. Whereas the research community has adopted a more complex view of writing, conceiving of it as an ability that is reconstructed by individuals in the context of significant social practices, and vindicates its dimension as an instrument of thought, in teaching of most of the primary and secondary schools in our country (as well as in many of our universities as is the case where we teach and research) generally speaking and despite some exceptions there persists a simpler view, that sees writing as a more or less complex procedure and circumscribes its functionality to communication and thus to a single generic procedure. This simpler view, in which writing is conceived of as a way of 'telling' knowledge that one already possesses (or is reproduced in a text), translates into teaching practices that are, at the least, restrictive, in the sense that they point to particular ends, but fail to take into account others, especially those that tend towards epistemic forms of writing. As a general rule, writing practices are rarely linked to the educational discourse that is meant to promote learning. As a consequence of this 'isolation', writing is seldom linked to the use of reading, listening or speaking to learn and is employed for the most part without a context or project that would give writing meaning. We make these assertions based on reviewing the research carried out in secondary education and higher education in our country. For example, in a study conducted in Spain (Mateos, Villalón, De Dios, & Martín, 2007) we found the reading and writing tasks most commonly created for, or suggested to, students (and which they themselves say they perform) are rather simple ones: taking notes, organising them, identifying the main ideas, underlining, summarising. These are tasks that refer to a single text, are regarded as rather easy by the students and require unsophisticated levels of written composition. Their key use is to reproduce information. This characterization is similar to the one Tynjälä (1998) provides when defining traditional academic tasks involving reading and/or writing in many European universities.

Despite being well-regarded because of their capacity to foster deep learning, the more complex tasks — synthesising two or more texts, commenting on texts, and writing essays — are performed much less frequently than the others. A detailed case analysis highlighted the difficulties that even university students with a good level of reading and writing competence had in synthesizing two texts (Mateos & Solé, 2009). All in all, these findings suggest that writing-to-learn tasks are consistent with a perspective that tends to conceive of writing more as a means of repeating knowledge than of generating it (for student perspectives on this, see Delcambre & Donahue, this volume). Such a view fails to foster an epistemic use of writing (or reading), which makes it unsuitable for developing academic literacy as a range of social and cultural practices around reading and writing in academic contexts, rather than individual cognitive activity (see Lea; Robinson-Pant & Street, this volume).

Also in our country, Castelló (1999), after analysing the writing aims, situations and strategies of students report at this level and in secondary education, concluded that the conceptualisation of writing as an instrument that is useful for knowledge-telling — first you think and then you write — is the most common among students. It is significant that in reporting their aims when using writing, only 1% connected it with learning as against 57% who link it with facilitating and improving memory, which is obviously related to the writing practices with which these students were confronted.

This and other research (e.g., Mateos & Solé, 2009; Tynjälä, 1998) reveals that the writing practices (the teaching of writing and the use of writing to learn) in which university students participate mostly lead them to use writing reproductively and thus favour a superficial approach to learning.

The way a particular student tackles a writing task is naturally mediated by the meaning she or he attributes to it and the way she or he represents it to him or herself (Flower et al., 1990). However, this representation is to a large extent constructed by participation in cultural practices involving writing. A certain conception of the written word, linked to a certain learning culture, helps to define the educational practices that are employed to ensure (academic) literacy in the sense in which that conception understands it. In these practices, individuals not only learn to write and to use writing in certain ways, but also learn, implicitly, what writing is, what it involves and how they can benefit from it. Conceptions or perceptions are thus key to students' success.

Research on Students' Conceptions about Writing

More and more people are insisting on the need to understand students' conceptions or beliefs about writing as a way of understanding the use they make of it and as an aid to promoting the use of writing as a knowledge-transforming tool (see Delcambre & Donahue, this volume). In this view, such beliefs act as filters, leading students to represent the task to themselves and approach it in a particular way.

The different ways students conceive of writing, their relationship with the strategies for tackling writing tasks, and the resulting written products have been investigated with different approaches built on different assumptions about the nature of the conceptions and even use different terms to refer to these conceptions. The methodologies employed to study them and the characteristics of the students studied also differ.

In this chapter we review research on writing conceptions from four of these approaches that can be considered the most outstanding ones from the cognitive and constructivist traditions in psychology: a metacognitive approach, a phenomeno-graphic approach, an 'implicit models' approach and an 'epistemological beliefs' approach. The first three approaches investigate writing representations directly. The epistemological beliefs approach, on the other hand, has a broader focus, as it looks at conceptions regarding the nature of knowledge and the process of acquiring it rather than at writing conceptions directly. Nevertheless, we think the contribution of this last-mentioned approach can be relevant in so far as beliefs about knowledge have an influence on writing.

Metacognitive Knowledge of Writing

The first steps in the study of students' writing conceptions in the field of cognitive psychology were taken by studies of students' *metacognitive knowledge* based on cognitive models of writing. This approach views writing as an individual problem-solving process, so interest is focused especially on the knowledge people have about their own cognitive processes that are involved in writing (planning, textualisation and revision) and the way this knowledge influences the control we exercise over our own writing. As we have argued elsewhere (Mateos, 2001), the very term used to refer to these representations is not neutral. The knowledge in question is conceived of as more or less accurate knowledge about one's own cognitive activity and not as beliefs or personal constructs. The object of these studies is to determine the degree of fit between what the subjects know about their own writing processes — the declarative, procedural and conditional aspects (what has to be done, how it has to be done and when it has to be done) — and what the scientific theories say on the matter. From this perspective, the development of metacognitive knowledge is seen as progressing from ignorance to more and more accurate knowledge of one's own processes and does not deal explicitly with how writing is conceived of globally.

Most of the studies that can be classified as based on this approach have investigated the metacognitive knowledge of primary and secondary students, with or without learning difficulties (e.g., Castelló, 1997; García & Fidalgo, 2004; Graham, Schwartz, & MacArthur, 1993; Raphael, Englert, & Kirschner, 1989; Welch, 1992; Wong, 1999).

Unlike those based on this approach, the studies based on the other three approaches mentioned above do not seek to describe the degree of knowledge students have of the cognitive processes of writing, but to investigate the ways in which writing is conceived of and interpreted. Another difference is to be found in the educational level of the students investigated. Whereas the metacognitive approach, as has been pointed out, has mostly concentrated its attention on primary and secondary students, the other three approaches have dealt principally with the conceptions of university students and, to a lesser extent, of secondary students. For the purposes of this chapter, which focuses on undergraduate students' conceptions and beliefs about writing, the results of these three last-mentioned lines of research are of enormous interest.

Writing Conceptions from a Phenomenographic Perspective

Studies employing a phenomenographic approach explore the experiential or phenomenic aspects (Marton & Booth, 1997) starting from the assumption that people experience writing phenomena in qualitatively different ways. The most commonly employed methodology consists in categorising the verbal descriptions of the phenomena of interest given by people in semi-structured interviews (Campbell, Smith, & Brooker, 1998; Ellis, Taylor, & Drury, 2006; Hounsell, 1984; Light, 2002), questionnaires or inventories (Boscolo, Arfé, & Quarisa, 2007; Lavelle, 1993; Lavelle, Smith, & O'Ryan, 2002; Lavelle & Zuercher, 2001), or the metaphors they use when reflecting on their experiences with writing (Levin & Wagner, 2006).

A similar approach may be found in Carlino's study (this volume), whose analysis aimed to understand the experiences of writing a thesis from the point of view of doctoral students.

Many of these studies make use of the distinction between superficial reproduction of knowledge and deep understanding (Marton & Saljö, 1976, 1997) in explaining learning, and the distinction established by Bereiter & Scardamalia (1987) between 'knowledge telling' and 'knowledge transforming' in their characterisation of writing models. In his investigation of undergraduates' conceptions of essay-writing, Hounsell (1984) found two types of conceptions: interpretative and non-interpretative. In the former, stress is laid on the construction of a personal meaning for the essay topic; in contrast, students with a non-interpretative conception see essay-writing in a mechanical and barely reflexive way. These conceptions have a bearing on the written products — students with interpretative conceptions tend to write better essays — and on the processes underlying them. Campbell et al. (1998) reached similar conclusions in their research into the way university students represent essays and the way of doing them: students who conceive of the task in more constructive terms are the ones who write more complex essays, engage in reconstruction more than reproduction processes, organise their ideas and construct arguments. Students with simpler conceptions write essays that are more reproductive.

The influential work of Lavelle and her co-workers on secondary students (Lavelle et al., 2002) and university students (Lavelle, 1993; Lavelle & Bushrow, 2007; Lavelle & Guarino, 2003; Lavelle & Zuercher, 2001) in which they set out to identify the motives and strategies with which students approach the task of writing was carried out within this framework. Lavelle (1993) designed and validated the Inventory of Processes in College Composition (IPIC), a 74-item questionnaire measuring five approaches to writing: elaborative, low self-efficacy, reflective-revision, spontaneous-impulsive and procedural. The elaborative and reflective-revision factors represent a deep approach to writing — the former on the dimension of personal and affective investment in writing; the latter on a more analytical dimension — while the other three factors represent a surface approach (Lavelle & Guarino, 2003). The questionnaire has been used in numerous studies and the results supplemented and validated by the use of interviews. Lavelle and Zuercher (2001) found that undergraduates with high scores on the elaborative and reflexive scales describe writing as a way of modifying their own view of the topic about which they are writing and report that they experience feelings of satisfaction and fulfilment when writing. Students with a surface approach, on the contrary, frequently report feelings of unpleasantness and avoidance in regard to writing. The work of Lavelle and her colleagues also shows that students who have a deep approach articulate their composition process better. More recently, using the inventory of graduate writing processes, Lavelle & Bushrow (2007) have identified seven independent factors in graduate students' approaches, some of which are the same as those in IPIC, while others are different. The results of this work have enabled two latent factors to be identified, one accounting for a deep approach, the other for a surface approach to writing. The authors also point to the emergence of an 'intuitive' strategy — which they identify with the factor of the same name — which the regression analysis reveals to be a predictor of the quality of the written products.

In summary, the conclusion to be drawn from the phenomenographic studies is that, although students' conceptions vary from one study to another, all the different conceptions can be reduced to two more global ones: one that is more superficial and reproductive, the other deeper and more constructive (Lavelle & Guarino, 2003). The results of this research strand show that the more constructive conceptions tend to be associated with more elaborate written products, whereas the more reproductive conceptions are associated with less elaborate products. Moreover, in all the studies, the former have been less common than the latter. Lastly, new dimensions have emerged in graduates' conceptions (Lavelle & Bushrow, 2007) which require further investigation.

Implicit Writing Models

Recently, writing conceptions have been studied also using an implicit beliefs or implicit models approach. Whereas the metacognitive and phenomenographic approaches deal only with the explicit aspects of representations, in this perspective conceptions constitute models understood as sets of tacit, but systematic, epistemological beliefs that underlie and restrict both the way we approach and the way we interpret writing situations. This is the perspective adopted by White and Bruning (2005) who have applied their implicit models of reading (Schraw, 2000: Schraw & Bruning, 1996) to study writing. They distinguish two implicit models of writing: transmissional and transactional. Writers with *transmissional* beliefs conceive of writing as a vehicle for transferring information from the text to the reader in a way that limits the presence of the author's ideas in the text. They also display little emotional and cognitive investment in the composition process. Writers with *transactional* beliefs, on the contrary, conceive of writing as the personal and critical construction of a text by actively integrating their own thought into the process, which translates into a greater affective and cognitive investment in the composition process. These different ways of conceiving of and approaching writing are related to differences in the written products. The results of these authors' work show that the texts written by students with low transmissional and high transactional beliefs were the ones that obtained higher scores on text quality.

The results of some research carried out by the present authors with secondary and university students (Mateos, Cuevas et al., 2011) point in the same direction. These studies examined the relationship between transmissional and transactional reading and writing beliefs, as assessed by the questionnaires developed by Schraw and Bruning (1996) and White and Bruning (2005), and the quality of a written synthesis of multiple texts. It was found that students with more transactional beliefs integrate and organise the information obtained from the different sources better, a result we find confirmed in Rinck and Boch (this volume).

Employing an approach similar to the above, Villalón and Mateos (2009) studied the conceptions of secondary school and university students about writing. They employed a questionnaire to look at facets such as the uses and functions of writing, the role of planning and textualisation processes, and the role of revising processes. This questionnaire, devised by the authors, explores both the beliefs students possess about writing and the actual practice they say they engage in as writers, as these are regarded as possibly complementary avenues for accessing students' conceptions about writing. Underlying students' reported beliefs and practices, as reflected in their answers to the questionnaire, there are two ways of conceiving of academic writing, one *reproductive*, the other *epistemic*. Whereas the former conception implies a mechanical and linear process, the latter considers writing as a learning tool that is able to fulfil an epistemic function. Underlying the reproductive conception there is the epistemological assumption of naïve realism, which leads the person holding it to think that writing must accurately reflect knowledge and therefore to endow it with a reproductive function. Making use of the well-known distinction established by Bereiter and Scardamalia (1987), this view would be akin to a 'knowledge-telling' model. Conversely, a stance recognising the importance of the active role of the writer and the planning and revision processes in generating new knowledge would be similar to a constructivist epistemology, granting writing an epistemic function, more in keeping with the 'knowledge-transforming' model.

The results of this study indicate that, although university students display a more sophisticated and complex conception of writing than secondary school students, neither group attained a fully epistemic conception. As found in the study by White and Bruning (2005), it would be no surprise if students were not wholly consistent in their responses and some students might even hold both conceptions simultaneously.

The Role of Epistemological Beliefs in the Production of Written Argumentations

Lastly, a number of studies have investigated the relationship between epistemological beliefs and the interpretation of conflicting information in tasks involving the writing of argumentative texts (Kardash & Scholes, 1996; Mason & Boscolo, 2004; Schommer, 1990). Research into these epistemological beliefs has been approached from various relatively independent standpoints (Hofer & Pintrich, 1997, 2002). Nevertheless, the different lines of research have put forward development models with very similar trajectories, ranging from simple, dualist and absolutist initial positions to much more sophisticated, constructivist and relativist positions. When university students have been given texts setting out different and conflicting points of view about a particular topic and have been asked to complete the text by writing the missing conclusion, it has been found that students who adopt a dualist and absolute epistemological stance experience greater difficulty in integrating aspects of the different perspectives put forward. Moreover, Mason and Scirica (2006) showed that epistemological thinking was a significant predictor of all three components of students' argumentation skills (generated arguments, counterarguments and rebuttals) for controversial topics.

A Research Agenda Regarding Students' Conceptions of Writing

Going back to the dimensions we proposed at the beginning to characterise the different popular and scientific conceptions of writing, we might say that the research into students' conceptions about writing carried out from the different approaches reviewed here has focused its analysis mainly on the dimension concerning what writing does and does not represent. Taken as a whole, this research has established that there are at least two ways in which students conceive of writing — as a tool for transcribing and reproducing knowledge, and as a tool for transforming and generating knowledge — although it has also shown that the more epistemic conceptions of writing are not the most common, even among university students.

However, the social dimension of writing have hardly been touched on in the studies conducted in this field from the domain of cognitive research, or have been treated as subsidiary to the previous dimension. This is completely different if we look to research in other domains that have a long tradition of studying the social dimension and focus on university writing and students' interpretations of writing in this context as shown by several contributions in this volume. As we have already pointed out, maybe it is time to start to joint efforts to bridge the gap between those different approaches.

The Relation between Personal Conceptions and Cultural Practices of Writing

Another important challenge of the reviewed perspectives is whether writing conceptions are global and undifferentiated for any type of writing or whether, on the contrary, we have different conceptions in relation to specific practices (writing to learn, personal writing, academic writing, etc.) that we construct as a consequence of our participation in different 'textual communities'. Most of the research carried out up until now from the cognitivist perspectives analyzed in this chapter has explored global conceptions of writing. Nevertheless some studies have examined the conceptions of specific writing tasks such as essay-writing (Campbell et al., 1998; Hounsell, 1984; McCune, 2004), synthesising multiple sources (Flower et al., 1990) and making summaries (Bosch, Scheuer, & Mateos, 2006), but only in a very few cases has this been done for the purpose of comparing the conceptions about different writing practices. In one such study, Light (2002) employed semi-structured interviews to investigate undergraduates' conceptions of creative writing and their own practice in writing various genres such as poetry, drama and fiction. The results indicate, on the one hand, that creative writing is conceived of as being unique and distinctive vis-à-vis other types of writing, personal, with less restrictions, more open to emotion and subjectivity. On the other hand, there exists an evident similarity, pointed out by the author himself, between the conceptions he calls respectively 'transcription' and 'composition', and the reproduction and transformation dimensions found in the research on writing (Bereiter & Scardamalia, *op.cit.*) and in other phenomenographic studies, such as those conducted by Hounsell (1984) on essay writing.

Again we should acknowledge that things are different if we look at research from social perspectives, focused on academic and university writing, which has a long tradition of investigating whether writing conceptions vary depending on the disciplinary communities in which this tool is used, as well as analysing student writing needs against a background of institutional practices, power relations and identities, with meaning being contested between the different participants involved in any writing task. This is indeed the direction being taken by some of the studies in this volume (Lea; Castelló & Iñesta; Robinson-Pant & Street; Delcambre & Donahue, among others) extending that body of research.

Acquiring and Changing Writing Conceptions

The research reviewed here supports the idea that the way students approach writing and the quality of their written products are related to the conceptions they hold

(Onwuegbuzie, 1998) and attitudes to writing (Knudson, 1995), the relationship between these variables and conceptions has rarely been investigated. We think there is a need to look at the possible mutual influence of writing conceptions and the more motivational and affective aspects of writing. Some studies that have taken this direction point to a relationship between writing beliefs and self-efficacy expectations (Maimon, 2002; White & Bruning, 2005), between beliefs about how to write well and the goals of writing (Silva & Nicholls, 1993) and between epistemological beliefs and attitudes towards writing (Charney, Newman, & Palmquist, 1995).

Also, given the role epistemological beliefs seem to play in writing, at least when the task consists of composing a text integrating different positions on a particular topic, it might be useful to look at the relations between such general beliefs about knowledge and more specific beliefs about writing, and their joint effect on writing. The work of Hammann (2005) and some of our own work (Mateos et al., 2011) has pursued this line of research.

Lastly, it seems necessary to take into consideration the fact that academic writing tasks — including most of those set students in research on writing and conceptions — are actually hybrid reading and writing tasks (essays, summaries, syntheses, etc., Bracewell, Frederiksen, & Frederiksen, 1982; Nelson, 2008; Spivey, 1997), so it makes a lot of sense to explore the possible relation between reading and writing conceptions, and between these and the quality of text comprehension and written composition. This is a little-explored area, perhaps because research on reading conceptions (Dai & Wang, 2007; Schraw, 2000; Schraw & Bruning, 1996) — an area on which we are currently working (Mateos et al., 2011) — has been less developed.

To sum up, as can be gathered from an examination of the research from the analysed approaches, important progress has been made in recent years at the conceptual level regarding the relevant dimensions for interpreting personal conceptions and the relation between conceptions and performance, etc.) — and at the methodological level — with undoubted achievements in respect of the instruments that can be used to explore these conceptions. However, the challenges facing us in our efforts to attain a deeper understanding of the nature, characteristics and effects of conceptions on academic writing are also considerable. This is an area of research that is not only promising, as its contributions and results constitute a palpable reality, but also has an arduous task ahead of it to achieve its purposes.

Acknowledgments

Preparation of this chapter was supported by grants EDU2009-14278-C02-01 and EDU2009-14278-C02-02 from the Spanish Ministry of Science and Innovation.

SECTION II

WRITERS' KNOWLEDGE AND PRACTICES IN EVOLVING ACADEMIC CONTEXTS

Chapter 5

Students' and Tutors' Understanding of 'New' Academic Literacy Practices

Anna Robinson-Pant and Brian Street

In this chapter, we will call upon aspects of the 'Academic Literacies' approach to student writing at university (see Ivanič, 1998; Jones et al., 2000; Lea & Street, 1998; Lillis, 2001; Scott & Lillis, 2008) in order to explore some of the changes we identify in the requirements and regulations laid upon both students and lecturers regarding writing practices. For instance, many UK Higher Educational Institutions now require students and their teachers to produce written documentation regarding teaching and research interactions, which were previously informally and orally negotiated. One question that these authors pursue is whether there is now greater explicitness and transparency regarding such expectations, explaining institutional norms and so on — in contrast to earlier research that addresses the implicit character of much knowledge regarding Academic Literacy. One effect of this change might be that there is now less space for negotiation and flexibility among participants — students and their tutors — as external institutional forces frame what they are expected to perform as academic writing. Before investigating these new practices in a UK university, we will briefly summarise the research approach known as 'Academic Literacies' and link it to issues in the wider university context that have been termed the 'New Orders'.

Academic Literacies: A Critical Perspective

Lea and Street (1998) have suggested that the activities and perceptions associated with student writing at university can be characterised in terms of three models: study skills, academic socialisation and Academic Literacies (see Russell & Cortes,

University Writing: Selves and Texts in Academic Societies
Studies in Writing, Volume 24, 71–92
Copyright © 2012 by Emerald Group Publishing Limited
All rights of reproduction in any form reserved
ISSN: 1572-6304/doi:10.1108/S1572-6304(2012)0000024009

this volume). Each successively encapsulates the other so that the Academic Literacies model incorporates the other two whilst offering a broader perspective on the writing process (see Table 5.1).

The **study skills** approach has assumed that literacy is a set of atomised skills that students have to learn and that are then transferable to other contexts. In the **academic socialisation** view, the task of the tutor /advisor is to inculcate students into a new "culture," that of the Academy. The third approach is **Academic Literacies**. This approach sees literacies as social practices, in the way addressed in New Literacy Studies (Barton, 1994; Gee, 1990; Street, 1984, 1996). It views student writing and learning as issues at the level of epistemology and identities rather than skill or socialisation. As Lea suggests, the focus then shifts onto 'meaning making and identity at the level of epistemology and what counts as appropriate knowledge' (see Lea, this volume).

In a recent paper based upon research with doctoral students in the United States, Street calls upon the Academic Literacies approach in order to explain the differences between the overt requirements that tutors and institutions make explicit regarding student writing and what he terms the 'hidden' features, in particular, 'the criteria that those in power would use to assess such pieces in the academic context' (Street, 2009, p. 2). Whereas dominant models of student writing (for instance, within English for Specific Purposes (ESP) and English as a Second Language (ESL) where

Table 5.1: Models of student writing in Higher Education.

1. Study skills:
   'Fix it'; atomised skills; surface language, grammar, spelling; pathology
   Sources: behavioural psychology; training
   • *Student writing as* technical skill and instrumental
2. Academic socialisation:
   Inculcating students into new 'culture'; focus on student orientation to learning and interpretation of learning task, for example, 'deep' and 'surface' learning
   Assumes one 'culture', doesn't focus institutional practices, change power
   Sources: social psychology; anthropology; constructivism
   • *Student writing as* transparent medium of representation
3. Academic Literacies, discourses:
   Literacies as social practices; at level of epistemology and identities
   Institutions as sites of/constituted in discourses and power
   Variety of communicative repertoire, for example, genres, fields, disciplines
   Switching re linguistic practices, social meanings and identities
   Sources: 'New Literacy Studies'; Critical Discourse Analysis; Systemic Linguistics; Cultural Anthropology
   • *Student writing as* constitutive and contested

writing is taught generically to students from a wide range of disciplines) have tended to emphasise formulaic lists of things to be covered, usually in terms of the structure of the essay (e.g. Introduction; Theory; Methods; Data), the 'Hidden Literacies' approach focuses on the less overt features that are called upon in judgements of academic writing that often remain implicit. Developing the pedagogical implications of research and theoretical insights within Academic Literacies, such as writing and identities (Canagarajah, 2002; Ivanič, 1998; Lillis, 2001), these 'hidden' features that students are introduced to include: framing, contribution (the 'so what?' question), voice, stance and signalling. While the current chapter is less about assessing student writing than about the institutional pressures and requirements, some of the same conceptual underpinning may be relevant, concerning the differences between overt, explicit requirements on the one hand and more implicit, 'hidden' requirements on the other.

The present chapter, then, considers whether there is now greater explicitness and transparency regarding expectations, meeting institutional norms, to be found in the regulations, and institutional pressures that serve to define what counts as student writing in particular and learning more generally at University. This new framework may be understood as part of the broader institutional pressure on Education as a whole that has been termed the 'new orders'. Before describing our case study and how it might be seen in this wider context, we now elaborate on the notion of the 'New Orders' and how it links with 'Academic Literacies'.

The 'New Orders': Work, Communicative, Epistemological

Street (2004) has attempted to locate the study of Academic Literacies in a broader conceptual frame that he refers to as the 'New Orders' — The New Work Order, The New Communicative Order and The New Epistemological Order. The orders, he suggests, require radical rethinking of what counts as literacy. How it applies to our understanding of student writing at university will lead us to revise what counts as literacy in this as well as other contexts and to locate our work in university within the much broader contexts within which these changes can be seen to be taking place. The rethinking, then, is as necessary for academics and researchers as it is for activists and practitioners: while the former have to accommodate to the needs of 'knowledge-in-use', the latter are being called upon to take account of 'knowledge-in-theory'.

The New Work Order

Gee, Hull, and Lankshear (1996) (and Holland, Frank, & Cooke, 1998), drawing upon the writings of economists and business theorists as well as critical sociologists, have attempted to characterise the New Work Order associated with globalisation of production and distribution (see Table 5.2). They consider the implications of these

Table 5.2: The new 'orders'

The New Work Order:
  Globalisation; flexibility; teams/projects
  Literacies at work

The New Communicative Order:
  Mix of literacy, oral and visual modes; 'multimodality'
  Multiple discourses in multidisciplinary teams

The New Epistemological Order:
  Crises of knowledge:
  1. *Within Academy:* postmodernism; reflexivity; local versus universal; critique of
      Enlightenment, modernism, science
  2. *Outside Academy:* marketisation of knowledge (knowledge as inert,
      information, 'quality' re product not learning process); 'knowledge in use'
      versus propositional knowledge; performativity (competence vs.
      understanding); ubiquitous sources of knowledge
  3. *Alternatives*: academics as 'practical epistemologists'; *critical eng*agement in
      real world projects/action, 'participatory'; rework university as forum for
      debate; critique bases of knowledge claims and frameworks

---

changes for the kinds of language needed in work and in educational contexts. These
changes represent the context within which contemporary literacy work is taking
place and force us to question the theoretical underpinnings of literacy itself. Work,
they suggest, is no longer defined and organised along Fordist lines, with mass
production on assembly lines and its Taylorist principles of work organisation and
discipline:

> There is now a shift towards forms of production which employ new
> ways of making goods and commodities, serving more differentiated
> markets, or niches, through segmented retailing strategies. There is now
> a great deal more attention paid to the selling environment at every level
> of production, from design to distribution. So while the old work order
> stressed issues of costs and revenue, the new work order emphasises
> asset building and market share. (Gee et al., 1996, pp. vii–viii)

Associated with these defining concepts are ideas about proper organisational
behaviour, including attention to flexibility and adaptation to change. Procedures are
put into place to ensure both flexibility on the one hand and uniformity and
guarantee of standards on the other. If consumers are perceived, through market
research and company predictions, to demand the same jackets or the same tomatoes
in shops across their travelling experience, then mechanisms need to be put into place

to ensure that wherever these are produced they conform to those standards. This Total Quality Management (TQM) has been a particular feature of the New Work Order that has impinged directly on the educational setting. TQM has provided models for quality control there too, imposing reductionist and unitised notions of measurement and of quality on educational outputs and 'products'.

A further organisational change in the New Work Order that has been of especial significance for language and literacy has been the notion of team working on projects, rather than hierarchical forms of organisation that simply pass orders down a chain of command. In the new project-focused work order, all members of a team combine to design, negotiate and develop 'products' for sale and distribution. In order to accomplish this, all members of a team have to be equipped with the discursive skills that such negotiation and development involve, such as ability to present and hear arguments, and to develop material for presentation on communicative devices such as overheads, slide projectors, computer displays and so on. Radical researchers confronted with these changes have particularly focused on the claims often associated with them that suggest a commitment to democracy. Words like 'collaboration', 'participation', 'devolution' and 'empowerment' — all cherished terms of oppositional groups, such as those working in Freirean literacy campaigns — are now used to indicate a partnership between managers and workers. Gee and his colleagues are highly suspicious of these claims and would have us examine them critically, while acknowledging that changes are indeed taking place in both the work order and the communicative demands associated with it. Attention to what counts as literacy in educational contexts, then, now needs to take account of such shifts and such critiques if they are to handle the complex communicative needs of the New Work Order. Interestingly, though, the warnings put out by Gee and his colleagues regarding how 'flexible' the New Order really is seem particularly appropriate in Higher Education where many participants might see the shift towards greater control and regulation as a move in the Fordist direction even as the higher order debates suggest the opposite. As we examine our research data, we will attempt to take account of these apparently diverse tendencies and to consider their implications for how PhD supervision practices are changing in the United Kingdom.

The New Communicative Order

A number of writers working in the area of social semiotics and visual design have suggested that in this new context, the reading and writing practices of literacy are only one part of what people are going to have to learn in order to be 'literate' in the future. They are going to have to learn to handle both the team work literacies described above and also the iconic systems evident in many communicative practices. These include the kinds of icons and the signs evident in computer displays like the Word for Windows package, with all its combinations of signs, symbols, boundaries, pictures, words, texts, images and so on (see Scollon & Scollon, 2004).

There is also a significant body of work on mediated discourse analysis (e.g. Norris & Jones, 2005; Scollon, 2001; Scollon & Scollon, 2003, 2004), semiotic remediation practices (e.g. Prior, 2001; Prior & Hengst, 2010; Prior, Hengst, Roozen, & Shipka, 2006; Shipka, 2011), resemiotisation (Iedema, 2001, 2003), recontextualisation (Linell, 1998, 2009) and semiotic approaches to language practice (e.g. Agha, 2007; Goodwin, 1994, 2000, 2007; Silverstein, 2005). While we signal this here, these traditions are less central to our analysis of New Communicative Order (NCO) and Academic Literacies than the account summarised here by Kress and van Leeuwen (1996). They subtitle their book *Reading Images: The Grammar of Visual Design* in order to suggest that this new approach to the semiotic order can apply similar 'grammatical' analyses as have been applied to language in its more traditional sense. By this, they want to indicate not so much a traditional focus on rules, knowledge of which sets the professional apart from the amateur, but rather grammar as meaning the way in which the people, places and things depicted in images 'are combined into a meaningful whole' (p. 1). The extreme version of their social semiotic position is the notion of 'the end of language' — that we are no longer talking about language in its rather traditional notion of grammar, lexicon and semantics, but rather we are now talking about a wider range of 'semiotic systems' that cut across reading, writing and speech. Whether the new regulatory frame can adjust to this conception of a wider communicative order needs further research and we will suggest here just a few of the directions and insights that arise from taking account of this particular 'order'.

The New Epistemological Order

This discussion is closely related to the third of the 'orders', the 'New Epistemological order', in that it entails questioning the very grounds on which we define and learn knowledge in the first place. This connects with Prior and Bilbro's challenge of the common understanding of 'academic enculturation' as 'one-way transmission of relatively stable cultural knowledge from experts to novices' and their proposal instead that it involves 'semiotic (re) mediation' (this volume). We will briefly indicate the features of this new 'epistemological order' before moving on to consider the implications for current shifts in the requirements in Higher Education regarding student writing and their implications for theory and practice in the field of literacy.

Barnett and Griffin (1997) have referred to Crises of Knowledge that are leading to a New Epistemological Order. Within the Academy, they suggest, postmodernism and reflexivity have led to a valuing of the local against the universal, including a critique of Enlightenment science and the kind of modernism on which much development work has been founded. Outside the Academy, meanwhile, the marketisation of knowledge has likewise led to a challenge to the dominant position previously held by universities as producers and guarantors of knowledge. Taking a longer historical perspective, the tension between what Clark (2006, p. 10) refers to as 'the two great engines of rationalism' — the ministry and the market, 'in their modern forms, state bureaucracy and managerial capitalism' — has been central in the development of the modern 'research university'. Clark (2006, p. 13) traces the changes in cultural and organisational practices through this 'insertion of academia within the market or rather, the cultivation of a market in academia' — where 'academia was treated as mining' — as far back as the 18th century. Analysing the shift from the traditional collegial structure of a 'self-regulating academic community' based on consensus-seeking decision making to 'an enterprising university which resembles a business', Jensen (2010, p. 10) identifies two types of 'knowledge organisation': 'the professional bureaucracy and the adhocracy' (*ibid.*, p. 14).

In our present commercial world, knowledge as inert commodity can be bought and sold for profit, measured as though it were inert information, and judged for 'quality' as though it were just another commercial product. As we saw above, 'quality' in the commercial sense now being applied to education refers to the object of knowledge itself but not to the process of learning, questioning and engagement in which receivers relate to it. This new knowledge is based in numerous, non-academic settings, such as large business corporations and leisure industry outlets, for whom the critical perspective of university approaches to knowledge is less important than whether it will sell in the marketplace. The University no longer — if it ever did — has a monopoly on the production, guardianship and legitimisation of knowledge.

Faced with this crisis of knowledge from multiple sources, Barnett asks what can be the role of the Academy in the New Epistemological Order. His response is of direct relevance to the research we describe below: the role of the researcher is to be that of a 'practical epistemologist', involving critical engagement in real world projects and action, doing 'participatory' work. At the same time, this involves reworking the university as a forum for debate. This forum offers a discursive space for critique of the bases of knowledge claims and frameworks in ways that for-profit knowledge industries do not. The practical epistemologist engages with knowledge in use not simply with propositional knowledge and he or she works *with* partners in real world contexts in the interests of equity and justice. Combining this task with knowledge of the New Work Order and of the New Communicative Order provides the contemporary activist and researcher on literacy with a very different agenda and framework than that envisaged in the modernist era of programmes to 'eradicate illiteracy'. Whether we are right to see the current shifts in requirements for learning at University as grounded in these new Orders, we will leave the reader to decide.

University Writing and the New Orders

Many UK Higher Educational Institutions now require students and their teachers to produce written documentation regarding teaching and research interactions, which were previously informally and orally negotiated. Cribb and Gewirtz (2006, p. 227) discuss these changes in terms of the 'technologies of audit', associating them with the 'managerial ethos', which is increasingly permeating Higher Educational Institutions. These new practices have often been introduced from a fear of litigation, which has intensified as students begin to pay higher fees and are positioned as 'consumers' within Higher Education. For instance, it is not unusual for minutes of doctoral supervision meetings to be taken by the student and agreed by the supervisor, then sent to a central administrative office as 'evidence' in case of an academic appeal by the student. Many of these developments are to be found elsewhere in Europe, as Thomson and Walker (2010, p. 11) note, and can also be related to the changing view of the doctorate as 'a qualification for other professional fields', rather than only a research degree: 'Doctoral education in Europe is seen to now require more direction and structure and not to be driven solely by intellectual curiosity'.

Similarly, research is now governed by formalised university research ethics procedures, such as the requirement for research participants to give written consent before involvement in interviews or other research activities. Other examples include the increasing importance of 'feedback' forms on undergraduate and postgraduate course teaching and how this influences teaching approaches/curriculum due to pressures to improve student satisfaction league tables at university/national level; plagiarism regulations and detection software — influencing how assignments are set ('plagiarism proof') and students' views of academic writing (such as increased fear of accidentally plagiarising if their university adopts a punitive approach); written codes of practice regarding supervision — defining expectations and roles; popular newspaper reporting on problems that students face as they move from school to university. Russell and Cortes (this volume) refer to these as 'bureaucratic texts within the "academic" institution', and we would see the examples above as fitting within the category of 'non-academic communities, non-scientific genres' that they identify on Figure 1.1. In this chapter, we are concerned to explore the interaction between the 'academic' and 'non-academic' communities in relation to these texts and practices (as indicated by the arrows in Figure 1.1). In contrast to Russell and Cortes, who mention only the 'scientists' (teachers) working in Higher Education who have to produce such reports, we take the starting point that students also have to engage with and produce these kinds of 'bureaucratic texts'.

We will go on now to look at how relationships between students and their teachers, as well as between researchers and their subjects, are being shaped by some of the new literacy practices (generated from outside the classroom) being introduced by UK Higher Education institutions. Through interviews with staff and students in a UK university, we analyse how doctoral students and their tutors engage with these unfamiliar literacy practices, alongside learning about academic writing within their courses of study. We also look at the ways in which university teaching and learning is changing in response to these new Academic Literacy practices associated with ensuring greater accountability and regulation of Higher Education. And we ask whether the theoretical frameworks outlined above, regarding 'Academic Literacies' and the 'New Orders', can help us to make sense of the shifts and to locate them in a broader theoretical as well as institutional framework (see Table 5.3).

Table 5.3: Academic Literacies and the 'new orders'

	New work order	New epistemological order	New communicative order
Study skills Writing as surface language correctness	Hierarchy and discipline; policing language	Atomised units of knowledge transmitted and tested; quality control, performativity	Include as units non-linguistic skills and modes — visual, gestural and so on, new policing of modes
Academic socialisation Writing as conduit	Multiple discourses in multidisciplinary teams; privilege exchange value	Learn new knowledge in old ways — elitist institutions — or in new marketised ways — wider access, knowledge in use	Learn/become socialised into new modes, for example, 'rhetorics of science classroom'
Academic Literacies Writing as contested	Flattened hierarchy, team work, new language skills; privilege use value	Critical reflexivity on language and knowledge as processes/resources; academics as 'practical epistemologists'	Critical reflexivity on uses of language and non-linguistic modes in representing/taking hold of knowledge

Investigating 'New' Academic Literacy Practices: Doctoral Supervision in a UK University

The following section is based on semi-structured interviews conducted with 10 doctoral students and 13 doctoral supervisors[1] in a UK university during early 2011. Students and supervisors were from a range of disciplines/areas of study, including development studies, economics, education, business studies, social work and law.[2] The majority of the students interviewed were in their first year of study and included

---

[1] Due to ethical considerations, we did not aim to identify whether any of the 10 students were supervised by the supervisors interviewed.

[2] In order to ensure anonymity of respondents, we have decided not to indicate the student or supervisor's department when quoting from interviews. There were however significant differences related to their departmental culture and discipline. We have indicated whether the student was 'home' (United Kingdom) or 'international' (from outside United Kingdom).

'home' (United Kingdom) as well as international students. The interviews focused particularly on the respondents' experiences of being supervised or of supervising doctoral students and explored the practices now associated with developing a doctoral study.

In this section, we take an Academic Literacies lens to analyse this data — looking at Academic Literacy practices as 'contested and constituted' (p. 3), in contrast to the dominant 'skills' discourse, and beginning from the notion that there is not one homogeneous Academy. We take a wider perspective on 'student writing' than simply drafts of the thesis or other formal papers, in order to focus on other texts and practices integral to PhD supervision — including notes from meetings, feedback (oral and written) and administrative documentation. In our analysis, we are interested to see how the 'new' Academic Literacy practices were shaping (or being influenced by) power relations between student and supervisor and between supervisor and the UK Higher Educational Institution. Building on Gee et al.'s (1996) discussion (see p. 6) around how 'flexible' the New Work Order really is, we also explore the possible tensions within Higher Education around whether the TQM is seen as moving towards or against a Fordist direction. Our account relates specifically to the UK context, but could be compared to differing cultural and institutional responses to the need to enhance and regulate doctoral practice that are described in this volume. For instance, Carlino (this volume) discusses the development of a doctoral seminar in a university in Argentina, which aimed to 'foster students' writing, together with exploring the emotional skills that become necessary when dealing with their PhD candidacies' (p. 217–234). In contrast to the 'top-down' monitoring systems described in our chapter, this intervention for supporting doctoral students appears to be developed by teaching staff rather than managers, in an attempt to address the isolation and lack of regular supervisory support — which Carlino suggests is commonly experienced by doctoral students in the social sciences in Argentina.

The Changing PhD: From Freedom to Structure

As discussed earlier in this chapter, the New Epistemological Order has particular implications for Higher Educational Institutions in terms of increased demands for greater transparency, accountability and 'quality control'. In the interviews, faculty members noted specific ways in which the doctoral programme or 'journey' had begun to change in response to these forces. Sarah described a 'shift to more structure and clarity' during the time she had been at the university and in particular that there was now a more prescribed structure for the first year of the PhD in her department, including formally assessed writing activities. Louise described the doctoral process as 'more professionalised now – previously it was quite idiosyncratic', noting that there was still a need for 'more parity of experience'. Though specific requirements varied between different subject departments, super-visors identified similar stages of the PhD process that had come to be defined by or associated with the student producing particular texts. These included the procedural paper (also termed 'upgrade' or 'transfer' paper and usually accompanied by a public presentation or seminar), which the student had to successfully complete in order to move from the MPhil course (first year of the doctoral programme) to the PhD course; the annual progress report (which formed part of a formal meeting between student and supervisory team) and depending on the student's field of study and research approach, a research proposal or forms to be approved by the department's research ethics committee before they could embark on data collection.

All the students interviewed also saw the PhD journey as broken down into these stages signalled by a deadline to produce a specific text, as Marcel (a third-year international student) explained, 'the first year was discovery. Second year-pressure of transfer paper'. This seemed to be a way in which the supervisor determined or controlled the pace of the PhD, as Rica (a first-year international student) explained, 'I have my personal opinion, for instance, when to do the upgrade paper. But I like to get their experience too. Now they will give me guidance. I hope deep down they will bring it into the discussion.' Although some of the students interviewed took the lead in determining the pattern and timing of individual supervision meetings, they all expected the supervisor, rather than the student, to decide when they were ready to prepare and present the procedural paper and the research ethics proposal. The only exception to this assumption that the supervisor should initiate action was with regard to the Annual Progress Report and meeting. By requiring the student to fill in their part of the report first and send it to the supervision team with a request for a meeting, the university had given the signal that this was the student's responsibility in the first place. Cath (supervisor) explained how the experience of learning to organise a team meeting was important for the student in relation to becoming a researcher: 'At the annual progress meeting, the student takes ownership of that. I am happy to feed into it, but the student must set up the meeting as it is their project. It is a good thing to learn to do that'. Along with the discursive practices of negotiating and presenting arguments in the context of team supervision, this experience could be seen as linking closely with our earlier discussion of the priority given to learning to handle teamwork literacies within the New Work Orders.

Alongside these stages prescribed by the university, there were other influences on how learning was structured during the PhD. Several supervisors mentioned that they had also taken their own experiences as doctoral students as a model, as Steve related, 'I went about supervision the way I had been supervised – through the grazing period, enjoy yourself, have some reading and freedom, then design about Easter. Data collection and analysis, digest and dissemination in the third year ... It was a model of practice that I knew from my own experience worked well'. Some of the older students challenged the university's prescribed stages and emphasised the need for more flexibility in the pace and structure of the PhD — as Kim (second-year UK student) commented, 'the job of PhD is not to be directed'. Phil (second-year UK student) related the current changes in the PhD structure and pace to the increasing tendency to see the aim of a PhD course as preparation for an academic or research career. He saw his own slower and rather 'haphazard' journey as related to his own position as an 'outlier' who had come to the PhD after, rather than before, a successful working life: 'The product of the PhD nowadays is to churn out qualified researchers. But if this is the aim, what will they produce from me? It's like a set of horseshoes – there's no demand for them, even if they are well made. It's an aesthetic not economic process for me'. From the perspective of the New Work Order, Phil's comments point to the ways in which the changing purpose of the PhD (where the PhD is seen as a 'product' in the commercial sense — see Thomson & Walker, 2010) has begun to shape the learning journey. Phil's interview revealed however the tensions between wanting a structure, yet also the flexibility to pursue his own interests and determine his own pace. He had only met his supervisors for 90 minutes during the previous year but insisted 'the problem is that I am not driving the process myself'.

Another major change identified by several supervisors was the requirement for a student to have two or more supervisors, rather than one. In some departments, supervisors and student were asked to fill in a form specifying the exact division of labour between the supervisors — whether this would be 50/50 or 70/30 or 80/20 overall and at defined points of the PhD (such as reading and commenting on drafts of the procedural paper). Some supervisors welcomed the idea of team teaching and as Cath described, this was for 'legal' as well as educational reasons: 'I am aware that 80% of complaints about PhDs are with the supervisor ... if the relationship breaks down, it helps having another presence in the meetings, to be a team'. She went on to point out that when her students were studying 'topics that need a lot of interaction', it was very helpful to have a team discussion from differing perspectives within the supervision meeting. Other supervisors had continued to interact with students on an individual basis and regarded the second supervisor only as 'backup' in case of problems or absence on study leave. As we will discuss later, some supervisors saw the writing of detailed supervision notes as integral to this relationship — so that even if they could not meet face-to-face as a threesome, there would be continuity between the individual discussions that had taken place with the student.

During the 1990s, a university code of supervision practice was developed, which now specifies the minimum number of supervision meetings that a student should expect, as well as requirements around the composition of the supervisory team, procedural paper and other progress monitoring mechanisms. Larry (supervisor) sees the code as 'writing down and codifying custom and practice' and discussed how this formalisation was necessary due to the changing conditions of both faculty and students: 'Its importance is partly because the pattern of induction to a PhD, the apprenticeship, is not as effective as it used to be. It couldn't be like that now as there isn't the time. The pattern of expectations on young staff now is more exacting'. He described by contrast how he had begun supervising students in a small research community with 'an excellent grapevine', including informal support and advice from more experienced supervisors. Whereas Larry saw the code of practice as trying to encapsulate the diversity of practice already there, Frank (supervisor) suggested that the code could influence supervisory relationships, encouraging more uniformity: 'The supervisory code of practice aimed to make it a more distant system ... It has all become too rigorous. If we lived up to the code of practice, it would be a cold and distant relationship which would not work'. Geoff (supervisor) openly resisted the code of practice as he felt the university was imposing a structure on his relationship with his students that left no space for negotiation: 'I don't like to say we are going to meet every 6 weeks as the university expects me to. I see no point in meeting if they have nothing to say. There is no point digging them up to see if they are growing ... I suspect the University would like me to contact them all the same, saying what I have to do and when, how many papers I should send to [the office]. They would like me to be more prescriptive, just so I can tick a box.' This view suggested that the code of practice could both reflect and contribute to an increasingly hierarchical relationship between the university and supervisor, and between supervisor and student.

The code of practice has been accompanied by (or perhaps generated) an array of handbooks and forms for monitoring the effectiveness of teaching and learning. Jane, a first-year international student, compared this favourably to the relative lack of administrative forms in her home country: 'I don't feel neglected here because of the procedures. It's a constant reminder, the forms. During the first few meetings we go through the handbook as the supervisor is goal oriented and we have an action plan for the whole year.' Jane associated the monitoring forms and minutes from supervision meetings as 'instilling the value of discipline' and talked about how learning these new Academic Literacy practices had made her 'more disciplined and goal oriented', linking the written practices she had learned with her changing identity as a student in the United Kingdom. By contrast, Marcel discussed the worry he felt about reminders from the central office to send reports and meeting notes 'as I like to keep my admin up to date', but also said that he wished 'there was more monitoring on me': 'Unfortunately my supervisor gives liberty to the student to manage their own pace. It doesn't work for me. I wish he was more strict'. Unlike Jane, he appeared to view the monitoring forms from the central office ('it is just to check that we are meeting') as completely separate from the teaching and learning situation that he saw as shaped by the individual relationship between him and his supervisor. Ironically — as his supervisor believed in more student control and flexibility within PhD learning — Marcel was reluctant to suggest to his supervisor an alternative way of working.

The move towards formal external mechanisms for monitoring student (and possibly also supervisor) performance could be seen as threatening or supporting or — as in Marcel's case, as completely separate — from informal monitoring and feedback practices within the supervision situation. Similarly, students and supervisors viewed the introduction of generic research training provision at a central level in relation to the kind of informal learning already taking place in supervision meetings. Recently, students have been required by the central office to fill in a 'training needs assessment' at the beginning of the PhD where they specify the courses that they will take (which have to total a certain number of credits by the end of the year). The relationship established between the student and the central administrative office that kept an account of their credits appeared to set up a polarised view of 'training' as learning for credits, as compared to informal and spontaneous learning within the supervision process. Anne (first-year UK student) described how she 'wanted more of a sense of freedom, yet there is the pressure to get points. They are treating us as children'. Marcel suggested that the credit system meant that 'people take courses whenever perhaps it is not the moment for them'. The training forms and accounts of credits earned were regarded by most of the respondents as quite separate from the learning related to their PhD project: for instance, Phil had attended courses simply to collect credits, yet also mentioned how he had taken Open University courses to develop the knowledge he really needed to pursue his study. The fact that supervisors were not copied into nor involved in interactions with the office about credits earned also seemed to reinforce students' notion that 'training for points' was separate from the process of learning to research and write a thesis. The dominant institutional discourse evident here — where learning (training) is quantified in terms of hours and credits — can be related to our earlier discussion regarding the 'reductionist and unitised notions of measurement and of quality on educational outputs' within the New Work Orders.

We have outlined above some of the academic procedures within the PhD programme in our case study university that had been developed in response to changes within and outside the Academy. These included the move towards supervisory teams, written codes of practice, new formal monitoring mechanisms and provision of generic research training. We have identified some of the new Academic Literacy practices that have been introduced and signalled the ways in which these both built on and challenged existing assumptions about the supervision process, including the notion of 'learning' and ownership. Several of these practices have resulted in setting up a more visible three-way relationship between the University (administration), the student and the supervisors — for instance, the training contracts established between student and central office where the supervisor had a minimal role compared to administrators. As indicated above, some staff and students contested the practices being introduced — particularly the implied assumptions around control of the PhD process and the relationship between and roles of student and supervisor. Whereas some of the new Academic Literacy practices discussed above had been disregarded by supervisors and students as 'guesswork' (notably the form quantifying the roles of first and second supervisor), others were identified as more integral to the supervision process, partly because they were seen as extending or paralleling 'existing' Academic Literacy practices. In the section below, we look more closely at two of these practices: writing notes and research ethics proposals. We explore how students and supervisors engaged with and mediated these practices in relation to existing Academic Literacy practices within the supervision process.

Writing Notes of Supervision Meetings

All PhD students were requested to send copies of notes on their supervision meetings to the central office — for a minimum of three meetings a year, as Kim described, 'I am required to send a bundle to the office once a year, a bureaucratic process. The office probably note it down, done, tick box'. Both students and faculty stressed the instrumental purpose of taking notes in relation to current concerns about litigation ('cover your back', Steve — supervisor) and, from the perspective of international students, to fulfil visa regulations ('to prove we are here', Jane). However, several people also mentioned that how far they documented meetings in enough detail to be useful in a case of an appeal depended on whether they felt there was likely to be any problem in future. A supervisor mentioned that she was meticulous about collecting evidence when she had a student who had 'more of a customer approach to what I was doing and I felt I needed to prove that the quality met standards' (Irene). Similarly, Felicity (a third-year UK student) described her note taking as a 'bit haphazard' but said that she would have taken it more seriously had she felt the need: 'I can see it would be good practice but my supervisor wasn't someone who was moving the goalposts ... I trusted my supervisor so there was no need for that'.

Phil (student) mentioned that he changed the kind of notes he wrote when he was sending them to the office afterwards, so that it was an account of what happened ('he said this and I said that ...'), rather than the usual 40 words he took for his own benefit, consisting of journal or article names. Adela (first-year international student) did not change the style of her writing for the meeting notes, but expressed her irritation at having to send them to the office: 'I feel it is none of their business what we discuss. This is science not administration, why should they read it?' This question of how or whether to adapt the notes for a different audience could be related to our earlier section regarding the researcher as 'practical epistemologist', and learning to accommodate to 'knowledge-in-use' as compared to 'knowledge-in-theory'. Several students observed that they were already making a transition into academic writing from their professional field and were still aware of moving these boundaries back and forth in their writing for different purposes. Felicity (student) emphasised the different kinds of writing she was working with while studying for the PhD: 'I am still working as a consultant so I am switching between styles constantly ... you don't reference so heavily as a consultant and you need to use lay language. I learned academic writing by replicating the voices from papers I read. You begin to learn the different voices and tone and then write in the same style'. The informal approach to learning Academic Literacies that Felicity described was similar to Frank's (supervisor) more formal teaching: 'I ask them to find a classical paper, take it apart and put it back together, a car mechanic job. We talk it through and then they write it. I ask, what is clever about this paper? Why did he/she write it in this way?'

With the move to team-based supervision, several people suggested that the meeting notes had served an important purpose in sharing and enhancing communication among the team. As well as filling in on discussions for a supervisor who had not been present in the meeting, the notes could help to ensure that a common understanding was reached. Rica (first-year international student) explained that she always met with both her supervisors at the same time and that one of her supervisors typed up notes as they talked. Afterwards, this supervisor would send these notes to Rica, to add to her own (typed) notes and her other supervisor's handwritten notes too. They would discuss by email any differences, with the aim of producing a collaborative account of the meeting: 'I like it as a non-native speaker. It can confirm what I heard orally through writing'. Like several other supervisors interviewed, Cath (supervisor) used written feedback on the student's drafts as a substitute for taking detailed notes herself during the actual meeting. She described how she and the other supervisor would meet before the meeting with the student to discuss their feedback and 'decide on a consensus so we don't give conflicting suggestions. We decide what we want to discuss'. She saw the note taking in the meeting as the student's role ('it's their responsibility given by the office') and asked the student to email these notes to both supervisors afterwards. Cath mentioned that she would 'take control if there are problems in a meeting or if something is in debate'. Supervisors varied in how explicit they were with students about the purpose of taking notes. Ray (supervisor) explained that asking the student to produce formal notes enabled her to see if they understood everything and that she justified the request [to the student] by saying 'if we don't write it down, I will forget what I said and if I ask you to do something different, you can check and point it out to me'. These examples illustrate the diversity of ways in which supervisors and students took notes and produced a written record of the meeting and/or feedback on work — and how the writing practices could serve to structure the oral interaction, as well as contribute to the relationship between the supervisory team and the student (particularly with regard to collaborative and participatory approaches).

However, not all students and supervisors viewed written notes or written feedback as an essential part of the supervision process, as Felicity explained, 'I was the one who communicated between them [the two supervisors]. Sometimes one would have a different perspective from the other and we had a laugh about it ... But I could remember everything in my head to report to one about what the other had said.' From the examples above, we can identify a range of practices involved in doctoral supervision, although the requirement to send written notes to the central office could be seen more narrowly as to impose or imply a hierarchy of written over oral communication. Unlike many of the other students interviewed, Felicity's supervisions were usually based on oral discussion, rather than any written work.

By contrast, Sam, a first-year UK student, suggested that the emphasis within supervision meetings on his written texts rather than more open-ended discussion meant that his supervisors did not engage with his overall ideas but gave micro-level feedback, mainly on his writing: 'Grammar must be correct, no short cuts. You have to back up all statements with evidence. You can't say anything without evidence. You have to make it clear that it is your own view. You can't say this is true. You have to say, I believe this is true'. These features are described by Street, in his 'Hidden Features' paper (2009) as 'surface', while the more in-depth requirements may remain 'hidden' as they seem to be for Sam, who was frustrated at what he saw as a hierarchy of who could produce knowledge: 'after four years I am fed up of not being able to say "I say this." Even for a PhD you still have to refer to other academics'. From Sam's perspective, supervision meetings and his relationship with the supervisors seemed to be constrained by the surface emphasis on writing before and during the meetings that would conceal the power relationship — the supervisors became positioned as the 'experts' because of the focus on academic writing (in contrast to other students who described themselves as more expert than their supervisors because they knew their topic best). He also suggested that the format of the notes that his supervisors expected him to write determined the pattern of work: 'I specify what has been covered and what I have achieved, then the goals for next time'.

Analysing the ways in which supervision meetings were structured, the student's written text often seemed to be the focal point as Michael (supervisor) described, 'The meeting was driven by work by the student. I make comments on that and talk about the comments at the meeting. The comments trigger the conversation in the meeting so neither of us felt we needed the minutes'. In this case, Michael considered that written minutes (required by the office) were an unnecessary addition to the process and perhaps could divert attention from the student's text. Irene (supervisor) had a similar stance but recognising the benefit of having a detailed record of the supervision meetings, she scanned all her feedback on drafts, filed these as pdf documents and sent to the student soon after discussing the feedback in person. Some students (both international and UK students) said that they found taking notes during the meeting difficult: 'I am struggling to participate and take notes at the same time' (Frances, a UK first-year part-time student). A solution to this difficulty was to record supervision meetings, though this also influenced the kind of 'talk' in supervisions too. From a supervisor's perspective, Irene described how she felt that 'sometimes you say things that may not be quotable, may not be precise or may be a frivolous remark, like "that was in the 70s" '. She advised students that they could check with her about particular quotations from the meeting transcript if they wished to use them (in a similar way to 'personal communication' notes) in their thesis or procedural paper. Taking notes at the meeting was regarded as sometimes changing the way in which supervisor and student communicated orally in their meetings. Some of the accounts of how minutes were constructed and confirmed also gave insights into the ways in which the relationship between the supervisors, student and the university was being shaped by these literacy practices (e.g. the collaborative nature of some of the note taking or issues around who decided an account was 'correct').

Aside from the requirement to take notes for the instrumental purposes outlined above, several supervisors and students mentioned that was an important part of the learning process of a PhD. Sarah (supervisor) described how she introduced students to note taking as a way into developing their analysis: 'I try to get them to think about the notes as a means of capturing the main ideas. I have one student who would write three pages of "he said this" and "she said that" but not draw out the main points'. Jane (student) saw the note taking as part of her professional development as a researcher, explaining that her supervisor had taken the notes in the first few meetings so that she could learn how to do this step by step. Jane also talked about the different approach to learning that has influenced how she writes, 'every supervision meeting she compels me to do self reflection. It is not people telling you what to do, you have to do it ... Here it is beyond the books you read. You have to find your own voice and position to frame the research'. Jane appeared to see the new practice of note taking within supervision meeting as part of this journey towards 'self reflection' and perhaps a way of making explicit some of the 'hidden' features of the research process.

In this section, we have explored how far writing minutes of meetings can be seen as a 'new' Academic Literacy practice. Analysing the requirement to send notes to the central office through the lens of the 'New Work Orders', this practice could be seen as reinforcing the notion of the student/supervisor relationship as similar to that of client/producer or as a means of producing quantifiable evidence of learning/ teaching for quality control. However, the diversity of practices discussed above reveals that for some respondents, writing notes was an integral part of doctoral supervision and the process of producing an account (whether this was done collaboratively, individually or based on feedback on drafts, digitally recorded or typed at the time) could influence the kind of learning they engaged in more deeply. Drawing on the Academic Literacy model, we suggest that 'writing notes' cannot be seen as separate from other communicative practices, including speaking and reading. The examples illustrate how discussion in supervision meetings, other kinds of writing and anticipating how texts would be read (for instance, the reading of notes by administrators) were all part of the process of writing meeting notes — communicative practices that as Kress and van Leeuwen (1996) argue embed literacy practices within other modes of communication. It was also clear that some respondents 'took hold' of this new Academic Literacy practice (writing and sending notes to a central office) so that it was meditated in relation to their own supervision practices, their approach to learning/teaching academic writing and how they viewed the relationship between student and supervisor.

Research Ethics Proposals

All students intending to collect empirical data needed to obtain approval from their departmental research ethics committee before they could begin the fieldwork. Anne (first-year UK student) suggested this was 'always there at the back of my mind because everyone talks about it: it feels like a hurdle but it probably isn't'. Unlike the other new requirements described above, the research ethics proposals and forms were requested and considered at a departmental level and practices varied across the university. In some departments, the student would deal directly with the research ethics committee, whereas in other cases, the supervisor would take a stronger role in advising the student on how to adapt their study to anticipate ethical concerns. As John (supervisor) explained, he anticipated that one of his students' proposed research study might be problematic and so advised her to change the research questions before submitting the proposal for consideration by the ethics committee.

The 'ethics proposal' was central to the process of gaining approval and supervisors and students talked about what made this text different from their other academic writing. Kim (student) said he had borrowed a proposal from another colleague and modelled his on that: 'I got a feeling that you have to be very refined in the ethical approach you are demonstrating'. He went on to say that it was not just a writing exercise: 'it changed what I did as well as how I talked about it'. Anne explained that she had already written a lot about the ethical issues that might arise in her research as part of other writing for supervision meetings, but that she had realised that much of this she did not need to discuss with the research ethics board. For instance, she had written about writing and ethical concerns about translation and representation of ideas within the text — 'But I gather that for the ethics committee, a general sentence about being aware of what I write would do'. Conversely, she had noticed that 'they put a lot of emphasis on ethical consent forms'. Although Anne considered the written form of consent to be 'irrelevant' in her research context (where many people would not be able to sign their names), she believed that she would have to engage with the agenda set by the research committee. As a professional moving into academia, she observed that previously she had had to make her own decisions about ethical issues: 'when I was writing very publicly, it was self-imposed monitoring, about removing names and sensitive information'. Elizabeth, a supervisor who had recently moved from another university, described how she was quite familiar with the genre of a research ethics proposal but had approached the Chair of Research to find out the specific practices advocated by this university: ' like whether it was opt in or opt out' (for obtaining consent).

As a supervisor, Michael felt strongly that the ethics committee procedures 'obstruct people from doing their research' and were problematic, being based on assumptions from what he termed 'the medical model' (which suggests that 'you can predict what will happen in the field') and the 'power model' (which he explained assumes that the researcher is 'all powerful'). As well as reinforcing these assumptions,[3] Michael pointed out that the ethics procedures in his department put more emphasis on gaining access to the research site than on the necessary continuous ethical scrutiny of the whole research process. Mary, also a supervisor, acknowledged that with regard to her own research, even though she had got consent from everyone possible at the beginning that by the end not everyone participating may have formally agreed: 'it is rather hit and miss from that perspective'. Several people observed that it would be impossible to monitor whether procedures had been followed in practice, particularly if the research was taking place outside the United Kingdom. Irene commented that some of the international students she supervised 'will probably continue with the same informal arrangements when they get back home, they just do the paperwork here'. Felicity (student) described how she had been required to fill in the ethics forms retrospectively — 'I was just writing up and had to get involved in this bureaucratic trivia. Someone in the department with responsibility for research ethics asked me to do it. That didn't go down well. I had to get people to sign consent forms for two years ago, just to tick the box'. These reflections suggested that the writing of a research ethics proposal or form could be seen as different in several respects from the writing of meeting notes: the purpose was not disputed or transformed (to provide the necessary paperwork for the university/researcher's protection), acknowledgement of an inevitable gap between

---

[3]For further discussion of these 'assumptions', particularly from a cross-cultural perspective, see Robinson-Pant (2005).

text and the ensuing 'action' and that writing an ethics proposal was different from other kinds of academic writing (even if this was also about ethics).

Although there was a strong view that research ethics procedures were required purely to protect the university and individual researchers, some supervisors commented on the educational value of writing an ethics proposal: 'I see it as a positive process. The form raises questions about their relationship with participants. It is important to get them into thinking about how to carry out the fieldwork' (Sarah). However, Anne (student) commented on how the ethics procedures seemed 'quite separate' from learning in supervision meetings — even when the discussion was also about ethical concerns. As with the example of producing meeting notes for an administrative purpose, the research ethics practices seemed to have brought a new party with a different interest into the student's research process — the university. As a supervisor, Steve saw the research ethics process as limiting his autonomy in his own research and his student's: 'I pre-empted the research ethics committee, they would have put their tuppence in for it. To keep control, I avoid them'. Steve's comments brought out the potentially hierarchical relationship between ethics committees and the supervisor, who could feel under scrutiny too.

Comparing the 'new' Academic Literacy practice of writing a research ethics proposal, we suggest that the process of learning this specific genre was characterised by more informal learning than, for instance, taking meeting notes. Students talked to their colleagues about their prior experiences with the ethics committee and shared proposals with each other. Although some supervisors gave advice on the proposal, the student was expected to communicate directly with the research ethics committee and in some cases drew on material provided by them on their website to develop their text. As with meeting notes, students and supervisors were aware that this new Academic Literacy practice drew in an additional audience for the student's project (the ethics committee) and this also added a new dynamic to the supervision relationship.

Conclusion

We began this chapter by looking at the implications of the New Work Orders for analysing changes taking place in UK Higher Education. We are aware that the 'new' practices such as we describe here in the United Kingdom (research ethics procedures and staged processes for doctoral degrees) are already long established in universities in other parts of the world, notably the United States. A comparative analysis across time and place would have provided a more complex picture than we are able to offer here — challenging, for instance, assumptions about the dominance of writing over oral practices in academia (see Canagarajah's (2002) ethnographic study of the University of Jaffna and the value attached to oral performance by academics there). As our data has revealed in relation to doctoral courses, the shifts taking place in the case study university could be seen as informed by similar values and principles to the

New Work Orders: the university's commitment to ensuring quality and equity translated into attempts to measure and quantify access to supervisors and produce documentation of meetings as evidence of learning. Paralleling the move towards teamwork and collaboration that we identified in relation to the New Work Order, the university was also putting greater emphasis on teamwork within supervision and in relation to the provision of training for doctoral students. Rather than remaining an individualised learning relationship between supervisor and student, the doctoral process had been restructured with more visible stages, procedures and formal learning activities that were common to all PhD students. Some of these changes could provide opportunities for students and faculty to learn to work collaboratively, both face-to-face and through other modes of communication than just writing. As we saw with both the meeting notes and the ethics proposals, in fact the writing was both framed by and in turn might sometimes have framed the spoken, non-verbal and interpersonal interactions. The concept of knowledge as quantifiable and packaged as 'training' — familiar from discourses around the marketisation of knowledge — also underpins some of the new Academic Literacy practices described by respondents in our study.

Analysing these institutional changes through the theoretical lens of Academic Literacies, we have begun to identify some of the contradictions and tensions around transposing practices from the New Work Order to the Academy. As discussed above, though practices such as producing meeting notes and writing ethics proposals could be seen on one level as aiming to ensure equality of opportunity, new hierarchies have thereby been created, privileging written over oral texts and moving responsibility for 'quality control' outside the supervision relationship to 'the office' or the 'ethics committee'. Rather than assuming that Academic Literacies are 'value free', simply 'skills' to be applied, the Academic Literacies frame can help us to analyse how such institutional power relationships are being constructed and play out through the new Academic Literacy practices. Like the 'hidden features' approach described earlier in this chapter, our analysis above could be extended in terms of pedagogy — with the aim of encouraging students and supervisors to recognise 'hidden' meanings and develop alternative purposes for these bureaucratic literacies.

Similarly the micro analysis of communicative practices involved can enable us to see whether teamwork is 'democratic' or 'participatory' and problematise terms that may be taken at face value within the New Work Order. As we saw in the examples above, though the intention of asking a student to take minutes of meetings may have been to ensure that they are more aware of their entitlement to quality supervision, in fact, the actual process of taking the notes and the relationship between student and supervisors influenced whether this was seen as a mechanism of control or empowerment. Whereas Sam, for instance, saw the goal-oriented notes he was obliged to take in terms of the supervisors' control of his learning, Jane regarded the same practice as integral to her development as a reflective researcher. Lea (this volume) raises similar questions around power, identity and authority in relation to the lecturers who are writing as students on a Postgraduate Certificate in Academic Practice course. Carlino (this volume) gives an insight into the emotional side of this process for doctoral students: how their experience of writing was shaped by feelings of anxiety and vulnerability around their identity as a student.

How flexible the 'New Order' is remains an area for further research — as we have seen, both students and supervisors can treat the new requirements as rigid and narrow prescriptions or as additions on the side, while they get on with the essential business of learning and research. In order to explore such processes further, we need to place the uses and meanings of written text within wider communicative and institutional interaction. We have suggested that in doing so, it can be productive to draw upon the conceptual tools offered by both the Academic Literacies approach and the complex analyses evident in the 'New Orders' research. Such an approach may provide a starting point from which further research in the new and complex situation faced by universities might be developed.

Chapter 6

New Genres in the Academy: Issues of Practice, Meaning Making and Identity

Mary R. Lea

Background and Context

This chapter foregrounds the changing context of higher education and, in relation to this, explores the potential value of taking an academic literacies perspective to help us understand more about new writing spaces in the academy. As such, it is both framed by but also develops further the field of 'academic literacies', which has been concerned with highlighting the relationship between language and learning in higher education, particularly in terms of understanding student writing (Lea, 2008; Scott & Lillis, 2008). This body of work draws on applied linguistics and social anthropology for its theoretical orientation towards the social, cultural and contextualized nature of writing in the university. Its use of the plural form, 'literacies', signals a concern with literacy as a range of social and cultural practices around reading and writing in particular contexts. Research findings suggest that to understand more about student writing it is necessary to start from the position that literacy is not a unitary skill that can be transferred with ease from context to context (see, Robinson-Pant & Street; Russell & Cortes, this volume). This points to the requirement for students to switch between many different types of written text, as they encounter new modules or courses and the writing demands of different disciplinary genres, departments and academic staff. It has unpacked this diversity primarily through ethnographic-type qualitative case study research, looking at student and faculty experiences of writing

University Writing: Selves and Texts in Academic Societies
Studies in Writing, Volume 24, 93–109
Copyright © 2012 by Emerald Group Publishing Limited
All rights of reproduction in any form reserved
ISSN: 1572-6304/doi:10.1108/S1572-6304(2012)0000024010

for assessment,[1] and the gaps between their expectations of the requirements of writing. In foregrounding the relationship between writing and learning, writing is conceptualized in terms of epistemology and what counts as authoritative knowledge in the different contexts of the academy.

The development of academic literacies as a field of enquiry has gone hand in hand with ongoing changes in global higher education, including increased diversity in the student body, the introduction of modular degree programmes, moves from traditional academic disciplines to more professional courses, e-learning and the globalization of the tertiary sector. These are having profound influences on the kinds of texts that students are being asked to produce for assessment. More recent research reflects the application of the principles of academic literacies to these changing contexts, which are resulting in new genres entering the academy, often when professional courses jostle with traditional, discipline-based programmes of study. Some developments have already been documented in terms of undergraduate study (Baynham, 2000; Rai, 2004) but, despite the prevalence of professional courses at masters level, little attention has been paid to post-graduate professional qualifications, the genres involved in such courses and the questions that this raises for understanding issues of meaning making, practice and identity in student writing. This chapter takes earlier work, which examines changing contexts (Lea & Stierer, 2000), as its starting point in interrogating a very specific space, when university lecturers themselves become student writers. It draws on data from a small research project in examining how emergent genres of writing articulate diverse literacy practices and academic identities. It raises questions about the inherent tension between professional practice-based knowledge and a theorised written assessment of that knowledge as this space is negotiated and contested by different participants, both those who teach on the course in question and those who study it. It will examine how — in addition to disciplinary identities — different experiences of writing before starting the course, values about writing in relation to professional identity and the models of writing associated with specific professional fields all suggest a contested space for writing.

The particular context under consideration is a postgraduate certificate in 'academic practice' for new university lecturers. The purpose of this course is to help academics to improve their own professional practice as university teachers. The people who study it teach in various different contexts, ranging across primarily practice-based subjects, such as nursing, more traditional discipline areas, such as history, literature, economics and those fields of study that combine elements of professional practice with more conventional academic subjects, for example, business studies. In the United Kingdom, teachers in higher education are not required to have a formal teaching qualification prior to taking up a teaching post. Historically, this is due to an implicit assumption that since applicants for teaching posts are already likely to hold a postgraduate qualification, and in many instances a PhD, then they will already be experts in their own subject areas; this alone should qualify them to teach others. This

---

[1]In UK English the term 'assessment' refers to the marking and grading of student work.

seems to be based on a belief that being a research oriented subject specialist equips an academic for teaching. During the past decade such a view has been challenged and, in large part in response to government-led initiatives in supporting teaching and learning, most UK universities have developed accredited courses for new teaching staff such as the one which forms the background of this chapter. These go some way towards addressing the potential disjuncture between disciplinary and subject-based research expertise and the practice of teaching.

The kinds of writing that the university teachers in question are being asked to do in their assignments, when they become 'students' on the course, closely mirrors those encountered in other masters level professional courses in marrying theory and practice (see Baynham, 2000; Rai, 2010; Stierer, 2008). There are some evident contrasts between these forms of writing and those that these teachers engage within their own specific disciplinary contexts. At some level, there are also similarities between the different genres; for example, presenting an argument and being critical and analytical are still explicitly stated requirements for the writing that the participants have to complete on this course. However, there are additional important and significant aspects of writing that are required in their assignments. These include reflecting upon their own professional practice as university teachers and using theory to relate to this practice. The main rhetorical task faced in their assignment writing is the integration of theory and practice. In addition, they have to consider the possible conflicts between the theory they are introduced to on the course and their actual experience of their own professional practice and be able to articulate this in their writing. Russell and Cortes (this volume) look at the relationship of texts and genres across academic and non-academic communities. Although their concern is with academic and scientific communities, rather than professional contexts, which is the focus of this chapter, they suggest that if we want to understand the 'situation of learning in relation to texts and their production' then we need to move beyond the linguistic to the social context. This elides smoothly with the claim being made here that, despite the apparent differences between the writing students have to do on this course and more conventional disciplinary contexts, issues of identity and meaning making are, nevertheless, at the heart of their writing practices. One intention here is that, in turning the lens on this very particular context, the chapter will illustrate how the theoretical and methodological approach, which underpins academic literacies as a field of study, can be usefully drawn on and developed to aid our understanding as new and unfamiliar genres claim spaces in the academy. Adopting a similar approach to Robinson-Pant and Street (this volume), it builds directly on the third model of student writing introduced by Lea and Street (1998), with its focus on meaning making and identity at the level of epistemology and social practice, and its exploration of what counts as appropriate knowledge in any particular context. There is also strong resonance throughout this chapter with Prior and Bilbo's focus on academic enculturation, literacies and identities and their argument that it is crucial to trace how people move across both multiple genres and multiple contexts. They point to the blurring of boundaries between academic and non-academic settings requiring more interrogation of how social practices and identities both shape and are shaped by academic enculturation. This chapter illustrates how assessment practices contribute to a contested arena where professional practice and academic theory collide.

Research Approach

The Open University offers its 'Postgraduate Certificate in Academic Practice' (PCAP) online and at a distance, not only to their own academic staff, but also to those teaching in other tertiary contexts. Working within an eclectic mix of subject areas, many have no previous experience of engaging in the kinds of genres which tend to be foregrounded in courses of this nature. Stierer (2008) likens the experience of university teachers using and understanding concepts from educational discourses in academic development courses as 'strangers in a strange land' (see also Russell & Cortes reference in this volume to the work of McCarthy, 1987). Nevertheless, it is through writing on the course in question here that they provide evidence of their practice-based development, becoming adept in a range of written genres to complete formal assignments and a final project, which involves an in-depth enquiry into their own practice. Participants are also required to be active contributors to online discussion fora; this adds a further dimension in terms of negotiating issues of ownership and authority in meaning-making practices but is not explicitly discussed in this chapter (see Lea, 2007, 2009). The extract from the assignment guide, below, is illustrative of the writing requirements in terms of foregrounding the relationship between theory and practice.

Throughout the course we expect you to develop a critical understanding of approaches to learning and teaching that are informed by current research in order to investigate your own practice.

In general, when your teacher marks your assignments, he or she will be looking for evidence:

- *of your critical reading of the relevant literature*
- *of your critical reflections of issues raised on the course*
- *that you have considered and appreciated a range of points of view (These will include research, other relevant literature and perspectives from other course participants).*
- *of your systematic examination of your own practice*
- *of your critical reflections upon learning and teaching issues*
- *that you have used research (expert and your own) to offer a rationale for your own view*
- *of how you have developed or plan to develop your practice (extract from Assignment Guide).*

One of the underlying principles of an academic literacies approach is that meaning making is at the heart of academic writing (Russell et al., 2009) and that central to this is attention to participants' practice. Lea and Street (1998) argue that student writing needs to be understood against a background of institutional practices, power relations and identities, with meaning being contested between the different participants involved in any writing task. They explored the different interpretations of faculty and students, concluding that there were fundamental gaps between their understandings of writing requirements. They suggested that the evidence for this was to be found at the level of epistemology, authority and contestation over different kinds of knowledge, rather than at the level of technical skill, surface linguistic competence and cultural assimilation (see also Robinson-Pant & Street, this volume). Lea and Street, and other researchers taking similar approaches to student writing (Ivanič, 1998; Lillis, 2001), articulated clear differences in understandings of writing tasks between students and their teachers; groups who were markedly different not just in terms of their access to disciplinary knowledge but to the role they occupied in the university. In the context discussed in this chapter, on first sight there is less distinction to be drawn between those who teach the course and those who are the students. The latter are already teaching and marking their own students work, so in many senses are part of the same community as those who are teaching the course; that is, they all teachers in higher education. This being the case, those less familiar with writing research which foregrounds the complexity and diversity of genres and practices (as represented in this volume) might expect that the written assignments would present few challenges either to the authors or to their readers. Indeed, such a perspective was the one taken by both tutors and students on the course who were surprised by the challenge the assignments posed as writing tasks. The data illustrate the variation in emphases that participants gave to aspects of the course and how these were played out in the writing process. These are explored below under the three inter-related themes of 'course concepts and practice-based knowledge', 'values and implicit models of writing', 'disciplinarity and emerging genres'. To contextualize these there follows some brief explanation of the project.

For some while the course team had expressed concerns that there were some students who were evidently struggling with writing their assignments. As a consequence, we obtained some internal funding[2] to explore this issue in more depth. There were two stages to the project. Initially all seven tutors[3] on the course were interviewed about the difficulties that they perceived around student writing. These interviews were transcribed and provided the framing for the next stage of the project. That is, drawing on a thematic analysis of the tutor interviews, a loosely structured check-list was drawn up which formed the basis of the interviews that were then carried out with 20 students. The interviews with both tutors and students were conducted by telephone and lasted for about an hour. When they referred to assignments in the course of their interviews, students were asked to provide electronic copies of these scripts. The assignments formed a further source of data. The themes discussed below emerged from a close reading, by both the

---

[2]The project was funded by the Open University 'Practice-based Professional Learning, Centre for Excellence in Teaching and Learning'.

[3]In the United Kingdom, 'tutor' is a generic term used to refer to anybody who teaches students whatever level of seniority (graduate teaching assistant, lecturer, senior lecturer, reader, professor) they hold in the academy.

researchers,[4] of all 27 interview transcripts and elements of some of the student assignments; but only where these where referred to directly by students in their interviews. The analysis was primarily interpretative and thematic; we did not undertake any close linguistic or genre analysis of the students' writing. However, the approach taken by Rinck and Boch on enunciative strategies (see this volume) could be potentially useful in taking forward research in a context such as the one discussed below, when so many different expectations and understanding of the assignment task collide.

Themes from the Data

Course Concepts and Practice-Based Knowledge

A central purpose of the Postgraduate Certificate in Academic Practice is to enable participants to reflect on their own practice, critique it and develop further their expertise as teachers. The balance between the value given to participants' practice-based knowledge and theories about teaching and learning are crucial. Students who were interviewed during the project described in detail how they went about writing their assignments and the reasons for rhetorical choices. For some, the central focus was on the course theory. The authorities cited in the course and the theoretical frameworks were the starting point for their thinking and writing. For others, the main focus of their thinking was their own practice: the experience and knowledge of practice was more central to their concerns:

> When you go to do the assignment you can relate that to your own practice. So it's kind of looking at your experiential learning and based on the theories and the models, but a lot of it is more about what you do in your everyday practice and I think that's how I managed to keep my scores up (quote from 'student' participant).

Some experienced difficulty in relating theory and knowledge of practice because they were neither used to writing about their practice nor reflecting or critiquing this practice, with one student describing the experience as 'rearranging mental furniture'. Others experienced a mismatch between their own valued practice and the course theory; this impacted on their writing, particularly when they found some of the theory not very relevant to their own teaching practice:

> I was doing it {i.e. using references to course theory} because I thought it was expected. I'm doing a series of tutorials soon and I'm not sitting there thinking 'now what would Biggs do?' I've not referred to any of

---

[4]The interviews were carried out by Dr Sylvia Jones, and I am grateful to her for her generative and insightful contribution at the data analysis stage.

the literature, I'm back to sort of 'right, this is the objective; this is what I want the students to go away with, how am I going to get that across?' (quote from 'student' participant)

For some students, the fact that they were required to provide references from the literature to support claims and statements about their own practice appeared to negatively influence their own processes of meaning making. This was because they were most concerned to meet academic writing conventions and expectations, finding support for their argument, rather than focusing on their own professional practice:

> Sometimes I found myself desperately wanting to make a point and foraging about on the net, googling, going to education sites trying to find some sort of support for something I wanted to say. (quote from 'student' participant)

The forging of the link between course theory, through appropriate references, and practice-based knowledge was often talked about pragmatically, to meet assessment criteria. Knowledge of practice had value in assessment terms only if framed by the course frameworks. This produced a dislocation between participants' own beliefs and practices and the way in which they represented these in their writing. Although they explained that their own view of practice and the basis for the validity of their points and arguments needed to be supported by theory found in the course, they did not necessarily own this perspective. For example, one person suggested that her role as assessed 'student' was in conflict with her identity as a professional teacher:

> That's all about the references. That is about having it reported by someone else rather than you just writing yourself, the 'its right' — because other people are saying its right as well. So it definitely wouldn't be scholarly if I wasn't referencing anybody, even though I could still be right. (quote from 'student' participant)

She describes the use of citation as being about 'somebody else's' perspective, rather than hers. There seems to be a tension here between this and her own knowledge drawn from practice; what she refers to as, 'it's right'. Although she sees both as valid — 'I could still be right' — she also suggests that writing without referencing cannot be deemed scholarly. This relationship between course theory and knowledge of practice is neither transparent nor straightforward. 'Starting from theory' and 'starting from practice' represent different orientations towards the course and different ways of making meaning. In terms of writing, an individual's own starting point for an assignment is significant because it influences and shapes the focus and argument in the text. Whilst providing opportunities to reflect on and enhance practice, the ways in which participants find themselves able to write as confident practitioners is often compromised by the necessity to view everything through the lens of the course theory. In this sense writing becomes more of a constraint than a possibility for interrogating and enhancing their own professional practice as university teachers.

Values and Implicit Models of Writing

One of the issues that emerged during the project was the significance of the values that individuals held around the status and type of writing that they expected in the course. This was clearly articulated by tutors' repeated use of the terms 'post graduate' and 'scholarly', in their interviews. These terms not only embodied implicit models of writing but also signalled possible rhetorical and genre patterns that were expected and valued in assignments, from the tutor perspective. The terms signified a standard or level of writing, with absence of this considered to be a problem:

> The fundamental problem around writing that I perceive is that it is actually at post-graduate level and it is scholarly. (quote from tutor participant)

Amongst the tutors there was general agreement about the highly valued features and characteristics of this scholarly or post graduate writing, as illustrated when a tutor described what she was looking for in assignments:

> to critically analyse the literature that they were reading, and integrate appropriately into their work in a way that both showed that they understood what they'd been reading, and could reference it appropriately, but more importantly that they could read things and be constructively critical about what they read, and not just take the quotes or the words of others at face value. And almost without exception, maybe one of my students, but all the others I've had real difficulty trying to get them to understand the concepts of ... first of all not just putting quotes in, and big chunks out of other people's work. Most of them actually have a good stab at referencing, but its just that to begin with there's a great tendency for people not to do that or indeed if they did put things in there was no attempt to any discussion or debates in their writing. (quote from tutor participant)

This quote, which typified tutor responses, would not be out of place with reference to perceived problems with first year undergraduate writing. It is maybe more surprising in relation to the writing of university teachers to find reference to a lack of evidence of critical analysis of course theory, of texts containing argument or of appropriate referencing as a way of discussing, debating or validating claims. These concerns are closely related to the priority tutors give to discussion of course theory:

> They really haven't grasped the importance of the theory behind what they're now referring to and talking about. (quote from tutor participant)

They see this as the 'starting point' for successful writing. They expect to see their students starting from the frameworks, concepts and information in the course readings and then relating these to practice rather than the other way round:

They're supposed to be analysing course materials that are in the course ... It's quite often the bit that they miss as well .... because of all the other stuff, because of the reflective practice.

For me it's the taking the material, and thinking about it in their particular discipline, and practice setting that for me makes the best kind of answer. (quotes from tutor participant)

Nevertheless, most tutors recognised the complexity of integrating critical analysis with reflection on practice and using an 'academic style' of writing:

I also think this course is more complicated because 'yes' there is a need to do that {i.e. critique the course material}, but there's also a need to do reflection on your professional practice, after all that's what the course is about, so possibly its about understanding how to combine that. (quote from tutor participant)

However, they still expressed concern when accepted referencing and bibliographic practices were not followed:

I would never have thought I would have had to discuss with the student about referencing at this level. (quote from tutor participant)

In contrast to their teachers, those studying the course didn't make any reference to writing in terms of 'postgraduateness' or being 'scholarly' in their interviews, unless specifically asked. This despite the fact that some were teaching on postgraduate courses and almost all of them were responsible for marking student assignments in their own subject area. Prompted in the interview with the term 'scholarly writing', their responses indicated that their understanding was affected primarily by differences in disciplinary and professional background. For example, a participant who taught postgraduates herself in a humanities subject was unsure how far the conventions of academic writing she was used to in that context could be applied to her writing on this course. She contrasts this, described as 'educational or social', with 'scholarly' or 'academic' writing, which is what she does in her own discipline:

The scholarly writing, or academic writing it's giving you a clear argument, it's the setting out the information, convincing the reader you know what you're talking about, and that they will know what you're talking about by the end, whereas I don't know whether either the educational, or social, I don't know whether that's what they're after or whether it's something different. (quote from 'student' participant)

Russell and Cortes (this volume) also highlight the complicated nature of genres involving the re-representation of practitioners' disciplines and professions. See also

Coleman (forthcoming) for her discussion of recontextualisation across academic and professional domains).

Students' description of scholarly writing varied considerably with emphasis on different features, including concerns about the acceptability of using a personal voice and ways of writing about experience:

> I think there's always been this problem that if you introduce the first person it can't be scholarly, and you can't have the appropriate jargon in there if you like, but I don't think that's the case. I think you can have a very scholarly piece of writing that can have a lot of personal experiential evidence in it, and I think it should be scholarly. It is a Masters course. (quote from 'student' participant)

Another student made a distinction between writing 'an academic piece' and writing about his own practice and saw these as distinct forms of writing. The issue of using references also emerged in terms of students' understanding of postgraduate or scholarly writing. Whilst they recognised that referencing authorities in the field was conventional academic practice they frequently admitted to being strategic in its use:

> When I was writing the assignments I was consciously trying to reference it to make it seem more academic rather than just a 'this is what I do'. (quote from 'student' participant)

Others shared the view of their tutors, seeing reference to the work of noted authorities in the field plus critical analysis as signs of postgraduate writing and expected to do this in their assignment writing. Rinck and Boch (this volume) suggest that students can be encouraged to see themselves as authors and be made aware of the rhetorical moves in their own text and, therefore, develop a set of tools with which they can interrogate their own stance, point of view and choices in their academic writing. In some sense one could claim that, as students, these teachers were doing something similar in their reflections but without having the advantage of an explicit linguistic language of description. The problem in the context being explored here is that there seems to be little overall consensus amongst those studying the course with regard to what was meant by writing in a scholarly way and, presumably what such a genre or genres might look actually look like. As a result, what it meant to be scholarly in one's writing appeared to be more problematic for them than for their tutors.

Disciplinarity and Emerging Genres

The lack of consensus between those teaching the course and those studying it is perhaps to be expected given the wide range of different disciplines and professions that are represented. Many of those interviewed (both students and tutors) had studied, across a range of fields of study, both academic and professional and, therefore, brought multiple understandings of written genres with them. They often held several academic qualifications that spanned different disciplines, for instance, a BA in Spanish plus a degree in Nursing or a degree in Anthropology and an MA in Systems Analysis and Multi-Media Design. The professional background of individual participants was equally varied, with many of the participants having experience of working in more than one profession. Consequently they were bringing myriad experiences of written and assessed genres and mapping these onto the educational discourses that they were being introduced to on this course.

Professions and academic disciplines draw on a range of written genres that shape the ways in which members of that profession or discipline communicate with one another (Bazerman, 1981; Berkenkotter & Huckin, 1995). The differences between genres are not only subtly nuanced but are heavily reliant on context and are much more than a set of rules for 'good writing'. They govern what can be said and how it should be said in a specific community. Although academic literacies research points to contestation over writing practices and would challenge the stronger version of such a perspective it does acknowledge that genres embed recurrent features of disciplinary communication. In much academic writing, features of genres shape how the arguments within the discipline can be made and how knowledge can be developed (Bazerman & Prior, 2004). Other authors in this volume focus in some detail on the analysis of genres and offer perspectives that are valuable in any consideration of those that are under discussion in this specific context (for further discussion of genre in this volume see both Chitez & Kruse and Russell & Cortes reference to 'Swalesian approaches' and 'activity and genre analysis'). An additional complication and particular challenge for participants in a course like the PCAP is that it requires engagement in, what are in effect, emerging genres, that draw on both disciplinary models of writing and writing about practice-based knowledge. They do not explicitly draw on or replicate writing in the workplace that the participants on the course inhabit in their professional lives. Additionally, academics who publish in the field, and whose work is foregrounded in the course, tend to adopt social science or humanities type academic genres and there are few instances of published work, which bring together theory and reflective practice in the ways that students are encouraged to do in assignment rubrics and criteria for assessment. Journal articles in educational development do not as a rule replicate the more critical personalised reflection on their own teaching practice that students are attempting here (see Peseta, 2007, for an exception). This might be because any orientation towards practice tends to become subsumed by or elided with more established and long-standing research into teaching and learning in higher education, with its concerns around theory, methodology and rigorous research approaches (Marton & Svensson, 1979). Although there is general agreement about the key conceptual underpinnings of taught postgraduate certificates in the field — as Kandlbinder and Peseta (2009) illustrate — it is ratherless straight forward to identify a stable academic or professional community (see Land, 2004, for discussion of diverse organizational cultures), or what writing valued genres might involve in line with the kinds of approaches articulated by, for example, Bazerman (1981) or Swales (1998). It is partly as a result of this that participants find themselves in a dynamic and developing situation in which several models of writing are operating and changing as practice-based learning itself evolves. Negotiating these genres requires engagement in complex processes of meaning making and the construction of writer identity, key concerns of an academic literacies perspective and articulated by Moje and Luke (2009) in their exploration of literacy and identity, 'strong academic writing, from the academic literacies perspective, depends on knowledge of self and awareness of one's identity enactments' (p. 434).

Whereas all participants spoke confidently about the writing they did in their disciplines and professions, they often contrasted this markedly with the writing they were required to do on the PCAP. For example, one student who wrote professionally in the areas of science and psychology tried to make sense of the differences between her field and the educational/social science field. This is all the more interesting given that both education and psychology draw significantly on social science genres and rhetorical patterns:

> I find writing in science and psychology given a title I can just research and write on it, that's fine. Writing for this course is slightly less easy because it's a lot more 'wafflie', and its not so fact based. I like facts ... but maybe that's why I'm struggling because I'm used to writing, and I've written hundreds and thousands of words in a specific, in a scientific, in a psychological way. (quote from 'student' participant)

Adaptations from their own discipline to this new context include how arguments are supported and knowledge constructed. Someone with a postgraduate degree in a humanities subject described the different ways in which she supported claims and made arguments:

> I suppose I was supporting why I was doing things by, in some cases, referring to the theory, in others referring to 'well I've done this before and it's worked' ... . Whereas in a {humanities subject} essay you would sort of do 'this is suggested, that's suggested, but if you look at this other new bit of evidence well that draws it more in favour of this one, therefore we'll go with that theory', and a lot of the other ones {assignments for the PCAP} were very much a 'this is the current thought on this. This is what people think formative assessment is, and this is why its important, and this is what I do in practice and actually use this'. (quote from 'student' participant)

Some, who came from practice-based areas, such as nursing, articulated the adaptation to a new genre in terms of lack of experience in what they called 'academic' as opposed to professional writing.

> I found that I didn't know if I had got the level right, you know my academic level ... I always have a bit of difficulty with the writing. (quote from 'student' participant)

Others recognized that there were particular models or styles in operation on the course, 'There is a house style accepted in the teaching profession', and tried to identify this to aid their writing, 'You know how there's method acting well I thought this was 'method assignment writing'. Others were unable to reconcile this assignment writing with their prior experience:

> I actually found it more difficult than writing research, or the assignments I wrote previously for my Masters' degrees. (quote from 'student' participant)

This particular participant had two Masters' degree in humanities and social sciences. She talked about enjoying the control she had over her writing in her own research projects, whereas in this context she said that she never felt sure that she had provided the 'right' information. Despite these disjunctures between disciplinary experiences and writing on this course there were those who did believe that having an extensive experience of writing in other contexts was helping them adapt to these new genres. For them, writing confidently seemed to involve some implicit or explicit recognition of features of emerging genres and being able to make sense of these in terms of what they were used to although this did not always mean that they found the writing straightforward. The three short snapshots of individuals below bring to the fore how issues of professional and academic identity are played out in student assignment writing. (Names and other details have been anonymised).

Cary

Addressing the assessment criteria was a particular challenge for Cary who taught student nurses. She explained how her own teaching was about 'learning in practice' but she felt that she was not able to easily map this perspective on to her assignment writing. This was because, in her opinion, the assignments did not align well with her actual experience as a practitioner. One of the areas that she had particular difficulty with was the use of some specific terminology. She believed that some of the course-based terms presented a particular theoretical perspective that did not sit easily with her own day to day practice, working with her own nursing students. In addition, Cary was unsure whether the theories of learning she had read about fitted in any way with what her students actually did in practice, which was the focus of her teaching. Consequently, when writing her assignments she referred to the theory because she was required to do so and not because she believed that there was really any clear relationship with her own professional teaching practice. Addressing the criteria for assessment proved to be particularly challenging for Cary. In her role as a teacher she was very familiar with the requirement to use the notion of reflection to integrate theory and practice; this is what she asked of her own students. Despite this, she found it particularly difficult to do when it came to writing about her own experience of teaching. We can conclude that even though, in this instance, the criteria draw on a language of assessment with which Cary — as a teacher — is very familiar, her experience as a student writer is rather different. The meaning of terms and concepts, for example, 'reflection', 'integration of theory and practice' and 'drawing on one's own practice', is neither obvious nor transparent but is clearly tied to the context of this particular course. As a consequence Cary finds herself struggling with how to frame and articulate course-based concepts when writing assignments concerning her own teaching practice.

Janet

Although they both taught trainee nurses, Janet and Cary had very different approaches to their assignment writing. Janet did not find writing the assignments particularly difficult. She believed that it was important for her writing to be critical and analytical, as opposed to descriptive. As she saw it, an element of the task was to read and engage with the literature and substantiate her own professional experience in relation to the publications by established authors. She adopted this approach even if she experienced a mismatch between the things she read and her own professional experience as a teacher. Interestingly, in her assignment writing she tended towards an impersonal style and did not use the first person — as illustrated in the extract of her writing, below — even though she had indicated in her interview that it was her own professional experience that was the starting point for her writing:

> Fry et al. (1999) describe experiential learning as 'learning by doing'. This appears to be appropriate for a practice based course such as nursing ... The author {this is Janet referring to herself} has adopted the approach of assessing each learner's prior knowledge by questioning and summarizing. (extract from Janet's assignment)

The approach she takes in her writing suggests that Janet is being influenced by another experience of academic writing, which may have required distance and detachment, rather than the more experiential, personal and reflective style that is encouraged on this course, as suggested in the assignment rubric:

Discuss how your perspective on student learning has been challenged and/or developed further since beginning the course.

You need to illustrate your answer with reference to

1. *your own experiences of learning and teaching*
2. *the online debates and discussion in your tutor group*
3. *published work and web-based resources on student learning.*

You will be expected to draw on your own experiences as both a teacher and a learner and on the full range of resources that you have accessed and read so far in your study of the course. (extract from assignment rubric)

Tamsin

The third case study offers a rather different context. Tamsin has a PhD and teaches in a research intensive university and also on a distance learning humanities course. She describes her first two assignments on the PCAP as 'straightforward essays'. This is despite the fact that they require her to undertake a significant amount of reflection on her own teaching practice and relate this to the published literature on teaching and learning in higher education. She describes how she approaches these assignments using evidence in the same way as she would in her own disciplinary context and searches for articles which back up what she is doing in practice. However, she explains also that writing for the course assignments does not reflect what she would actually be doing in practice. Although they are connected, when it comes to assignment writing she would give more authority to the literature, what she refers to as 'other people's writing'. She makes a distinction between her 'practice' and her 'writing'. Her own interest is in the interaction between two different ways of viewing or experiencing the world — theory and practice — but she doesn't really draw on her actual practice in her assignment writing:

> I would see myself as doing something quite different in the writing than I'm doing in practice. I think they have a dialogical relationship with each other but the justification in the writing is largely based on other people's writing. What I am actually interested in more than my professional development is the interaction between the theory and the practice, which I don't directly use to justify my writing although it has a quite close relationship with it. (quote from 'student' participant)

Tamsin brings her experience of writing from humanities, which may be predisposing her towards theory rather than her own experience as a teacher. She describes her own experience of writing in her own academic contexts as 'using other people' to say what she wants to say. She explains how she finds the personal reflection difficult since it requires a very different way of writing from that which she is used to in her own subject area. As she says, she does not 'feel as confident in the conventions of this genre'.

Tamsin appears to be drawing on her own implicit models of writing from her own experience of disciplinary writing and mapping this on to the assignments she has to do for this course. She approached the assignments as 'essays', which might suggest someone who is strongly immersed in her own disciplinary ways of writing, and yet she also expressed frustration about the lack of 'opportunity to explore your own interests and doubts'. This was because she seemed to believe that the course theory took precedence over professional experience. Despite some familiarity with the social science nature of the educational discourse on this course, possibly because of her own disciplinary background, she still feels frustrated by the ways in which the assignments are framed. For example, she would like to have seen something she describes as 'more open ended'. Despite these misgivings, Tamsin talks about the way that the readings have had a direct influence on her own practice. This contrasts with the experiences of Janet, who was starting from her own professional practice and looking for something in the course readings to relate to in her assignments.

Ivanič, in her research with student writers, offers a compelling case for viewing writing as central to the 'discoursal construction of identity' — that is, the ways in which writing functions reflexively both to constitute and to express identities (Ivanič, 1998, 2006). Although Cary, Janet and Tamsin had, thoughtfully, adopted different approaches, all expressed self-doubts in their ability to write on this course. In their interviews, their sense of identity as a writer and their related struggles with meaning making are dominant. None of them felt that they were particularly successful in managing this emerging assignment genre with its requirement to merge concepts and theories from academic sources with reflection on professional expertise. In addition to the explicit attention to the theory/practice dyad, they needed to take on different identities simultaneously in their writing. These included being a student but reflecting on one's professional experience as a teacher; being a teacher but reflecting on one's experience through the lens of a learner; being a professional educator, being a disciplinary/subject-based specialist. Traces of these different identities ran through students' assignment writing, raising questions of power and authority regarding claims around knowledge in this particular disciplinary space. How is what counts as authoritative in a practice-based professional context such as this one determined in textual practices, without recourse to a shared, historically established, disciplinary knowledge-base? Should writer authority be given through the articulation of experience in practice or through the theorizing of this practice in a body of literature around academic development which, as a field is, arguably, still in its infancy, certainly in any comparison with traditional disciplines? Can an academic literacies frame alone help us to understand more about pedagogic contexts where knowledge is articulated and given authority through the recontextualisation of professional practice, or do we need to embrace other theoretical perspectives, as Coleman (forthcoming) argues, and as Russell and Cortes indicate (this volume)?

New Directions

This chapter has built on a tradition in which academic literacies researchers have been interested in unpacking micro-social practices, which are deeply embedded in the writing activities of the academy (Robinson-Pant and Street take a similar approach in this volume). This has made them particularly sensitive to both researching and theorizing new genres of writing as they emerge and the different interpretations and understandings of texts and practice of participants in any specific literacy encounter. This focus on textual *practice* is central to the field — both conceptually and methodologically — but it also dovetails productively with overlapping and related approaches, which are signalled across this volume. Academic literacies have now moved beyond its initial concern with undergraduate writing practices to embrace a diverse range of new contexts in and around the academy. In this respect Lillis and Curry (2010), in their study of international scholars writing in English, argue for the need to consider the specificity of the contexts in which written texts are generated, including who is involved and what is consequential. Tuck (2011) explores grading student writing from the perspective of the mainstream university teacher who undertakes this work, concluding that institutional contexts constrain the possibilities for engaging in a range of productive feedback practices around writing. Lea and Stierer (2011) examine how university lecturers' engagement in everyday writing practices, as they complete routine workplace documents, signals their maintenance of power and authority in a rapidly changing, managerialist university context. Robinson-Pant and Street (this volume) consider the significance of the new work order in examining the requirement for postgraduate students and their supervisors to record and make their practices visible in the production of written documents demanded by the university. Lea and Jones (2011) suggest that the processes of meaning making involved in digital textual practices in higher education are still largely hidden and are not being taken account of in student assessment. Similarly, Williams (2009) explores the power of popular culture in students' practices of reading and writing online. All these studies move the literacies framing on to embrace new domains and illustrate how powerful genres emerge in the relationship between the creation of texts and their associated practices in and around the academy. The significance of both context and practice, which has been foregrounded in this chapter, is always central to their analysis. Genres always emerge in relation to particular contextual configurations, drawing a range of texts and practices into the literacies frame (Lea, 2004; Lea & Street, 2006). As Russell et al. (2009) remind us in their discussion of genre and the contrasting perspectives of 'writing in the disciplines' and 'academic literacies', 'The focus on the minutiae of texts and practices in understanding meaning making is given by the ethnographic roots of this field, and particularly Hymes' (1974) ethnography of communication, resulting in the foregrounding of an institutional perspective which takes precedence over a disciplinary or subject based focus'. This institutional perspective is central to any understanding of genres as social practice, with its attention to the value placed on aspects of textual practice by different participants in the academy. This sits alongside Prior and Bilbro's claim (this volume) that any enquiry into academic enculturation must always include attention to participants' social, personal and professional trajectories and to spaces that may not be 'culturally marked as academic or disciplinary'.

We are only beginning to understand the complexity of the written genres that are emerging as people engage with new contexts within higher education and the implications in terms of practice, meaning making and writer identity. This has been illustrated in this chapter, specifically with regard to the changing landscape for professional postgraduates and the intersection with practices in their wider professional world. It is reasonable to predict that we are likely to find more of these unfamiliar spaces as academic, disciplinary and professional boundaries shift and blur and, in addition, as new technologies enable a range of different textual knowledge making practices. In facing this challenge both researchers and practitioners will need to focus the literacies lens more tightly on micro-practices and, at the same time, widen the lens to pay more attention to the institutional practices that are implicated in the emergence of new genres, both in and outside the academy.

Chapter 7

Enunciative Strategies and Expertise Levels in Academic Writing: How Do Writers Manage Point of View and Sources?

Fanny Rinck and Françoise Boch

Introduction

In research writing and the writing that is part of university research training, students have great difficulty adopting the specific image, figure or stance of the author that is expected in these genres. In line with the many studies conducted on the writer's investment in the text, or the notions of attitude, ethos, position and authority (Campbell, 1975; Delcambre & Laborde-Milaa, 2002; Delcambre & Reuter, 2002; Donahue, 2002a; Hyland, 2002; Ivanič, 1998; Rinck, 2006a), we intend to show the writing strategies through which this authorial stance can be approached in texts. We adopt a developmental view: how does this stance develop with the degree of expertise of the writer, from initiation to research for undergraduate students to the research writing of experienced researchers? Our approach is a textual one that can provide linguistic resources to help students to write. However, it deals also with enculturation issues. The aim of teaching research writing is not simply to expect students to adopt the 'author-researcher stance' that the researchers adopt in their texts. A developmental view can provide critical perspective on the teachers-researchers' expectations in our context of French higher education, as seen also in the question of the academic and scientific texts and communities posed by Russell and Cortes (Chapter 1, this volume) and the question of the nature of the academic enculturation posed by Prior and Bilbro (Chapter 6, this volume).

We will present here a summary of our research on stance in research writing. This research has been conducted for several years on the basis of written corpora of

University Writing: Selves and Texts in Academic Societies
Studies in Writing, Volume 24, 111–127
Copyright © 2012 by Emerald Group Publishing Limited
All rights of reproduction in any form reserved
ISSN: 1572-6304/doi:10.1108/S1572-6304(2012)0000024011

novice students, doctoral students and researchers, as well as interviews with students. Detailed data are provided in Part 3.2. Research on stance represents an ongoing trend in discourse analysis; our approach to stance is based on both 'genre theory' and 'enunciative linguistics'. As detailed in Rinck (2006a), we define stance as a genre-specific reader expectation and we hypothesise that the enunciative features are relevant to describing how stance is manifested in the texts. We will focus here on two aspects of stance in research writing: how do writers manage point of view in a text that should be 'objective'? And how do they refer to what has already been thought and written? For each aspect, we will outline expert strategies and student difficulties. Our work therefore allows us to examine students' enculturation to research writing and to question training in, and through, research writing. What needs should be targeted and what should be the teachers' expectations regarding stance in students' research writing?

Context

Our research group, LIDILEM (Linguistique et Didactique des LanguesEtrangères et Maternelles) was created in 1987, at l'Université Stendhal, a university with domains in literature, languages, linguistics and communication science. Situated in the French Alps in Grenoble, its 150 researchers make it one of the largest linguistics and didactics research groups in France. It is within the context of this group that our research team has worked on research writing and writing in university research training for over 10 years. By research writing, we mean the writing produced by researchers with the aim of constructing and disseminating academic knowledge, as explained in Chapter 1 by Russell and Cortes (this volume), in France we refer to *écrits scientifiques*, which encompass not only physical and natural sciences but also the Social Sciences and the Humanities. By writing in research training, we mean the very diverse pieces of writing that accompany students' paths through university. At university, teaching is based upon research and sometimes requires students to undertake research work. In France, and particularly in the Humanities, initiation into research is an important part of a university career. This initiation occurs progressively from the first or second year of the *Licence* (undergraduate degree) to the doctorate, and the university offers the students pedagogical support to supervise them as they undertake this work.

The students are guided by a tutor, but the aim for them is to follow an individual process: they choose a research question and determine an issue for investigation. They must read existing literature and undertake analysis within various methodological frameworks depending on the discipline (corpus analysis in Linguistics, archive analysis in History, field work in Sociology and Educational Science, experimental situations in Psychology, etc.).

Writing is key in this initiation to research: the students must produce research or research-based writing. As discussed in the present volume by Russell and Cortes, in some cases, it is research writing — namely for the more advanced students heading towards professional research (the genre of the thesis, but also the genres of professional research such as articles and paper proposals); in other cases, the writing is not that of researchers but 'trainee' research writing (*écrits de recherche en formation*) as Reuter (2004) calls it. Its features are, in part, based on the writing of researchers (definition of key questions, theory, methodology, analysis...). Russell and Cortes (Chapter 1, this volume) suggest that the aim is to 'to think scientifically', even if not all students are heading towards professional research, as outlined by these authors: this research-based writing also has the aim of enabling students (and practitioners) to acquire skills that will be useful whatever the professional sphere they intend to enter. In France, the term 'reflexive writing' is often used: tools for thinking that should encourage 'critical thinking through writing' and that aim to foster the real appropriation of knowledge rather that its mere restitution. In other words, this writing aims to encourage 'knowledge transforming' rather than 'knowledge telling', to use Bereiter and Scardamalia's (1987) terms. This writing encompasses various genres: study and research work, work placement reports, dissertations and professional dissertations.[1]

For example, where primary and secondary school teacher training is concerned, future teachers undertake work placements in which they play an active role: learning support and class observation for the novices (undergraduate level) and classroom teaching for advanced students (Master's level). Along with this, they produce a report or dissertation on a topic of their choice (e.g., how best to facilitate the process of learning to read? how to present an argument in a science class?) that they will explore through theoretical reading and their work placement experiences. For those training these future teachers, the aim of these reports and dissertations is for the students to bring into perspective their pedagogical practice as trainees and the theoretical works of reference (in educational science, psychology, sociology and in the didactics of different disciplines). If this is achieved, these reports and dissertations can be viewed as good tools for learning how to apply reflective practice to a professional context: the ability to question practice, to use existing tools and to evaluate their relevance.

Our study is at the intersection of academic literacies and students' vocational training. It focuses on training in and through research and concentrates on literacy practices and writing as a central part of this process. We consider academic literacies from a developmental perspective, as cultural, socio-institutional and cognitive familiarisation with the genres of research and research-based writing used in academic and disciplinary communities. In this context, writing constitutes a tool for learning and for thought. It is a locus for both personal development, and the building and assessment of knowledge: these are essential dimensions of academic enculturation, beyond writing abilities (see Prior & Bilbro, this volume). The academic genres in which we are interested are in some cases professional genres (those used in the professional sector of the research in question, e.g., articles or

---

[1]These so-called dissertations are not only PhD dissertations but also Master's dissertations.

paper proposals) and in others, 'knowledge transforming' genres, considered as vocational for example reports or dissertations of teachers-in-training (see, e.g., Crinon & Guigue, 2006).

We take the standpoint that the analysis of these different genres at different levels of expertise can allow students to be supported in their training as writers, not only with a view to their success within higher education, but also to encourage abilities in personal reflection that can be of use to them within the professional world. Such an analysis must enable a better grasp of the literacy development of students and allow their difficulties with research and research-based writing to be identified. It must also allow the differences between genres to be questioned as well as the expectations of university lecturers regarding the written production of their students within initiation to research.

Aims and Methods

How can we help students to familiarise themselves progressively with research writing and offer a vision that is more than simply a set of norms to which they must adhere, which would run the risk of heightening writerly insecurity (Dabène, 1987), that is, feelings of inadequacy or writer's block? How can teachers, on the one hand, better guide students towards success at university, whilst, on the other, more generally, allowing writing to become a real tool for learning and thinking?

Linguistic Description

We shall put forward here a synthesis[2] of some of the work carried out within our team on writing in research and initiation to research, in different genres and at different levels of expertise. This work falls within the scope of several fields: studies in academic literacies (a body of work referred to in French as *didactique de l'écrit dans l'enseignement supérieur*, or the didactics of writing in higher education), and studies in scientific discourse (born of Social Studies of Science and Rhetoric of Science); studies in text production and its teaching/learning (e.g., Barré de Miniac, 1996b; Piolat & Pélissier, 1998) that have shown the importance of textual genre, the role played by writers' representations of the genre they are to produce and the role

---

[2]In the context of this chapter and edited collection, we are privileging European references, purposely leaving aside the numerous U.S. studies on this subject, despite their great value. Two reasons led to this choice. For one thing, our U.S. colleagues are better situated than we are to carry out this type of theoretical review of the Anglo-Saxon literature. For another, given the long U.S. tradition of research about academic writing, we thought that the volume's readers would doubtless be already quite familiar with those references and might find value in discovering other work in this vein, less well known overseas, and sometimes using methodologies or targeting particular angles than those typically used in the United States.

of correction and revision; discourse analysis and enunciative linguistics,[3] which provide tools with which to offer detailed descriptions of writing strategies as shown in our work (see Boch & Rinck, 2010; Rinck, 2006a).

More specifically, we shall concentrate on two aspects here:

1. Point of view: how do writers take responsibility for assertions and manage point of view in a text that should be objective? Which authorial stance is characteristic of research writing?
2. Sources: how do writers refer to what has already been thought and written? How do they position their research in relation to existing work? We make a distinction between these two aspects but they are obviously linked: the way in which the author refers to what already exists plays a role in the image that they present of themselves in their text. These two aspects have been identified as being, on the one hand, an important locus for difficulties in the context of studies on students writing[4] and, on the other hand, essential aspects in the rhetoric of academic and research writing.[5] More generally, in terms of university literacy and literacy development, the issues at stake regarding 'point of view' and 'sources' are the following: how can we enable students to find their voices in their writing and to position themselves as subjects of their writing rather than effacing themselves behind fragments of received knowledge? How can we make writing into a real tool for appropriating knowledge in such a way as to allow the progression of personal reflection?

Pedagogical Perspectives

Regarding 'point of view' and 'sources', the advice given in classes of initiation to research and in the books aimed at novice researchers presents several problems (Boch & Grossmann, 2007). It insists on normative aspects of a technical nature (how to insert a reference, how to write a bibliography), does not always correspond to the actual practice of researchers (e.g., the idea that all subjectivity must be eschewed in research writing and the use of 'I' strictly avoided), and can be contradictory in the eyes of the students: one must take up a point of view, but avoid all subjectivity; one

---

[3]For an overview of the field, see, for example, Maingueneau and Charaudeau (2002) and for some fundamental texts Benveniste (1974), Bakhtin (1977), Anscombre and Ducrot (1988), Kerbrat-Orecchioni (1980).

[4]In the Francophone context, the following special journal numbers devoted to writing in higher education that give substantial space to these questions of point of view and sources can be mentioned: Delcambre and Jovenet (2002); Delcambre and Laborde-Milaa (2002); Boch and Grossmann (2001a); Boch and Reuter (2004); Pollet and Boch (2002).

[5]See Rinck (2010a) for a summary of the linguistic approaches to academic discourse and Boch and Rinck (2010) for a special volume of a journal devoted to *Enonciation et rhétorique dans l'écrit scientifique* (Enunciation and Rhetoric in Academic Writing).

must quote, but not too much; one must put forward one's own ideas, but constantly refer to external authorities.

To reach better-founded recommendations and provide genuinely useful support, our analysis is based on the description of the writing strategies of undergraduate students, advanced students who are novice researchers, and experienced researchers. We also carried out interviews with the undergraduate students who produced a piece of research-initiation writing in their 3rd year. All the pieces of writing that we have analysed were written in French within the field of the humanities (disciplines: Linguistics and Didactics of French). We used several corpora: 20 research-initiation reports produced by 3rd year students (Boch & Grossmann, 2001b, 2002; Rinck, 2004, 2006b; Rinck & Pouvreau, 2010); a corpus of 22 research articles published in scientific journals and written by doctoral students (Rinck, 2006a, 2010b; Rinck, Boch, & Grossmann, 2007); a corpus of 110 articles published in scientific journals and written by experienced researchers.

The aim of our work is to describe actual expert strategies, so as to avoid unfounded recommendations (for example, the cliché that 'I' should never be employed). We also intend to describe the difficulties faced by students and to question what can reasonably be expected of them. We use this descriptive work within training at different levels, so as to help students with these two issues of 'point of view' and 'sources'. Thus, rather than telling them that they must 'cite sources', it is possible to show them texts and make them aware of the different ways of referring to existing work, as well as of the effects produced by adopting one strategy or another. We believe that linguistic descriptions are also useful in training higher education practitioners: norms of usage are very rarely the object of conscious knowledge, and thus descriptions can be helpful in understanding how texts work, in identifying what leads to negative judgments, in questioning ways of evaluating particular problems and in knowing how to advise the writer rather than simply penalising their work.

We first examine the point of view of the author and then ways of dealing with sources, and for each aspect will provide information concerning expert strategies and student difficulties. In conclusion we question the differences between genres and levels of expertise, as well as academic expectations and the elements involved in providing effective support.

Effacement Énonciatif and the Image of the Author

Who Is Speaking in Research Writing?

Studies on how students position themselves in research-initiation writing often highlight the space devoted to accounts of experience. The paragraph below illustrates this (Rinck & Pouvreau, 2010).

> Afin de réaliser au mieux ce travail, je me suis posé plusieurs questions, dans le but de trouver un domaine d'observation qui serait le plus adapté, et le plus intéressant possible.(…) Après avoir trouvé le sujet

de mon dossier, il me restait à formuler ma problématique. J'ai alors décidé d'analyser de façon plus précise mon domaine de recherche. Tout d'abord, je me suis aperçu que les difficultés de cet apprentissage étaient multiples, puis je me suis dit que chaque élève était unique, et qu'alors, ils ne possédaient pas forcément tous les mêmes prédispositions à cette acquisition qui paraît longue et complexe.

In order to complete this work to the best of my ability, I asked myself several questions, with the aim of finding the most appropriate and most interesting area of observation. (...) After having found the topic for my project, I had to define my research issues. I then decided to analyse my research area more precisely. First of all, I realised that this learning process had multiple difficulties, and then I thought to myself that each pupil was unique, and so, they didn't necessarily have all the same predisposition for this acquisition, which seems long and complex.

This paragraph, situated in an introduction, is entirely centred on the student's 'I'. It is characterised by a narrative of the stages of the research process (*après avoir* [after having]; *j'aialors* [I then]; *tout d'abord* [first of all]; *puis* [then]; *alors* [and so]. The student presents her aims in axiological terms (with the interest of the object and the precision of the approach as key values) and with ameliorative terms (*réaliser au mieux de travail* [complete this work to the best of my ability]; *domaine d'observation le plus adapté possible le plus intéressant* [the most appropriate and most interesting area of observation]; *analyser de façon plus précise* [analyse (...) more precisely]. She recounts her choices and observations using verbs of intellect (*j'ai decide de* [I decided to]; *Je me suis aperçue que* [I realised that]; *je me suis dit* [I thought to myself]. This type of experience account suggests the discrepancy that can exist between the writing of students in initiation to research and that of experienced researchers. To better grasp the differences between the genres, we shall examine the positioning of the author-researcher in expert research writing.

Who is speaking in research writing? This question has been much discussed in the field of Social Studies of Science, where it has been shown that 'scientific style' is characterised by impersonal utterances such as 'substance A acts upon substance B' (Latour & Fabbri, 1977, p. 81).[6] In enunciative linguistics, reference is made to *effacement énonciatif*, literally 'enunciative erasure' (Philippe, 2002; Rabatel, 2004). Indeed, the observable tendency in research writing is that facts seem to recount themselves. This tendency is considered to be a specificity of 'theoretical discourse' in the typologies of discourse founded on enunciative criteria (Benveniste, 1966/1974; Simonin-Grumbach, 1975 and Bronckart, 1985). As Bronckart (1985) explain, reference (what is being spoken about?) in theoretical discourse is constructed as

---

[6]'le style scientifique se caractérise par des énoncés impersonnels tels que: «la substance A agit sur la substance B'.

follows: on the one hand, this type of discourse has the mimetic mode of seeking to express truth, and, on the other, it presents a form of enunciative erasure in the sense that all reference to the enunciative situation (who is speaking to whom, where, when) seems to be blocked. Theoretical discourse seeks to be cut off from, and autonomous with regard to, the situation in which it was produced.

Enunciative erasure is a linguistic feature: discourse is never actually cut off from the situation in which it is produced. However, enunciative erasure is exploited by theoretical discourse as a way of objectivising what is said by presenting it as independent from the situation of production; it is a discourse that is centred upon its object (the 3rd person is predominant), without deictic terms (traces of the I-here-now) and that aims to give universal truth value to what is being asserted.

The rhetoric of science has allowed progress to be made with regard to the question of knowing 'who is speaking'. Aside from name and signature, the author's presence in her/his text is relatively slight. Nonetheless, traces remain, as evidenced by the numerous studies of personal pronouns in academic and research writing. The presence of personal pronouns calls into question the idea that 'no one is speaking' but does not, in itself, allow more to be known about 'who is speaking'. To determine who is speaking, or which 'personae' (Campbell, 1975) we are dealing with, it is important to go beyond the simplistic opposition between objectivity and subjectivity (Kerbrat-Orecchioni, 1980) and the frequent confusion between objectivity and neutrality. Academic writing is most definitely produced by an author (or authors). It aims in many fields to be objective, and enunciative erasure is a process that has the effect of objectivising discourse. It is not, however, a neutral piece of writing: etymologically speaking, neutral means neither one nor the other, or the absence of position, which is not the case in writing where the issue at stake is that of arguing in favour of a point of view. The subjectivity that appears in academic writing should be described in terms of both enunciative erasure (Grossmann & Rinck, 2004; Rabatel, 2004) and the marking of subjectivity. For example, the impersonal form does not indicate a lack of position and, on the contrary, can even serve to make strong affirmations (e.g., 'it is obvious that').

How, then, is point of view constructed in writing that seeks to objectivise? Enunciative linguistics has shown the value in distinguishing between deictic subjectivity and modal subjectivity (see Rabatel, 2004 and, for research writing, Grossmann & Rinck, 2004; Rinck, 2006a). Deictic subjectivity links what is said to the person speaking, in their capacity as a physical entity, with the faculty of expression, who says something at a given time and place (I-here-now); modal subjectivity refers to the commitment made to what is said. As we have seen, in academic writing deictic subjectivity is often erased (enunciative erasure) because the ideal of universality requires what is written to remain true regardless of who wrote it and of the spatial or temporal context. Conversely, every utterance includes modal subjectivity: in an utterance such as 'water boils at 100 °C' there is a universalising commitment of the kind 'it is known that'. It is through this modal subjectivity and the forms of modal subjectivity specific to academic writing that the author asserts, gives nuance to and strengthens their claims, and that the reader can follow the author's reasoning and know what they are taking individual responsibility for.

However, this distinction between deictic and modal subjectivity needs examining in more depth: the clause 'I think that' falls within the scope of both types of subjectivity and could be seen as a way of giving nuance to an affirmation: making it acceptable with regard to the assumptions made about the reader's reaction; specifying that in epistemic terms it should not be considered as a general truth. Such formulations are rare in research writing (Fløttum, Dahl, & Kinn, 2006), but show that the study of personal pronouns can be interesting: indeed, observing not only their frequency but also their co-text can provide a good basis from which to better understand how affirmations are made in academic writing, when an author chooses to foreground their presence, and with what effects.

In this way, Fløttum et al. (2006) developed a typology of the roles of the author in the research article, on the basis of all the pronominal markers of the author in three languages (French-English-Norwegian) and according to the verbs and other lexical items associated with them. They identify three roles taken on by authors in their texts: the writer (*in this section, I shall present...*), the researcher (*the study we conducted*) and the arguer (*I would defend the idea that*). The analyses carried out in the context of the KIAP project with the help of this typology show that practice varies according to discipline and, to a lesser degree, according to national culture. It also varies depending upon the level of expertise of the writer (Fløttum & Vold, 2010): in articles written by doctoral students, the role of the writer is very present, showing their concern with being reader-friendly. This reader-friendly dimension to doctoral students' articles could either be considered to be an effect of their status as novices in the field of author-researchers that will gradually disappear as they acquire more experience of research, or else the sign of the evolution of the genre towards standards placing particularly importance upon this dimension (Rinck, 2010b).

Student-Authors

When used in training students, linguistic description can allow them to focus their attention on the author's stance in the academic genre, so as they can better understand what is expected of them and manage to analyse their own practice as authors, and better control the image that their text conveys of them as authors. The work of our research team has focused on different linguistic aspects in expert research writing within this perspective. Work has been carried out, for example, on: evaluative markers (the most used markers and the ritualised values of clarity and novelty); verbs of positioning, used in these same texts, to show an opinion or point of view, intentions or choices and scientific contribution (Tutin, 2010); the way of indicating theoretical filiation (Grossmann, Tutin, & Garcia da Silva, 2009) and of distinguishing ones position from other works (Chavez, 2008); the way of setting out the state of the art within an introduction so as to situate one's research object (Boch, Rinck, & Grossmann, 2009). In this way, it is in fact the rhetoric of research writing in its ensemble that can be described. Students can therefore be made aware of this in the context of support provided in the writing process, thus giving them strategic tools to work on rewriting their text with reference to expert practices.

Enculturation to academic genres is progressive. Our work has shown, on the one hand, that students need to develop a command of the phraseology characteristic of research writing; for example, experts, rather than employing a formulation such as *nous avons été stupéfaites de constater* [we were astounded to note], characteristic of novice writing, will prefer turns of phrase such as *il est étonnant que* [it is surprising that], *il est frappant de constater que* [it is striking to note that] or *nous avonsconstaté* [we noted that] (Rinck & Pouvreau, 2010). In the same way, the expression of agreement in *nous soutenons totalement la pensée de [nom d'auteur]* [we entirely support [author's name]'s thinking] belies a certain awkwardness in expression that influences the author's stance due to the degree of assent that it implies. The teacher advises an alternative formulation: *nous adhérons sans réserve à l'analyse de* [we subscribe unreservedly to [author's name]'s analysis] (Rinck, 2006b).

Alongside the analysis of writing in initiation to research produced by students, we also included interviews conducted with these students throughout this process (Rinck, 2004). These interviews show that the students have confused representations of research writing.[7] The latter is seen as neutral and objective, but nonetheless some of the students are aware that they are expected to *mett[re] des choses personnelles* [include personal things] as one of them put it. They therefore experience the necessity of positioning themselves as a confusing requirement: *c'est quand même personnel mais je trouve qu'on n'a pas trop eu l'occasion de dire vraiment ce qu'on pensait du sujet* [it is still personal, but I think that we didn't really have the chance to say exactly what we thought about the subject], *on ne s'introduit pas vraiment dans ce qu'on dit, on ne dit pas vraiment ce qu'on pense soi* [we're not really present in what we say, we don't really say what we think ourselves], *on ne peut pas donner son avis* [we can't give our opinion], *de toutes façons nous on ne peut pas élaborer des theories, on n'est pas professionnelles* [anyway, we can't put forward theories, we aren't professionals], and the necessity to take up authors read: *c'estparadoxal, on nous demande de mettre des phrases qui ne sont pas à nous et aussi de les retravailler* [it's paradoxical, we're asked to include sentences that aren't ours, and also to rework them], *ce qui est dit est tellement mieux dit* [what they say is always worded so much better] (Rinck, 2004, 2006b).

Students' difficulties in asserting themselves as authors in their research initiation writing are due at least in part to the fact that this kind of writing requires a progressive appropriation of genres that impose a characteristic lexicon and phraseology, both for enunciative erasure and for the marking of subjectivity. Furthermore, as shown by interviews with students (Rinck, 2004), they have an unclear notion of the genres of reference and seem suffer from a writerly insecurity already observed in school and professional spheres (Dabène, 1987; Lahire, 1993), faced with expectations presented as being evident whereas in fact they are not, and faced with the fact that their writing is the locus for assessment and competitive selection. The issue for those training them is therefore to provide support in the

---

[7]Reuter (1998a) highlights some of these representations showing how they act as obstacles in writing.

writing process that takes the academic context into account, as well as the difficulty that students have in constructing their own thoughts within existing frameworks to which they are asked to conform, without these being made sufficiently explicit.

References to Other Points of View

References to other studies and points of view are another essential feature of research writing. They influence the image conveyed of the author that we referred to in the first part of this chapter: in expert research writing, the author presents him or herself as being capable of mastering a domain or a research issue, of establishing the theoretical background, of indicating his/her theoretical affiliation, of discussing accepted conceptions and of proposing new ones. We shall show that it would be futile to try and model the practice of novice writers on those of experts. We will begin by looking at the strategies at work in the writing of initiation to research, with undergraduate students, in comparison to research writing. We will then offer an account of a study comparing research articles written by doctoral students with those written by more experienced researchers.

Comparing Novice and Expert Practices

The comparison between research writing (researchers' articles) and the writing of initiation to research (3rd year students' work) focused upon what we designated as *discoursd'autrui* [the words or voices of others] (DA), in reference to Bakhtin's (1977) dialogism. The starting point for the descriptions was the general idea that research writing is a multi-reference work (Grossman, 2002) that gives over a large space to DA and that modes of reference to DA are varied. Citation is, indeed, but one means amongst others — no doubt the most explicit — to indicate building on what others have said (Boch & Grossmann, 2002; Grossmann, 2003). Figure 7.1 set out in Boch and Grossmann (2002) presents the typology retained as the basis for analysis.

Different linguistic criteria allow these categories to be distinguished. In *allusions*, the writer mentions studies without claiming to summarise their contents: 'In Linguistics, the studies that marked the end of the 1980s can be mentioned, for

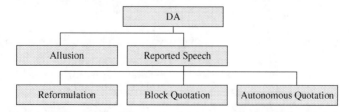

Figure 7.1: Typology of modes of reference to *discours d'autrui*.

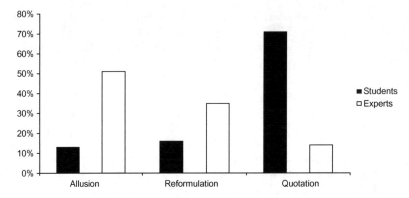

Figure 7.2: Respective weighting of allusion, reformulation and quotation in novices and experts.

example Cruse (1986) or Winston, Chaffin and Hermann (1987)'. In *Reported Speech* (RS) the writer indicates that he/she is summarising, reformulating or citing the words of another. Three categories of RS can be distinguished. *Quotation* creates an autonomous space on the enunciative level, whereas *reformulation* allows the writer to include the words of the other within a discourse for which they takes responsibility. *Block quotations* allow the cited segment to be both integrated and highlighted by scriptural markers, through the use of italics and quotation marks. In sum, if we detach ourselves from the RS label, which tends to mask the main oppositions rather than foregrounding them, it seems preferable to distinguish *allusion* — allowing shared knowledge, or non-essential elements, to be placed in the background whilst still situating the research within an identifiable epistemic space — from *reformulation* and *quotation,* which each express a specific way of building upon what has been said by others.

Figure 7.2 shows the contrast between expert (research articles) and student practices (research-initiation reports).[8] Two tendencies can be noted in expert practices: the high level of allusion (51%) and of reformulation (35%) compared with citation, used less frequently (14%) and in specific contexts (to give a definition or create an aesthetic effect by reproducing a strong turn of phrase).

Allusion and reformulation mean that expert research writing can be defined as a discourse with author's names (DAN) to which, from time to time, these authors' words are added (reported speech of others, in the form of reformulation and quotation).

In the case of novices, the features that have been highlighted in many studies are the abundance (or even proliferation) of quotations and the fact that they are inserted in a way that leads to a disjointed patchwork (Donahue, 2002b; Kara, 2004;

---

[8]See Boch and Grossmann (2002) for further details on the data.

Pollet & Piette, 2002; Rabatel, 2002). Overwhelmingly, quotations are used to justify an assertion or a choice, and to introduce a new idea, with the awkwardness that stems from a lack of command of the requisite phraseology and — more problematic as far as the argument is concerned — a tendency to make quotations into arguments of authority (Boch & Grossmann, 2001b, 2002; Rinck, 2004, 2006b). The priority needs for pedagogical intervention are to enable students to avoid confusion regarding how to take responsibility for the claims they made and to learn to use the thinking of the authors that they have read to further their own thought.

Is it appropriate to expect students to adopt the expert model for research writing, which consists in reformulating rather than quoting the authors read? A training programme built on this model will prove necessary for future researchers but in the initial stages of learning is far from easy. As Boch and Grossmann (2002) have shown, 'recourse to quotation appears to be linked to sociolinguistic constraints, to forms of insecurity that only greater command of the content but also a change of *position* can lift'.[9] Furthermore, the use of quotation can allow students to 'familiarise themselves with the concepts of the field of reference' and to take on an author-researcher voice and a rhetoric specific to academic discourse by borrowing from other authors. Quotation as practised by students thus seems to be a good tool for progressing towards the reformulation characteristic of expert practices. In this way, a potentially reprehensible practice, such as the profusion of quotations, can in fact be exploited to positive ends, if we accept that demands must be prioritised and emphasis placed on those that can genuinely help students to think through the act of writing.

Comparing Articles by Doctoral Students and More Experienced Researchers

We have seen that expert research writing can be considered as 'discourse with authors' names' that often mention previous works without always outlining their content in detail. On the basis of this idea, we sought to describe all the processes that enable an author to state that points of view and approaches exist: in other words, that something has already been thought or written about his research object.

This study, presented in Rinck, Boch, and Grossmann (2007) and in Rinck (2010b), focused on published research articles, some written by doctoral students, some by more experienced researchers. An important point to be made is that whether a text has been written by a novice or experienced researcher, if it has been published in a peer-reviewed journal, it has therefore been deemed admissible and is considered to comply with the norms of a community, in accordance with the principles of the peer-reviewing process. The specificity of doctoral researchers' articles can therefore not be considered in terms of deficiencies to be improved upon

---

[9]'le recours à la citation apparaît lié à des contraintes sociolinguistiques, à des formes d'insécurité que seule une meilleure maîtrise des contenus mais aussi un changement de *place* peut permettre de lever'.

and can allow us to reflect upon enculturation both on the level of the genres of the research discipline and upon the socio-institutional status of the PhD student novice researcher.

Our typology of reference to 'what has already been thought or written' distinguishes six categories.

1. Author cited, with no other reference (no date, no document), often in an inflected form (noun or adjective). For example, *Searlian theory*.
2. Document cited (book or article) in the traditional format: author(s) + date, with complete references in the bibliography. For example, Ducrot (1995); according to Sperber and Wilson (1989); Chevrot et al. (1983).
3. List of documents (when reference is being made to several documents, either by the same or several authors). For example, see Goudaillier (1887, 2002) (cf. Rossi, 1971; Di Cristo, 1978).
4. Names of schools of thought (*praxematics; according to cognitivists*), disciplines or research fields (*a rhetorical classification; in the linguistics of proper nouns*).
5. General terms without specifying the research field (*the diverse approaches; the analyses; the descriptions; certain definitions; these conceptions/positions; for some; two main interpretations*).
6. Erasure of the source: reference to a collective 'one' with no explicit mention of author or document, often in a passive form (*a question that has already been raised often; the proper noun is most often considered to be*) or more rarely in a impersonal form (*it has long been considered*).

The specificity of doctoral students' articles compared to those of more experienced researchers concerns first the number of references of all types. Figure 7.3 shows the average number of references in research articles for each group of writers (doctoral students versus experienced researchers).[10]

Doctoral students' articles contain far less references than those of more experienced researchers (with an average of 39.5 references for the former, and 73.3 for the latter, and a statistically significant difference[11]). Furthermore, the number of references is more homogenous from one article to another with doctoral students and their articles never include less than 8 references. With other experienced researchers, there is greater variability and it is not impossible to find articles including only two or three references. Qualitative analysis shows that doctoral students limit themselves to references that are of direct use to their argument without always linked them to a more general context. The eight references represent, however, an appropriate minimum through which their texts comply with the canonical models of research writing.

---

[10]Data were as follows: a corpus of 22 research articles published in scientific journals and written by doctoral students (Rinck, 2006a, 2010b; Rinck, Boch, & Grossmann, 2007); a corpus of 110 articles published in scientific journals and written by experienced researchers (Rinck, 2006a).
[11]Mann–Whitney U test, $U = 140.5$, $p = 0.0279$.

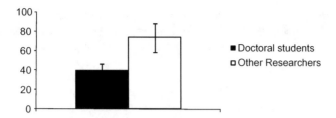

Figure 7.3: Average number of references in the articles of doctoral students (D) and other researchers (O). *Note*: The error bars on the graph (standard error) indicate the variability around the mean.

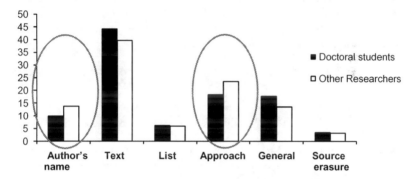

Figure 7.4: Percentage of each type of reference to sources in articles of doctoral students (D) and other researchers (O). *Notes*: The ellipsis indicates the categories for which the difference between doctoral students' articles and those of other researchers is statistically significant. Mann–Whitney U test, $U = 139.0$, $p = 0.0254$ for the names of authors, $U = 109.5$, $p = 0.0032$ for the names of approaches.

The analysis of modes of designation also supports this hypothesis of a canonical use of the genre of the article by doctoral students. The six modes of reference to sources presented above are distributed as follows in the articles of doctoral students and other researchers (Figure 7.4).

The distribution of types of reference is very close overall between the two groups of writers: in particular, the references to texts taking the form 'author name + date' are the most frequent. Two significant differences arise, however, where 'author name' (*Saussurean linguistics*) and 'approach' *(the structuralists)* are concerned: these two modes of reference to sources are significantly less frequent in doctoral students' writing.

Doctoral students, therefore, adhere more to the norm according to which explicit references are made to textual sources in the 'author + date' format. Omitting the explicit reference and mentioning only the author's name is a process that could seem to run contrary to conventions but is representative of typically expert practices. It testifies to the writer's capacity to make a name function as an 'emblem of position' and could be attached to a 'knowledgeable' posture as it puts into play a discourse of complicity. In doctoral students' articles, mastering the norm takes precedence and their status does not allow them to play with these standards.

As for the contrast between usage of names of approaches between doctoral students and other researchers, this can be explained by knowledge of the field. With names of approaches, it is no longer a question of designating an enunciative source (the bibliographical reference, the author's name) but of mapping out the research field by identifying theoretical positions, designated by labels — either endorsed by their representatives, or of an ad hoc nature. This stance therefore requires a global overview of the field. However, such designations contribute, in turn, to creating this stance (Grossmann & Rinck, 2004; Rabatel, 2004) and the difficulty facing doctoral students is perhaps less the knowledge of the field than the need to feel legitimate in taking up such a position, that is, that of an author offering a panoramic view of the field and providing a synthesis of its main tendencies.

Conclusion

Our work is based on a linguistic approach to research and initiation to research writing. It allows us to identify the textual strategies used in constructing an author-researcher point of view and dealing with sources, and to analyse entrance, or enculturation, into research writing from this perspective, comparing writing strategies at different levels of expertise.

Linguistic description should enable advice to be given to students for the writing and revision of their texts in a more specific manner than simply making recurrent demands such as 'you must put forward a personal point of view but not be too present in your text' or 'you must cite your sources, but not cite too much'.

The analysis of the students' writing and the interviews conducted with them show that their difficulties are linked in part to awkward phraseology that can be evaluated negatively as they indicate insufficient command of the genres. This awkwardness could, however, be probably corrected thanks to guided observation of expert writing and of characteristic patterns of phrases. It no doubt poses less of a problem than the students' insecurities: they feel helpless in face of confusing or even paradoxical representations of what research writing is.

Linguistic observation can act as a basis from which students can be made aware of the way in which expert writing functions, so as to better control their own practices and to work on rewriting, considered essential in expert models of text production. This observation can also serve as a springboard for questioning the stakes of research writing: above and beyond, academic demands such as citing sources or using quotation marks, how and why is it important to document oneself, to take on board previous knowledge and to define one's position with a field? Or to adopt an overt position by making distinctions between the assertions for which one takes responsibility as an author and those made by others?

Moreover, our work allows us to question expectations within the academic context. Is the author-researcher stance in expert writing a good model against which to evaluate 'trainee' research writing? (Reuter, 2004) Is it a good model to use when training novices? How can the 'spontaneous' practices of novices be used to develop training tools that build on these practices and progressively guide students towards expert practices?

The analysis of literacy practices and their development in the specific sphere of research writing shows that enculturation is the progressive familiarisation with genres in use and their respective conventions, that is, not only with ways of writing by also with ways of doing and thinking (Carter, 2007). It is also a socio-institutional issue linked to the insecurity of the writers in the context of learning and evaluation, and to the legitimacy required to present oneself as the author of research.

The issues in supporting the learning of research writing must be defined at the intersection of two constraints: on the one hand, that of passing on academic heritage (the conventions specific to research writing within a given discipline), and on the other, that of fostering training by thinking through writing (writing as a tool for self-development as a writing subject and an epistemic subject, a tool for knowledge building and a tool for analysing professional practices).

The author-researcher stance expected in research writing is a very specific stance, linked to a specific discursive community, that is, that of the researchers in the field. What stance should be presented as positive in initiation to research? To what discursive community do such genres belong? Are other models of texts and writerly stances than those of traditional academic genres used in the context of currently successful professional Masters training programmes? While training in research writing is a strong need within graduate schools, the link between universities and the professional world also requires us to think about what, in the academic sphere, can prove useful training for other spheres of application.

Chapter 8

Academic Writing Activity: Student Writing in Transition

Isabelle Delcambre and Christiane Donahue

Introduction

This chapter will focus on the writing students describe as they move through levels
of higher education in two institutional contexts: a small group of universities and
disciplines in France and Belgium, and a single university and several disciplines in
the United States. The studies done in each context provide insight into student
perception of the writing produced, the challenges and obstacles, and the transitions
that the students experience. The writing they are describing is named, in the United
States, "academic" writing and in France, "university" writing for undergraduates
and "scientific" writing for masters level and beyond, the point at which students are
learning to write theses and dissertations, much closer to actual research scholarship
(see also Rinck and Boch, this volume).[1] Our purpose here is to explore their sense of
this writing in ways that allow us to describe their experiences in writing as they move
through higher education, as well as the writing activities they perceive and how this
perception develops our understanding of academic-scientific university genres. The
work across two cultural contexts sharpens and highlights our understanding of each
context while drawing on different traditions of study.

---

[1]"Scientific" is a term that applies to all disciplines in France, not only the hard sciences.

University Writing: Selves and Texts in Academic Societies
Studies in Writing, Volume 24, 129–149
ISSN: 1572-6304/doi:10.1108/S1572-6304(2012)0000024012

University Writing: Texts Specified by Disciplines

In this section, we offer background about the institutional contexts of the two studies: the authors' situations, populations studied, and the traditions of writing research and teaching that frame the studies.

The French and Belgian study took place as part of a funded project carried out at l'Université de Lille III in France, where the didactics research group Théodile-CIREL is organized. This group includes researchers from Lille, Paris, and Belgium. It was a collaborative effort with the research group LIDILEM at l'Université de Grenoble in Grenoble, France. The students included in the study were from these institutions. The U.S. study was situated at a small public liberal arts college in Maine, and carried out by the director of first-year writing and a team of scholars from six different disciplines. The students in the study attended this college from 2004 to 2008.

U.S. Research and Teaching Traditions

In the United States, the attention paid to writing in contexts other than the first year of university studies has developed over time in two complementary strands, the "writing across the curriculum" strand and the "writing in the disciplines" strand. The first is generally understood as supporting the use of writing to learn curricular material in any discipline and the second is generally seen as focused on entering into writing in a particular discipline, although of course there are overlapping interests (see Russell, Lea, Parker, Street, & Donahue, 2009).[2] What that "entering in" might look like is the subject of much debate and discussion, as various researchers support different approaches — an epistemological approach, a convention-driven teaching approach, or a genre approach, to cite the most frequent divisions (see, Prior and Bilbro, this volume, for an in-depth discussion of the different ways academic enculturation is modeled).

The U.S. WAC and WiD fields have been in some ways insular from other fields that study student learning generally at the university, although they have much to exchange. In more recent years, U.S. writing researchers have broadened their knowledge base, consulting with researchers from various disciplines who affect scholarship of teaching and learning, researchers in the field of education, and researchers focused on the sociology of various fields — education, science, and so on. Certainly the overall work in this domain is affected by the types of U.S. institutions of higher education in play: "research one" universities, liberal arts colleges, community colleges, public comprehensive institutions, specialized (military, maritime, environmental ...)

---

[2]A prime example of this is the "WAC" Clearinghouse's deep and ongoing attention to both WAC and WiD. In fact, McLeod and Maimon argued the two strands are fully complementary, and positions WAC as the umbrella, with WiD as a part of WAC (cited in Petrucci, 2002).

institutions[3] have different sets of needs, structural openness, and resources. In addition, an ongoing strand of publications has focused on higher education in general, and writing, reading, and critical thinking always figure in these discussions (cf. *Clueless in Academe, Academically Adrift*, etc.).

In this section we will briefly overview the WAC and WiD strands, discussing them in terms of research and practice. The field is vast, and this is simply a provocative highlighting; the story can be told in many ways.

The practices associated with WAC are diverse and productive, and appear in a variety of settings. They are notable for their embedded nature: a course is not generally a "WAC" course but rather uses time-tested WAC strategies to accomplish goals in the course. These strategies can range from brief in-class writing activities to journals used for an entire course (for an example of the range of activities, see http://writing2.richmond.edu/wac/wtl.html). Their underlying purposes include supporting the learning of the course material via the unique affordances offered by writing, and supporting students' acquisition of writing as a meaning-making tool.

Research has supported the effectiveness of these different "write-to-learn" practices. J. Langer's work in particular has supported this development (see, e.g., "Learning through writing: Study skills in the content area," 1986). Bangert-Drowns, Hurley, and Wilkinson report, in a 2004 meta-analysis of 48 school write-to-learn programs in the United States, that there is evidence to support writing to learn as an effective technique, if the activities involve metacognitive work and are used over time. Rivard's (1994) meta-analysis of the literature about writing to learn science, while critiquing its focus on postsecondary contexts and its tendency toward poorly developed empirical studies, offers a review of evidence that supports using expository writing to increase science learning, and expressive writing to improve students' engagement in learning the material and supporting scientific problem-solving (pp. 973–974).

WiD practices are adopted in different ways, again, broadly speaking. They tend to be either convention-driven or epistemology-driven. For the former, practices include attention, in courses in different disciplines, to the features associated with writing in a field: conventions of genres, of citations, of structures. For the latter, practices might be more associated with exploring the ways in which writing and the construction of meaning are intertwined and how these work in a particular disciplinary worldview. In both cases, practically speaking, institutions in the United States offer designated writing-intensive courses, or courses entirely dedicated to writing in a discipline ("The Art of Science Writing" or "Advanced Writing in Sociology" ...).

In terms of the research basis for these practices, we find divisions as well. U.S. models of writing in the disciplines work have been studied extensively within the "writing studies" domain and within domains of a broad variety of disciplines.

---

[3]See glossary.

In addition, some of the research about writing has grown out of attention to the needs of students for whom standard U.S. academic approaches to writing and language are not primary (e.g., speakers of English as a second or other language). Each research model supports different practices.

One of the most well-known scholars in the "conventions" perspective is Swales, whose groundbreaking careful dissection of the moves made in scientific writing defined a shift in understanding. His initial work has been taken up in many scholarly projects for decades. The international fields of English for academic/ scientific purposes draw heavily on this kind of work to offer students methods for developing as scientific writers (for further discussion, see Russell and Cortes, this volume).

In contrast, the more epistemology-driven research we find by writing scholars such as Carter, Bazerman, Prior, or Russell, to name a few, uses activity-theory models, cultural-historical activity-theory models, or social cognitive models to bring out the complex and transformative relationships between written words, disciplinary knowledge construction, social context, and individual negotiation. Several of these models are described in detail in Prior and Bilbro (this volume), who offer insights into their evolution and their current status in the field. These research strands have influenced writing activities in the United States beyond the first year, although less clearly. The complexity of the models makes them resistant to "application" directly in classroom practice, but should lead to fruitful discussion with faculty from other disciplines precisely because the basis for discussion is epistemology.

One particular approach to studying evolutions in students' practices and perceptions of writing as they move through higher education is the longitudinal study. There are hundreds of studies of university student writing in the United States, although the modes of inquiry have trended largely toward ethnography and case study. In the past 10 years or so, longitudinal studies in particular have become prominent modes of inquiry in the United States, although there were certainly hallmark longitudinal studies well before (cf. McCarthy, 1987; Chris Haas, 1986). These studies have surfaced in part because of increasing attention in the field of composition to the question of knowledge transfer, and in part because of increasing critique of the generic first-year writing course and deep interest in understanding what is happening with different student populations at key points of transition: from college to the professional world, but also from high school to college and from U.S.-style "general education" (a slate of courses students at most universities must take outside of their major field of study in order to ensure broad contextual knowledge of ways of seeing the world) to work in a major. The U.S. study detailed later in this chapter is in the longitudinal category, and seeks to further our understanding of students' writing experiences as they move through higher education.

European Writing Research and Teaching Traditions and Evolutions

In Europe, especially in francophone countries, research about writing at the university is rather recent, though broader questions about studying at university have been explored for a long time in sociological studies (see, e.g., *Les Héritiers* published in 1964 by Bourdieu and Passeron[4]). But the problems students encounter with language practices and discursive genres at the university have been taken in account only for 20 years, due to the transformation of the university in the late 1980s. The university had to cope with the affluence of many "new" students, essentially caused by increasing success on the Baccalaureat (which is the exam at the end of secondary school and serves as the first university grade, sufficient to enter University), following Lionel Jospin's Law on Education (1985) and his wish to see 80% of students succeeding on this exam, the economic crisis, the search for university degrees to face the unemployment of young people, etc. (Boch & Frier, forthcoming).

Specific to writing in higher education, there is a history of research, even if it is not extensive. We will present here, specifically, studies coming out of two main French research centers, Grenoble[5] and Lille.[6] Many European studies on writing at the university could have been cited here, but we have chosen to focus on French research as it is perhaps less generally well-known.

In the 1980s, early French studies focused mainly on describing the genres of academic discourse (thesis, text commentary, synthesis, internship reports, etc.). These descriptions were often particularized by focusing on certain features of academic discourse such as the problems of citation (Boch & Grossmann, 2001a) or of the reformulation of other writers' discourse (Delcambre, 2001) and on enunciative features, such as the marks of the author's stance (or "the discoursal self" as Cazden (2009) calls it), that is, the image that the writer constructs of himself as a writer, which denotes more or less control of implicit standards (Delcambre & Laborde-Milaa, 2002; Laborde-Milaa, 2004) or the construction of an author's figure (Rinck, 2006b,c), that is, "the self as author," according to Cazden's categories.

These descriptions aimed to define, from textual analysis, the potential difficulties students would encounter while writing introductions or research questions, while gathering and introducing appendices, and so on, or to better know the practices related to personal work (taking notes, rewriting).

Originally, these studies were done by researchers enrolled in linguistics or didactics of writing; they are corpus-based, gathering students' texts selected for their specific problems, or research texts (research articles, conference proposals) identified as possible models for the writing required of students and as means to better understand their writing problems or even to understand how the students' products can help change university writing practices.

However, the interest of linguists in research articles has produced a methodological scission: researchers enrolled in linguistics in France are moving increasingly toward quantitative analysis based on large corpora[7] that identify specific rhetorical

---

[4]See Gruel, Galland, and Houzel (2009), a recent publication, on these topics.
[5]Lidilem (EA 609), Université Stendhal-Grenoble3.
[6]Théodile-CIREL (EA 4354), Université Charles-de-Gaulle-Lille3.
[7]See the study named "Scientext" and its Website, http://scientext.msh-alpes.fr/scientext-site/spip.php?article1.

functions, while the didacticians continue to work mainly on the students' productions or what they say about their writing (see, Rinck and Boch; Carlino, this volume, for alternate perspectives).

Meanwhile, some of these studies have focused early on disciplinary and epistemological dimensions of writing, and explore the links between writing and disciplines, whether in secondary students' productions (Reuter, 2007), or university students' and researchers' productions (Reuter, 1998a). This disciplinary dimension is common to both linguistic and didactics fields, as they have often made comparisons between university disciplines in constructing their research data.

Finally, as another common purpose, these didactics and linguistic studies question the practices in the institutional contexts of written productions. Writing to learn/to be evaluated (area of teaching and learning) is thus distinguished from writing practices of researchers (who aim to develop and to communicate new knowledge) and from those of advanced students when they learn about research at master's or doctoral levels (what Reuter (2004) named "research writing in training"; see also, Rinck and Boch; Carlino, this volume). The question of areas of practice (teaching, research, research training) is thus an important concept for describing the transitions and the complexity of the links between disciplines and writing.

Recently, a new field or research, named "University Literacies," in reference to specific writing and reading practices at the university, has emerged, crossing two major and ancient fields of research, linguistics, and the didactics of writing. The French study presented in this chapter is grounded in the University Literacies approach. This field of research is related first to the linguistic analysis of scientific discourse[8] that aims to show how scientific activity is built up through its speech (Rinck, 2010b; Rinck and Boch, this volume). Thus, many French studies have focused on describing the writing of researchers or PhD students, highlighting different phenomena, including theoretical framing (Boch, Rinck, & Grossmann, 2009), reference to others (Grossmann, 2002), enunciative positioning (Rinck et al., 2007; Rinck & Boch, this volume), and the issue of the scientific author (Grossmann, 2010). These studies have extended and deepened the detailed depictions of the rhetorical moves made in scientific writing (see, e.g., Hyland in the United Kingdom or Flöttum in Norway), offering powerful insights into the construction of successful scientific texts as well as the evolutions in their function.

They often focus on disciplinary comparisons. The hypothesis of a disciplinary identity of discourse genres, already validated for subject matters quite different from each other, is also true when epistemological foundations of the disciplines and institutions are considered relatively close (such as language sciences and literature).

The field of University Literacies is also linked to the didactics of writing, a theoretical field (Delcambre & Reuter, 2010) which considers writing and reading as issues, explicit or implicit, of teaching and/or learning (from elementary school to the

---

[8]In the French sense, that is to say, research writing, whatever the discipline, sciences or humanities.

university). This does not mean a focus on possible mechanisms of teaching and learning. The didactics of writing is a scientific framework that allows specific description of the acts of writing and the texts, leading to asking some specific questions (for instance, how writing is involved in disciplinary contexts) while not treating others, such as the cognitive processes or social determinations of writing activity. As we see in other chapters in this volume (Mateos & Solé; Russell & Cortes), those dimensions are quite interesting, but they are not central for the didactic approach.

First, a researcher who adopts a didactic point of view considers writing as involved in teaching and learning, and therefore takes into account the status of the writers: they are students or teachers, whose positions toward knowledge are different (Chevallard, 1991) but need to be considered in relation to each other in research studies.

Similarly, one would consider this writing to be located and situated in a didactic way. It is important to distinguish the textual genres and modes of writing according to the writing situation. It may be a situation of assessment or a situation of private writing (e.g., "taking notes"). Indeed, according to these different situations, the content of teaching/learning does not have the same status: in the first situation, knowledge is institutionalized; in the second situation, it is reformulated.

Finally, analyzing practices from a didactic point of view leads to considering the academic disciplines in which these practices and actors exist, as a possible factor of variances in the modes of writing, the standards, and the writing strategies. In fact, the main specificity of this theoretical point of view is the importance given to changes in the content with which students (and teachers) write. These different contents belong to different disciplines, and so define them. So, one of the didactic issues is the link of these practices to the different disciplines that organize them. An epistemological and institutional description of these disciplines (academic or research disciplines[9]) is the basis of a didactic analysis of writing at the university. Reuter has proposed the concept of "disciplinary awareness" as a link between disciplines and the modes of teaching/learning: the way the actors are aware of the disciplinary dimensions of working (i.e., of writing), the way they reconstruct the disciplines in their own contexts (Reuter, 2007/2010, p. 41; see also, Prior & Bilbro, this volume).

Thus, the two points of view, linguistic and didactic, which are the basis of the University Literacies field, join in giving a central role to epistemological and disciplinary dimensions in writing practices at the university. We add here a brief commentary on the phrase "University Literacies," which is a quasi translation of the English phrase "Academic Literacies," a framework detailed elsewhere in this volume, in particular in the chapters by Lea and by Robinson-Pant and Street. Even

---

[9]We propose to consider that at the university, teaching disciplines have to be distinguished from research disciplines, the "institutional" context being different. Thus, the contents taught as Psychology, Language Sciences, and so on, are partly different from the theoretical and methodological issues a researcher deals with.

though there are many common dimensions between the two fields, the choice of the French phrase is linked to the specific meaning of "academic" in the French tradition, which is rather negative. "Académique" work is often understood as formal, conventional, even pretentious. Thus, "university" literacies refer to the institutional sphere of discourse production, gathering the discourses whose purposes are teaching and learning and the scientific discourses of researchers (or researchers-to-be as PhD students).

Shared Theoretical Aspects: Discursive Genres, Contexts, Writing Practices

The two traditions described above are grounded in complementary theoretical frames that inform our understanding of writing practices, genres, the effect of context, and the interaction of these in studies of what university students say about writing in different disciplines.

For us, as for many others in this volume, writing is described less as a singular activity than as plural practices, linked to sociological, historical, cultural backgrounds, writing being included in multiple other practices. Therefore, writing is not described as the very moment of transcribing, but is integrated to "a before and an after that determine the conditions of possibility, the functions, the uses, the meanings and the values" (Delcambre & Reuter, 2010, p. 20) of the situation in which the writer is engaged.

These practices occur in, are shaped by, and shape contexts. In a French didactic perspective, three interconnected systems can be proposed as three contexts that weigh upon writing practices: the "schooling" system (here university level), the pedagogical system, and the disciplinary system. These three contexts render writing practices functional. They "become tools, or objects, essentially in relation to teaching, learning, and evaluation, and are shaped in a way that makes them as easily managed as possible in *school spaces* (determining temporality, spatiality, tools, media, length, genres, and so on)" (Delcambre, 2010).

The *"school system"* (in the sense Vincent (1994) presents, the *school form*), is an organization of social relations, specific to the relationship of teaching and learning at school, which is different from other modes, rather informal, such as the family or experience-based modes of teaching and learning (Reuter, 2007/2010, p. 111). Is the university the same system as school? It is an open question.

We also find writing practices to be structured by what Lesne (1977/1994) calls a *pedagogical work mode*. He defined three different pedagogical work modes, according to the various relationships to knowledge and to power between teachers and students, and the pedagogical means the teacher uses. These modes have a powerful effect on the frequency, form, modes of connection, and modes of evaluation of writing practices. And finally, writing practices are inscribed in/with *disciplines* (and at particular points in a disciplinary curriculum). It's quite difficult to define the notion of discipline (see the debates about this notion in sociological studies (Fabiani, 2006) for example). But we can propose that a discipline is a social and historical construction, organizing contents, devices, practices, tools, etc., in the purpose of teaching and learning (Reuter, 2007/2010, p. 85). In the university, disciplines may also be seen as linked with theoretical and methodological frames, and thus differentiate disciplines to be taught from research disciplines. We can thus see these practices as disciplinary objects or tools that are at the heart of disciplinary work. Each practice (analyzing, commenting, observing, experiencing, etc.) has its function in a discipline, with different genres specific to those disciplines. As we situate writing practices in these three contexts, we see their specificity for university work, as contrasted with extra-scholastic practices, shaped by their own contexts and socio-institutional spheres (Reuter, 1996).

Thus, and it will be of certain interest in our text, the disciplines are contexts that determine writing practices, as well as they are in turn shaped by specific writing practices or specific genres of discourse; how are students perceiving and experiencing these different factors, as they move through higher education?

The role of genres is central. In the genre theory on which the French study reported here is built, "The genres of discourse are cultural products, specific to a given society, developed during its history and relatively stable. They govern the speech of members of the society engaged in endless situations of social life. [...] (Delcambre, 2010). These genres of discourse are built from categories of linguistic production that do not rely on internal approaches that classify texts by different organizing principles, but instead are framed by various contexts, including utterances, institutions, and histories.

This concept of genre is grounded in Bakhtin's (1986) articulation of linguistic productions as shaped by historical and social dimensions — his well-known definition of genres as relatively stable utterances shared in particular situations. "Any verbal statement," said Bakhtin, "[...] actualizes a genre of discourse; that is to say, manifests both a common dimension and an 'individual form'" Genres of discourse are thus not formal text typologies of the kind often described and developed in earlier research about writing in both France and the United States.

The U.S. study shares this bakhtinian understanding of genre, although the notion of genre is less central to the part of the study reported here. The contexts evoked above are also shaped differently for the U.S. work: while the disciplinary context is shared, the question of school context has not been taken up in the U.S. study. Instead, it takes as context both the discipline and the unique shape of U.S. curricular stages: general education and student "major" or student learning toward a discipline, and considers the theoretical framework of some writing to learn scholarship. This scholarship is central to understanding parts of the relationship between writing, learning, and disciplines.

Briefly, the writing to learn scholarship has provided some key theoretical points of support. Grounded in the 1960s and 1970s in the work of Barnes, Britton, and Rosen (1971), among others, it countered the transmission model of learning to focus instead on "knowledge in action" and the dynamic learning roles afforded by writing. Of course, different types of writing demand different levels of cognitive engagement, and produce different kinds of learning (see on this topic

Bangert-Drowns, Hurley, & Wilkinson, 2004; Mateos & Solé, this volume, among others). In addition, the learning afforded by writing is not automatic but dependent on particular factors in any learning context (Newell, 2006). More recent work on modeling student writing as learning, in particular as connected to disciplinary contexts, is drawn from Lave and Wenger's development of participation models. They consider increasing participation, its "use value" (Newell, 2006, p. 243), as a complex way to analyze integration over time, its phases, its relationship to knowledge, to context, and to the individual as social. The U.S. study reported here offers insights into this integration over time, and the French study offers insights developed from surveying students at each of the various points of undergraduate and masters' work.

Two Empirical Studies in Dialogue

This section presents the results of two studies, one in France and Belgium, and one in the United States. These two studies serve here as concrete examples of some of the students' experiences, the writing activities they perceive, and how that perception helps us to understand their university writing in each country. These experiences index both shared concerns and differences. The studies will lead us back to considering theoretical frames in these cultural contexts, in a way we believe is useful to broader discussions of writing in disciplines in different culturo-institutional contexts.

The two studies are methodologically different in their approach. The French study focuses on describing students' representations of the written student texts produced at the university in a given level of study in five disciplines, with student processes as a secondary interest. Its overall purpose includes exploring, in the French *didactique* tradition, the relationships between writing, disciplinary context, and level of studies. The U.S. study is of a much smaller group, and focuses on a broader set of questions, including not only students' written experiences but also their sense of what develops from context to context and the way they understand the relationships between courses, disciplines, writing, and learning. Globally, the two studies offer different ways to understand concrete manifestations of the students' writing experiences as theorized in Part I.

French Study via Questionnaire

We present here a recent three-year study about University Writing Practices in France (and Belgium), funded by the French National Research Agency.[10] The main objective of this study is to describe *the perceived links between university writing and the disciplines* by inventorying the kinds of university writing students report doing

---

[10]ANR-06-APPR-019.

(academic and scientific writing) and some of their reported writing practices. In addition, it aims to describe the characteristics of academic writing at *different stages* of the university cycle in order to identify aspects that represent continuity and discontinuity between the different text genres required according to the level and/or the discipline and to identify the thresholds students cross.

This study is based upon collecting students' and teachers' discourse about writing as empirical data. In this chapter, we will focus on the students' responses to an extensive questionnaire, presented below.

The Students

We collected and studied 456 detailed questionnaires, representing six disciplinary spaces and several different universities: History (Lille), History (Brussels), Psychology (Lille), Educational Sciences (Lille), Language Sciences (Grenoble), Modern Literature (Créteil); and five different levels: L1, L2, L3 ("Licence," undergraduate), M1, M2 (master).

The Research Questions

The structure of this survey allows us to focus on two main issues and therefore on the results linked to them:

- Are the writing practices described linked to the disciplines in which they take place?
- What are the perceived continuities and/or the discontinuities among writing practices along the curriculum?

The Questionnaire

The first part of the questionnaire, useful for our chapter, is presented in the appendix. The second part is focused on exam assignments, on the support students feel they need, support they encounter, and support they lack.

Students were first asked to make a list of the written texts requested by their program, identifying the representative writing of their studies (at the level where they were when they completed the questionnaire) (see below in the appendix, questions 1 and 2). Our treatment of this data aims to identify links between writing, discipline, and education level, establishing the writing the most frequently cited or quoted prominently in each group.

We then studied the standards associated with the writing that is considered representative of the discipline by the student, through different questions: we distinguished between standards that students want to respect (question 3) and those that they suppose are implemented by teacher-scorers (question 4).

Third, students had to identify the ease or difficulty of the genres of discourse with which they have problems or are comfortable (questions 5 and 6). Then they were asked about the writing in which they encounter new problems (specifying the type of difficulty, ease, newness) (question 7).

In this chapter, we will focus in particular on the responses to the questions about representative text and about standards, and only secondarily about the ease or difficulty students identify.

The Curricular Differences

We identified whether there are links between the texts students say they have to write and their level of study, in order to point out thresholds or transitions in university writing, from the point of view of the students.

From the disciplinary standpoint, the identification of representative disciplinary genres is more or less clear, depending on the discipline. The academic disciplines that are the most clearly identified through the texts they configure are those which have referential disciplines in high school or middle school (literature, history) in France, and where the teachers claim a continuity in the writing, from high school to the end of the academic curriculum, in particular the French academic genre which is the "dissertation" (the essay). This interesting result for our purposes has to be linked to other findings discussed below.

The main finding related to the curriculum variable is that the analysis of the representative texts the students designated allows us to contrast undergraduates with masters degree students. The students who are at the very beginning of the program identify less than the more advanced students the genres that are adequate and common to many of their experiences; advanced students identify very similar genres.

For a third of the students at the beginning of the curriculum, there is some difficulty in identifying a representative document of the discipline. They report experiencing a blur as to what kind of writing is required, or they report such a multiplicity of types of writing proposed by faculty that they hesitate to identify one or two as "representative."

However, the "essay" is mostly chosen by the students of L1, the investigation (or survey) by the L2, synthesis and internship report by the L3.

On the contrary, the "thesis" is the representative writing students at the masters degree level choose; it is clearly a designation relevant to this level, but it is also a genre or a designation that is not disciplinary. It is cited in all the disciplines as the specific writing of this level of study.

The Standards are Linked to the Stages of the Curriculum

From the responses to the question "Among the pieces of writing that you have to produce at university, which is the one that seems to you the most representative of your discipline of study or of the courses you are taking?" we were able to establish four profiles of responses:[11] those whose principal aim is to "answer adequately,"[12] those who think that the most important is to "write clearly,"[13] those who say they are focused on "writing from others' texts,"[14] and finally those who are interested by "self-expression"[15] when they write academic texts.

If we establish the links between these profiles and the curricular dimensions of our survey, we see interesting results: writing based upon others' texts (or against) is really a masters' level writing practice; the L1 students are mostly involved in self-expression, or concerned by the search for an adequate answer, while the L2/L3 students are focused on the clarity of writing.

Evolutions Inside the Licence Cycle

The difference between the first year and the second/third years is important because it lets us think that there may be transitions within a cycle, not only when the students enter the masters level. We find the same opposition when we analyze the students' discourses about difficulties. Students who declared they have mainly essays to write (in literature and history), say that they do not encounter difficulties with this genre in the first year; on the contrary, mention of difficulties appears in the second and especially in the third year. We think that the continuities between secondary school and university in these disciplines, manifested by the continuity of the main written genre, the essay, produce an illusion of ease, in the first year, due to a weaker disciplinary awareness. The students discover, as they progress toward the last year of Licence, that this supposedly well-known genre of discourse is not so easy, that the teachers' expectations are more complex than they thought.

U.S. Longitudinal Study: Interviews

Another path for ongoing questioning of students' experiences at transitional points is to study students longitudinally. In this particular case, unlike in the French study, the key experience in terms of moving through higher education studied is from general education to work in students' majors. Our specific research questions in this project were:

- How can the institution's writing culture be described based on the experiences of the students in the study? Who is writing what, and in what contexts?

---

[11]We have determined 43 scores for each item with which we made a factorial analysis based on correlation. The interpretation takes into account the closeness of the variables.

[12]This profile is identified by the correlation between the scores given to the "accuracy of the response" and to the importance of "knowledge."

[13]"Writing clearly" is linked through the scores of the "clearness of the discourse", the "links," and "formal clarity."

[14]This profile characterizes the scores of "Reformulation," "references," "quotations."

[15]"Self-expression" is identified by the scores of "style," "originality," "personal opinion."

- How does each student's writing change over time? What patterns are exhibited in student writing over four years? What patterns are correlated with disciplines, types of assignments, genres, other factors?
- *Is there a difference between students' ability to write well and their awareness of how well they are actually writing?*

The Students

The study involves 20 students from 11 disciplines: Business Economics, Community Health, Creative Writing, Early Childhood Education, Elementary Education, English, History, Interdisciplinary, Psychology, Secondary Science Education, and Rehabilitation Services. The students stayed with the study for the full four years. They turned in everything they wrote, and were interviewed at the end of the second and fourth years of their studies, and surveyed at the end of each year. Each interview lasted between 30 and 45 minutes, was tape recorded, and was fully transcribed.

The Tools: Interviews

The interview questions focused on three major domains: the students' experiences with writing in general education and major areas of disciplinary study; the students' understandings of writing and its functions; and the kinds of writing experience students brought with them to college.

The interview results have been analyzed by coding types of responses, looking first for similarly themed nominal groups, then adjectival groups, and finally forms of subject positioning. The results are thus not an analysis by discipline as done in the French study reported above; here we have 20 students, and the most productive approach is closer to case study of each student than to a report of statistically significant results.

Preliminary Suggestive Findings

The tabulated interview replies here focus only on relevant questions for this chapter:

- What differences do you see in writing in different disciplines?
- What is the relationship between learning and writing in your classes?

The purpose of writing in college was largely seen by the group as: to demonstrate understanding; to communicate; and to increase depth of thinking. Less frequent purposes included: to prepare for a career, to improve writing skills, to analyze, and to have something for which you can be graded.

Students used a broad range of strategies to approach assignments, from outlining (9/20) or peer discussion (6/20) to breaking the assignment into sections (3/20) or allowing themselves time (1/20). The drafting approach ranged from writing two drafts, by computer or by hand, to "writing immediately." Students reported that over time, this process changed minimally if at all, although some did claim to have improved their editing ability, to have developed a process, or to have improved small points of their process (citation, preparation ...).

The kinds of writing knowledge students cited as useful, as they moved from one course or activity to another, were low and heterogeneous. Broad useful abilities included "format" (6/20), "process" (6/20), and "analysis" (5/20), with a few students mentioning content, citations, or mechanics. Specific abilities, cited most often by only one student, ranged from knowing how to do citations in Education or structure in Art to style in History or group writing in Science.

Students were expressive about the relationship between writing and learning: 8 of 20 cited writing for its role in developing future comprehension or demonstrating knowledge. Aside from these two categories, the replies fragmented, ranging from "making connections" or "digging deeper" to "remembering material more effectively."

These results suggest broad areas of interest for further study. The close readings provide additional insight into ways students' perceptions are connected to disciplines and to their writing practices.

Evolution Seen in Close Readings of the Interviews

The evolution of the students' writing and critical thinking as they move through their courses of study is of course always a complex and complicated process; content, assignment, reading, teacher emphasis, and student's disciplinary affiliation, among other factors, are interrelated. What students say in the study interviews is itself sometimes evidence of their critical thinking. In the first year, students describe writing criteria as arbitrary, associated with different faculty members and their requirements. By the fourth year, students articulate these criteria as related to the discipline of a course. They have shifted from idiosyncratic individual issues to subject-related understandings of writing's shapes and frames.

How Writing Is Perceived?

In the study results, students' advances, regressions, and lateral developments over four college years become clear in their written work more than their interview narratives, which tend to reflect their impressions of a more "seamless track towards growth." In fact, from the part of the study not reported here, in which we analyze the students' texts over time in relation to their interview comments, we find that the texts show a stronger evolution in terms of the writing-knowledge-constructing relationship and the student's subject positioning than do the interviews. In their interview statements about writing and knowledge, shared themes become clear, but these themes do not appear to suggest that students are aware, in many ways, of the writing-knowing relationship.

Most striking is students' persistent understanding, after four years of college, of knowledge as an object, something that can be "kept" or "contained" by writing. One student notes, "Writing things down and really thinking about your writing really makes you remember stuff better, so I know I won't forget certain elements of the classes that I'm taking ..."; for another, "it kind of imprints it [the knowledge] and makes you know it even more" (writing as capturing knowledge). Writing the material down creates a permanent repository he can return to: "as a learner, you sort of have the brain connections that get disconnected once you're done taking the class ... if I had that paper I could read it over and really remember what I did ... instead of having them [the ideas] lost forever." Allen suggests that it helps to look back on written essays as knowledge transcribed and deposited on paper: "If I tried to figure out, what was that reading, I can look at the paper I wrote about it too."

The three also return frequently to writing as proof of knowledge, evidence of learning, or mastery of content, supervision: "writing serves 'to make sure you've done the necessary work,' 'to make sure you did the reading,' 'to make sure the professor knows you understand the material,' 'it's more of a test to see that you've, you know the, you know what you have to know, you've done the work, you've done the reading.'"

Their Relationship to Disciplinary Writing

Another key theme shared by the three students is that of differences in expectations between their general education courses and their disciplinary courses. For one student, "scientific writing is, to do it well is really difficult and it takes lots of practice [...] conducting our own research but then having to put findings, and writing statistical analyses, being able to interpret it concisely and effectively is hard." She suggests that in her general education courses the expectations are lower, and the rules are more relaxed, "I can talk much more in the first person in different types of writing [...]; personal reflection and things like that." This particular issue could of course point to real differences in the courses or to students experiencing differently based on their own investment.

Students identify disciplines partly through shared writing approaches; a student suggests, after stating that he never took a single writing course in college, that he ended up a philosophy major because it is so similar to English "it [my interest in English] kind of morphed into philosophy for me ... which is just a lot of reading and writing anyway." The discipline is defined here by its activities rather than its epistemological particularities.

Each student also articulates his or her views much more specifically and with maturity in the fourth year; this is matched by changes in the written texts; but the essential positions the students take about writing and knowledge do not change. There is a change in ease of describing advanced topics. A student, for example, suggests "I had to do a paper on Gandhi and how we can view him through the cargo cult paradigm of colonialism." There is equally a shift in expression about knowledge as expansive — too much to say, too many ideas ("It was hard not writing a book on it ..." says one) — and the work to learn being synthesis and analysis ("How to fit together all those pieces ..." or another student's statement, "the level of analysis I'm expected to do is much more based on numbers and proof and not being allowed to say certain things if there's not at least one little detail to back it up").

The "scientists" express awareness of research as review of the literature versus research as "one's own" — experimental, carrying out one's own work. One student is particularly articulate about this difference by year 4: "A good chunk of what I have to write are research papers for any of my classes, my own research or just looking at other people's studies."

Conclusions

While it is clear that, for institutional, social, and historical reasons, writing development in higher education has evolved in some ways differently in the United States and France, we would suggest that studies of students' awareness of writing in their university work is a powerful point of exchange.

May we read, through the French results, a learning journey? This would mean that during the first-year course, the students are more concerned with types of writing as products and less with the strategies for producing their texts. Maybe the attention to the correctness of the answers they give through their texts, to the self-expression they think their texts must reveal are the signs that they conceive a reader whose focus is assessment. Later, as the levels change, as they become more and more acculturated, they pay more attention to the process. The clarity they told us they attempt may be seen as a conception of a reader who has to be convinced. Eventually, the masters students put their priority on entering a scientific discursive community, on mastering its codes and standards, on developing the disciplinary identity and awareness that we detailed in Part I.

This study also points out a clear evolution in the students' discourse: according to the representative texts they identify, students move from the perception of a great diversity of genres (and sometimes, a difficulty to identify typical genres) to the universality, so to speak, of the masters thesis. According to what students say about the norms they keep in mind as they write, we have been able to identify a slow transformation of their representations about what is central in academic writing, that is, writing with or against others' discourses, making references, and re-formulation. These results confirm that learning to write has to be considered all along the curriculum, and especially at the masters level, where new writing genres and new standards occur. They confirm also that university writing, although it seems in continuity with secondary school traditions (the case of the essay), must be reconsidered, by students as well as by faculty, and even more closely when there is no clear continuity (when students discover really new genres of discourse); (see also, on these issues, Rinck & Boch; Carlino; Dysthe; Chitez & Kruse, this volume). A bakhtinian understanding of genre helps us to see how dynamic, blurry, and interactive this process can be (in the U.S. study) and is perceived to be (in the French study).

The U.S. study highlights students' practices as writers in contexts that are more or less disciplinary. We see in their language a relatively diffuse understanding of the relationship between language and knowledge — in this case, disciplinary knowledge — and yet, a strong understanding of the writing-learning relationship. The frames that have been long in place for WAC and WiD pedagogies and reflections in the United States assume that students must be aware of their progressive movements into and around different disciplinary conversations; the U.S. study suggests that their writing might allow us to see traces of an evolving enculturation before their talk does, although we are at the bare beginnings of such possible conclusions. In addition, we don't claim to know whether performing an interaction without full awareness or accompanying epistemological shifts in talk is indeed actually "learning." We saw in earlier work reported in Part I that learning via writing is not automatic, and more importantly that increasing participation over time as a complex way to analyze phases of integration and relationships among knowledge, context, the individual, and the social; might the relationship in the U.S. students' text and talk be a glimpse of one kind of complex layering?

The two studies' results draw us back to the questions from which we began this chapter. Complementary results include the students' focus in both contexts on the need to show their knowledge via their writing, which could be linked to university demands — although we might find these results if we studied students in secondary school as well. Maybe, as Vincent (1994) suggests, "school forms" are at the heart of this result. Students also share concerns about "style" though that notion is not very clear. Students in both contexts shared, as well, the fact that they were discovering what "scientific" or "university" writing is, its features and specificities. And finally, they shared difficulty in their efforts to discuss or reference disciplines in their epistemological dimensions; students stayed in the realm of activities, although in the French study there was a difference between the undergraduate focus on writing as product and the graduate focus on writing as process. This shared result suggests that the students are closer to the convention-driven models of university writing than to the epistemological ones.

Finally, the relationships among learning, writing, and disciplinary awareness (as defined by Reuter), seem to be a rich field for further exploration, based on the two studies reported here. What is the role of writing in learning, and to what degree must students have a deep understanding of this role? Do students who see writing as an assessment tool, a knowledge demonstration, or a container for knowledge risk losing out in the college classroom? Do students in a model of higher education that includes "general education" and specific disciplinary studies have more difficulty developing a crucial disciplinary awareness? Or perhaps is this an issue more related to how much of a discontinuity students experience between one level of studies — say, secondary to postsecondary — and another? We hope that this fruitful dialogue is only beginning, here, leading scholars across cultures to share questions, frames, methodologies, and results as we explore students' writing in the coming years.

Appendix : The First Seven Questions of the French Questionnaire

Questionnaire: Written Texts and Writing at The University

(ANR-06-APPR-019)

This questionnaire is proposed to you as part of a research on the writings produced at the university, which aims to better understand the possible difficulties encountered by students and to consider what improvements could be made to make academic writing easier.

Department:
Year in school (check off the box):

Licence 1° année	
Licence 2° année	
Licence 3° année	
Master 1° année	
Master 2° année	

Question 1
In your current studies, what types of writing do you produce?

Question 2
Among the pieces of writing that you have to produce at university, which is the one that seems to you the most representative of your discipline of study or of the courses you are taking?

Question 3
In the writing you produce at the university, to what do you pay the most attention?

	Expressing personal opinion
	Originality
	Clarity of discourse—introductions, conclusions, examples
	Formal clarity (handwriting, formatting, paragraphing...)
	Technical correctness (syntax, word choice, spelling, etc.)
	Discussion of required reading
	The accuracy of your answer
	Reformulation of the texts you read
	Style
	Articulations (connections, transitions) among the parts of your text or between concepts, ideas presented
	Citations (citing authors, citing excerpts from texts)
	Knowledge

Indicate the five most important dimensions, from number 1 (most important) to number 5 (least important).

Question 4

Indicate the three dimensions of writing which determine, according to you, the grade you receive from the person who corrects your writing. Classify these in order of importance.

Dimension 1

Dimension 2

Dimension 3

Question 5

When you have to produce a piece of writing at the university, what piece of writing seems to you to be the most difficult?

And what are these difficulties?

Question 6

When you have to produce a piece of writing at the university, what piece of writing seems to you to be the most easy?

And what are these facilities?

Question 7

Do you have the impression, this year, to be encountering writing that poses new problems for you, as compared to previous years?

o Yes
o No

If Yes, indicate the type of writing and the key new problems.

[...]

Thank you for taking the time to reflect on these questions.

If you could give us some additional information, it would be interesting for us to know

– Your name
– Telephone and/or e-mail

so we can contact you for further interviews.

And, if you agree, would you kindly give us some additional information, which will of course remain confidential?

Birth date:

Profession if not full time at school:

Institution:

Baccalaureat exam — which one taken and date

What program (major) were you in last year?

PS: We guarantee the anonymity of all the information you provide in this questionnaire.

Chapter 9

Writing Cultures and Genres in European Higher Education

Madalina Chitez and Otto Kruse

Introduction: Aims and Definitions

The Local and the Global in European Writing Cultures

In this contribution, we will look at writing cultures in European higher education and try to summarize what we know about their differences and commonalities at a national level of comparison. The pressures toward globalization and the dominance of English as a publication language in many disciplines (Ammon, 2003; Lillis & Curry, 2010) have led to an increasing awareness of intercultural differences in writing. In education, however, the standards of English have not had the same impact as in science publication, and most teaching is done in the respective national languages. Student papers still follow standards that are specific for their national teaching culture, and student mobility may severely be hindered by confusing terminologies and differing conventions across countries. A "dissertation," for instance, is an essay form in France and not a doctoral thesis as elsewhere. Similarly, the "mémoire" in France is a thesis, while in most other countries, it would be used to refer to autobiographic texts. An "essay" in the German-speaking countries is a witty commentary on any topic in the sense of Montaigne but not a text with five paragraphs or with a well-structured line of scholarly argumentation as in the Anglophone world. Such culture-specific meanings of almost identical words are common in the field of writing, and Donahue (2007) has shown that these "false friends" can obstruct useful communication very effectively if readers are not aware of the differences.

University Writing: Selves and Texts in Academic Societies
Studies in Writing, Volume 24, 151–175
ISSN: 1572-6304/doi:10.1108/S1572-6304(2012)0000024013

Looking for the origins of the differences in European educational cultures, one has to go back to the 17th and 18th centuries when Latin was replaced by national languages and when educational systems were forced under governmental control so that each country started to go its own way. Since then, all European countries developed their own educational systems characterized by their own learning philosophies, institutions, academic degrees, writing practices, and genres. Each of them makes use of writing in a different way. Writing cultures are embedded in learning arrangements, as Russell and Foster (2002) have pointed out, and they are "local" in nature, which means that little cross-national discussion and transfer takes place.

Today, globalization has started to reverse this trend, now leading to standardized ways of teaching and to an increasing pressure to comply with worldwide trends. The creation of a common European higher education area, as initiated by the Bologna process, has led to a unified degree system (in three cycles), to a shared European Credit Transfer System (ECTS) grading system, to common quality standards, and a unified qualification framework. All participants are supposed to comply with the aims of the Bologna Declaration of fostering student employability and international mobility.

Although Bologna is not directly connected with didactical objectives, it carries new teaching philosophies with a preference for student-oriented instead of a teacher-oriented learning and for competence-driven instead of knowledge-driven teaching (see also, this volume, Dysthe; Castelló & Iñesta, for further discussion of the Bologna Declaration). Writing as a form of independent learning is certainly in line with the Bologna teaching philosophy although it is not mentioned explicitly as such. Still, we can observe that writing is increasingly used for learning and, probably even more, for assessment. Generalizations about these developments are not easy to make as the point of departure for each country is different. Besides that, changes are difficult to detect as most innovations in the teaching of writing happen at the level of institutions and study programs and are rarely communicated to a wider public, not even within the respective universities.

One of the impacts of internationalization and the Bologna reform on higher education that can be taken for granted is a constant change and a destabilization of existing writing cultures. The past decade probably brought more change to higher education in Europe than the whole preceding century. For the intercultural study of writing, this means that the national baselines of writing cultures are superimposed by a set of newly acquired genres and writing practices. In this situation, diachronic studies of genre evolution would be of great help in understanding these linguistic, functional, and practical changes.

Differences in higher education are not only the result of distinct national educational systems but also of differences in languages. Due to the European Commission, the EU has 23 official languages and more than 60 regional and minority languages, some of them with semiofficial status. Alongside globalization, we find also a revitalization and revalorization of minority languages, many of which are used for teaching. In almost all European countries, several languages are in use, not to speak of the languages imported through migration. To "promote multilingualism with a view to strengthening social cohesion, intercultural dialogue and European construction" is part of Europe's official language politics (European

Commission, 2008). Language planning and the management of linguistic diversity are matters of great priority in the EU. It is not clear how much of the cultural differences in Education are due to language and how much to the social/educational system parameters, but it is obvious that the high number of languages is an interesting challenge for effective communication about writing across cultures.

To complicate things even further, there are groups of countries that are more closely related to each other either by language, by history, or by regional proximity, like the German-speaking countries, the Scandinavian countries, the Anglophone countries of the United Kingdom, the Slavic countries, or the Romance countries (from Romania to Portugal). Other countries, like Switzerland, use three official languages that are connected through one educational system. Spain, as another example, has one official and three semiofficial languages.

We will develop, here, four examples for national writing cultures in Europe and sketch the particular features of these cultures within their educational systems and histories. We will try not to be too detailed but rather typify these cultures in order to grasp the essential connections between genre use, writing cultures, and educational systems. We hope to identify the basic roles genres and writing can have in national educational systems. To come to valid conclusions, we will first go through a series of theoretical issues and explain how writing cultures can be studied in the complex system of a multilingual and multifaceted world like Europe. We will look at the following questions, in an effort to offer a snapshot of the intriguing complexity of different European writing cultures and what this can tell us about the nature of writing, genres, and intercultural comparisons:

- What are writing cultures? And how may they be studied?
- How do writing cultures relate to genre?
- How can we trace genre systems through history and different cultures?
- How can we study genre differences and what do these differences mean?
- Which differences in writing cultures can we expect between countries and which not?

Writing Cultures and Contextual Levels of Writing

In our analysis, we use the term "writing culture" to refer to the fact that each educational system creates its unique mixture of educational genres, writing/learning practices, assessment procedures, instructional materials, expectations towards writing, and required writing competences, in varied relationships with the genres and practices of professional or scientific domains (see, this volume, Russell & Cortes; Prior & Bilbro). Students entering a study program soon learn basic techniques of note-taking, e-mail correspondence, essay writing, and library work. They get acquainted with literacy practices that are used for learning, communication, documentation, and knowledge construction. Through writing, they learn how to think and argue in their discipline, and through reading, these learning processes are supported and verified. Through feedback on their writings, they learn about quality standards and through instructional materials about conventions and expectations. Seminar discussions help them grasp the epistemological principles of their disciplines and the logic of argumentation. These learning processes have been well documented in a variety of studies on disciplinary socialization in the Writing Across the Curriculum framework (for instance, Langer & Appelbee, 1987; Poe, Lerner, & Craig, 2010; Thaiss & Zawacki, 2006; Walvoord & McCarthy, 1990, for recent evolutions in this discussion, see, this volume, the treatment of academic enculturation offered by Prior & Bilbro; see also, this volume, Carlino; Robinson-Pant & Street; Castelló & Iñesta).

Disciplines, however, are not the only contextual conditions that influence writing. We may describe writing cultures in higher education at several levels of educational systems organization and thus correlate them with different contextual aspects of writing. Individual writing is an integral part of complex psychological, social, institutional, and cultural configurations, which determine what, how, and why people write. In Figure 9.1, we try to single these factors out in order to make them accessible to our analysis. We use "academic writing" as a term covering student writing in the sense of Russell and Cortes (in this volume).

Figure 9.1 may help understanding different layers of context in which academic writing is integrated. The individual writer, in the core field at the bottom, is not a socially isolated social being as early cognitive approaches have suggested (see, for instance, Kent, 1999) but part of many contextual factors that determine his or her actions and thoughts.

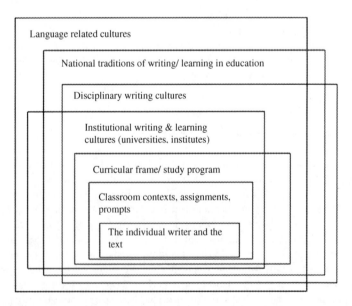

Figure 9.1: Contexts of academic writing (modified from Jakobs, 2005).

First, writing in academic settings usually relates to certain class experiences, and writers are likely to react individually to a particular prompt or an assignment. Writing may also be influenced by the teacher and his or her values or attitudes. If we find differences in a comparative study, they may to a larger or lesser degree reflect such differences in classroom experiences and assignment types.

Second, writing is influenced by the curricular arrangement within a study program. Curricula usually coordinate and integrate learning processes and may influence student writing by favoring certain genres and writing practices. If we find differences in a comparative writing study, we should be aware that they might be the result of differences in study programs and their curricula.

Third, study programs are part of even larger organizational structures as they are hosted by a certain university type. This type may vary from junior colleges to Ivy League universities and from art schools to institutes of technology. Writing is handled differently in each of these university types and curricula as well as classroom experiences are influenced by their organizational cultures.

Fourth, writing may be influenced by the discipline(s) the study program belongs to or is related to. Disciplines are very influential in shaping assignments, writing practices, and genres. Disciplines are, however, not entirely subsumed under a certain university type as, for instance study programs of economy may well be part of a traditional university or a polytechnic university.

Fifth, there are national writing cultures into which writers are born and in which their literacy development takes place, as we pointed out in our first section above. Primary language acquisition leaves its traces on the way people write, as do secondary and higher education. There are also certain traditions in using writing practices for teaching in higher education and of preferring certain genres to others. Some differences in student writing in comparative studies may well be related to national differences.

At a sixth level, finally, there are differences in languages. Writing is influenced in many ways by the language, not only because language provides a basic system of grammar, lexis, and idiomatic but also because it determines to a certain degree perception and thinking. Connor (1996, p. 10, 2002) claimed that even if the Sapir–Whorf hypothesis of linguistic relativity in its strong version ("language controls thought and perception") seems not to be valid any more, it may be acceptable in a weak version ("language influences thought and perception"). Some of the original approaches to contrastive rhetoric like Kaplan (1966) or the work of Galtung (1981) have followed the path that language results in certain "thought patterns" or "thinking styles" that are typical to certain nations or language cultures, approaches that have since been questioned or nuanced. Though there is no doubt that there are national specifics in writing related to language and to educational system, it is not clear how to separate influences of these two, that is, of the fifth and sixth level in Figure 9.1.

For comparative studies, it is important to be aware that each of these contextual factors at the six levels may be involved when in a contrastive study differences in writing between nations or languages are found. Such differences may be related to course assignments, curricular writing instructions, institutional specifics, disciplinary writing cultures, as well as national or language-related aspects. What complicates things further is the fact that all these factors are not independent of each other. National peculiarities in writing may be associated with different classroom or curricular arrangements, with specific interpretations of disciplinary work or with institutional factors. Thus, higher-order differences are usually accompanied by or may even completely be explained by lower-order differences.

Genres and Writing Cultures

As a core aspect of writing cultures, we will focus on genre. Many aspects of writing cultures are crystallized in genre. Genres are connected to all major aspects of writing cultures; they are part of writing practices and instructional systems in student writing; they point out what kind of learning experience students should gain from writing and guide their thinking; they define the kind of writing competences students are expected to acquire and form habits of knowledge recall or knowledge construction in assessment procedures (for additional reflections on genre specifically, though organized in different ways, see, this volume, Russell; Prior & Bilbro; Carlino; Delcambre & Donahue).

In its broadest sense, the term "genre" refers to regularities in language use and to typical distinctions between texts. These regularities and distinctions, however, are not simply stylistic variations but reflect different social actions attained through language and different pragmatic expectations on what texts may accomplish (Hyland, 2000). In a narrower sense, genres may be seen as recurrent text patterns that are used for defined purposes in certain social environments (Bazerman, 1994; Miller, 1984; Russell, 1997, and Russell, in this volume). This definition stresses not only the instrumental or action-related nature of genre but also its embedding in social, professional, cultural, educational, political, technical, and so on contexts (see, this volume, Prior & Bilbro; Delcambre & Donahue; Dysthe).

Genre theory has developed rapidly over the past 30 years and has benefited from contributions of different origins. Bakhtin (1986) probably was one of the first to apply genre theory to everyday language. According to him, genres are created in a process that is governed by "dialogic rules," in which the writer and the social context are continuously negotiating the right use of textual forms. There are three basic approaches to genre theory that have been distinguished by Hyon (1996) and subsequently used for classification by many others. Though they seem to converge lately as Swales (2004) noted, it is worthwhile to look at their different ways of conceptualizing genre (Johns, 2007).

The New Rhetoric Approach: Miller's (1984) influential definition of genre as typified rhetorical action in recurring communicative situations has been ground-breaking for the North American adaptation of the term. Miller (1984, p. 151) stresses that a definition of genre "must be centered not on the substance or the form of discourse but on the action it is used to accomplish." What seems stable about genre in her eyes is not the language but the situation in which language is used. Bazerman (1994) and Russell (1997) extended the model to integrate genre theory into the concept of "activity systems" in Leontjew's sociohistorical sense (Leontjew, 1979), thus replacing the more static term of "situation." Bazerman (1988) was able to demonstrate that genres like the research article may have trajectories that go over several centuries in which they grow and modify. Russell (1997) expands the scope of the term to the use of educational genres and discusses aspects of cultural transmissions of genre knowledge (see Russell, this volume).

The ESP Approach: Swales (1990, 2004) provided a model for analyzing genre that is connected with the teaching of English as a second language in academic contexts (see Russell, this volume). Swales analyzed many corpora of academic genres like research articles, grant proposals, theses, dissertations, and reprint requests in order to understand how these genres work and how they are used in academic discourse. Swales (1990, p. 58) states that "a genre comprises a class of communicative events, the members of which share some set of communicative purposes. These purposes are recognized by the expert members of the parent discourse community and thereby constitute the rationale for the genre. This rationale shapes the schematic structure of the discourse and influences and constrains choice of content and style." His definition of genre, however, is not only functional. He also notes that "exemplars of a genre exhibit various patterns of similarity in terms of structure, style, content and intended audience. If all high probability expectations are realized, the exemplar will be viewed as prototypical" (Swales, 1990, p. 58). This "typicality" of structure, style, content, and so on is what linguists have to find out about.

Swales relies strongly on the term "discourse communities" as structured, hierarchically organized groups with shared interests. Swales (1998, p. 21) criticized this concept himself when referring to the facts that it is difficult to delineate a discourse community (is it related to a university, a discipline, a faculty, a specialized group of researchers?) and that it is hard to use the term for all genres (it may account for well-established genres but not for emerging genres that are not yet in possession of a stable community) (for additional critiques of this framing, see Prior & Bilbro, this volume). More than the others, the ESP approach has led to linguistic research on text features of genres, for instance, Hyland (1999, 2000) on academic discourse or Bhatia (1993) on legal writing; see also Russell, this volume, for a review of the question.

The Systemic Functional Approach: A third genre tradition goes back to Martin (1984) and is based on Systemic Functional Linguistics (SFL) as Halliday (1985) devised it (see also, this volume, Russell's description of SFL). It is also called "genre-based literacy approach" or the "Australian school of genre" or the "Sydney School." SFL has to be seen as a "descriptive and interpretive framework for viewing language as a strategic meaning-making resource," as Eggins (2004, p. 2) put it. It is a complex system of functional grammar that delineates a large analytic framework for studying texts. Martin (1984, p. 25) places special emphasis on the genre term in this approach and defined it as a "staged, goal-oriented, purposeful activity in which speakers engage as members of our culture." To view genre as a "goal-oriented" and "purposeful" activity accounts for the functional nature of genre and genre parts. The term "staged" means that every genre fulfills its purpose not at once but in several steps. These steps are the base of a functionally defined or "schematic" structure. SFL sees it especially important to analyze these steps und uses them for teaching purposes. In terms of teaching applications, while the New Rhetoric approach to genre is mainly used in undergraduate composition courses at US American universities and the ESP approach teaching English as a second or foreign language, SFL has been developed in secondary education, especially with students of poor educational background. Although the functional approach seems to be in line with the two aforementioned theories, it has one tendency that seems incompatible with the other approaches. Its reliance on decontextualized "key genres" such as description, explanation, exploration, narrative, and so on, which are seen as the prime elements of teaching, does not find support with genre theories that avoid closed classifications. European traditions that follow this line are Björk and Räisänen (1996) and Gruber et al. (2006) who both use a two-stage genre theory in which an open and a closed classification are connected. Both groups call the closed classification system "text types," while they use the open system "genres."

Almost all genre theorists like Miller (1984), Martin (1984), Bakhtin (1986), Bhatia (1993), Bazerman (1994), Russell (1997), Devitt (2004), and Bawarshi and Reiff (2010) stress the strong ties of genres to the cultures in which they are used. Cultures seem to provide genres for different purposes and may be characterized by their dominant genres and genre expectations. Genres tap many aspects of culture. They represent, as Bazerman (2003, p. 131) notes, "a constitutive mechanism in the formation, maintenance, and enactment of society, culture, psychology, imagination, consciousness, personality, and knowledge, interactive with all the other processes which shape our lives." Genre theory helps us, as Devitt (2004, p. 27) points out, to go beyond the "more immediate context of situation of a particular genre" and look at networks of genres in their political, social, or economic contexts.

Genres are not to be thought of as isolated or singular events. They differentiate, split, merge, or compete with each other. Hybrid genres are quite common as are "dead" genres, which are not in use any more. Bazerman (1994) speaks of systems of genres when interrelated genres are used by a professional group (see also, this volume, Prior & Bilbro; Russell). Bhatia (2002, p. 10) refers to a "constellation of closely related and overlapping genres" which he calls "colonies of genres." The term "genre family" is used by Nesi et al. (2008) to classify similar genres in higher education. From a corpus of student texts, they identified about 100 genres that they group in 13 families like "critiques," "essays," "case studies," or "research reports." Looking at genres within cultures allows and demands focusing not only on the meaning of single genres but also on their interplay and interrelations.

Genres in Academic Writing

Academic Genres in Developmental Perspective

Genres are both functional and traditional: they are historically grown prototypical text patterns shaped by many exchanges within communities in their attempts of communicating effectively (Bazerman, 1988; Hyland, 2000). It is widely accepted that the linguistic setup of genre reflects their rhetorical purpose. Genres adapt to changes or otherwise disappear when more suitable genres take over.

Texts fulfill multiple functions in academic communities and genres determine, to a large extent, how these functions are interpreted and carried out. Knowledge construction and communication as well as learning and grading depend on the use of established genres, and these genres determine what kind of performance is expected and how it is valued. Genres in education are part of a larger network of activities and they are closely connected to writing practices (Foster, 2006). The time granted for writing, the way assignments are given, what is expected from the writers, the consequences of writing, and the grading procedures associated with each genre vary greatly. Writing practices, in turn, are embedded in curricular structures and are part of general teaching principles.

In academic writing, the term "genre" has become important not only for understanding the nature of writing but also for understanding the social contexts in which writing takes place. It is not only that genres are shaped by the social contexts, but genres also shape the social contexts by influencing their members' thought and communication patterns (Bazerman, 1989). Genres develop in stable communities with repetitive tasks but, in turn, they also give these communities stability.

The development of educational genres appears as part of a more general evolution of texts when looked at under a linguistic perspective and as part of the evolution of the university and its educational demands when looked at from sociohistorical viewpoint. Both kinds of evolution have been object of critical and analytical meta-discussions that had been set in motion by ancient rhetoric and later been carried on by disciplines like pedagogy, linguistics, and writing. Genres are dynamic. If they are functionally connected to human purposes and actions, they have to be flexible in order to adapt to changing action systems. And vice versa: If they were static, development could not take place (Devitt, 2004, p. 89).

Still, genres are also a factor of stability in language use, if not to say of conservatism. Stability of genre results not only from repetitive situations and rhetorical actions but also from expectations of those who use genres. Another factor of stability is teaching. A myriad of how-to books explains over and over again how essays, CVs, seminar papers, and so on work. The persistence of genre is of major importance in education. Genres like the German "Aufsatz" (Kruse, 2007) dominate secondary education for about 200 years. This essay form has been introduced as an assessment tool and defended this place ever since, even though education itself has undergone fundamental changes. A genre that is agreed on by all stakeholders in education is likely to resist change for a long time or at least changes slowly and moderately.

The kind of developments and changes genres undergo probably are best characterized as evolutionary with the implications of gradual rather than evolutionary change processes and of some kind of survival-of-the-fittest process running in the background. Bazerman's (1988) analysis of the first 135 volumes of the "Transactions of the Royal Society," the first research journal in history, gives a good account of the development of a genre. Bazerman demonstrates that a variety of tasks had to be solved to make research communities accept a textual form documenting research. Credibility, relation to other's research, reporting results, dealing with, and describing methodology were among the most prominent issues that had to be dealt with. He claims that same group of researchers who invented the experiment also had to invent the methods to report on the experiment. The genre itself, in reaction, influenced experimentation enduringly, as experiments ever since have to be carried out to provide the necessary information demanded by the research report.

Historical genre research has its merits in providing background information on how certain genres have to be interpreted or how national peculiarities in writing cultures can be understood. For Germany, Pohl (2009) has presented a historical account of the *Hausarbeit* (a synonym for "seminar paper") in which he traces academic writing back to its roots in 18th and 19th century and reconstructs its roots in early seminar teaching. Similarly, Kruse (2005a, 2005b, 2006a) described the turn from an orally based higher education to a writing-centered kind of teaching based on new literacy practices of paper and thesis writing.

Academic Genres in Intercultural Perspective

Intercultural research on academic genres has several roots. One of the first to comment on differences in academic discourse was Kaplan (1966) in a contrastive study of student writing in L2, which became a landmark publication for contrastive rhetoric in ESL/EFL. He identified major differences in text organization of students with different origins, which he attributed to culturally acquired thought patterns. While paragraphs of native English speakers seemed to be organized in a straightforward manner, all others showed digressions in the way ideas were arranged. He hypothesized that these differences may be attributed to such global units like the English, Semitic, Oriental (Chinese and Korean), Romance, and Russian cultures.

A similar idea followed Galtung (1981) who differentiated between a Saxonic, Gallic, Teutonic, and Nipponic style. To him, differences seemed to go back to "intellectual styles" rooted in the academic traditions of these cultures. Clyne (1987) compared a large corpus of sociological and linguistic texts from German and English writers with respect to the use of macro-propositions, organization of arguments, length of text sections, and uniformity of conventions. He noticed a higher degree of digressiveness in German texts, which he interprets as a typical tendency to what is called "Exkurs" in German (a side step to another topic providing additional or background information) and to a lack of text organization. German texts also seemed to be more asymmetrical and use less macro-propositions.

A next generation of comparative studies used more refined research strategies to come to conclusions about national differences. The linguistic units they studied were influenced by the aforementioned research but also included new variables like the use of topic sentences, self-reference, hedging, text coherence, nominalizations, meta-communicative statements, reader versus writer orientation, and use of reporting verbs. For a review of the findings contrasting English, French, and German, see

Siepmann (2006); for an explanation of the field's shift in method and framing and the move to renaming its work as "intercultural rhetoric," see Connor (2002).

Many of these studies face the problem of validity in that it is not always clear how to generalize the results. Are they pointing toward national differences in mentalities or thinking styles? Are they reflecting peculiarities in academic cultures or education patterns? Or are they caused by differences in languages and language use? It has been demonstrated that variability within nations/languages may be higher than between them. A significant difference in, let's say, the use of hedges between two cultures/languages, might apply to discourse from the social sciences but not from technology.

As Donahue (2009) has suggested, attributions of distinctive features to nations like "In Turkey, they write like this ... " are problematic as every country is internally diverse and, within any language and context, there are hundreds of distinct discourses. Rhetorical strategies do differ deeply in different regional cultures and contexts, but those differences must be understood in the context of the multiple constraining factors, one of which is disciplinary contexts (cf. Donahue, 2010; Hyland, 2000).

A research strategy allowing to integrate more contextual aspects into contrastive studies from Russell and Foster (2002, p. 6) provide a list of 10 common themes that comparative writing research in higher education has to take into account. The first five themes are characteristics of the educational system: disciplinary specialization; educational traditions and ideologies; the degree of centralization; the role of writing in tracking, selection, and examination of students; and finally, the attitudes and orientations toward writing. The second set of themes is connected with the teaching and learning of writing in the classroom: transition from school to disciplinary conversations, problems in handling intertextuality, functions of writing assessment, language policy, and the teaching of writing (explicit or not). All these issues form important context variables necessary to understand the activity systems underlying writing and genre use in higher education.

An example for a well-grounded comparison of national writing cultures is the research of Foster (2002, 2006). He studied student writing in Germany on two teaching visits through his own teaching at two different guest universities and through interviews with students and faculty in both Germany and the United States. Methodologically, he used a case study approach and compared five pairs of students in similar situations (year of study, discipline, and kind of university) with each other. His results indicate that the German kind of writing gives undergraduate students more autonomy in writing, demands more self-directed long-term planning, and introduces students faster to the academic writing in their disciplines than its American counterpart. Even though his focus was on writing practices and student roles, he de facto compared the dominating genres of both countries, the seminar paper versus the term paper. Both papers organize student roles differently, demand different actions, and integrate writing differently into learning.

Another instructive study connecting first-hand cultural knowledge with data from a corpus analysis has been carried out by Kaiser (2002, 2003) who compared writing and genre practices in Literature Studies and Linguistics in Germany and Venezuela.

Kaiser started analyzing guide books and instructional materials from both cultures. Next to the fact that such materials seemed much more popular in Germany than in Venezuela, she noticed a strong emphasis on good style in Latin America while German guides warned their students not to be too literary or place too much emphasis on style. While the Latin American guide books emphasize the need of good language and original thought, the German ones emphasized independent academic/ scientific work and the verifiability of facts. The genres proposed in both cultures were noticeably different, the Latin American guide books describing the ensayo, *comentario de texto and trabajo final* (essay, text commentary, and final thesis), while the German ones were dealing with the *Seminararbeit Hausarbeit Thesenpapier and Protokoll* (seminar paper, home paper, thesis paper, and seminar protocol).

A more text-based study by Donahue (2004, 2008) used comparisons of essay writing in France and the United States. The essays came from fairly identical writing practices in two similar situations of 12th grade and first-university year. Donahue stresses the fact that while there can several surface differences between students' writing strategies and features be observed, there are also powerful commonalities between them. Her study of 250 French and US student essays study showed statistically significant higher frequencies of the French texts in:

- the use of one of three organizational patterns (identified in the study, not proposed a priori): between thesis-antithesis-synthesis, for/against, or yes/but;
- paragraph structures using the French "alinéa" (moving to a new line with each shift in ideas within a paragraph);
- presence of a hinge turning point statement isolated in the middle of the essay, moving from "thesis" to "antithesis" or for-against;
- the use of the multivalent pronoun "on," a usage clearly linked to the linguistic affordances of the language itself; and
- the pronoun "we," as lead explicit subject positioner.

The US students' essays in contrast showed a statistically significant higher frequency of

- a thesis clearly established from the beginning (84%);
- paragraph structure created by indenting each new paragraph;
- an organizational structure following five-paragraph-essay or comparison-contrast conventions;
- the use of passive voice; and
- the pronoun "I" as lead explicit subject positioner.

The study also identified strong shared features across all first-year university student (13th grade) essays. The students used a broad variety of negotiating movements in their writing, taking up, and adapting multiple existing elements:

- echoing the prompt
- adopting and adapting the stance

- approach of the text read
- working closely with commonplaces
- situating the self with respect to the assignment and text, partially taking it up but partially redirecting it

More important than national differences seemed to be the differences in the institution, in the assignment given, in the student's level in school, and in the texts read for the assignment. Students' texts, as complex, rich, negotiating discursive acts, shared more across different situations than the large differences in the writing cultures of the countries studied would have us expect. Some of the differences between the texts may be accounted for by differences in the genre interpretation in both countries. The dominance of the thesis in the essays of the American students seems the product of essay teaching as does the dominance of the thesis-antithesis movement in the French essays.

An approach to compare academic discourse in Germany, Italy, and France is the work of a research group rather than of individuals. A collection of papers published by Dalmas, Foschi Albert, and Neuland (2009) is the result of a research conference on differences in French, German, and Italian discourse and provides background information on all three educational systems and their respective writing traditions. This collection tries, what is not very common, to compare three cultures with each other and it demonstrates that such comparisons demand a higher degree of coordination and collaboration than is usually the case in contrastive studies. Part of their results will be reported on in Section The case of Italy.

Exploring Major Educational Genres across Europe: Four Examples

The Case of France

The French educational system has been historically highly centralized, something that has only recently undergone dramatic changes at the postsecondary level. The roots of the educational system go back to Napoleon reforms around 1800 when he closed all universities and replaced them by rigidly controlled schools. Though universities had been reopened soon again, the centralized structure remained. Together with Prussia, France was the first country to introduce a school system preparing for the university. While Prussia used the *Abitur*, a school-leaving examination since 1787 and revised it in 1812, France introduced the *Baccalaureat* in 1808. Both examinations were created to regulate university entrance and secure a sufficient quality of school education.

French higher education is almost entirely public and almost entirely subsidized. It currently follows three key tracks, only one of which is identified as "university": the elite track (*écoles préparatoires* for two years, then examination-based entry into the *Grandes Ecoles*); technical studies; university studies. Teacher preparation was its own track for several years after an earlier reform but has recently been merged into the university track. This is interesting for our work in this chapter, as the teacher preparation institutions have been a focal point for much of the research on writing in higher education.

Recent reforms have decentralized parts of the system, giving university presidents much more autonomy, enabling competitive systems of larger and smaller groupings of universities with different ratings, implementing a peer review system for departments and programs, and focusing funds and attention on student success in the first year. These reforms promise to change many long-established practices in French higher education, for better or for worse.

Attention to writing is deep and intense in secondary school. Students are taught to write, according to the *Bulletin Officiel*, three main types of writing: (1) argumentative or deliberative writing (e.g., analytic and close reading exercises, text commentaries, and dissertations); (2) inventive writing; and (3) functional writing (summaries, syntheses, and reports). While official curricular guidelines emphasize these three domains, teachers in fact report focusing primarily on the first and second, because the end-of-secondary school examination (the *baccalauréat*) only requires the first two. These are taught primarily through examples of good and poor writing, lessons focused on specific approaches for writing a particular essay, repetition of the same kinds of essays and assignments, and imitation (Reuter, 1996). In addition, students are taught using "*corrigés*" in-class analyses of completed essays that identify strengths and weaknesses. Finally, the role in France of teaching reading through close analysis has a strong effect on students' understanding of writing (Donahue, 2008).

Entering postsecondary studies is in many ways less of a threshold in France than in other countries, at least at first (see Donahue, 2002a, although recent research suggests this might be particularly true for certain fields like literary studies; see, this volume, Delcambre & Donahue). The most notable immediate changes in expectations are often in terms of length and development rather than radical shifts in genres. University studies broadly do not always call for writing other than in exams, and these are highly normed and focused on verifying knowledge acquisition (Ropé, 1994). One particular strand of university studies, the teacher preparation track, has its own unique set of text types, linked frequently to students' fieldwork, student teaching, and curriculum development experiences.

What students are asked to write depends on many factors, but there has been little systematic study of the genres of writing that are required. One of the few such studies that offers a small window into some of these genres is reported on in Delcambre and Donahue, this volume. For that study, "according to the theoretical frame of Bakhtin's speech genre theory, one of [Delcambre and Donahue's] hypotheses is that disciplines, taught at the university, provide the contexts that shape the writing produced by the students and expected by the faculty. Thus, they consider these kinds of university writing to be genres of discourse, produced in different contexts: the institutional context (secondary v. post-secondary, university v. teacher-training institute ...), the context of the year of study with its specific demands, the context of the discipline, etc." (2010). And indeed, the study did support students' tendency to consider quite different pieces of writing as representative of their discipline (Delcambre, Donahue & Lahanier-Reuter, 2010, p. 2), and their responses suggest that "the disciplines also influence the standards students pay attention to when they are writing."

The following higher education writing types appear in various studies from 1998 to 2008, although these types were not themselves the object of study; they were incidental: "Long" essays, theoretical commentaries, reformulation of theoretical texts, conference proposals, literature reviews, abstracts, summaries of theoretical texts, exams, analysis and interpretation of visual information, and specific segments of written texts: introductions, appendices, and the development of a research question.

Writing instruction continues to be intense in the elite tracks, most notably in the "*écoles préparatoires.*" In these programs, students write and revise constantly, in multiple subject areas, using primarily the *dissertation* and *commentaire* forms. A small percentage is then admitted to the Grandes Ecoles, but the rest may use their two years in the "*prépas*" to count toward a university undergraduate degree. They thus enter the third year of studies with a different preparation.

By that third year, there is a shift in the university studies to intense writing in many majors, shaped by work students do to complete their programs. This work, from the few studies we are aware of, appears to be fairly different in different disciplines. Students who go on to MA-level work encounter even more rigorous writing demands, as the requirements move from exams to written reports, theses, and seminar work. Simultaneously, genres of writing converge toward a small similar set by master's level, moving away from the diversity of earlier years. Explicit teaching of writing happens at these stages in some disciplines, though not in a systematic way; the teaching is linked to particular professors' styles as well as to courses in research methodology that become particularly important in later stages of studies. C. Barré de Miniac (1996a, p. 12) has suggested that the main reason French students do not complete MA and PhD degrees is their inability to manage the writing (see also, this volume, Carlino; Dysthe; Castelló & Iñesta for similar insights into this challenge in other countries).

Finally, a third track that offers explicit writing instruction is the technical track of higher education. Students pursuing degrees in technical fields will systematically be asked to write a broad range of texts that are designed to improve their ability to express themselves clearly. One of the most frequent genres is the "*synthèse de documents*" that requires reading several documents and synthesizing the information to draw a conclusion. But many other forms of writing appear in these courses, generally required in students' first year.

As Daunay, Delcambre, Dufays, and Thyrion (2007) suggests in his article on French higher education writing in the disciplines, the university system in France did impose at one point a required first-year course called "*techniques d'*expression" whose purpose was primarily to work with students on surface features of text production, organization, and the very French "*méthode de travail*" that should serve students in every task. But this program was fairly quickly abandoned as faculty recognized that generic skills-based learning of writing was not very useful and did not transfer. A new effort in the 1990s introduced courses in *"méthodologie universitaire"* (Hassan, Daunay, & Fialip, 2006), but these were more broadly focused on acculturation to university work in general. Boch (in Donahue, 2008) suggests that her University of Grenoble linguistics program offers students a required course in the first and the second year, called *pratiques de textes*, designed to support students' communication, reading, and research abilities, but she emphasizes that it is difficult to talk in general about French universities and student writing, given how diverse and fragmented these practices are even within a single university (see also, this volume, Rinck & Boch).

If we consider writing practices in the way they are defined in the next section in the case of Germany, that is, if we equate writing practices with the writing processes students follow or are taught, then we know the least about this aspect of French higher education writing. We do have insight into the types of texts produced, through studies done about students' difficulties with writing in different higher education tracks and through studies such as the one reported, this volume, by Delcambre and Donahue and based on extensive questionnaires given to students. But, as mentioned above, these studies were not focused on genres or text types as such; they describe them in the process of identifying the context in which student difficulties appear. These difficulties "can not be considered simple technical difficulties, but are tightly linked to writers' representations (their representations of writing and of themselves as writers, of academic expectations about the writing to be produced, etc.), to the expected text genres, and to the frames these genres propose for written production, in particular with respect to discourse content and types of knowledge, and finally to the forms of support and evaluation that accompany the learners' writing, forms that are themselves based on teachers' representations of writing and learning" (Delcambre & Boch, 2006).

In this same proposal, Delcambre and Boch (2006) clearly specify the importance of considering genres of writing in higher education as inseparable from considering disciplinary context: "writing difficulties are intrinsically linked to the new discourse objects, the academic discourses themselves, that students discover at the university (difficulties thus associated with the content of discourse). The notion of genre is key, here, for thinking simultaneously about the articulation between the linguistic, textual, and socio-historic dimensions of writing, in a Bakhtinian line of thinking. Speaking of genres requires us to see the interrelated nature of the challenges of discourse organization, linguistic choices, and conceptualization or mastery of content, and is thus central to responding to the need to take into account the specificities of types of knowledge in the analysis of writing difficulties."

Finally, there is abundant research in this domain that explores one of the most important struggles faced by students in higher education: the use of sources and interaction with source material in students' written work (see, this volume, Rinck & Boch; Dysthe; Castelló & Iñesta; Delcambre & Donahue). This struggle is not uncommon in the world, but there may be aspects of French education that render it even more challenging. In particular, students are generally not taught much in secondary education about citation and are sometimes encouraged to stay close to the wording of both texts they are reading and the language of assignment prompts.

In higher education contexts, they are confronted with new knowledge, new demands to position themselves with respect to this knowledge, and sometimes little instruction about how to do this.

The explicit call in France to teach students to write in university studies was made in 1998 by Dérive and Fintz: "We must stop considering students entering the university as having already mastered writing [...] On the contrary, we must make acculturation to university writing inextricably linked to acquisition of disciplinary knowledge; we cannot think of one without the other and we cannot pretend we are evaluating only the second" (p. 48). That call is currently being taken up, in particular through the formation of writing and learning centers.

The Case of Germany

Germany's educational system has, similar to France, been remodeled in the beginning of the 19th century and thus set an end to the traditions universities had followed since their foundations in the 13th/14th century. The basic parameters of this new system remained stable for roughly 200 years, until the Bologna process again introduced a fundamental system change. Different from France, Germany's education system always had been (and still is) decentralized with fairly independent universities as agents responsible for the organization of teaching, for examinations, and research. Even after Germany was united in 1871, education legislature was left to the states and not to the federal government. To this day, the federal government provides only a legislative frame for higher education, which has to be filled out by each of the 15 states.

Historically, the lack of a capital like Paris or London had led to the foundation of a large number of rather small universities, each funded by one of the small counties or kingdoms that formed Germany. In spite of this fractured national situation, universities were in constant exchange with each other and shared a set of common principles for regulating admissions, teaching practices, internal organization, and graduation routines (Clark, 2006; Rüegg, 2004).

A decisive date for the restructuring of the universities were the reforms introduced by Wilhelm von Humboldt in 1809/10 in Prussia, one of the larger German kingdoms, after Prussia had been defeated by Napoleon in 1806. In a historical situation of great need for reforms, Humboldt managed to restructure not only primary and secondary education but also teacher's education and higher education in less than two years. With a relatively small set of regulations and directives, he was able to convert the universities to research institutions by providing them with research facilities like botanical gardens, observatories, or research labs. This process also allowed Germany to integrate the natural sciences into the universities that had been practiced in the academies or in private societies only. Humboldt gave the professors a strong stance by guaranteeing liberty of research and teaching. And he committed the universities to connect research and teaching, a directive that proved to be very powerful in drawing a line between school and university and demanding from professors not only to reproduce or hand down knowledge but factually to produce it (see Kruse, 2006a, for a more full account).

What proved to be essential for the kind of writing cultures resulting from this development was the creation of the research seminar (Clark, 2006; Kruse, 2006b; Olesko, 1988; Pohl, 2009). At the beginning, seminars were small institutions within one of the university faculties that provided more intensive training for a small group of selected students than ordinary studies did. Seminars received extra funding for maintaining a library and providing scholarships for the students. Teaching was based to a large extent on activities of the students themselves. They had to do independent reading, present at class, discuss papers, and do research. The most important feature, however, that was to become the basis for learning in every seminar, was writing. Each seminar participant had to submit one or two papers per semester, which was then read and discussed by the seminar group. Writing, for the first time in university education, became the main teaching and learning agent. Seminars soon proved to be an ideal institution for recruiting future researchers (Paulsen, 1921). A large part of the rapid university development in 19th-century Germany was owed to the constant output of research-trained graduates that had passed through the seminars. Along with the seminar, education specialized. While all degrees until 1812 were provided for one of the four faculties, the seminars paved the way for the rise of disciplines like in history, pedagogy, theology, or philology. The sciences too profited from founding seminars (Olesko, 1988) before they changed the institutional form of the seminar into institutes and laboratories.

In the course of a century after Humboldt's reforms, seminars changed from a selective teaching institution for a small group of students to a standard way of teaching that was offered to nearly all students within the philosophical faculty (which covered all disciplines except medicine, law, theology, technology, and art). It became similarly popular in law schools but not in the technical disciplines and medicine. In 1914 at the university of Heidelberg, the seminars already covered around 30% of the classes in theology and 44% in philology (Jarausch, 1991). Around 2000, right before the onset of the Bologna reform, Ehlich and Steets (2003) found in a survey among professors at the University of Munich that roughly 50% of all courses in the first part of the study programs (which roughly equals the BA) and roughly 60% of the courses in the second part (which roughly equals the MA) required the submission of a seminar paper ("Hausarbeit"). For disciplines like theology, law, philosophy, and sociology, however, more than 90% of the professors reported that they demanded a seminar paper (at the BA and MA level) in their courses. Disciplines like economy, psychology, and mathematics had lower rates at the BA level but also scored around 80% at the MA level. The lowest rates had medicine (below 15% at both levels) and the natural sciences (between 20% and 35% at the two levels). For all others, however, learning at university had become mainly a matter of writing (see, this volume, Castelló & Iñesta for a report on the writing in two university disciplines in Spain, and Delcambre & Donahue, this volume, for results from France).

What resulted from this development is a writing culture in which student writing seems a natural part of student activity. Students have to write "academic texts" from the very beginning of their university studies. The genre that has been introduced with the seminar, the "seminar paper" or, more popular in German, "Hausarbeit" (literally: "home paper") has a tremendous importance for teaching. Writing a seminar paper is more or less equal with academic writing, even if there are a few more genres that are traditionally covered by this name. Kruse (2007, 2010) offers the following categorization for academic genres:

- transition genres (e.g., excerpts, notes, and transcripts)
- research genres (e.g., research article, literature review, and reports)
- documentary genres (e.g., laboratory report, research protocol, and seminar protocol)
- educational genres (e.g., seminar paper and portfolio)
- professional genres (e.g., technical report and medical report)
- popularized genres (e.g., features and reportage)

All these genres may play a role in academic writing, but the seminar paper is by far the most dominant one. What is striking in German higher education is the fact that no essay-like genre exists. Typical for an essay would be a text format of three to eight pages that can be written in class or within a few days. It is essentially argumentative in nature and needs no extensive researching or reading but relies on the readings and discussions from the course it is written for. In Germany, essays are dominant in secondary but not in higher education. The writing practices associated with the seminar are characterized by the following:

- the seminar focuses on a fairly narrow topic, sometimes on a research field or an open research question;
- participants are introduced to the research field in class;
- they choose a topic from a list of subthemes and start independent work on this topic;
- it is expected that they define their topic and narrow it down to a manageable research question;
- most seminars require an oral presentation of the readings and, in fact, most teaching in seminars is done by the students themselves;
- a seminar paper has to be submitted at the end of the term or at a certain time (up to several months) later;
- individual or group work is both possible;
- supervision traditionally is scarce and limited to the weekly office hours of the professor; other kind of writing support is usually missing; and
- feedback will only be given after the paper has been submitted.

As interesting as seminar teaching is from a writing-in-the-disciplines perspective (see, this volume, Prior & Bilbro; Russell), it also has prevented change. The routines of seminar teaching and its unquestioned dominance have made it appear a "natural" way of teaching even after the onset of mass education when the number of seminar participants increased considerably and supervision became even more scarce than before (see Kruse, 2003, for an illustration). For many students, writing became more associated with stress than with the opportunity of independent study (Dittmann, Geneuss, Nennstiel, & Quast, 2003; Keseling, 1997; Kruse, 1997). It was not until the 1990s that the routines of seminar writing had been questioned and new support structures were demanded or introduced. A first summary of newly founded writing centers and newly introduced pedagogical measures was edited by Kruse, Jakobs, and Ruhmann (1999) as the result of the first national conference of writing in Germany. The introductory chapter of this book (Kruse & Jakobs, 1999, p. 31) criticized the lack of specialized educational programs in writing pedagogy and of research in this field.

Genre research in Germany follows the lines of the most commonly used genres as described, for instance, by Ehlich (2003), like notes (and note-taking) (Steets, 2003), excerpts (Moll, 2002), seminar protocols (Moll, 2003), or summaries (Keseling, 1993). Most research, however, has been devoted to the study of the seminar paper. Corpus studies analyzing the research paper show that it is a very variable genre that has a few common features only. Gruber et al. (2006, p. 250) who studied seminar papers in three different study programs at the University of Vienna noticed that the expectations of professors to the quality of seminar papers varied considerably but that they could easily agree on the following rather formal aspects of seminar papers: consistent style and layout, academic style, clear and consistent structure, argumentation and an own point of view, and finally the use of and a proper handling of sources (these results are also interesting in relation to, this volume, Rinck & Boch; Delcambre & Donahue). Steinhoff (2007) compared a large corpus of seminar papers with papers from researchers and with a sample of journalistic texts. The study allows looking at the developments of student writers depending on the number of papers written.

The Case of Italy

Italy provides an example for a writing culture that has remained in the oral traditions of university teaching much longer than France and Germany and has only recently started to turn to a text-based kind of teaching. It is not clear what may have caused this delay. To this day, the *corso universitario* (lecture) and the oral examination have remained the dominant kind of teaching (Hepp, 2009). Though writing in secondary education is well elaborated and makes use of a wide variety of genres, writing at the university level was factually nonexistent until recently as Boscolo and Carotti (2003, p. 198) stated,

> Whereas elementary school children practice many genres (e.g., personal and expressive writing, records of personal events, reports of school activities and text re-elaboration), the variety of genres is progressively reduced in middle and particularly high school, where students write compositions almost exclusively. These may focus on literary and historical questions, where students are required to elaborate what they have learned from the study of literature and

history. Compositions may also be about topical subjects, where students are asked to express and sustain their own points of view.

Only the *tesi di laurea*, the final thesis, was demanded in all study programs as part of the final exams. As students were not prepared for such a task, the qualities of the *tesi di laurea* were questionable.

An important impulse for a new writing culture came from Umberto Eco's (1977) book *Come si fa una tesi di laurea* (*How to Write a Thesis*), which has seen almost 20 editions since its first appearance in 1977. It is well matched to the writing tasks of thesis writers in the humanities but does provide useful knowledge on the organization of the writing process and its relation to research for other disciplines as well. Even more important is the fact that it paved the way for many other guide books that introduce thesis writing to other disciplines or to special questions like argumentation or reporting research (see Sorrentino, 2009, for a review).

Until 1984, the *tesi di laurea* was the only thesis in use in Italy. It marked the end of the four-year study programs and was accompanied by a set of oral examinations. It also had the function of a dissertation as, until 1984, there was no such degree as the English PhD or the German Dr. phil. (Dell'Aversano & Grilli, 2009). When Italy joined the Bologna declaration and introduced the BA/MA degrees in 2001/2002, a new genre, the *prova finale*, was introduced as a thesis for the bachelor's degree, while for the master's degree a *tesi di laurea magistrale* was created (*ibid.*). Hepp (2009) notes, however, that this does not necessarily mean a doubling in the overall amount of writing as the time investment for both papers has been restricted so that both together would maximally equal the former *tesi di laurea*. Finally, A *dottorato di ricerca* (doctoral program) was added so that today a third kind of thesis is in use.

The discussions starting in the 1990s in Italy resulted in many small initiatives that introduced innovative kinds of writing in academic contexts, similar to France and Germany. The point of departure for these developments, however, was a different one as it did not build on a similarly established set of writing practices and genres as in France or Germany. New developments seemed to be centered on a genre called *tesina*, literally translated as "little thesis." The tesina seems to equal a seminar paper while for the essay in Italian the term *saggio* is used. The term *tesina* suggests that it is seen as a small thesis to which the same criteria apply as for the thesis itself (see, for instance, Bennati, Fanfani, Palesi, and Zunino, 2009; the same term is used in Spain. See Castelló & Iñesta, this volume), but it is also used for the essay of the final examination at the gymnasium where the essay character may be dominating. There is an abundance of descriptions on the web about *tesina* writing, which is united by the fact that it is mainly an argumentative genre that may rest on research but is not reporting own research. In the sciences, however, it may also be interpreted as a kind of the research article with its typical IMRAD structure (see, this volume, Bazerman, Keranan, & Prudencio; Russell; Robinson-Pant & Street; Carlino).

At some universities, organizational structures have been created to support student writing, like the tutoring system at the University of Siena (Bennati et al., 2009) or the writing program at the University of Pisa (Dell'Aversano, 2006; Dell'Aversano & Grilli, 2005).

The Case of Romania

Educational genres in Romania are not rigorously defined. In Romanian school-books, for example, genres are approached holistically, being divided into the dramatic, epic, and lyric category. They are also referred to as "literary genres," whereas in the area of academic writing, the term "genre" is not used.

The treatment of genres at the secondary level is different from higher education and there is little continuity between the two levels of education (see Delcambre & Donahue, this volume, for similar trends in France). At the secondary level, students, who had been exposed intensively to writing-to-learn genres during elementary school classes (e.g., *dictare*/dictation, *autodicatare*/self-dictation, *notiţe*/note–taking, etc.), continue practicing some of the reproductive genres. This is the case of the note-taking genre family (Nesi et al., 2008, p. 23), which contains genres such as the follows:

- simple notes: copy of the notes on the blackboard
- discourse notes: notes made by students during the teacher's/professor's lesson/ lecture
- reading notes: notes on reading texts, which are either class or home assignments

The domination of reproductive genres in the Romanian primary education can be related to the prevalence of teaching methods, which are "based mainly on memorization and reproduction of the knowledge previously acquired" (Iatcu, 2000, p. 238). It can be considered a teacher-centered system, which today the Bologna process tries to transform into a student- or learner-centered system.

At the secondary level, students are also familiarized with genres demanding more challenging writing tasks. They can be grouped into three main categories: (i) creative writing, (ii) argumentative writing, and (iii) formal writing. The most common and frequently used form of creative writing is *compunerea* (composition). *Compunerea* can be defined as a descriptive, argumentative, or narrative essay on a given topic with a free structure. Teachers value when such texts contain poetic imagery or have a highly original narrative plot. This genre is more frequent at early stages of the secondary education and it almost disappears in the final years.

The category of argumentative writing is represented by numerous literature-dependent genres at the Romanian preuniversity level. *Comentariul literar* (literary interpretation) is a typical Romanian type of school text that is often used in the evaluation of the written argumentation skills of the students during their literature (target language: L1) and language lessons (target language: L2). It is a controlled piece of writing in which the students write something about a given literary text. *Comentariul literar* normally includes the argumentation on the genre affiliation of the text to be interpreted and comments on its structure and expressivity. *Caracterizarea de personaj* (characterization) refers to the type of text in which the physical and moral features of a literary character are detailedly described. *Analiză literară* (literary analysis) is the most complex written composition. It may share elements with *comentariul literar* but it also presents elements of the characterization. In addition, it can include a *rezumat* (summary) of the text, which has the characteristics of a usual summary but students have to pay extra attention to the features of the indirect speech.

Finally, school curricula also require students to learn to produce certain real-life genres that are considered to be useful in the future. These types of texts are rather functional: *cerere* (request), *invitație* (invitation), or *scrisoare* (letter). The students have to consider the specific structure of each text type and the various compulsory elements to be used (e.g., closing formulae for formal letters) (see Vargolici, 2004, for details).

It is interesting to note that nowadays, curricula (e.g., Iancu, Bălu, & Lăzărescu, 2009) and exam requirements have gradually introduced genres that are internationally recognized but that are new to Romanian students. Among these genres, the argumentative or "opinion" essays are extremely challenging. What makes it more difficult for Romanian students is the fact that they have to adapt to new writing requirements without being offered the correspondent terminology and genre descriptions (a challenge shared by French students as described in Delcambre & Donahue, this volume). Sometimes, the genre is simply "translated" (Harbord, 2010, p. 2) as in the case of the borrowed term *eseu*/essay that replaces the familiar term *compunere*. In this way, the traditional Romanian genre *compunere* has been transformed into a new genre family with different subtypes, structures, and connotations (Table 9.1).

Similarly to the French educational system, the Romanian *Bacalaureat* marks the transition to the university level and the accompanying new set of genres. Thus, students have to adapt to new writing practices that start to be more research-oriented. In other words, they do not write only texts on the basis of given information or literature but they are also expected to do more independent work such as researching on a topic, selecting, and commenting on subject matters. The writing is both reproductive and self-managed, note-taking genres coexisting with seminar papers. The latter has similar characteristics to the German *Seminararbeit* but it also is related to the research paper (Opariuc-Dan, 2010). It requires a research hypothesis, research goals, previous research, data analysis, and interpretation.

Table 9.1: The genre family *compunere*/composition in Romanian secondary education

Genre family *compunere*		
compunere traditional	compunere as essay	compunere as literary interpretation
– free structure	– specific structure	– specific content
– "poetic" language	– recommended connectives	– literature-dependent
– no specific markers	– linguistic markers	

The structure of such papers has developed only recently under the influence of foreign writing cultures. Moreover, the use of the same genre in foreign language classes, especially English, has also influenced genres in Romanian language. In fact, students of humanities, who are more exposed to genre use (portfolios containing genres such as argumentative essays, story, journal articles, and formal letter) have better writing skills than the science students, who only have to write genres such as scientific reports and problem-solving papers. Nevertheless, the reality is that the majority of the Romanian students have great difficulties in preparing a final bachelor's or master's paper since very little assistance is offered to them during the writing process. Generally, the supervision focuses on content and information structure whereas WID and WAC are completely ignored.

Conclusions

The four examples presented in the last chapter say a lot about the differences in genres and genre use in European higher education. To come to a conclusion about where to locate the origins of these differences, it is necessary to consider at least three different factors.

First, there are historical factors related mainly to modernization processes of the universities in 18th/19th century and, later, in the 20th/21st century. The first turn represents times when adaptation of university teaching to new societal developments was necessary and different solutions were favored. At the beginning of the 19th century, Enlightenment had changed the very base of social and intellectual life in Europe and the beginnings of industrialization demanded a closer connection of higher education with the technological development. The tasks universities had to solve at that time were the creation of new internal structures, the integration of the sciences into the disciplinary structures, and an opening of the universities for research. France, Germany, and the United Kingdom found different solutions for this (see Rüegg, 2004), which were adapted from many of the other European countries. The second historical moment that demanded change was the beginning of mass education in the second half of the 20th century. The change from elite to mass education confronted the universities with the need of developing new organizational forms, teaching philosophies, and training methods. Finally, and this is a third point, all European universities were unexpectedly affected by the top-down reform of the Bologna process, which imposed a historically unequalled change process on higher education. As the point of departure for this reform is different for each nation, the meanings and the directions of the changes differ. Little is known about the transformational processes of higher education in Italy and in Romania at both historical periods. While Italy has reformed its higher education in several steps since the 1960s, Romania had passed through a long stage of agony in its Stalinist era and then had to catch up in a relatively short with the new developments in higher education.

Second, the genres used in a certain educational culture are a factor of stability. Though genres are, as mentioned above, flexible and open to change, expectations and routines are not. Once genres are conventionalized and part of larger activity systems, they tend to resist change. This accounts for the difficulties of dealing with seminar papers flexibly as in Germany or of introducing argumentative genres in Romania where not too long ago expressing an own opinion bore a great personal risk. As helpful and socially connecting a well-established genre in higher education may be, as difficult may the introduction of new genres like the Italian theses prove to be. Free negotiation of genre features, as has been mentioned above, applies to many activity systems but not necessarily to educational genres that are regulated by universities or by state/federal laws.

More attention has to be given to how such innovative genres are introduced and delineated. For all European countries, the introduction of the BA/MA structures brings about the need to define what a BA thesis and what a MA thesis should be. Currently, no general norms or descriptions are available, neither within nor between countries. Genre design is a task of the future.

Third, genre evolution is a process that does not respect traditions nor wait for genre designers. As the French example shows, there is an abundant variety of new genres flooding higher education in spite of the traditional genres that still exist. Genre evolution is driven by introducing more flexibility into teaching, by connecting teaching closer with professional fields and by internationalization. For teaching, this means importing genres from professional fields or from other cultures. The management of genre development is a task that needs more specialized writing programs and writing centers at European universities but also more cooperation between the existing ones in order to allow a purposeful exchange of genre knowledge between the European countries.

Monocultures as exemplified in the German dominance of the seminar paper are likely to prevent the diversification of genres and make it difficult to import missing genres like the essay. For cultures like Italy and Romania, it is more a problem of introducing such new genres that interfere less with traditional ones but reach acceptance and provide a certain degree of comfort for all actors. Genre awareness and a deeper understanding of what genres accomplish in education are factors that supposedly play a crucial role for creating new teaching directives in the future. It will be necessary to gain an understanding of literacy practices that allows to purposefully select, create, and design genres for special purposes and, vice versa, better understand what the use of certain genres may add to literacy development.

Acknowledgments

We acknowledge Christiane Donahue for her contribution of the section of the chapter, "The case of France," on writing practices in higher education in France.

SECTION III

RESEARCH ABOUT WRITING FROM
A TEACHING AND LEARNING PERSPECTIVE:
FOSTERING THE DEVELOPMENT
OF IDENTITIES AND ATTITUDES

Chapter 10

Texts as Artifacts-in-Activity: Developing Authorial Identity and Academic Voice in Writing Academic Research Papers

Montserrat Castelló and Anna Iñesta

Introduction

Academic writing is considered nowadays as a socially and culturally situated activity (Castelló, González, & Iñesta, 2010; Flowerdew & Peacock, 2001; Johns, 2002; Lea & Stierer, 2000), inserted in a (micro) context of specific communicative situations which, in turn, make sense according to the (macro) historical and cultural context in which they take place. This is related with an equally situated conceptualization of language as a cultural and psychological tool (Mercer & Littleton, 2007) which, through its mediating role, allows the mind "to go beyond the skin" (Wertsch, 1991).

The previous considerations become even more relevant if we acknowledge that writers participate in several communities that are, in turn, embedded in complex systems of activity. Becoming aware of the tensions and contradictions that are inextricably involved in those systems of human activity is key to this social participatory practice, especially when writers are students trying to deal with learning within academic and, in our case, scientific communities.

In this chapter we present the approach to teaching and learning academic writing that we have implemented in an educational intervention in the academic community of Psychology. Our aim is threefold. First, we explain and justify the theoretical assumptions underlying the educational decisions about teaching and learning academic writing that account for the educational intervention. Second, we present and discuss the key principles and characteristics of such intervention. And finally we conclude by presenting some of the findings obtained in different studies we carried

University Writing: Selves and Texts in Academic Societies
Studies in Writing, Volume 24, 179–200
ISSN: 1572-6304/doi:10.1108/S1572-6304(2012)0000024014

out to assess the impact of the aforementioned intervention. While doing so, we use some examples to illustrate the students' struggles for writing as members of a disciplinary community and for developing an authorial identity, as well as their efforts to make their voice visible in their texts through the use of discursive resources such as citation or their dialogue within their own community of learners reflecting on successive versions of their peer's texts.

Texts as Artifacts-in-Activity

To clarify what we mean when we refer to texts as *"artifacts-in-activity"* (Prior, 2006), we begin by outlining the characteristics of the texts that our university undergraduate students have to write. Academic research paper writing (ARPW) implies two complex processes. On the one hand, students need to be able to think and act as researchers when developing their research study. On the other hand, they need to appropriately communicate the results of their research in the specific genre of the ARP. Following the classification proposed by Russell and Cortes (this volume), this genre has the particularity of being halfway between the academic texts (produced as part of the degree/university studies and to be read mainly by professors and/or tutors) and the scientific ones (produced with the objective of being published and thus read by the corresponding research community).

Moreover, successful ARPW requires students to be aware of what we may consider as the general functions of the academic writing. First, they need to use writing to accomplish an epistemic function, involving the construction and transformation of knowledge (Bereiter & Scardamalia, 1987; Galbraith, 1999) and having in mind the lines of thought in which the corresponding field of research is structured. The epistemic role of academic writing does not happen in a vacuum and neither is it exclusively based on the individual characteristics of the writer. Instead, it takes place as part of a joined construction of meaning, of a synchronous and asynchronous nature (i.e., inserted in a historical dimension), which the writer must be aware of.

Second, they must be aware of the dialogic function of academic writing, which refers to the dialogue established with other members of the academic-scientific community, and through which writers must position themselves, aligning with one or other approach, and therefore with the authors that subscribe them (Bakhtin, 1986; Bazerman, 2004c; Dysthe, 1996; see also Dysthe; Bazerman, Keranen, & Encinas, this volume).

Third, students need to know that research writing also serves the function of establishing and maintaining influence networks, in such a way that each text reveals the influence that the writer attributes to the different voices invoked through the ways in which intertextual dialogue takes shape (Nihalani & Mayrath, 2008).

Fourth, students should reflect on the communicative function, which involves the dissemination and sharing of this knowledge with other members of the community through the channels designed for that purpose (Swales, 1990, 2004). This communicative function is enhanced according to the fulfillment of the readers' expectations with regard to the previously mentioned functions and as regards the degree of adjustment to the conventions of the discourse genre, which, in turn, depends on the writer's position in the academic community. Actually, our students are encouraged to submit their final texts to a scientific journal in Psychology once revised and edited by their tutor who, in most cases, may appear as the second author. Obviously, not all students take this final step but the educational intervention is the context in which they develop the competences necessary to progress in such attempt in the near future.

And finally, academic writing contributes to the students' construction of a social identity as academic authors and researchers (Ivanič, 1998, 2005; Albertinti, 2008) which takes place through the dialogue that writers establish with the different actors involved in the more or less explicit co-authorship process of their texts and which is quite unfamiliar to our students (Bazerman, 2004a, 2004c; this has been also pointed out by Carlino in this volume regarding doctoral students).

The complexity involved in ARPW as outlined above invites us to abandon the seemingly "flat" conceptualization of texts as end-products of thought. Instead, we propose that texts are "artifacts-in-activity" (Prior, 2006), that is, central ingredients around which the meaning construction process that the research and writing activities involve is articulated and whereby the author's discoursal identity is forged and made visible to the readers. This implies considering texts as semiotic artifacts, that is, as a specific type of "mediating means" as they are conceived by Activity Theory (Engeström & Sannino, 2010), and being aware that they have "some sort of actual provenance: a place and situation in which they were elaborated; people who have literally or metaphorically read them before, and also a cultural shaping, in terms of the genres and discourses from which they are drawing (Ivanič, 2005, p. 4)". Moreover, from this conceptualization texts become a "second stimulus" in Vygotskyan words (Vygotsky, 1997, p. 212) in the sense that when students have to confront an academic writing task (first stimulus), texts can operate as tools or artifacts that may be filled with meaning and turn into new mediating signs that may help students to reframe the writing task. All the above boils down to the idea that texts may be considered as problem spaces in which specific tools are used and which, eventually, end up being outcomes.

However, such conceptualization of academic texts (as well as the writing regulation practices derived from it) is far from obvious to the students. This is why the learning activities proposed in our educational intervention aim to increase the complexity of students' representations of ARPW by showing them the need to strategically regulate the writing process. In the following section, we develop in more detail what we understand by writing regulation, the second key element articulating our educational intervention.

Academic Writing Regulation, Co-Regulation, and Socially Shared Regulation in Communities of Practice

As writing research has extensively shown, one of the most outstanding challenges that instructional proposals focusing on academic writing at the university have to face is to promote students' acquisition of strategies to efficiently manage and regulate their own writing activity (Caffarella & Barnet, 2000; Castelló, 2000; Englert, Mariage, & Dunsmore, 2006; Graham, 2006; Tynjälä et al., 2001). In short, acquiring such strategies requires students to reflect on their intention and objectives when writing every particular text, and to regulate their writing practices so as to fulfill these objectives.

Needless to say, students at the university have already incorporated strategies that allow them to solve writing demands associated to telling what they already know — Bereiter and Scardamalia's (1987) knowledge-telling — but most of them have not learned how to manage more complex demands which require them to adjust the knowledge of their own rhetoric and discursive objectives so as to produce complex academic texts (Castelló, 2000; Castelló et al., 2007). More specifically, such demands require them to deal with the hybrid combination of reading and writing processes involved in meaning construction (Nelson, 2008), as well as with the fact that the primary purposes of such processes evolve parallel to the development of research expertise. Indeed, for beginning researchers (as is the case of our students), the reading and writing processes are oriented to learn about the research field, a knowledge-construction process that Dysthe (this volume), following Bakhtin, considers undissociable from the active understanding resulting from "the juxtaposition and interanimation of many voices."

With the acquisition of expertise in the area of research, these increasingly focus on constructing an argumentative architecture which supports their position at the same time as it makes sense within the conceptual bounds of the specific academic community (see Nelson & Castelló, this volume).

Such challenges cannot be adequately addressed merely by applying any planning or revising techniques or by being familiar with the macrostructures or the linguistic features of the research papers. The need to cope with and ideally make the most out of the complexity of these processes requires the implementation of writing regulation strategies that are inextricable from the representations of the text that the author/s may have constructed (Castelló et al., 2010) as well as from the successive drafts that the author/s produce and that constitute the actualization of "rehearsed texts" (Camps, 1992). Indeed, both the stage in the development of the argumentative architecture that the author has reached and the specificities of the draft that materializes it determine the kind of writing strategies to be implemented. From this perspective, therefore, what student researchers need to learn is not only what linguistic resources — such as, for instance, boosters and hedges — are but when, how and to fulfill which objective their use is required while proceeding in the writing research activity (Castelló, 2000; Castelló & Monereo, 2005).

This requires the implementation of interventions designed to go beyond the teaching objective of equipping students with de-contextualized and declarative knowledge on writing strategies. Certainly, if we are to provide students with keys to strategically regulate their ARPW activity beyond our classes, educational interventions need to be designed so as to allow students to intentionally use the writing strategies learned at precise moments and in the precise way so as to make their case convincingly before the academic community.

Developing the competence to make this type of judgments may be said to be related to the author's enculturation into "academic regulation", a notion that Walker (2007) proposes to refer to the processes of co-regulation involved in the acceptance of a research paper in a discourse community forum. We aim to explicitly promote this academic regulation which, by means of collaborative writing and revision activities, takes the form of two complementary forms of regulation: *co-regulation* and *socially-shared regulation* (Castelló, 2008; Castelló et al., 2009; Järvelä, Hurme, & Järvenoja, 2007; Volet, Summers, & Thurman, 2009). On the one hand, co-regulation is conceived as a shared process whereby the less experienced writers internalize their own self-regulatory strategies thanks to dialogue with other members of the community and specially thanks their tutors' guide and scaffold. On the other hand, the notion of socially-shared regulation refers to the fact that each student should regulate their writing activity while participating in a particular community of practice usually making decisions and revising collaboratively with their peers.

All these academic writing regulation modalities aim to develop students' awareness and knowledge regarding: (a) the content they are writing about and the establishment of new conceptual relations; (b) the discursive mechanisms and linguistic resources that are valued in each specific community; (c) the emotional and identity-related dimensions involved in academic writing regulation.

Authorial Identity and Academic Voice

Different approaches have been interested in the relationship between academic writing and identity as well as in how identity is instantiated in texts (Farmer, 1995; Ivanič, 1998, 2005; Prior, 2001; Wenger, 1998) and several studies have shown the relationship between academic identity and the possibility to develop a reflective knowledge of how, when and why to produce some specific texts (Donahue, 2004; Gee, 2005; Ivanič, 2005; Prior, 1998, 1995, among others). Our approach to identity — mostly influenced by the work of Ivanič (1998, 2005) — is dynamic and relational instead of static and individual, situating the individual writer in relation with the social dimension of his/her contributions within the academic-discursive community. In line with this conceptualization, we assume that identity is relational and discoursally constructed at least by the three processes defined by Ivanic: by address ("the way we are talked *to* by others"), by attribution ("the way we are talked *about* by others") and by affiliation ("the way we talk *like* others") (Ivanič, 2005). At the same time, "identity" is constructed through subject positioning, that is, through a process of self or subject construction (see Ivanič, 1998, pp. 10–11, for further discussion of ways of talking about "identity"). Therefore, we do not consider "identity" as a static product, but as a continuous process of identification.

In the case of ARPW, we argue that this identity manifests in what has been called authorial or academic voice (Castelló et al., 2011), which in turn, can be considered as both an individual and social construct (to further explanation about voice multiplicity see also Nelson & Castelló, this volume). Specifically, the individual dimension has to do with the fact that the author's presence is shown in certain strategic uses of the language related with the enunciation process (Benveniste, 1970) or positioning (Hyland, 2002) (for a detailed discussion on positioning see Rinck & Boch, this volume). Complementarily, the social and situated dimension has to do with the author's awareness of his/her words' power to represent or differentiate him/her as a member of a community (Gee, 2000, 2005) and, consequently, of the need to dialogue, adjust or differentiate his/her own discourses taking into account the characteristics of the context within which the differed dialogue may take place. As Spivey (1997) highlighted this social dimension of identity implies that writers — psychology students — were positioning themselves relative to others whose work they read. As they wrote these papers for psychology, they were "trying on" what some have referred to as "possible lives" as they were positioning themselves (at least for a time) as particular kinds of psychologists.

Moreover, a specific author's voice not only invokes the voices of those other dominant discourses in the corresponding academic field but requires the critical expropriation of others' discourses so that these may be intentionally used in the construction of new meanings (Farmer, 1995; Prior, 1998, 2001) that must be inserted and that, at the same time, receive their meaning within the network of texts — voices — populating the disciplinary dialogue. In this sense, writers "re-present their discipline (...) in what they write (to "discipline" their thinking and their activity)" (Russell & Cortes, this volume). These processes may also be related to an academic enculturation which Prior and Bilbro (this volume) consider a dialogic, socially and culturally situated open system involving "semiotic (re)mediation" (Prior & Hengst, 2010) with other social spaces and activities.

Recent research has revealed further complexities in the construction of an academic voice in paper research writing. Indeed, most of the studies focusing on academic voice have based their conclusions on the textual analysis of the final versions of academic papers (Hyland, 2002; Koutsantoni, 2006), therefore inferring the writers' decisions from the final result. The results obtained in Iñesta's (2009) study analyzing the writing activity of expert researchers as it developed in their word processor screen, however, have revealed a more dynamic notion of voice, presenting it as a complex construct that becomes visible in the decision-making process involved in text construction or "crafting". From this perspective, then, and adapting Prior's (2006) concept, we could say that academic voice appears as a "trace-in-activity" of the researcher's social identity as an academic writer, a social identity that is expertly crafted through the situated and intentional use of discursive resources according to the writing goals and the particularities of the writing situation.

In addition, the results obtained in that study suggest that expert researchers address both the discoursal dimension of authorial voice crafting (selecting the best possible resources to, for instance, imprint the necessary emphasis on an idea) and its social dimension (taking other voices as well as the readers' point of view into consideration when selecting the resources mentioned in the previous example) implicitly, that is, without making any explicit reference to finding these challenging.

Something similar concluded Matsuda and Tardy (2007) in a study — from a different perspective — in which they reported how expert writers, when acting as blind reviewers, try to find traces of author's identity by means of identifying and situating their voices as members of a community through an implicit process. Results from reviewers' interviews and written review reports indicated that the reviewers' constructions of the author's voice are related to their stance toward the author. In identifying discursive and non-discursive features that led the reviewers to construct the author's voice, they propose the notion of *markedness* that refers to the reviewers' attention not to those textual features that were conformed to discursive and generic expectations ("unmarked"), but to "marked" features of the text — that is, those features which departed from the discursive or generic expectations in some way (see also Nelson & Castello, this volume, for a further development of this discussion).

While the expression of voice seems to require explicit attention on the part of non-expert academic writers (Castelló et al., 2011), these results allow us to hypothesize that expert researchers and writers' unawareness of the challenge that addressing these voice-related aspects involves to student researchers could explain (a) why such aspects remain more implicit for student research writers or newcomers into a discursive community and (b) why educational interventions have not usually focused on them (except for some well-known exceptions such the work of Dysthe on multivoicedness to which we have already referred to and some of which are summarized in this volume).

Fostering the Development of Students' Authorial Identity and Academic Voice in Writing Academic Research Papers in Psychology

Taking into account the aforementioned framework, we have conducted a series of studies to develop and analyze different teaching-learning interventions aimed at fostering the development of students' authorial identity and academic voice in ARPW. The current design of the intervention is based on some workshops we initially implemented with doctoral students in 2006. We have continued to develop these workshops, refining their theoretical framework as well as revising both the sequence of learning activities and the interactive and relational dynamics among the participants (Castelló, 2008; Castelló et al., 2009, 2010; Castelló, Iñesta, Pardo, Liesa, & Martinez-Fernández, 2011). Before presenting the interventions, we briefly characterize the context in which they were developed.

Contextualizing the Intervention

In the past few years, the Spanish Higher Education system has been immerse in a challenging process aimed at adapting to what is known as the Bologna process, that is the convergence in a European Higher Education Area (EHEA), as many other countries (see for instance Dysthe; Chitez & Kruse, this volume). The changes required for this convergence to be possible are both structural (such as those related with the length of the studies) and methodological (such as the need to modify the conceptualization of teaching and learning as well as the instructional practices in the classroom).

Briefly, the latter changes are confronting university teachers with the need to promote critical thinking and students' awareness of and reflection upon their learning process as well as with the need to develop the necessary teaching strategies to help them construct new knowledge. When adequately addressed, these new demands are frequently met by means of increasing students' writing, which is used as a way for them to show their learning process during the courses. Despite this new scenario, writing remains to be scarcely taught at the Spanish university (Mateos & Solé, this volume; Solé et al., 2005) although attention to writing practices is starting to increase partially thanks to the creation of educational innovation centers in most of the universities.[1]

One of the most important curricular changes at a Spanish national level is the requirement for students to write a graduation thesis, also called the end-of-studies dissertation. Students have to write this kind of texts at the end of their undergraduate studies. Despite the compulsory nature of this piece of writing, its final form, the process of writing it, its features and demands vary from one study program to another. The panorama is even more complex since, except for some disciplines (Architecture and some Engineering degrees), there is no tradition in most of the Spanish universities of this writing practice at the undergraduate level. As in other European countries (see Dyshte; Chitez & Kruse, this volume) writing courses are not usual and teaching writing is placed inside disciplines, if taught at all.

In this context, our University[2] was pioneer in establishing this requirement as part of the Undergraduate Degree Program in Psychology curriculum 15 years ago. In this case, the final text is supposed to be an ARP presenting the results obtained in a research project developed during the two final semesters of the program. The Tutors, all of them teachers of different subjects in the undergraduate degree, discussed the features of the research project students had to carry out, developed guidelines and agreed upon a common framework of minimum requirements for this final text. Nevertheless, the focus of such guidelines was on the research activities and it was implicitly assumed that writing would not be a problem if some clear guidelines about the final text structure were provided. But the reality was quite different and students not only revealed problems to write this type of academic research paper, but showed blocks, anxiety and negative feelings that prevented them from writing and led them to postpone the completion of the written text.

---

[1]These centers provide educational counseling to teachers, helping them to rethink their teaching practices.
[2]Ramon Llull University, Barcelona, Spain (www.url.edu).

The Educational Intervention

The characteristics of the educational intervention have been synthesized in two tables, each focusing respectively on its conceptual underpinnings (Table 10.1) and on its contextual characteristics (Table 10.2).

Regarding its *conceptual underpinnings*, the educational intervention focuses on three key aspects already presented: seeking to help students develop a complex conceptualization of texts as artifacts-in-activity, regulate their writing activity and develop an authorial identity and academic voice. At the same time, we seek to place dialogue at the center of the teaching and learning experience to promote the students' awareness of their disciplines' communicative practices and, consequently, the emergence of a metalanguage to talk about them as well as about the meaning-construction process through writing (Lillis, 2006; Street, 2005).

The class group functions as a community of learning trying to construct discursive knowledge (linguistic resources, genre conventions ...), *social knowledge*

Table 10.1: Conceptual underpinnings of the intervention

Key elements in which the intervention focuses	• Development of complex conceptualization of texts as "artifacts-in-activity" • Acquisition of strategies to regulate the writing activity • Development of academic voice and authorial identity

Key psychological processes in the intervention	• Dialogue
	   • Peer-to-peer
	   • Students-tutor
	 • Reflection
	 • Awareness of the specificities of students' own writing process
	 • Acquisition of writing regulation strategies
	 • Enculturation into the discursive and knowledge-construction practices of the disciplinary community
	 • Personalization and internalization of discourses and academic writing regulation

The role of the class-group	A community of learning trying to build new knowledge through participation
Knowledge construction	• Discursive knowledge • Social knowledge • Metalinguistic knowledge

Table 10.2: Contextual characteristics of the intervention

Group size	A total program cohort of 120 students organized in seminars of 12–15 students
Duration of the intervention	9 months (last 2 semesters in the Undergraduate Degree in Psychology)
Number of face-to-face sessions in which the intervention translates	18–20 1.5-h sessions
Actors involved in the students' academic research paper writing process	Students
Actors involved in the educational intervention (course)	Tutor (disciplinary expert) Students
Tutor's (disciplinary expert) role	Participates in the educational innovation project that implementing the intervention involves Participates in a teaching community grouping all tutors involved in supervising the end-of-studies dissertation (self-as-a-teacher) Participates in the disciplinary research community (self-as-a-researcher) Provides students with tips regarding writing regulation strategies and practices Provides students with topic-focused insights Provides students with individual counseling focusing on emotional dimension
Type of feedback provided and received in peer-tutorial sessions	• Direct feedback • Indirect feedback • Critical feedback
Teaching and learning tasks	• Analysis and discussion of research papers with the objective that students learn the language and the specific ways of communicating which characterize their (psychology) scientific community • Writing of their own academic research paper • Revision of a peer's academic research paper and provision of feedback • Revision of own academic research paper having in mind a peer's feedback

(relationship of writing practices to the community), and *metalinguistic knowledge* (metalanguage to talk about practices and the meaning-construction process) through participation.

As for class-group size, the kind of processes that we aim to engage students into require working with small groups of up to 15 students and the intervention develops along approximately nine months, coinciding with the last year in the undergraduate studies. Meetings take place every fortnight during the nine months (therefore arriving at an approximate number of 18–20 meetings).

The actors involved in the students' ARPW process are, of course, the same students, and a tutor (a psychology teacher who plays the role of disciplinary writing expert).[3]

Both students and tutors participate in different activity systems and are active members of different communities that in some cases could interfere or interact with that of the educational sequence. Tutors are committed to research in varying degrees of intensity and, being used to publishing scientific papers, they regularly participate in their scientific community. Moreover, tutors also participate in a teaching community in which they have to share and discuss decisions about how to develop the didactic sequences or about their own role as supervisor. At least in these two different communities related with that of the students' writing practices, tutors put into action a network of different selves (Ivanič, 2005) that can be understood as different manifestations of their identity. Students also participate in different activities and communities and have developed discursive selves when trying to learn and communicate in different courses and disciplines.

Regarding the type of feedback, students were taught to offer a combination between direct, indirect and critical or more open suggestions (Cho & Mac Arthur, 2010). Direct suggestions could be related to the authoritative ones; they refer to a direct and close suggestion to improve the text (*"you should change that sentence in that sense" "you would modify the structure starting in this way ..." "you should add a reference"*). Indirect feedback refers to the analysis of some texts problems or difficulties without a clear suggestion of change (*"I think this point is not enough justified" "This section seems to me a bit unclear" "this idea is a redundant with these other one"*). Critical feedback could be related to a dialogical model since suggestions are formulated as possibilities to discuss and to argue (*"this section seems not enough clear: maybe it would improve by means of adding examples, further explanations or rephrasing it. What do you think?" "The discussion is too much centered in one single perspective. Is it the only one you know or do you consider it is the only one relevant in this case?"*). According to some previous research results on feedback (Cho & Mac Arthur, 2010; Dysthe, Samara & Westrheim, 2006; Topping, 2010, see also Dysthe, this volume), we encourage students to combine these types of feedback depending

---

[3]In this case "tutor" can be equated to full-time professor, usually senior. They are called tutors since they work in seminars, with small groups of students and without a specific psychological content to teach, other than doing research and writing the academic research paper.

on the nature of the identified problem. Moreover, in previous studies we found that fellow feedback between doctoral students was only effective and useful for text improvement if students were able to define the nature of the problem and to ground their decisions about changes on arguments relating some actions to the defined problems (Castelló et al., 2009, 2010). For this reason, we also encourage our students to try to define and discuss accurately the nature of the problem before taking any decision regarding changes in text.

Finally, regarding the different teaching and learning tasks proposed to the students, research papers in Psychology — similar to those that students have to write — are discussed with the objective that students learn the language and the specific ways of communicating that characterize each scientific community. Students' voices join those of their tutors in such a way that they have the opportunity of acting as members of the community and being recognized as "belonging." From these discussions, a set of recommendations and quality criteria emerge as a consensus of what is important to have in mind when writing.

The interventions focus on practices but include texts as part of these practices, as artifacts evolving with and through the overall activity. Regulation of the students' activity that occurs through the internalization of social practices is mostly promoted by means of the *writing tutorial sessions*. Before each tutorial session the students read their peer's text and thought about suggestions to improve it, the tutorial session allowing them to share and discuss these suggestions. The tutor helps them to improve revision strategies and offers his/her own suggestions about what needs revision. In this sense, writing regulation is implemented in co-regulation contexts, externalizing, and becoming part of the instructional scaffold within the meaningful activity. Each of these writing tutorial sessions ends with a collective analysis of the changes required, the most conflicting aspects of writing that constitutes an opportunity to socially share the regulation of writing activity.

Regarding the content of feedback, in the discussion sessions and in the writing tutorial ones, students are confronted with the linguistic and discursive resources commonly used in Psychology. These resources refer to the maintenance of a stance and a writer's position (Hyland, 2005a; Nelson, 2008), the establishment of a dialogue with other texts and authors that takes account of intertextuality (Bazerman, 2004c) or, in Dysthe's words, of multivoicedness since the students are exposed to different voices (Dysthe, 2002, see also Dysthe in this volume) and the evidence of a structure and text organization coherent with the content and the writer's position (Swales, 1990, 2004). In each session, reflection about the characteristics of these resources, their contribution to the text and specially the social and contextual analysis of when, how and why they could be used, was promoted.

Discussing Some Findings

To analyze and assess the impact of the intervention we rely on a methodological approach combining different types of data, mostly qualitative in order to obtain a comprehensive picture of the participants' knowledge, identity development and writing practices.

Regarding the *participants' knowledge*, at the end of the intervention we developed a questionnaire designed to assess students' learning and comprehension of the most outstanding contents discussed in the class sessions. The items referred to academic research paper organization, linguistic resources necessary to make the authors' stance explicit and intertextuality mechanisms such as those used to dialogue with other voices and authors and those to imply readers in the proposed argument (Castelló et al., 2011). Students were also interviewed six months after the intervention to explore how they conceptualized writing academic research papers and whether they considered themselves as authors with particular voices when writing academic research papers. Observations and notes were also collected during the planning meetings with tutors as well as records of informal discussions with tutors (recorded immediately after every interaction).

To assess the students' *writing practices* we took into account the evolution of the successive versions of texts. This involved assessing both peers and tutors' revision suggestions, as well as the related changes that students introduced (or not) in their texts. In other words, we tried to analyze traces of changes in texts and relate them with the suggestions and the discussions with peers and tutors in each specific community of practice. To conduct this analysis, peers and tutors' suggestions were categorized according to the nature of change they referred to (writers' stance, intertextuality, and text organization) and the type of feedback (direct, indirect, or critical). The different drafts produced of every text were analyzed to identify traces of whether text evolution was related to peers' or tutors' suggestions. With this kind of analysis we aimed at unearthing how texts evolve, taking into account their provenance and the mediating effects on students' practices.

Finally, we also assessed the quality of the final texts both from an educational and from a reader-based approach.

Some quantitative analysis were also conducted, which confirm that the text quality increased in each version and that better texts were related with higher rates of revisions and more students' satisfaction (for further explanation of these analysis and results, see Castelló et al., 2011). Nevertheless qualitative analysis carried out helped us to gain a profound understanding of the students' construction of knowledge, the sense and the meaning they attribute to their writing practices. This kind of analysis has also thrown light into certain contradictions and tensions that appeared all along the intervention and that had been rarely highlighted by teaching and learning academic writing research. In most cases, these contradictions may be considered as problems or conflicts but also as the engine that makes learning possible (Engeström & Sannino, 2010).

In the following sections, we focus on these contradictions and tensions that offer a comprehensive picture of the students' learning and help us to reflect on the strengths and weaknesses of the educational intervention implemented. We found three major categories in which these contradictions can be grouped: the first one refers to students' efforts — in some cases successful but not in others — to construct their authorial identity; the second one has to do with how students relate the need and interest of their own writer's positioning with the use of some linguistic resources in texts, and the last one with the tension between considering texts as artifacts versus texts as objects in students' revisions.

Constructing an Identity When Participating in Different Communities

Difficulties regarding the construction of an identity as a research writer, or at least as an academic research writer arose, most of the times, when students had to manage different and sometimes contradictory constraints related with the different communities in which they participated or to which they aspire to belong. One of these is the learning community, where students and tutors have a clear and well-known, although not always explicitly defined, role. Some of the rules and norms of this community have to do with assessment — a grade at the end of their writing process should indicate the quality of the students' performance — and with the authenticity of the activities, namely their sense and meaning. In this respect and highlighting the complexities involved in distinguishing between academic and research writing (see Russell & Cortes, this volume), some students clearly claimed that they could not be assessed as *real* scientific authors since they were *beginners*, so they considered themselves as new — and still non-legitimate — participants in the academic community of researchers (Lave & Wenger, 1991; see also Bazerman, Keranen, & Encinas, this volume, to enlarge the characteristics of legitimate peripheral participation although in a different context, the one of the Non-Native English Speakers – NNES – when writing scientific papers in English). However, at the same time they valued their participation as student-writers in the learning community as relevant and fully legitimate. It seems they clearly distinguish they have a different commitment and role in both communities, which is obviously a potential source of conflict when constructing an authorial identity. Nevertheless being aware of potential conflicts is the first step to be able to analyze and solve them when they appear. Comments such as *"it was too difficult for me to feel the text as being mine"* [R, 22:24]; *"We are still beginners writing this type of texts, we are just starting"* [A, 12:13] or *"Tutors know how to write research papers; she is involved in writing papers; our classmates know the same as we do, we are all students"* [S, 33:15], collected through interviews are representative of this dual participation and of this awareness of its potential impact on students' authorial identity.

Besides the acknowledgement of this dual participation, we have evidences of how students solved some conflicts between communities as these appeared during the educational intervention. This is shown, for instance, in the evolution of Mark's[4] text at the beginning of the introduction section. The conflict underlying the student's decisions is revealed in the rationale behind the changes introduced in each new

---

[4]All the students' names have been anonymized.

version as well as in the contradictory nature of the tutor's suggestions and those provided by the classmate.

As displayed in the writing sequence (Table 10.3), in the first draft, Mark included an introductory story in his paper, and while no changes were suggested by his classmate, his tutor considered the introductory story as unnecessary. In the second draft, he removed the story but, this time, his peer considered the beginning of the paper to be too abrupt. In the final draft, he decided to include an introductory story again, combining practitioners' and academics' tone.

During the interview with the student, we could ask him about the reasons for the radical change in the beginning of the text from Draft 1 to Draft 2. He explained that he wanted his paper to be relevant for academics and practitioners alike, and that is why he had included, in the first draft of the paper, an introductory story aimed to frame the research topic from the practitioners' perspective.

On the contrary, his tutor had asked him to remove the introductory story and produce a more "to-the-point" paper, directly beginning with a discussion of the different definitions of the subject. And finally, he wrote a more classic introductory paragraph, in the fashion of a social sciences academic tone.

Table 10.3: Description of Mark's writing sequence

Steps in the writing sequence	Action	(Potential) Implication/s on the draft
1	Elaboration of Draft 1	It includes an introductory story aimed to frame the research topic from the practitioners' perspective
2	Reception of feedback from peer	No change is introduced in the Introduction
3	Reception of feedback from his tutor	The introductory story is considered unnecessary
4	Elaboration of Draft 2	The introductory story is replaced by a more formal beginning, focusing on the definitions of the subject
5	Reception of feedback from peer	The beginning of the paper is considered too abrupt and a new introductory paragraph is proposed, which is more in line with the academic discourse community than the first introductory story
6	Elaboration of 3rd and final draft	The introduction includes a much more "catchy" introduction, combining both practitioners' and academics' tone

When faced with these contradictory suggestions, the student both incorporated and resisted the professor's written suggestions, trying to find a satisfactory solution which is consistent with Prior's consideration that participation into a community promotes at the same time reproduction and transformation of social practices (1995). The student found a balanced solution, which fitted the constraints of the tutor and his own objective of writing a paper relevant for academics and practitioners alike. The theoretical consideration that identity is a relational construct is played out in examples like this, showing how participants experiment with different representations of the text as output and try to find out the best way to present their research and themselves as participants in that field. A yet unexplored aspect is the students' feelings when faced with these contradictions and with the at times urgent petition to modify their text. This student, for instance, declared feeling very stressed out when having to change the whole text in three weeks before its submission.

Difficulties to Relate Writer's Positioning with Linguistic Resources in Texts

A great number of difficulties appeared when tutors and peers frequently asked students to position themselves. Their difficulties focus on deciding consistently upon which discursive mechanisms — structural, grammatical, and rhetorical strategies — need to be used to establish their positioning in each section of the paper. Despite the need to establish writer's positioning, it cannot be ignored that one of the academic requirements in research papers has to do with the presentation of knowledge as relative argument based on accumulated evidence. This implies being able to make a complex balance of assertion, caution, and evaluation of existing positions (Read & Francis, 2001), which has shown highly conflicting for our students.

The following examples display some of these conflicts in students' understanding of what writers' positioning implies and why this is an important feature of academic research papers. The first one refers to an unsuccessful example of writer's positioning that appeared frequently in our context. In this case, the student was working on a paper on dissociation and revised different sources with the objective of integrating them into a coherent synthesis. This structure repeats in all the sections in such a way that it is not possible to find out the writer position.

> Richard (2007) argues for dissociation as a process in which experiences and psychological interpretations are not related and meanings are altered. He explains how experiences are distorted and interpretations for personal and interpersonal experiences are subtly but deeply altered. In addition, Steinberg & Schnall (2002) suggest [...] dissociation is an adaptive behavior to face up with tensions or traumas. On the other hand Bernstein y Putnam (1996) argue for different levels of dissociation which imply memory loss and disconnection from the context. (M1)

To which the student reviser comments: "Ok but, do you agree or disagree with those authors' assumptions?"

When the student was asked whether he agreed or disagreed with the discussed authors' assumptions, the student answered: "*I agree, obviously!*"; and he was very surprised to realize that this was not self-evident for the reader. From his perspective the very act of citing those authors and explaining their assumptions was sufficient sign of his own (agreeing) positioning. We may take this as an extreme example of lack of awareness of the discursive mechanisms to make visible the writers' positioning.

Quite a different type of conflict is represented by the following example in which Carol comments on the writer's positioning of his/her classmate. In this case, Carol asked for a hedge, which is a quite interesting recommendation, but what is even more interesting are the arguments she used. First, she asked for a citation as a way to reduce the writer's agency with the statement; then she considered necessary to hedge the statement because it compromised the writer's neutrality, which seems far from considering hedges as a help for writer's positioning.

> It is considered that functional loss is the most serious consequence of spinal cord injury, although pain has a direct influence on the recovery of the optimal level of daily living activity, <u>negatively affecting patients' quality of life, including mobility and sleep</u>. If we analyze the population of spinal cord injured patients, we observe that many of these experience more than one type of pain. Many treatments have been used to alleviate pain and improve patients' quality of life, but drugs doses are very high and the degree of patient satisfaction is moderate to low. This indicates that the pharmacological treatment of pain <u>is not successful in reaching these objectives</u>.

> Student reviewer comment: "Very strong language to use. Without a citation, it sounds like hyperbole that could compromise your neutrality. If there is no cite, could you try to hedge?"

Examples from interviews also show these students' difficulties in finding how to make the writer's position evident, and in some cases it seems that students consider authorial identity to be a fuzzy concept that is not linked to any linguistic or discursive resources except citation and intertextuality. This was the case of this student:

> To make my position, my stance clear I work on my reading notes; first I add the authors' citation and I mix different ideas from several authors. That's the way I construct my text and my particular stance. It's like a jigsaw. (R_24:28)

A different step in the construction of authorial identity is shown when students were able to solve the conflict mostly by developing a strong feeling of community belonging through the dialogue with other authors who linked him — as author — with the scientific community.

> I am there as author when my text is not bizarre or sounds weird. I mean it is scientific based, networked with other authors which in turn, are also linked to other ones ... (A_34:18)

Texts as Artifacts-in-Activity versus Texts as Objects in Students' Revisions

One of the things that appeared as extremely difficult for our undergraduate psychology students was to understand that successive versions of their texts do not need to become "the text" in its final version as quickly as possible, that is to consider texts as evolving artifacts and mediating tools that allow them to evolve as authors in turn. Most of the suggestions they made to their mates during the revisions as well as the comments they offered during discussions reflect this idea of texts as objects that should be changed only so as to fit the constraints of what could be considered a "good" text (which is also revealed as a very narrow and fuzzy concept in itself). This is clear at least in two different dimensions: 1. The use of citations and their function in texts and 2. The type of suggestions students offer for revising texts

1. The use of citations and their function in texts

Most of the students' suggestions about changes in texts were devoted to citation (97% out of the total of comments and revision suggestions), and more precisely to the need to introduce other voices in texts only as a way to enhance the authority to the writer's own voice (94%). It seems that, from the students' perspective, each sentence — especially in the introduction section — should have its own reference in such a way that there exists no room for a writer's elaboration of ideas or formulation of his/her own conclusions. In those cases, instead of valuing writers' positioning and offering ways to improve it, peers asked for citations when they were not sure whether the writer was the author of a certain idea or whether it had been extracted from a particular source. The suspicion that most of the times it might be the latter case made reviewers suggest the need to include the necessary citation. The following examples are highly representative of these students' conceptions.

In the first one, the reviewer considered that even some very general sentences should be authoritatively supported by a citation. What is interesting here is not that the reviewer claims for citation but the function attributed to this citation as an authoritative support for the writer's opinions, which should not be expressed without being supported by some voices of the scientific community:

> In current society, we observe that the increase in life expectancy of older people has a direct impact in the likelihood of developing dementias such Alzheimer's disease. [AR, 2.1.Intro]

Student reviewer comment: "You should check if there's some authors saying this and you should cite them in order for this not to seem as a personal opinion"

Something similar happened when reviewers asked the authors of their revised texts *"to look for authors that support what you are saying"* or in a more direct way demanded *"where does this idea come from?"*

In the following excerpt, the need to support all the claims made lead the student to ask for a citation each time a new sentence started; so, after a dot, the reviewer student asked if the new sentence could be attributed to the same author(s) or a new reference should be introduced, even when the sentence is an explanation of the previous one:

> Jaenes, Godoy & Román (2009), in their studies about Marathon men, demonstrated that they developed a resistent personality (RP), characterised by high scores in control, commitment and challenge. More specifically, the higher is the mark of a marathoner, the higher is his score in RP. Therefore, they are individuals who think of themselves and their environments as something interesting and important, find meaning to their actions in their life plan (commitment) and believe that what improves their lives is change, growth and learning instead of the comfort and security of stability. [SP. 1.1. Intro].

> Student reviewer comment: "In this last sentence, is the reference the same as the one appearing in the previous one, that is Jaenes, Godoy & Román (2009)?"

Students' comments on the dialogic function of references are less frequent but when occurring, as in the following two examples, a discussion between different voices and approaches is possible as well as the possibility to recognize that these voices could contribute in a different way to display the writers' intentions and positioning:

> Another author who confirms this theory is Gonzalez Lopez (2006) who, in accordance with Yubero Jiménez (2000), pointed out that tales could be used as a strategy for learning .... [PC 1.3. Intro]

> Student reviewer comment: "I think that he is not confirming the theory but introducing new ideas".

In other cases, as in the previous one, reviewers are able to focus on the type of dialogue that the writer establishes (or not) with other voices and especially with those who were explicitly cited in their texts. In these cases, a reviewer could point out that the writer's stance is not clear (*"Although you have many references it is not clear where you put your emphasis*") or that there is no dialogue or relationship between the different voices ("*I can't see controversy. Do all these authors have the same point of view? Do they share yours? Are they related in some way?*")

2. *The type of suggestions students offer when revising texts*

As for the type of suggestions students offer to their classmates, even though they were taught about the usefulness of critical and indirect suggestions that help discussions and reflection on different possibilities, more than 84% of the students' comments were categorized as direct indications for change with only one possible option. Comments such as: "*you should change that*"; "*I would put that here ....*" "*You need to say/clarify that ...*" are by far the most frequent when they analyze their peer's texts. Besides, in some cases, they tend to indicate local changes in words or sentences, such in this representative example:

> The scarce londitudinal studies revised suggest that deficits in face recognition remain stable at least one year in which it didn't improve with the improvement of symptoms which are characteristic of the illness (Addington & Addington, 1998; Kee et al., 2003). [RA 1.1. Intro]

> Reviewer comments: I would change the word "deficit". Change the expression: "at least" by" during". I would delete all the sentence: "in which it didn't improve with the improvement of symptoms which are characteristic of the own illness"

In other cases, students directly rewrite whole paragraphs or offer indications about how to modify overall sections. Besides, in all that cases there is a lack of comments and arguments about why these modifications are suggested, for what purposes or under which criteria some expressions are considered more convenient, although students were taught to do that and the impact and usefulness of different types of feedback were discussed in class. It seems that students tend to assume there is one single "correct" way to write and that revising texts has to do with finding that correctness. Nevertheless, in many cases (a 48% out of the total), when they realize that they might be too directive, they try to excuse themselves saying something like:

> *In doing this very detailed revision, I just want to offer you what I consider to be suggestions, this is not the absolute truth. We will comment on that during the class session, ok?*

This type of comments — which were frequent in tutorial sessions when discussing their own texts — shows a discontinuity between two conflicting ways of interpreting texts as objects and outcomes of the writing activity. Although students participate in a community of learners where texts has been considered as evolving objects to reflect on and at the same time instruments to achieve their writers' objectives, they also have the representation — probably from previous experiences and from their participation in other systems of activities — that academic texts are normative, should use a specialized lexicon and a fixed structure. These conceptions seem to enter into contradiction with the possibility to reflect upon the linguistic resources and to use them strategically to position themselves, to reach their objectives and finally to develop their identity as academic writers and not only as reproductive students.

On the contrary, this is the focus of most of the tutors' comments (out of 75%), which ask for thinking about aims and objectives instead of offering direct solutions. More than half of the tutor's comments are accompanied by an explanation of their understanding of the text and the writer's intentions (56%). On the basis of such reflections some suggestions are provided in an indirect way and when changes are directly proposed they are always justified, namely almost all the tutors' feedback is indirect or critical. This procedure could be interpreted as the tutors' intention to turn the object text — understood as a raw material — into a mediated tool of the activity (Engeström & Sannino, 2010). In such a way, the text becomes an artifact to be transformed and which in turn might be able to transform the subject, the student, as evidenced in the following examples:

> Is a text in which the topic is explained but not argumentatively supported. Now it is time to work on the text to turn it into more argumentative addressing research readership.

> The first two paragraphs frame the topic, situate the territory; they are great and the third paragraph represents a jump in which — as in the first draft — you explain what tales are. On page 5 the topic of the influences is continued, but the intention is not clear; for instance, we know that they facilitate socialization but? We know that they like them but, in what sense?

> Since the text does not talk about the existence of a problem, it seems that the objective has no sense. Do we want to research into something we already know?

Concluding Remarks

We have presented our approach to teaching and learning academic writing focusing on the development of an intervention where students were asked to write an academic research paper. This approach is supported by the theoretical consideration of academic writing as a social and cultural practice and from this perspective we aim at promoting constructive and expansive learning as defined by Engeström and collaborators (Engeström & Miettinen, 1999; Engeström & Sannino, 2010). Therefore, we understand that learning to write research papers is a matter of enculturation into a new disciplinary community since this enculturation must help students become acquainted with epistemic stances (ways of knowing) and identities (ways of being) of the academic and disciplinary community (Dysthe, 1996; Marilyn & Larry, 2004; Prior & Bilbro, this volume). Nevertheless, we expect that our students not only reproduce social practices but that they learn strategies to transform them (Prior, 1995), by means of being aware of the constraints and characteristics of these discourse communities, deciding how, when, and why to use linguistic and discursive resources to position themselves and learning to regulate their activity taking into account their role in the different communities in which they participate.

On the basis of the consideration that tensions and contradictions are the engine of constructive and transformative learning (e.g. Engeström & Sannino, 2010), we have analyzed whether these contradictions are interpreted as conflicts by the same participants and which actions were implemented to solve or to deal with such conflicts. This analysis led us to identify three major types of contradictions and some of the conflicts they originate from. The first one refers to the students' efforts to construct their authorial identity; the second one has to do with how students relate the need and interest of their own writer's positioning with the use of some linguistic resources in their texts, and the last one has to do with the tension between considering texts as artifacts versus texts as objects in students' revisions.

We found evidences of how students dealt with these contradictions which illustrate both the major difficulties and the successful actions they carry out to give sense and meaning to their writing practices. These evidences, adequately situated in their context, help us gain a deeper insight of the sense and meaning that students attribute to the proposed practices and to better understand which mechanisms account for reflection and learning which would ultimately benefit the development of more adjusted teaching and learning sequences and support the students' development of authorial identity and academic voice.

We would also like to point out the role of tutors in the development of this type of learning. Most of them confessed that although they were active members and writers of their own academic and disciplinary communities, they were unaware of how this activity is acquired or developed. Moreover, they expressed their satisfaction when given the opportunity for making their implicit knowledge about text, language, and patterns of their community participation explicit, not only as a means to help their students, but also as a way to develop their own academic identity.

Shifting between communities and adjusting participation in each case has been challenging for all participants, that is, for students, tutors, and also for us as researchers and is still a matter of reflection and growth. We have tried — not always successfully — to take advantage of these challenges and conflicts making them explicit and discussing how different selves and communities could be interwoven. We will be glad to add a community of readers to these networks.

Acknowledgments

We are grateful for funding from the Ramon Llull University — FPCEE Blanquerna — and *Generalitat de Catalunya* (Government of Catalonia-Spain).

Chapter 11

Multivoiced Classrooms in Higher Education Academic Writing

Olga Dysthe

Introduction

In this chapter, I will focus primarily on the teaching and learning of writing at university level that has been inspired by a dialogic theory framework. I here use the term 'academic writing' about student writing which has as one of its major aims to become 'scientific' (Russell & Cortes, this volume). The central issue is how academic enculturation is fostered through institutional, literate practices that weave together writing, reading and talk (Prior & Bilbro, this volume). 'Dialogue' and 'dialogic' are notoriously multifaceted and complex terms that are interpreted in different ways. The most recent comprehensive discussion of dialogue and dialogism is found in *Rethinking Language, Mind and World Dialogically* (Linell, 2009). Linell defines dialogism as a meta-theoretical framework for explaining human sense-making: 'It is a general epistemology and/or ontology for sociocultural (human) phenomena: semiosis, cognition, communication, discourse, consciousness, action in the world, i.e. for the social, cultural and human sciences and arts' (p. 28). Linell lists a number of traditions leading up to dialogism in the 20th century: phenomenology, philosophical hermeneutics, pragmatism, symbolic interactionism and cultural semiotics and activity theory (p. 401). My work has primarily been inspired and informed by the Russian philosopher of language and literature, Mikhail Bakhtin, an influence I share with a great number of writing researchers, for instance, Nystrand, Bazerman, Prior, Halasek and Lillis, just to mention a few. Some of them also participate in this volume, for instance, Bazerman, Castelló and Iñesta, Delcambre and Donahue, Prior and Bilbro; see also Russell and Cortes for an overview of traditions in writing research.

University Writing: Selves and Texts in Academic Societies
Studies in Writing, Volume 24, 201–216
Copyright © 2012 by Emerald Group Publishing Limited
ISSN: 1572-6304/doi:10.1108/S1572-6304(2012)0000024015

On the one hand, Bakhtin sees dialogue as an all-pervasive dimension of human language and communication; it is part of the human ontology: life itself is dialogue. His dialogism is also an epistemology in the sense that he contends that new knowledge is always created through dialogue and that all our utterances are dialogic, involve addressivity and are part of a chain of communication; they never exist in isolation. On the other hand, Bakhtin also sees dialogue as an ideal to struggle for, counteracting the forces of monologism that will reduce multivoiced dialogue to 'the authoritative word': 'The authoritative word demands that we acknowledge it, that we make it our own: it binds us, quite independent of any power it might have to persuade us internally: we encounter it with its authority already fused to it – it demands our unconditional allegiance' (Bakhtin, 1981, p. 343).

Bakhtin himself recognised the monologic dominance in traditional education and used 'pedagogic discourse' as an example of the authoritative word. By 'authoritative', he means discourses where there is no room for doubt or critical questioning. Instead, he poses 'the internally persuasive word' which is based on a confrontation between different voices where ideas are tested through dialogue (Bakhtin, 1981, 1984, 1986; Matusov, 2007). In higher education, this ties up with the Humboldtian ideals of fostering critical and independent thinking, a connection that has been shown by Otto Kruse's investigation of the link between seminar pedagogy and writing in German universities in the 19th century (Kruse, 2006a) and has recently been discussed in the context of the Bologna process in European universities (Dysthe & Webler, 2010).

My work has also been influenced by the Norwegian social psychologist Ragnar Rommetveit who developed similar ideas to Bakhtin's dialogism in the late 1960s before Bakhtin was known in the West. In his seminal book, *On Message Structures* (1974), he outlined a model of communication premised on the intersubjectivity of the conversants (for instance, writers and readers) and the reciprocity of their perspectives. Particularly relevant in this chapter is his emphasis on participants' 'temporarily shared social reality' as a prerequisite for dialogic communication. Implications of this for multivoiced writing and feedback practices will be discussed in the case studies.

The overarching question of this chapter is: *How can multivoicedness in students' writing be facilitated in higher education and how do students benefit from this?* There are various ways of providing students with opportunities to interact with voices in their writing processes, and a major focus is on feedback. I have chosen to foreground the meso level,[1] that is, design issues and institutional practices. The rationale for this is twofold. First, because decisions made at the meso level

---

[1]Dirknick-Holmfeldt, Jones, and Lindstrøm (2009) have argued that the meso level need to get more attention in educational research as the focus in research has largely been on the micro and macro level. 'The meso level at its simplest can be thought of as the level of interaction that was intermediate between small scale, local interaction and large-scale policy and institutional processes' (p. 11). A meso-level approach to networked learning practices, which is their particular concern, would investigate how to design for a specific type of desired learning in different settings and to identify the basic conditions that allow for such learning as well as understanding how technologies and infrastructures afford and mediate the learning that takes place (*ibid.*)

determine to a large degree what is possible or not possible for students to do. Second, this level has been less researched than the micro level.

The outline of the chapter will be as follows: After a description of the national context for the studies and a discussion of the theoretical concept of multivoicedness, I first present findings from two studies relating to graduate/postgraduate student writing: Writing groups for doctoral students and multivoiced supervision of master's students. Second, I draw on two studies from bachelor programmes, one in history and one in law: Digital portfolios and feedback practices in a traditional university course and new and changing teacher roles in a digital age. In the final section, I discuss the challenge of making such feedback practices mainstream and relate this to the question of the impact of research. Writing research based on a socio cultural framework tends to prioritise small-scale, qualitative, interpretive case studies, and so do the studies presented in this chapter.[2] Such studies are useful from a strategic point of view, and findings can be compared across contexts even though generalisations cannot be claimed.

The case studies in this chapter are all from a high ranking research university in Norway and they are conducted within the field of educational research. There has been little interest in researching writing in departments of Norwegian or English in Norwegian universities, which may be surprising given the strong standing of composition research in English departments in the United States. Norwegian writing researchers have primarily been located in education (particularly in the field of higher education and teacher education) and in applied linguistics.[3] Writing research in education is often an integral part of an effort to improve students' teaching and learning environment, while in applied linguistics, there is often a more narrow text focus. An interesting feature of Norwegian universities is that an interdisciplinary course in 'university pedagogy' is compulsory for all new academic staff. This means that research-based knowledge about writing, feedback, supervision and technology is in demand. Our experience is that young Higher Education (HE) teachers see the importance of writing and feedback in their own career both as researchers and as teachers and are interested in ways of facilitating multiple perspectives from teachers and peers in their own students' writing of texts. In such a setting, case studies make sense.

Contextualisation

Norway is a small European country that is outside the European Union but still has been part of the Bologna process from its beginning. Student writing and writing instruction are deeply situated practices and cannot be understood apart from the macro and meso factors that shape them. The situation of student writing at

---

[2] Because all the case studies referred to in this chapter are either published or submitted, those interested in the methodology can find this by going to journals/books referred to.
[3] Norwegian writing research was introduced by Igland and Ongstad in *Written Communication* (2003a, 2003b).

Norwegian universities before a major reform in higher education in 2002 (the quality reform) can briefly be characterised as low demands at undergraduate level and very high demands at master's level. Undergraduate students had traditionally little or no compulsory writing except the final exam (in most cases, a sit-down exam of 6–8 hours). Training in sustained writing was lacking, and this became a problem for many graduate students.

The Bologna process has affected higher education across Europe and is also referred to by Chitez, Kruse, and Donahue and by Castelló and Iñesta (this volume) as the new context for academic writing in Europe. A major aim of the Bologna process was to align the education systems in order to facilitate student mobility. The members agreed to a 4-2-3 structure from bachelor to PhD, modularisation of all courses and a common credit system European Credit Transfer System [ECTS]. Norway has been in the forefront of implementing Bologna, and the quality reform was a direct result of this. Our bachelor level was reduced from 4 to 3 years; to compensate for this, the quality reform introduced more structured study programmes in modularised courses, more student active teaching, closer follow-up of students and more varied assessment forms. Research evaluation of the reform documented considerable increase in compulsory student writing at undergraduate level as well as in graduate courses, the proliferation of portfolios (which had been virtually unknown before the reform), increased amount and more systematic teacher feedback to student writing, more peer feedback and extended use of virtual learning environments (Dysthe, 2007, 2009). One of the unintended consequences of the increase in compulsory writing, particularly when coupled with continuous assessment, was that students reported to read less and also that they acted more strategically, that is, putting in minimum effort in all ungraded writing assignments.

Writing in Norwegian higher education follows the European tradition where it is integrated in disciplinary courses. This also means that 'writing teachers' are virtually non-existent and that it is the teachers in the disciplines who teach writing; if taught at all. A similar situation is described in this volume by Castelló and Iñesta in Spain; Delcambre and Donahue in France; and Chitez and Kruse in other European countries. An overall finding that can be drawn from my research studies about writing and feedback practices is that after the restructuring due to Bologna, the design of the study programme, the assessment form chosen and the use of digital technologies are the most decisive factors in shaping students' writing experiences. More attention is now given to planning study programmes as well as study design of courses. While individual teachers used to have a lot of freedom to design their own courses, after 2002, there is a Study Programme Committee for each discipline that secures more uniform and collective decisions about course content, progression and pedagogy; sometimes also writing assignments. If digital portfolios are chosen as the assessment form in particular courses, students in these courses will invariably write regularly. Other courses have just a final exam. Supervision and tutoring models as well as feedback formats may also be decided at a level above the individual teacher. This means that multiple voices may be *facilitated* by course design and models of supervision at both bachelor and postgraduate levels; in which case, it will affect *all* students.

The challenges of creating collaborative learning opportunities and of community building, however, require new ways of thinking and leading, and it is still up to the teacher how to use the opportunities afforded by the study design and the technology. I have chosen examples to illustrate some new trends in our country relating to how the choice of study design, technology and assessment may foster multivoicedness in ways that were unthinkable before when the autonomy of each teacher was almost limitless. This is another reason why my examples focus more on the meso than on the micro level. There are many studies in international literature of similar practices by individual writing teachers, but what is new are the efforts to make this more mainstream. Before presenting the case studies, the key concept needs to be explored theoretically.

Multivoicesness — A Bakhtin Inspired Concept

The key term of this chapter is closely associated with Mikhail Bakhtin's theories of dialogue. While 'dialogue' in everyday language primarily has been used in the narrow sense of face-to-face oral communication, Bakhtin is mostly concerned with the juxtaposition and interanimation of many voices. It is precisely the difference and the struggle between the diverse voices that constitute the great potential for meaning-making according to Bakhtin. This sets him apart from earlier dialogue theoretians from Socrates to Habermas, where consensus was a major goal (Burbules, 1993). Dialogue does not just happen because two or more people exchange information (Sidorkin 1999); it is the tension between conflicting and actively agreeing voices that constitute the productive aspect.

Bakhtin distinguishes between active and passive understanding. The latter affords no expansion of the dialogue; it is reproductive, contributes nothing new and does not lead to new insights. In the following quotation, Bakhtin explains what he means by *active understanding* and how the confrontation with different points of view and 'alien' voices and conceptual systems leads to new elements in our own understanding and thus also in our own discourse:

> Thus an active understanding, one that assimilates the word under consideration into a new conceptual system, that of the one striving to understand, establishes a series of complex interrelationships, consonances and dissonances with the word and enriches it with new elements. [...] It introduces totally new elements into his discourse; it is in this way, after all, that various different points of view, conceptual horizons, systems for providing expressive accents, various social "languages" come to interact with one another. The speaker strives to get a reading of his own word, and on his own conceptual system that determines this word, within the alien conceptual system of the understanding receiver; he enters into a dialogical relationship with certain aspects of this system. (1981, p. 282)

Related to this is Bakhtin's distinction between what he calls the 'authoritative' and the 'inner persuasive' word or discourse; a distinction also explored by Prior (1998) and Matusov (2009). By 'authoritative' Bakhtin means discourses where there is no room for doubt or critical questioning, while the 'internally persuasive' is based on a confrontation between different voices where ideas are tested through dialogue: 'The authoritative word demands that we acknowledge it, that we make it our own; it binds us, quite independent of any power it might have to persuade us internally; we encounter it with its authority already fused to it'. In contrast, 'the inner persuasive word is half-ours and half-someone else's' (Bakhtin, 1981, p. 342). This means taking a critical stance, 'experimenting with the text, questioning the author, imagining alternatives, evaluating diverse discourses, and challenging the text'. There is a constant struggle with others' internally persuasive discourses and for hegemony among ideological points of view, approaches, directions and values (*ibid.*, p. 345). In academic disciplines, where truths are always contested and where critical thinking and the ability to take a stance and to argue are highly valued, multivoiced discourse becomes particularly important. Students, however, often feel that what counts at exams is the ability to reproduce the authoritative word. This creates a tension and even a contradiction that also was seen in the case studies.

A classroom with students is always *potentially* multivoiced because it consists of people with different backgrounds and different viewpoints, but it takes a special effort from the teacher to design for multivoicedness and to facilitate the potential both orally and in writing. In this respect, 'multivoicedness' has the same Janus-faced duality that characterised 'dialogue'; it is simultaneously a *fact of life* (in classrooms as elsewhere) and a *goal to be pursued.*

Multivoicedness is also associated with the term 'polyphony'. The latter comes from music where a 'homophonic' composition is hierarchical with an overarching, melody voice and where the other voices are subservient. Bakhtin calls Dostoevsky's novel 'polyphonic' because the author gives his characters their own voice. When Bakhtin distinguishes between monologic and dialogic texts, he does not mean that just one voice exists in the monologic, but that there is a main voice that marginalises all the others. In academic writing, we want students to take authority of their own text; in doing so, they need to be familiar with and respect other voices. The philosophical basis for a monological text philosophy is idealism, and the linguistic presupposition is that the author is able to have complete semantic authority. For Bakhtin, this is impossible; nobody owns the word alone, as the text is always inhabited by other voices. When Bakhtin still talks about monological texts, it is when the author has suppressed the multivoicedness.[4] A closely related concept is 'intertextuality' (Bazerman 2004a), but I choose in this chapter to concentrate on multivoicedness. Rinck and Boch (this volume) refer to a number of studies contrasting expert and student writers' practices regarding how to position themselves among other relevant voices.

---

[4]In the article 'Revisiting dialogues and monologues', Tone Kvernbekk argues that monologues have been undervalued and that non-responsiveness is an ethical issue (2010).

Critical reading and writing are core competences in higher education. In order to create multivoiced texts, students need to be exposed to different voices. This may take place by reading texts related to the topic,[5] or by written and oral interaction with the teacher(s), peers and other knowledgeable people. Reading-to-write has always been a must in academia. Going back to Humboldt, the root of the modern European universities, students were supposed to spend most of their time pursuing knowledge through studying written sources. But as Otto Kruse has documented in his research on the Humboldtian seminar tradition, students were supposed to write regularly and to give and get what we today would call oral feedback from professors and fellow students in seminars (2006). The rationale behind this practice sounds familiar: the importance of different perspectives to the development of critical thinking and knowledge production. With mass education, this ideal of a community of teachers and students, which was the ideological foundation of the seminar, became largely restricted to postgraduate students, and even at that level often replaced by the supervisor–student dyad.

One of the major changes over the last decades has been the rediscovery of the crucial importance of the student writer's interaction with 'live' voices in the writing process at all levels, thus facilitating multivoicedness. Because the teaching of writing is organised in specific courses in the United States, it has been relatively easy to implement this in the design of such courses, for instance, peer discussion of drafts in class and writing groups of all kinds (Gere, 1987; Nystrand & Brandt, 1989; Tannacito, 2004). Such activities have therefore become mainstream in the teaching of writing in US higher education and can no longer be designated as a 'new trend'. However, in Europe and other parts of the world where writing is integrated in the disciplines and where the teaching and training of writing as a consequence will 'eat' of the time allocated to disciplinary content teaching, it is still common to leave the responsibility for multivoicedness in the process of writing to the individual student. Some other modes have developed over time; however, see, this volume, for instance, Carlino; Castelló and Iñesta. The introduction of digital technologies has also made it much easier to design for transparency and interaction among students while in the process of writing. The degree to which teachers and students make use of this varies a lot. In the first case study, students exchange texts through email, but they meet face to face in order to discuss their drafts. In the two last cases, the virtual learning environment (VLE) is a crucial part of the study design.

Postgraduate Writing Groups as Entrance to Academic Writing at PhD Level

> Group supervision in graduate education: A process of supervision skill development and text improvement. (Samara, 2006)

---

[5]'Text' is here used in an extended sense of multimodal text.

The background for this research study carried out by Akylina Samara (2006) was a national survey among doctoral studies in social science, which revealed disciplinary isolation as a major reason for the high percentage who did not finish. Carlino (in this volume) relates similar problems in the Argentinian context. One early hurdle that delayed the Norwegian doctoral students' progression in Samara's study was a compulsory essay in philosophy of science. She therefore chose this context for initiating cross-disciplinary writing groups. Students could choose their essay topic and had to present the finished product in a 45 minutes' public lecture. An open invitation to all PhD students resulted in 13 participants in a three-hour writing workshop held by Samara, which focused on the genre and on writing group processes. Three thematic groups were organised: economy and modelling, qualitative research methods and ethics. None of the students had any experience in writing academic texts except their master thesis and they had never had direct writing instruction. Some were quite sceptic to sharing texts in writing groups. The groups met for a three-hour face-to-face session every week and the activity focused on peer feedback to essay drafts. Samara participated in the two initial sessions in each group. Instructions and 'rules' were initially modelled on the rich literature on writing groups from the United States, but were modified to meet the specific needs in the group. Each group reported regularly to Samara and she also interviewed group members and had access to submitted drafts. The study drew on previously published writing group studies, for instance, Dochy, Seegers, and Sluijsmans (1999), Lonka (2003), and Peterson (2003).

The findings confirm the importance for students of getting access to different perspectives on their own texts. Particularly important for developing multi-voicedness and critical testing of their own perspectives and viewpoints were the oral discussions of drafts in the groups. Students themselves said they were more reluctant to express disagreements and challenges in writing than orally. Face-to-face dialogues gave them opportunities to follow up arguments and a chance to modify their positions. This was important because they often developed their own perspectives through meeting opposition. By listening to others, they also became more certain about what they actually thought themselves and they got several chances to reformulate. This is a very commonplace experience, but it is interesting that no arena for such dialogic exchanges had been available for them as PhD students (see also Carlino, this volume).

Another finding had to do with defining and developing the genre of the critical academic essay. Philosophy of science was taught by philosophers and the students who came from very different traditions in the social sciences had great problems finding out what was expected from them. Through discussing the assignment in the writing groups as well as reading peers' attempt at different formats and ways of structuring the text, they came up with their own way of solving the task. The confidence gained in this communal forum was very important for them when they made their first public presentation as PhD students.

Not all the groups functioned equally well. One problem was when groups failed to keep a regular meeting schedule. Another was 'free-riders' who were not willing to spend sufficient time on fellow students' drafts but still expected substantial feedback on their own. These are common findings regardless of institutional level. But the study also showed a discrepancy between what PhD students wanted of institutional support and what they got. Students clearly stated that such groups should be an integrated part of the study programme offered to PhD students, while the prevailing attitude among faculty leadership was to leave it to the initiative of students themselves. The establishment of research schools, however, has gradually changed the traditional privatisation of responsibility at PhD level in Norway and other Scandinavian countries, also regarding writing. Case studies like the one by Samara have provided knowledge about how such groups can be productive. Even at master level, the writing of the thesis used to be a lonely affair with varying degree of supervision, but after the quality reform, master programmes provide a lot of support. The next case is an example of how a new supervision model changed teacher and student practices.

Foregrounding Student Voices — A Fragile Success Story

> Multivoiced supervision of Master's students: a case study of alternative supervision practices in higher education. (Dysthe, Samara, & Westrheim, 2006)

Graduate and postgraduate supervision has got much attention internationally over the last decade, and Norway is no exception. One major reason is that the traditional one-to-one supervision practice often failed to give students the support and the challenges needed to write their thesis. To design for multivoiced teacher and peer supervision was one way of meeting this situation.

A new supervision model was tried out with three cohorts of students in a two-year master programme in education from 2002 to 2005, and a research study was conducted to document and analyse the results of this innovation The model consisted of a combination of three supervision arenas: regular meetings of student colloquia, supervision groups consisting of two to three supervisors with their master students (four to six) and individual supervision. The student colloquia met once a week and had a wide agenda: discussion of theory and method, discussion and feedback of early drafts as well as sharing of personal issues. The supervision groups met every third week. Two or three students' drafts were discussed each time (distributed electronically three days ahead). These meetings were strictly structured, with clear leadership, rules and routines, while the colloquia were more informally structured. Individual supervision meetings varied in frequency and primarily dealt with longer texts.

An overview of the findings of the research study comparing the particular contributions of each of the three supervision arenas are presented in Figure 11.1

Student colloquia	Supervision groups (8–10)	Individual supervision
(5–7 students)	(2–3 supervisors and their master stud)	
Multivoiced	*Multivoiced*	*Dialogical and monological*
Students give and get feedback	Students give and get feedback	Student get feedback
Peers provide	*Two (3) supervisors & peers provide*	*Supervisor provide*
a 'safe haven'	– divergent voices	engagement in
a place for	– disciplinary knowledge	– project
– emotions	– authority	– the student
– sharing problems	– structure	sharing of responsibility for
– support and encouragement	– interesting discussions	progress and quality
a first filter for new ideas	– strategic focus	
Feedback characteristics	*Feedback characteristics*	*Feedback characteristics*
Low threshold (easy to share)	High threshold (anxiety of sharing unfinished texts)	– generally low threshold
Supportive and critical	Supportive and critical	– focus on all levels of text
Focus on writer's concerns	Main focus on ideas, method and theory	– several versions of same text
Real readers (audience)	Many perspectives, many ideas and suggestions	– revisions expected
Peers are good at	Supervisors good models for peer response strategies	
– reformulation		
– questions		
– confidence building		

Figure 11.1: Characteristic aspects of three supervision arenas[6].

Only students' own experiences of multivoicedness in the different arenas will be highlighted here. First, the colloquia functioned as 'sorting-out' arenas for ideas and texts in very early stages, and students relied on discussion with their peers to decide whether ideas were worth pursuing or discarding. If in doubt they brought them to the

---

[6]For a comprehensive analysis, see article in *Studies in Higher Education* (Dysthe et al., 2006)

supervision groups. Second, the colloquia provided a structured space for students to share their fears of failure and their desires to succeed, their frustrations and their joys (Lee & Boud, 2003). The colloquia seemed to have an important function in forming the students' academic identities. In this safe and nurturing environment, they learnt that the mixture of fear and desire, of failure and success that each of them thought was particular to them was a common denominator instead of an individual problem. Learning to handle conflicting emotions and to turn potentially debilitating fear and ambitions into working energy was reported to have been very important for the participants' progress. The multivoiced peer feedback thus had a distinctively different role to play than the multivoicedness of the supervision groups, offering a space not just for the disciplinary but also for the personal dimension. There has been an increasing awareness in the literature about writing of the emotional side of writing, aspects that have been privatised and under-communicated (McLeod, 1997). Students also highlighted that the development of trust and community in the colloquia were prerequisites for the success of the high stakes supervision groups.

Key factors in the supervision groups were mutual obligation and engagement, regularity, structure and clear leadership. One of the clearest finding was that in spite of students' initial reluctance to engage time and effort in fellow students' texts, they agreed on the benefit of giving and getting feedback. Students themselves mentioned multivoicedness and co-construction of knowledge as most important in the groups. Similarly, Carlino (this volume) found that it was useful for Argentinian graduate students to engage in other students' work by giving feedback, particularly in groups. Another finding in the Norwegian study was that the participation of two or more supervisors in each group added considerably to the variety of perspectives and also towards legitimising disagreement. Interestingly, although not surprising from a Bakhtinian point of view, the latter was seen by the students as a particular asset: 'Actually I prefer it when there is disagreement between the supervisors; this helps me think better and more critically'. And another student added, 'Teachers should disagree more often'. What they both experienced was that divergent thinking sparked more creativity than consensus and that dialogic co-construction of knowledge is a strong element in academic knowledge production.

Systematic use of supervision groups has been rare in the humanities and social sciences where there is a strong culture of individual projects. In the natural sciences, however, students often work in research groups with several researchers whose projects are interdependent. Rommetveit (1974) wrote about the importance of TSSR, 'a temporarily shared social reality' among dialogue partners. This also turned out to be a crucial factor for the success of the model described above. Students needed to learn about each others' project in order to give productive feedback, and oral project presentations were built into the study design from the very beginning. It was a surprise for students to discover how much they learned from engaging in peer projects, even when quite different from their own.

The research evaluation of the new 'multivoiced supervision model' concluded that it was a success story in the sense that both the master students and the supervisors agreed that students improved their writing and finished faster. The grades were also higher than in previous cohorts. It was a 'fragile' success, however, because the implementation of such a model required a degree of theoretical alignment and practical commitment from the teachers that disappeared when the department expanded. From being the model for all, it became a choice for 'dialogically minded' supervisors. Nevertheless, the model has been influential and also inspired similar projects in other universities.

Writing at Bachelor Level — Potentials of Multivoicedness in Digital Portfolios

> Digital portfolios and feedback practices in a traditional university course. (Dysthe & Tolo, 2007)

> New and changing teacher roles in a digital age. (Wake, Dysthe, & Mjelstad, 2007)

The next examples of how study designs may foster multivoiced communication are from history and law. History is a pedagogically traditional university discipline in the sense that the design usually consisted of lectures, seminars and sit-down written exams. The history department in this case study, however, introduced digital portfolios in a number of bachelor courses from year 2000. The rationale was that students could not learn history without continuous writing; this was how they learnt 'to think like a historian'. Because the existing virtual learning systems were not designed to suit their pedagogical purposes, one of the teachers developed a new VLE called KARK (the name of a thrall in Norse sagas), purpose-built to handle teacher and peer feedback.[7]

Feedback from the teacher was dependent on students' posting their feedback to two peers first; a common way of making sure students read fellow student texts. All texts and comments are visible to all students registered on the course and all teachers in the department. The public nature of the comments in Kark is a feature possible in all VLEs, but the extent of access was a conscious pedagogical choice by those who designed the study programme. Students had access to all peers' drafts and feedback in their own course, and teachers had unlimited access. The rationale for full transparency was to give students, as well as teachers, the chance to learn from each other's voices. Interestingly, the department leadership reported that the quality of teacher feedback had improved as a result of their access to colleagues' comments. Students soon discovered who were the best writers and feedback providers and not surprisingly prioritised reading those. The evaluation surveys that were carried out each semester showed that students consistently rated highest the learning effect of reading fellow students' text and teacher comments. Giving feedback scored second and peer comments third.

---

[7]For a description of KARK and its functions, see Wake et al. (2007).

The teacher role was affected by the digital portfolios. Since students had to comment on two peer texts before getting teacher comments, the teacher also had to read and evaluate student feedback and decide whether or not to comment on their comments: 'In the beginning teachers and TAs only commented when we disagreed. This was clearly a mistake and we started to acknowledge good student comments, for instance: 'Very pertinent comment- I totally agree'. This was enough to give students the assurance they needed. It may seem like a minor issue, but it actually turned out to be a very important part of our job' (Teacher D) (Wake et al., 2007). The portfolio system made writing the backbone of the study design in the courses where it was introduced, and it was no longer up to the individual teacher to choose assessment format. Writing assignments structured students' work and therefore the negotiation of assignments also became a collective task. Teachers reported that their role was changing. In another traditional discipline, law studies, changes for *students* were even more revolutionary.

A Complete Change of Pedagogical Design in Law Studies

Productive learning in the study of law: The role of technology in the learning ecology of a law faculty. (Vines & Dysthe, 2009)

Multivoiced e-feedback in the study of law: Enhancing learning opportunities? (Vines, 2009)

After the quality reform, the Faculty of Law completely redesigned its study programme. Instead of relying on lectures, self study and comprehensive sit-down exams, a structured weekly cycle was implemented for years 1–3 consisting of a lecture, a writing assignment discussed in groups, peer and tutor feedback on texts submitted in the VLE. Student writing was moved from the periphery to the centre of the study design. As a result, an amazing quantity of student text was produced, the failure rate at exams was reduced and grades improved (Vines & Dysthe, 2009).

Electronic feedback became an intrinsic part of discourse and assessment practices in this bachelor programme. In a micro-ethnographic study, Vines examines how electronic-mediated peer feedback shapes and is shaped by the broader sociocultural context (2009). His point of departure is that earlier research shows that networked technologies *per se* do not guarantee educationally productive dialogues. Andriessen et al. (2003) claimed for instance that the quality of student networked dialogues was often quite poor: 'Participants seem to be keen at avoiding conflict, do not really discuss the plausibility and strength of produced information and are not much concerned with the argumentative quality of the resulting text' (p. 107). This conclusion is echoed by Arnseth and Ludvigsen (2006), Rourke and Kanuka (2007) and others who found that much research on computer-supported collaborative learning (CSCL) reports a lack of discussion, argumentation and challenging ideas and that ambiguity, disagreements or diverging ideas are seldom resolved in any productive manner.

Vines analysed more than 1,800 electronic student feedback utterances produced by law students as response to mandatory assignments in three courses in year 1 of law. He categorised peer comments as affirmatory, evaluative and challenging feedback. By comparing and contrasting the core differences of these, Vines argues especially for the productive learning aspects of challenging feedback. Even though confirmative and evaluative feedback may be useful by providing motivation, reformulation of their own ideas and examples of other styles of writing, it is the *challenging* feedback where the response giver represents a contrasting and critical voice, which is productive in the sense that the writer is moved to new ways of thinking and writing.

> The overall findings suggest that systematic multivoiced e-feedback offers students unique opportunities to develop their own authoritative voice and grow as independent thinkers who are able use the unique voices they meet as raw material for their own meaning-making in the discipline. Here it is important also to underline that this is a long-term goal that may only be accomplished because the feedback system is integrated in the teaching and learning system over the three first years. (*ibid.*, p. 23)

The new design of the study program in law 'represents a break with a long tradition of the student as a solo performer who focuses on competition and therefore keeps things for herself' (*ibid.*). Vines underlines the importance of structuring and integrating e-feedback into the curriculum, but he also outlines measures that are necessary if students are to get the full benefit of multivoiced e-feedback, for instance, better training in what it takes to give challenging feedback and 'closer consideration of the balance between just learning the exam genres and fostering independent thinkers for future work in highly demanding professions' (*ibid.*).

Discussion of Future Challenges

In this chapter, I have drawn on six case studies from a research university in Norway in order to show how facilitating multivoicedness, particularly in connection with feedback, has been a major element in the improvements of students' writing and learning environment in several disciplines over the last decade. The term itself may be rejected by teachers as esoteric educational language, but exposing students to multiple perspectives is widely acknowledged in higher education as important for improving students' critical thinking and implicitly also for their writing. In most European universities, however, it is left to the individual student to actively engage with the diverse voices in their writing process. This is where 'my' case studies differ and present an institutional challenge. They document that institutional initiatives not only facilitate but also ensure students' active engagement with multiple voices through the design of study plans and pedagogical use of technology. Such initiatives, however, presuppose academic leaders who are interested in and knowledgeable about teaching. A broader notion of academic leadership, based on *collective responsibility* for students teaching and learning processes and learning outcomes, seems to be emerging at post-Bologna universities. One of the consequences is an increasing interest in educational research, which may be used to underpin institutional decisions. I will briefly discuss feedback research and theory as an illustration of how different types of research may be useful at meso and micro level.

There has been a lot of research on feedback over the last decades and a number of meta-studies have concluded that feedback greatly impacts the quality of student performance and effectively promotes student learning across disciplinary areas (Black & Wiliam, 1998; Hattie & Timperley, 2007; Shute, 2008). Such studies have had an impact in higher education; not only in the United Kingdom where feedback has become one of the indicators of study quality, but also in Norway where there is a considerable increase in teacher feedback. But what research message is being heard, beyond the fact that feedback is important? Feedback research seems to have three different theoretical foundations. The first is predominantly behavioural and focuses on effective delivery of feedback to students. The second is based on constructivism, emphasising student autonomy and self-regulation, and the third is based on sociocultural perspectives and highlights the importance of joint activity (Dysthe, 2009; Dysthe, Lillejord, Vines, & Wasson, 2011).

One major challenge for the latter perspective is the difficulty of documenting the *effect* on student writing of dialogic feedback practices in ways that clearinghouses can use to promote 'evidence-based' practice. Theoretically grounded case studies like the ones in this chapter cannot easily be synthesised, and thus, they make less impact on educational policy. Haswell (2005) has criticised writing research for lacking studies that are replicable, agreeable and data supported, and he has recommended a shift in methodologies. Mixed method studies may be one of the answers, but in my view, it is also important to find new ways of synthesising qualitative studies. One reason is that while meta-studies and quantifiable findings may influence leaders and decision makers at macro and meso level, case studies have a greater potential of influencing teachers' practices. Teachers need rich documentation and thick descriptions in order to fill new study designs with best practice at the micro level of everyday interaction with students and their writing. My claim is that theoretically grounded case studies of writing and feedback practices may provide inspiration as well as guidance for change.

Bakhtin's distinction between 'the authoritative' and 'the inner persuasive word' is an example of theory that makes sense for practitioners. The authoritative model of feedback has been the default model for most teachers in higher education, based on the authority of the expert and on the conduit metaphor of communication (Reddy, 1979). The pedagogical problem may then be reduced to effectively informing students of what they need to do with their text. The dialogic model, as shown in the theory section, is based on a different epistemology where the development of knowledge is dependent on joint activity and on the testing of divergent perspectives. Without an understanding of the theoretical rationale, teachers may find this an ineffective use of time. However, when Bakhtin emphasises the productive power of multiple viewpoints, diverging voices, disagreement and even provocations, this resonates well with ideals of writing in higher education — where knowledge claims are always contested. An important part of academic socialisation of students is therefore to help them deal with opposing viewpoints and perspectives. Multivoiced feedback that challenges the writer and suggests alternative ways of thinking and writing is therefore crucial to the core of higher education values. Case study research from a variety of disciplines may show ways of implementing this at both meso and micro levels and thus improve student writing.

Chapter 12

Helping Doctoral Students of Education to Face Writing and Emotional Challenges in Identity Transition

Paula Carlino

> Learning is particularly drenched in deep emotional issues, precisely
> because learning expands us beyond the secure realms of habit and
> prior senses of the self into new areas of competence and participation.
> (Bazerman, 2001, pp. 185–186)

Introduction

The difficulties that postgraduate students experience in order to bring forth their
theses have been documented in numerous studies (e.g., Ahern & Manathunga, 2004;
Kiley & Wisker, 2009; Lundell & Beach, 2002). As a consequence, the PhD
completion rate is between 50% and 60% in Australia (Martin, Maclachlan, &
Karmel, 2001) and the United States (Council of Graduate Schools, 2007). In
Argentina there are no systematic data but the estimated rate is much lower
(Jeppesen, Nelson, & Guerrini, 2004). Developing a thesis is, therefore, a goal that
eludes many, especially in the fields of social sciences and humanities (Ehrenberg,
Jakubson, Groen, So, & Price, 2007).

What is it about the writing of a thesis that makes it so difficult to complete?
Besides requiring of the candidates the acquisition of conceptual and methodological
knowledge, it is also an unfamiliar genre which demands a new kind of writing.
Furthermore, doctoral research also entails the development of personal capabilities

University Writing: Selves and Texts in Academic Societies
Studies in Writing, Volume 24, 217–234
Copyright © 2012 by Emerald Group Publishing Limited
All rights of reproduction in any form reserved
ISSN: 1572-6304/doi:10.1108/S1572-6304(2012)0000024016

(e.g., tolerance for uncertainty and perseverance in the face of failures). These are needed to address critical creative work (Lovitts, 2005), to cope with the disorientation caused by working in a field in which they often have little experience and references (Delamont & Atkinson, 2001) and to be able to persevere in an uncertain undertaking which shows no signs of reaching a successful fruition until close to the very end (Styles & Radloff, 2000).

Research shows that the main obstacle in social sciences is the weak academic integration (Lovitts & Nelson, 2000, Tinto, 1993) or the scarcity of exchanges (Delamont, Atkinson, & Parry, 1997). This may be linked to thesis work performed outside of a research team, the irregular dedication of those who lack scholarships (Evans, 2002), and the isolation that they experience (Miller & Brimicombe, 2004). Furthermore, many candidates feel disheartened by the magnitude of the task, given the fact that it does not usually show intermediate-range achievements (Manathunga, 2005). They often doubt about their ability to finish their theses (Appel & Dahlgren, 2003; Carlino, 2003; Castelló, 2007; Ngcongo, 2000). Such problems are enhanced when there is no supervisor especially committed to holding frequent meetings with the students in order to guide them through the stages of their work. This situation is endemic in the field of social sciences in Argentina (Carlino, 2005b).

In line with these studies, the core idea of this chapter is that the production of a doctoral thesis brings to bear challenges beyond conceptual, methodological, and writing knowledge. Delving into a research culture and being accepted as a full member involves learning new modes of doing and behaving, in a process of academic enculturation and identity transformation (McAlpine & Amundsen, 2008; Prior & Bilbro, this volume; see also Castelló & Iñesta, this volume, for the relationship between social and authorial identity). This slow change is often accompanied by the tensions and emotions that are typically activated in humans when they are exposed to the gaze of members of the community which they aspire to join (Boice, 1993; Britton, 1994; Carlino, 2003, 2005b). This is especially true when the candidates are unsure as to whether they can successfully carry out what the task will demand.

Several universities in the world have implemented institutional mechanisms to improve the writing development of PhD candidates (e.g., Aitchison & Lee, 2006; Cargill, 2004; Chanock, 2007; Dysthe, this volume; Dysthe et al., 2006; Rienecker, 2003; Rose & McClafferty, 2001; Rubdy, 2005; Zuber-Skerritt & Knight, 1986). Although some workshops allow for the exploration of the feelings involved in the doctoral experience (Lee & Boud, 2003; Lonka, 2003), it is not common for writing to be used as a way to reflect on the difficulties encountered.

In this chapter, I analyze a seminar that sought to create an environment in which these emotions could be shared through the work of academic writing. First I outline the status of writing in Argentine universities. Second, I describe the tasks undertaken in the seminar, their theoretical foundations, the participants and the graduate program. Then, I specify the corpus and strategy of analysis used to characterize the emotions involved in the experiences of these doctoral students, followed by the transcript of some of their voices in order to illustrate the topics that emerged. Finally, I briefly explore the relationship between the emotions which came to light through writing and the action of writing about them.

Writing in Argentine Universities

In Argentinian university Social Sciences and Humanities divisions, writing is usually required for assessment purposes, but is seldom supported in the disciplines. Viewed as a prolongation of a generalizable skill that should have been previously learnt, it is taken for granted. For that reason, students often receive scant guidelines and feedback. Since university teachers rarely consider academic writing as a learning tool, undergraduates are rarely given the opportunity to draft and rewrite afterwards (Carlino, 2010, in press). Conceived of as a medium of communication to convey already-formed thoughts, writing is regarded as "a textual product rather than an intellectual process" (Carter, Miller, & Penrose, 1998).

In contrast, the doctoral seminar described in this chapter acknowledges and nurtures the epistemic power of writing. In addition, based on a situated learning approach of academic enculturation (see Prior & Bibro, this volume), it has been designed to help students take part in the practice of writing precise texts for specific audiences, instead of teaching a general decontextualized technique.

The Doctoral Writing Seminar

A 33-hour writing workshop was developed over a 20-month period and delivered in two parts:

1. 4 classes of 3 h over a 2 1/2 month period and
2. a year later, 7 classes over a 6-month period (4 meetings before the summer vacation period and 3 meetings afterwards).

This temporal arrangement was aimed at working with students' different needs due to their progress in their postgraduate study. The second part of the workshop was intentionally split by a vacation period to allow for plenty of time devoted to writing.

The seminar included several different tasks focused around the process of writing, group and peer reviewing, and rewriting two scientific texts. During the first year of candidature, when they had not even defended their thesis proposal, students were asked to write a dissertation abstract as if their dissertation were finished. The purpose of this task was to encourage writing as an epistemic tool to develop their research problem and plan their theses work as a whole, taking into account the coherence among aims, research questions, methods, foreseen findings, and relevance of their prospective study. A year later, in the second part of the seminar, they had to write an abstract and then a paper with work in progress regarding their theses and find an appropriate scientific conference to submit it and present it.

Additionally, they were assigned several "subjective" reflective texts: an initial autobiography of themselves as writers, before the beginning of the workshop and after receiving by e-mail the professor's autobiography, a letter telling their experience as doctoral students at the beginning of the second year, and at the end of the first and the second parts of the seminar, two reflective and evaluative accounts about their work in the seminar.

Besides the written assignments, the workshop started with an exploration of several PhD theses and thesis proposals in Education. Because these texts are not easily available for students in the Argentine context (in fact, research proposals constitute an "occluded genre" (Swales, 1996)), the professor brought them in a bag and distributed them to groups of three students. The task was to analyze and extract their features (number of pages, structure, type of information and relative extension of each chapter, titles, subtitles, verbal tense and person used in each, forms and functions of citations and their location, etc.). This analysis lead to a discussion about who the readers of these texts are, what purposes their authors have, what function is fulfilled by each part of the dissertation, whether its intention is explanatory or argumentative, etc. The need to insert the PhD contribution within the theoretical debates of a field of study was also elucidated, dismantling the stressful belief of original work as absolute novelty but requiring entering in an established conversation at the same time. To sum up, during the first and second classes, we characterized the thesis and the thesis proposal genres as social practices within specific communities, and abstracted the similarities among texts understanding that they are instituted means to accomplish similar writers' aims.

Linked to this genre analysis, the IMRD structure was explained considering the function that its parts (Introduction, Method, Results, and Discussion) serve in the research disseminating actions of a scientific community. We listed the text types which constitute the academic genre set (research report, thesis, conference paper, research proposal, abstract, etc.) and pointed out how the IMRD structure was expanded, condensed, or cut across them. To show the relevance there is in learning to write an abstract, its central role in the academic writing practices was highlighted. We discussed when, who, in which situations, for what purposes, etc., abstracts were written and read in the investigative world (see *scientific academic genres* in Russell and Cortes' Figure 1.1, this volume).

The second part of the seminar began with an exploration of different calls for papers in Education conferences that students were asked to gather in advance, in order to choose one conference to present their dissertation work in progress. A shorter but analogous genre analysis was performed with conference proposals.

Over the entire workshop, the task of giving and receiving peer critique was assigned as regular homework. This was modelled on the shared review that took place in most of the classes, in which two or three students delivered copies of their drafts to be collectively read and reviewed. During this joint activity, multivoiced feedback (Dysthe, this volume) was coordinated by the professor, who commented on the drafts after the students did. In addition to giving her viewpoint, she synthesized students' responses, highlighting agreements and discrepancies among them. Participants were advised to comment first on content, structure, and substantive aspects (e.g., clarity, coherence, thematic progression, adjustment to genre expectations, and authorial image). They were also taught to pay attention to the consistency among the components of the research design (Maxwell, 1996).

Sometimes, the group also offered indications about how to modify certain portions of the text. In addition to textual problems, the positive aspects had to be pointed out. In all cases, reviewers were encouraged to justify their suggestions. The student authors whose texts were the focus of feedback were advised not to respond to comments during the session and, instead, to take notes about them. They would have to consider them in order to rethink their drafts afterwards.

At the end of each part of the seminar, the students' work was assessed through an individual portfolio in which they included a sequence of the drafts they wrote, the feedback they received, the improvement plan for their texts, along with their initial autobiography, the letter with their experience after one year of doctoral training, and a reflective account about their involvement in the different tasks during the seminar.

The professor made explicit that the philosophy of the workshop was not normative. Academic writing could not be reduced to following rules. Instead, the seminar attempted to promote the development of genre and rhetorical awareness. This meant that the improvement of students' drafts was usually a matter of taking into account the relationship between the authors' intentions and the effects that textual choices may have on the likely audience. It was necessary to develop an understanding of its probable expectations (the typical discourse actions this audience would expect in a definite situation), and the initial description of the genre would help on this. Therefore, the challenge was to learn to envision the point of view of the reader in order to minimize the gap between the writer's purposes and the reader's anticipated response.

Pedagogical Framework

The coursework included in the writing workshop was designed taking into account different and complementary contributions:

1. The concept of writing not only as a rhetorical and communicative practice but also as an epistemic process (Flower, 1979; Hayes & Flower, 1986; Scardamalia & Bereiter, 1985). Further, the idea of writing as pertaining both to the "context of justification" and to the "context of discovery," in terms of Popper's epistemology (1934; Carlino, 2006).
2. The analysis of scientific genres, both in their textual features (Hyland, 2002, 2003; Swales, 1990) and as social activities (Artemeva, 2008; Bakhtin, 2002; Bazerman, 1988; Maingueneau, 2002; Miller, 1984).
3. The pedagogy of academic writing, which emphasises the need to teach how to give and receive critical comments on a piece of writing within a nonthreatening low-stakes situation (Aitchison, 2003; Caffarella & Barnet, 2000).
4. Central issues of research methodology such as the search for coherence among the different parts of the research design (Maxwell, 1996; Rienecker, 2003).

5. The concept of academic integration as a central factor in "doctoral persistence" (Lovitts & Nelson, 2000; Tinto, 1993) and how writing groups can relate to it.
6. The idea that learning (Bazerman, 2001; Pichon-Rivière, 1971) and academic writing (Bloom, 1981; Britton, 1994) are stressful challenges and, in particular, the experience of doing a thesis as part of a process of identity change (Lee & Boud, 2003; McAlpine & Amundsen, 2008) plenty of emotions (Manathunga, 2005; Morrison-Saunders, Moore, Newsome, & Newsome, 2005) and not just as a cognitive issue. Related to this, the role that text-work can play in identity-work (Kamler & Thomson, 2004) and the usefulness of creative writing to deal with emotional issues related to learning (Creme & Hunt, 2002).

The Students

Since 2005, the seminar was iterated with five cohorts of part-time Education doctoral students, having five to eleven students at a time. Most of them were over 40 years old and had a professional rather than academic career, although several of them had defended a master thesis (in Argentina this is not a requisite for doing a PhD). Only 5 students were under 30 years old studying on a full time basis inside a research group.

The Graduate Program

Argentina has an established tradition in Laboratory Sciences PhDs but a shorter history regarding Education doctorates. This means not only that the doctoral program in which this seminar took place was in its early stages but also that the available dissertation supervisors were few, overloaded with work and usually not full time professors in the same university where the doctoral program was being taught. Team research, co-authorship with supervisors, and learning from advanced students was seldom expected. At the same time, the idea of what PhD work entails was under construction and therefore not a given in the academic culture.

In this context, the writing workshop examined in this chapter was part of an unusual three-year long dissertation seminar in which students were guided to elaborate the thesis proposal and assisted to begin their thesis work with the help of other professors and through assignments other than the ones analyzed here.

Corpus and Method of Analysis

The material analyzed in this chapter involves the reflective notes included in the portfolios of the doctoral students. Using an interpretative-qualitative approach, the analysis aimed to understand the experiences from the point of view of those who were involved. The students' notes were read, initially as separate cases and later seeking common themes among them. This coding process became more precise in several re-readings of the material that aimed to arrange themes in general categories. Finally, the writing of this chapter also helped to further refine themes and coordinate them in relation to one another.

Students' Reflections on the Seminar Tasks

The most recurring themes that emerged in this data analysis were the insecurity of doctoral students, their sense of vulnerability when observed by others, the workshop as a stimulus for writing, and the temporary building of self-confidence every time they achieved their goals. Other themes that appeared in student texts include gaining a more accurate understanding of doctoral work during the workshop; getting to know the academic community which they long to be a part of; the anxiety they experience when writing, knowing that their text will undergo many changes until they achieve what is expected; their relief upon perceiving that the workshop allowed them to express their personal feelings of incompetence without making them feel guilty; the pleasure they got out of certain writing assignments versus the painful challenge of others; the overcoming of certain writer's block as a result of the workshop assignments; writing as a method for thinking and not only for communicating, and the contribution of peers in revising their own texts.

To illustrate how the experience of writing as a PhD student "is drenched in deep emotional issues" (Bazerman, 2001), I provide quotes from students reflective notes, which were submitted in their portfolios at the end of each part of the workshop.

1. Students perceived the assignment of writing their "autobiography as writers" at the beginning of the seminar as an opportunity to reflect on their personal history and see where they were in terms of the challenge of the doctoral thesis. The thesis was seen as part of a rite of passage in which members of a community would assess them personally and not just their written product:

   > [I believe that writing one's autobiography is] Very valuable because it encourages you to hold a very personal dialogue with yourself [...] Very valuable in terms of exposing oneself to others, almost like a drill-practice [...] of the baptism of fire that comes when you introduce yourself in (academic) society, a presentation that has a personal charge as strong as a doctoral thesis.

   > it allows you to clarify the "symbolic" starting point for undertaking the task of writing, one's relationship to writing and the emotions that it provokes, in order to have them in mind when it comes to writing something as emotionally demanding as the thesis.

The assignment also encouraged students to get to know one another and to strengthen their mutual bonds:

> By reading the [autobiographies] of the other students, I got to know them professionally, academically and personally in a way that I would not have been able to otherwise, thus increasing the group's trust.

> it increased my expectations of the course. I really enjoyed exchanging these writings, and it was also a useful tool in terms of the familiarization and unity of the group.

Although it was not written in their portfolios, some students expressed that receiving the professors' autobiography at the beginning of the seminar was an unusual welcome. They also declared that the autobiography assignment laid the foundations for an atypical course, in which the personal "nonacademic" issues were also taken into account. Nonetheless, a few of the students felt uneasy because the assignment exposed them publicly:

> The task of writing an autobiography as a writer is an uncomfortable one, since it inevitably brings up issues about certain aspects of one's private life.

2. Skimming and analyzing theses and thesis proposals aided students in getting an idea of the written pieces they would have to submit and gave them a clearer understanding of the uses given to the pieces by the community they wish to become a part of. This knowledge had a reassuring effect:

> "Looking" at other people's theses helps diminish the reverential fear that slowly grows in academic circles. For me, in particular, it really kept me grounded to think about the specific people who would be reading my thesis – something I hadn't thought of in the past. The reader I imagined was academia as a whole, and this was an obstacle to writing, since it is impossible to write for such a vast, plural public.

> it allowed us to look at different styles, structures, presentations [...] to see how they resolved things and understand that it can be done.

3. Writing a 400-word dissertation abstract (including "findings") before starting their dissertation seemed like an impossible task at the beginning. The professor invited students to approach the assignment as both a fictional writing game and a tool to develop their thesis proposals. Very soon, the students saw the assignment as a license to write without inhibition because it was a "game" with no losers. After three classes of writing, revising, and rewriting their abstracts, the students appreciated the task for several reasons:

> like a fun, motivating game [...] moving forward on what didn't "yet exist" and willed to be brought into being. I got excited about it and it

encouraged me to come up with definitions and to take a chance on some answers [...] I felt like I could play the simulation game [...] Maybe this 5th version won't look anything like the final one but right now, I can say it helped me make progress and keep me going [...] Preparing the abstract forced me to make decisions about my thesis and made me feel like "it can exist."

The process of imagining the finished thesis was not only relieving but also inspiring:

It's like making the task of imagining something official, allowing yourself to go faster than you usually would go in order to "be there" before you arrive, and thus get an idea of the dimensions and acknowledge one's problems and the necessary steps.

Imagining that the thesis is already done can really calm you down, but most of all, I thought it was great to write about something that is, to a certain extent, fictional, imaginary, unreal.

Writing the abstract encouraged students to consider the different components of their intended research as a whole, and to check that they formed a coherent unit in advance:

it was a very useful strategy for rethinking certain global aspects of the research that we are about to undertake [...] to anticipate some of the central work themes

it gave me a global vision of how to develop the thesis, allowing me to perceive theoretical inconsistencies and methodological issues that had not yet been resolved and to evaluate the quality of what I had proposed to investigate.

It also made students ponder over possible outcomes of the research they were envisioning and assess its significance:

It helped me get better organized and allowed me to think about my hypotheses, as well. Up until now, I had only thought about the goals.

It made us think about the potential findings and sketch an interpretation of them.

The task of writing the abstract was considered to be very useful in prompting students to develop their thesis proposal:

it forced me to come up with a better definition of my subject of study and the main question I wanted to answer.

> The abstract has "yanked" on my outline plan and has forced me to go back to it time after time, increasing its communicability.

> When I look at the first abstract I handed in and compare it with the last one, I see that in a short time, I made significant advances in organizing my ideas for the thesis.

Many students appreciated the task because observing their progress boosted their self-confidence:

> When I started the workshop, I was in a very particular, complicated stage of non-productiveness in terms of my doctoral thesis project [...] Today, after three or four versions of the abstract, I am in a totally different situation. I am not convinced that the summary fully expresses the research that I am going to do, but I do believe that I am going to find the topic [...] The workshop gave me a push; it awakened my curiosity and my confidence.

> it allowed me to clarify my own ideas about my thesis project, to get over the writer's block [...] and to increase my self-esteem to some degree because I was able to effectively produce and make some progress in my thesis project.

After several rewritings, some students felt they had a decent written product to show outside the seminar. The abstract of their future dissertation was perhaps the first tangible structured *logos* after a creative process only experienced as chaos:

> it allowed me to start writing about what I imagine will be my thesis. It was the first thing I managed to send to my thesis advisor and her feedback was positive [...] This was the push that helped me unblock myself and put my ideas down in the abstract.

> [the abstract served as a] tool for communicating with actors outside the workshop [...] the "cover letter" of my progress in the Thesis Workshop and in meetings with my advisor.

4. The collective review of abstracts in class along with peer critique between classes served many purposes.[1] In the first place, it "taught" students that no good work

---

[1] Group or peer review and giving/receiving feedback are very rare tasks in school or university curriculum in Argentina.

is born finished: recursively drafting one's ideas was an expected academic practice, not a sign of failure or incompetence:

> I learned to deal with the imperfections of my first drafts and thus overcome my desire to write the first draft as if it were the last.

> I started to understand that, for now, there is not a definitive version, accepting that a reading or comment from my professors or fellow classmates can mean "shuffling and dealing a new hand" [...] I feel like I have experienced a major change: I can no longer write a report, a communication or any professional text in the same way I used to.

Some students realized that giving and receiving feedback to rewrite a text was a typical activity of the social community they aspired to become a part of. This was empowering for them:

> it put me in the position of the colleague and commentator of others, giving me a level of protagonism in the critical assessment of the texts [...] having the chance to offer and receive criticism trains us in the academic dynamic of reflective criticism, with the criteria and requirements that are used in this environment.

Most students began to understand that receiving feedback from the professor and peers was an opportunity to develop their thinking and improve their abstracts:

> I realized that when readers did not fully understand my ideas, it was because I had not fully elaborated them at an intellectual level.

> My peers contributed with new ideas and perspectives, along with questions that I hadn't thought of and mistakes I hadn't caught.

> my recent entry in the social sciences limits my ability to evaluate all of the aspects that should be considered in the research. Therefore, writing the abstract and analyzing it with a peer have played a fundamental epistemic role for me, allowing me to come down to earth in terms of my unrealistic expectations.

> When I received suggestions, it made me want to start writing right away.

When students became aware of the effect their texts had on a reader, they realized that this knowledge was useful to redraft them to shorten the distance between their intentions and their achievements on paper:

> The chance to have someone else read what you have written seems very important to me because you always know what you want to say

but you may not always be sure what it is that you have actually expressed.

Choosing what to leave and what to take is very complex, and it is even more when you revise and see that you are not totally sure if the writing's rhetoric is clear to the target reader. Peer feedback is a good way to overcome this issue.

Giving and receiving feedback also facilitated the students' integration with their peers:

in general, I felt there was a lot of mutual respect and relevant contributions. It was useful for me to feel like I was part of a network.

It helped us to continue to build up the team as a group of doctoral students, to get to know each other and to stop being so afraid of giving or receiving criticism.

For some students, their accomplishments boosted their confidence:

It was helpful for me to read other abstracts from a critical point of view and realize that I could make specific contributions.

the exercise of feedback and re-reading helped me increase my confidence and also made me feel self-assured when the time to rewrite arrived.

At the same time, other students stated that in the first part of the seminar they or their peers felt highly exposed to their critiques. They provided several suggestions on how to deal with this:

sometimes I feel that making comments or interventions to other people's texts - especially if they have more experience and a longer academic career- can be bothersome [for them] or cause some silent displeasure.

the group had some misapprehension about "being critically reviewed." Sometimes we couldn't finish the exercise because we were defending a position instead of critically analyzing whether the suggestion made was relevant or not.

it would be great if the first abstract analyzed could be rewritten and presented again in the next class. This way, the author wouldn't necessarily feel like he or she did a bad job in comparison with the other [classmate abstracts] presented afterwards, as mistakes are minimized thanks to this initial presentation. [This would allow] the author of the abstract to find his or her way out of a situation that is not always a pleasant one.

5. A year later, for the first assignment of the second part of the seminar, students wrote a letter reflecting on their experience as doctoral students ("Progress, obstacles, struggles I have overcome, and battles that I have not yet fought"). Six months later, they assessed this assignment in the second portfolio and found that it had been highly valuable because it legitimated the difficulties as being inherent to a doctoral student, allowed them to notice their accomplishments, and "authorized" the personal feelings in the dissertation research process:

> The task of reflecting was a very useful one [...] because I had arrived to the workshop after some stressful months of discouraging experiences: thesis advisor's change, lack of motivation, feeling like "I can't do it". So, stopping at a point along the way, looking back and writing about it was [...] great for my self-esteem and therefore gave me the energy to continue.

> it allowed me to gain more awareness of what had happened between the two workshops and also allowed me to informally express what I was feeling or what was happening to me, integrating the work process with the day-to-day complications.

> I wrote the letter a few days before defending my thesis proposal, with the concomitant anxieties and insecurities about the work I was doing. By pausing and reflecting, I became aware of the progress I had made since my Master's work, and this made me feel more confident about having to expose myself to defend my project.

> It was a pleasurable experience, one that brought back childhood memories of "writing a letter to you."

> Your suggestions for self-reflection on our own practices of academic writing continue to be so stimulating and engaging that I can assure you I don't consider this an academic "burden" but rather a discharge, a chance for an analysis that enriches our learning [...] it is a very pertinent strategy for opening up a space that requires the commitment and the personal involvement of all the participants.

6. The main task of the second part of the seminar was to choose an academic conference to submit a paper containing work in progress related to the students' dissertation. For many of them, it was the first time they ever presented a paper at a scientific meeting. The seminar fostered their writing abilities to reach this goal, as a stimulus on the long path toward their theses. Their reflective notes in their

portfolios revealed topics similar to the ones mentioned in their accounts of writing a fictional dissertation abstract during the first part of the seminar. The differences that emerged were related to the new audience that guided their writing. This was experienced as an opportunity to participate in an authentic disciplinary community practice in the immediate future and not only after they had finished their dissertations, which represented both a tangible accomplishment and a menace to their emotional comfort.

In the first place, the deadlines of the chosen conference helped students organize their agendas and discouraged procrastination and digression:

> in the beginning, I experienced this as pressure, but in the end, it was an incentive. In addition, the pressure helped me set deadlines and start writing …

> Having short, middle and long-term objectives allowed me to better organize my work schedule and kept me motivated.

> it served as the antidote to becoming dispersed in my writing.

> Since the form and the deadlines were so clear-cut, I was forced [...] to delegate [other tasks] and to postpone everything "except my thesis" [...] If I hadn't had to present a paper in the conference, my thesis would probably have gone much slower [...] During these two months, the fieldwork with secondary sources for my thesis advanced at this rate thanks to the decision to present part of the document analysis at a Scientific Conference.

Writing the conference paper encouraged students to move forward in their dissertations:

> [it turned out to be] the kick-off towards my fieldwork [...] By writing the conference paper, I learned to sacrifice relevant information, to select and prioritize contents, to meet deadlines.

> it was the workshop's most important contribution [...] It brought significant progress in my thesis – the document analysis stage. This advance allowed me to redefine [...] the number of cases that I am going to use, amongst other things.

> it helped me to think about the chapters of my thesis, since it forced me to consider which of the partial results or what part of the theoretical framework would be useful to publish, and at the same time it led me to put together an outline of the thesis's structure.

On the other hand, having to expose themselves to wider audiences aroused new fears:

> The assignment of writing for an upcoming presentation outside the workshop environment, for an audience other than the professor and the group of my peers, was challenging and stimulating [...] but at the same time, I was struck with doubts: What if they don't accept it? What if I'm not up to it and I get turned down ...? I didn't voice these doubts; I kept them inside ... until this moment.

> it means exposing yourself and this forces you to work on your self-esteem and on your psychic balance.

However, the work in the seminar aided students to face this short-term challenge with more confidence:

> the experience of working on the abstract during the past year [in the first part of the seminar] was linked with the writing of the paper, helping me to gain confidence since there was already one part "that I knew how to do."

The continuous experience of giving and receiving feedback helped mitigate some of their insecurities:

> Above all, I am losing my fear of writing and of receiving criticism. Instead, I have learned to value criticism as a significant resource for my thesis work.

> This workshop has taught me [...] to listen to the comments of my colleagues in a "safe" environment and then reflect on these comments. Also, it allowed me to feel more confident when I defended my doctoral proposal ...

> In my case, the revision process in 2008 [the first part of the seminar] was very different from this one. This year, I wanted to have my colleagues review my work as much as possible. As I got to know them, their opinion meant more to me, since not only each of them addressed different areas, but all of their comments were enriching ...

Students also became aware of the need to develop some personal skills like patience and tolerance for failure:

> it was made evident to me [...] that I need to be perseverant and "patient" with myself when I want to communicate something to my academic peers on paper.

Their accomplishments helped them feel more confident in their ability to work toward their academic goals:

> it was very important in terms of thinking about what I had to say regarding my thesis. Up until then, I didn't think I had the material [...] and, because I "had" to do it, a topic appeared along with "something to say" [...] I wonder if I would have made a conference presentation if it hadn't been for this workshop.

> [These assignments] helped me to get rid of my "fear" of academics and the related "demands" and to be more confident in my work. In other words, it allowed me to "get myself out there" [...] Writing the conference paper has allowed me to reaffirm my identity and to value what I am producing ...

> I know that I still have a long way to go, but writing the conference paper helped me come down to earth by moving on from the project into reality, at least in its smallest form of expression.

In short, the students realized that writing for the academic world was usually distressing because it involves interaction with others whose acceptance and welcome the writer seeks:

> We learned about technical aspects of academic writing, but we also understood how our subjectivity is at play in these processes.

> writing gets you in touch with deeper issues: to put yourself to the test to make the other person understands you, that is, to make him/her accept you and welcome you.

Students also became aware that developing their writing skills was part of a transition toward the identity change they desire so deeply:

> this is about constructing a new professional identity through written work and it gets me very excited ...

Although the workshop gave students the opportunity to notice tangible achievements and thus reinforced their belief that they could in fact overcome the multiple obstacles they would face, a few stated that their anxiety was so immense that they would need a more extensive writing support:

> This workshop positively mobilizes personal efforts towards writing and allows you to achieve specific goals in a short period of time.

> Although all these tools are useful, the process continues to be very "anxiogenic" and frustrating at times. That's why I believe that the

more technique you acquire, the greater chance you have of dealing
with these feelings.

In sum, allowing that students' feelings of incompetence were made explicit and
offering postgraduates varied support to overcome them was experienced as an
opportunity for a long-term reflection on whom they were and whom they desired to
become.

Conclusion

This chapter has examined the rationale, syllabus, and outcomes of a doctoral
seminar which was aimed at fostering students' writing, together with exploring the
emotional skills that become necessary when dealing with their PhD candidacies. In
turn, this had the goal of facilitating academic enculturation. Based on various
theoretical concepts, the workshop combined scientific with reflective writing,
nonthreatening peer review with authentic high-stakes audiences, and genre
awareness with process approach. The twofold purpose of the seminar allowed the
candidates to address epistemic and communicative writing while aiding them in
acknowledging that writing as a PhD student entails enduring social exposure with
feelings of anxiety common to most students. Helping students to achieve visible
results after laborious cycles of drafting, receiving feedback, and redrafting
gave them an experiential model for their entire dissertation process. This gently
exposed them to the literacy and emotional challenges that they will recurrently face
during their academic careers.

According to the reviewed literature, writing workshops used to focus on technical
and general skills. To the contrary, current initiatives tend to be based on genres as
situated social practice and on writing groups' approaches. There are also a reduced
number of doctoral programs that discuss emotions linked to the process of writing.
Within this framework, the seminar examined in this chapter offered an uncommonly
long experience of developing research writing along with writing about threats and
opportunities brought on by the writing of a PhD thesis.

The analysis of the postgraduates' reflective notes specified some of the tensions
that students faced when trying to participate in an activity hosted by the disciplinary
community that they aspire to enter. These tensions were brought on by
disorientation involving their own identities. The tensions that their emotions
expressed could have worked as internal obstacles. However, the seminar attempted
to make them explicit and shared to enable them to become one of the engines that
make learning possible (Castelló & Iñesta, this volume). Students' texts also showed
that the seminar gave them the chance to learn about academic writing and
participate in new scholarly genres, as well as gain exposure to the social and
emotional tools which are necessary to face this task. Interweaving writing to think,
writing to communicate, writing to participate, and writing to find out about oneself
has probably strengthened each of these separate undertakings.

Thus, this chapter has provided data on which to evaluate the acknowledged
anxieties experienced by doctoral student writers and by learners in general. The

question of whether making room for reflective writing has enhanced the development of academic writing as a result of its meta-cognitive effect (Castelló, 2007; Lonka, 2003) has been left open. Nevertheless, it seems evident that the seminar helped students advance their research goals as part of a process of academic enculturation. Their progress, combined with the awareness that difficulties are inherent in the task and by no means a sign of personal failure, has increased postgraduates' self-efficacy and promoted sustained motivation.

This seminar also illustrates a pedagogical innovation to make disciplinary practices more visible (Prior & Bilbro, this volume). In addition, the present case study can contribute in the direction advocated by Dysthe (this volume), to underpin institutional decisions and impact on educational practices.

In brief, two main ideas have been developed in this chapter: (1) Learning to write for the academic world involves threats and opportunities experienced with deep affect. (2) A lengthy seminar which takes into account writing and emotional issues can foster this learning. Both theses argued in this chapter require research to ascertain whether they receive support outside the Argentine context in which they have been explored.

Chapter 13

Facilitated Immersion at a Distance in Second Language Scientific Writing

Charles Bazerman, Nancy Keranen and
Fátima Encinas Prudencio

With the emergence of English as the dominant language of international science (Ammon, 2001), non-native English-speaking (NNES) scientists who have not had extensive experience in an English-speaking country are caught in a bind. To participate in international science — that is to communicate findings and discuss latest research developments, methods, and theories with colleagues in their specialties globally — they need to have written and spoken fluency not only in English, but the scientific English of their specialty, with the idioms of the specialty that both signal expertise and facilitate rapid, precise mutual understanding. That is, they need a clarity and univocality of expression using the specialized lexis and phrasing so as to make their ideas understood with enough ease so to allow the readers to maintain focus on the scientific issues rather than problems of language and translation. No general course in English, nor even a specialized one in scientific writing, nor even one that uses authentic materials and tasks, can provide enough depth in the language of their specialty. Nor can any course provide enough hours of motivated practice of sufficient challenge to develop the level of competence and fluency necessary for high-level participation in their specialty in English. Language courses can only provide preparation and support to facilitate actual practice in immersive situations, but at some point, those immersive situations must become the site of writing practice and development.

The bind goes even deeper, in that learning and doing the science within a particular linguistic context is the actual means for learning the specific language that embodies the ideas and reasoning of the field. Conversely, gaining ease with the

University Writing: Selves and Texts in Academic Societies
Studies in Writing, Volume 24, 235–248
Copyright © 2012 by Emerald Group Publishing Limited
All rights of reproduction in any form reserved
ISSN: 1572-6304/doi:10.1108/S1572-6304(2012)0000024017

language is also gaining facility in recognizing and formulating the thinking of the field. The language is a means of talking about and expressing what one is doing, elaborating specialty-appropriate thought and argument, so one learns the language hand in hand with doing the science. This is a process even native speakers must go through as they move from introductory courses to the more intense, nuanced, and refined discussions of graduate work and then practicing science, situated not in the authoritative certitudes of lower schooling, but the emergent, uncertain, and contended world of the research front or unsolved applications (see Prior & Bilbro, this volume, for elaboration of the academic enculturation process.). Second language speakers, even though they may be highly talented and have advanced in their science as far as schooling and scientific practice in their native language allows, may be able to access the most current finding and ideas, as well as the most current framing of research questions only within international discussions likely to be in English. Since most specialties of science are conducted as international inquiries relying on international communication, communicated in English, full participation is dependent on the ability to read and write scientific English with a nuanced understanding of the language of the specialty. Of course, this problem is most severe among graduate students and scientists working within languages that have only regional presence (such as the Eastern European languages), but even within scientific communities using the largest and most robust international languages other than English (such as Spanish and Chinese), students in many disciplines must learn to read the English language literature of their fields, and publication in English becomes an important advantage, if not a requirement as their careers progress (see Meneghini & Packer, 2007, for a recent discussion of this problem with alternative solutions). The language shift disrupts their ability to talk and write about what they already know and places obstacles in engaging in and learning from the most advanced discussions (see Chitez & Kruse, this volume, for the complexity of scientific cultures and the role language plays in it).

The language difficulty may have a further effect of increasing anxiety about one's ability to participate adequately and not be judged poorly, an anxiety that further impedes the ability to step forward into the discussion to advance one's science and one's experience as a scientific communicator. The problem is further compounded for those who have limited opportunity to participate in international laboratories, and must learn to participate in international English medium science at a distance, only through the virtual worlds of texts and the Internet (setting aside further issues of connectivity and bandwidth). In short, those at the fringes of English language international science must make the most of limited and distal opportunities to interact.

In this chapter, we offer some conceptual resources to understand the challenges facing NNES scientists in participating international scientists. We then describe an intervention we developed to help a group of Mexican scientists to face these challenges. The concepts and intervention were based on a research study of the attitudes and histories of NNES scientists who have successfully been able to publish regularly in English (more elaborated findings from this study are to be found in Keranen, Encinas, & Bazerman, 2012, and other forthcoming publications).

Prior Studies of the Position on L2 Scientists

A growing literature in English for Specific Purposes and English for Academic Purposes has examined the difficulties and strategies of NNES scientists attempting to publish in English. Flowerdew's series of interview studies, in particular, reveal both the dilemmas and strategies of NNES scientists needing to publish in English despite limited English writing abilities. Flowerdew's initial quantitative survey (1999a) and a follow-up interview study (1999b) identified obstacles faced by Hong Kong scholars in making effective arguments in English, including limited vocabulary, rudimentary style with little nuance or flexibility of expression, with special problems in introductory and discussion sections along with qualitative articles in general. In a further in-depth study of a single subject in attempting to publish a single article, Flowerdew found that the obstacles went beyond language proficiency, to difficulties in maintaining ongoing engagement with the relevant research communities (2000). The subject had done both his masters and Ph.D. work in an English-speaking country and had substantial comfort in English as well as some of the specialized lexis and locutions of his field, though his eventually accepted essay did need some language revisions. The greater revisions, however, concerned the structure and argument, issues not that different from those faced by L1 scientists seeking their first publications. The revision process, however, was exacerbated by the distances and communicative obstacles, including lack of access to his advisor. Flowerdew invokes Lave and Wenger's (1991) theory of communities of practice to explain the problem of being on the periphery without regular communications that would support legitimate peripheral participation (LPP), despite extended experience within an English-speaking research unit.

The problem of being at the scientific periphery again surfaced in Flowerdew's (2001) interviews of applied linguistics journal editors. Although these editors were sympathetic to the plight of NNES scholars and provided editorial support, they found difficulties with submitted manuscripts not just at the surface language level (which could be remedied by editorial support) but also with parochialism and absence of authorial voice, both of which could have their origins in the limited engagement with scholarly discussions. Nelson and Castelló (this volume) consider in greater depth the difficulties in developing academic voice. An even greater obstacle to engagement occurs when editors and reviewers stigmatize the capabilities and quality of work of writers whose texts show evidence of EFL difficulties (Ammon, 2000, 2001; Curry & Lillis, 2004, 2009; Flowerdew, 1999a, 2008b; Li & Flowerdew, 2007). Authors' perception of stigma creates a further psychological burden (Flowerdew, 2008b). Similar problems have been found with Korean scientists (Cho, 2009) and Spanish-speaking scientists in Spain (St. John, 1987) and Mexico (Englander, 2006, 2009).

In order to overcome these difficulties and to begin to engage in international science, some NNES scientists have been found to use a variety of techniques and strategies that indicate they are not just victims of marginalization. Rather, they can be self-conscious, strategic, persistent actors (Belcher, 2007; Okamura, 2004, 2006) attempting to improve their position and interaction within a social system through a variety of supports. Some of the supports include seeking the help of other people who can assist them in overcoming the language barrier, such as editors and proofreaders (Burrough-Boenisch, 2003; Flowerdew, 2001; Harwood, Austin, & Macauley, 2007; Li & Flowerdew, 2007; Lillis & Curry, 2006; Misak, Marusic, & Marusic, 2005). The contributions of editors, however, sometimes lead to significant changes in text and intention (Hartley, Branthwaite, Ganier, & Heurley, 2007).

Other strategies involve attempting to understand the norms, genres, practices, and patterns of language use within the articles in their specialties (Buckingham, 2008) and developing reading strategies that overcome language difficulties (Burrough-Boenisch, 1999). One language-based strategy is to reuse phrasing found in the literature — this ranges from writing new sentences and sections using sentence and phrase patterns used by other authors to patching together existing phrases (or "patchwriting" as termed by Howard, 1993) to totally copying of entire sections, varying only to present their specific methods and findings (Abasi & Graves, 2008; Flowerdew & Li, 2007; Okamura, 2004, 2006; Pecorari, 2003).

On the other hand, others have a more passive attitude, not understanding their challenges and not seeking to improve their language skills and engagement, thereby entrenching their marginal positions (Wang & Bakken, 2004).

Our Larger Project

The ideas and applications presented in the remainder of this chapter were developed in conjunction with a research study (described more fully in Keranen et al., 2012 and other forthcoming studies) aimed at understanding how some NNES scientists nonetheless come to have successful publication careers in English. For this purpose, we conducted a series of interviews with professors and graduate students in physics and mathematics at a major research university in central Mexico. These researchers and theorists were at different stages of their careers, from young researchers just starting out to publish internationally to senior scholars with long lists of international publications. What we found among our interviewees were varying histories, but most containing increasing interactive engagements with English language scientists early in their careers, which bootstrapped their opportunities to learn and practice English in the context of their science. These included international residencies early in their careers, working in English-speaking laboratories and regular attendance at international conferences. They also reported continuing collaborations with international English-speaking teams along with ongoing correspondence with English-speaking colleagues. While some had near native English fluency, others reported regularly having difficulties in English, ranging from patterns of errors to difficulties in expressing ideas clearly — but those with difficulties relied heavily on their collaborators and editors to either produce or correct the prose. High levels of English language publication seemed to correlate with higher levels of immersion in social and collaborative networks of English language scientists, who provided language opportunities and support as well as scientific. Those earlier in their publication careers were just starting to build those networks and engage in such interaction.

In a workshop based on our analysis of these findings, some of the participants had barely begun this international engagement and showed the kinds of problems described elsewhere in the literature: limited language skill, lack of confidence, obstacles to publication, little conference attendance and little visiting experience in English-speaking labs and universities. While they had advanced well within the academic word of Spanish-speaking Mexican undergraduate and doctoral programs, and also were able to read research publications in English, they had not found a way to enter into the international communication system. They also seemed to lack much of an understanding of how to proceed to engage in international science and seemed to suffer from a kind of timorousness and passivity (as Wang & Bakken, 2004, noted in their subjects). In short, the non-publishers were at the social margin while the high English publishers seemed immersed in the world of international science.

The Problem of Immersion

As the study and workshop developed, we found it useful to describe the fundamental problem as one of gaining immersion in the rich and motivated language experiences that would lead to further specialized L2 language learning that would then support further immersion and engagement. NNES scientists seem to have high practical, experiential and emotional barriers keeping them from those bootstrapping interactions that would lead to communicative fluency and publications, and they need to find ways to overcome those barriers. Those that have overcome these barriers have had fortunate early experiences that have helped move them from the periphery to more central roles in the relevant networks of scientific activity of their field — where they are able to further build their knowledge, language skills, and engagement with cutting edge problems.

In second language learning, Krashen (1981) has hypothesized that the amount of comprehensible input within intensive interaction (which would be concomitant with immersion) facilitates fluency and high levels of performance. Similarly, Long (1996) has hypothesized that interaction is central to acquisition. Schmidt (Schmidt, 1983; Schmidt & Frota, 1986) also has long argued through detailed case studies that while high levels of interaction facilitate fluency, targeted instruction still has a role in focusing attention on grammatical precision. While such studies consider the degree of learning under immersion conditions, they do not examine what immersion means, what its social mechanisms are, what drives people to engage in it, and how immersion is experienced by the language learner (Cummins, 1998). Immersion has also been invoked as a justification for various Internet-based innovations that support engaging interaction between second language learners and native speakers (Oliva & Pollastrini, 1995), but again, there is little consideration of the meaning of immersion. A few topics within the applied linguistic research world do bear some relevance — such as the value of time on task (Collins, Halter, Lightbown, & Spada, 1999), frequency of processing (Ellis, 2002), and correspondingly the amount of input and output; yet, even these tend to be studied only within a controlled classroom experience.

The concept of dual immersion has, similarly, been adopted as an innovation in primary and secondary education, originally developed to meet the particular cultural and political needs of Canada, but adopted in many other regions with a variety of heritage languages (Johnson & Swain, 1997). Dual immersion (where students study at least two languages both of which are used throughout the rest of the curriculum) is largely defined by school hours using each language and other curricular measures. The benefits of dual immersion have been documented with educational assessments (Cummins, 1998), and the sociopolitical dynamics on the effectiveness of dual language for immigrant children have been examined (Valdes, 1997). Yet, the social and psychological processes that form the immersive experience remain little understood.

A lack of in-depth understanding of immersion limits our ability to consider ways to help people engage in it — particularly adults who face obstacles to naturally occurring ambient immersion. Further, since few NNES scientists have the opportunity or resources for extended residencies in L1 English-speaking scientific environments, it would be useful if we could find ways to consider how interactions at a distance through traditional print and newer digital technologies could provide some degree of immersive experience at a distance. As we will elaborate below, we believe immersion is constituted on both a psychological and a sociocultural level. Accordingly we will examine the psychologically based studies of immersion that have arisen out of the virtual realty and gaming worlds, sociocultural theories from education, and sociological studies of the organization of science. We will then draw an analogy to social networks to synthesize these strands and apply them to the interactions at a distance available to the NNES we studied. We end with a description of a workshop we designed on the bass of this analysis.

Research into Immersion in Gaming

As the study and workshop progressed, we found ourselves using the analogy of immersive virtual reality to consider how one can become immersed in a situation not physically present, When we in fact investigated the literature on computing and virtual reality, we found research that associated an intense immersive experience with a sense of presence (Dillon, Keogh, Freeman, & Davidoff, 2000; Freeman, Avons, Pearson, & Ijsselsteijn, 1999) or actually being in a live, materially embodied situation (Pine & Gilmore, 1999). This idea of potentially very broad application has been most explored with respect to digital gaming. The gaming literature perceives the concept of immersion as underdefined, but has begun to explore its psychological components (Brown & Cairns, 2004; Ijsselsteijn, de Kort, Poels, Jurgelionis, & Bellotti, 2007). Interviews with gamers reveal three levels of involvement: engagement, engrossment and total immersion (Brown & Cairns, 2004). The first level of engagement requires access (including the necessary skill to participate) and the desire to spend time with the environment, which in gaming is associated with the task being interesting and providing adequate response and rewards to the players' actions. Engrossment, the second level, adds an emotional component that is correlated with an investment of time, attention and effort, giving rise to a state of concentration described as "zen-like" and that leaves one drained after stopping. In the final stage of total immersion, the players lose sense of the reality around them and all they think about is the game; moreover, this tends to happen only when they empathize with the game characters, seeming to take their part or transfer their consciousnesses into the character. The authors associate these higher levels of involvement with the concept of flow (Csikzsentmihalyi, 1990).

Ermi and Mäyrä (2005) and Douglas and Hargadon (2000) also associate immersion with flow and identify three components contributing to high degrees of immersion: sensory, challenge, and imaginative. Challenge exists in relation to level of skill, pushing one's limits but not beyond, as in the Zone of Proximal Development (Vygotsky, 1978). High levels of challenge are also associated with high use of working memory, taxing one's resources (Grodal, 2003).

Several authors have also noted the importance of familiarity of environment or "discernability" allowing the player to recognize the meaning of stimuli and the anticipated effect of their actions (Douglas & Hargadon, 2000; McMahan, 2003; Salen & Zimmerman, 2004). This is also a theme of flow research that sees necessary conditions as skill, challenge at the limits of skill, a recognizable and limited environment, and rewards coming directly from actions (Csikszentmihalyi, 1975, 1990). Within flow states there is rapid problem solving and maximum learning. This coordinates with neurological findings that associate learning with heightened emotional states (Hinton, Miyamoto, & Della-Chiesa, 2008). But if there is little appropriate skill, worry, or anxiety sets in, interfering with engagement, and if there is little challenge, boredom or relaxation may keep engagement low, mitigating the kind of attention that would lead to learning and deeper involvement.

Immersion in Language Learning in Real Life

So what does this gaming research have to do with language learning? Of course, this research about gaming is seeking to recreate the kind of presence that occurs in real situations where flow occurs simply by being part of the events that surround us. The prototype of language immersion is an adult second language speaker living and working in a second language situation in which all transactions must be carried out in the second language. One must constantly listen, speak, read, and write in the second language and give up dependence on the first language. Beyond time on language learning tasks and extensive practice, one's interactions are framed in the second language — directing one's thought, motives, and spirit toward a way of life within that second language.

When we negotiate meaningful life activities, we are fully attentive as we produce language to meet challenges that provide us immediate feedback and rewards. Further, most of us (not having delusional dissociation) identify with ourselves in our actual situations even more than we do with the most engaging fictional game characters. Our communications are accompanied by the many emotions of success and failure of interaction. Fortunately, the good will of interlocutors and the flexibility of situations often allow us to repair failures and to improvise alternative solutions — both of which support maximum learning. As we warm to situations, language may flow, and we produce more meaningful language than we thought possible. As situations succeed, our attention turns more to the engaging, immersing activities that motivate us and less to the language that was a barrier.

All this is consistent with what the gaming research tells us about the psychological attention and emotions associated with immersion. However, real situations are composed of social relations and activities and not just synthesized audio and video, and we have important material and social stakes in the outcomes of the interactions. As very young children, we may be shy in front of others, but most of us learn to stand straight and give socially acceptable responses. While many of our interchanges may with time become routine and unchallenging, we seek spontaneity, discovery, and fun through friendships, play, and engaging works. When we are met by challenge, our language grows as we incorporate language we hear around us, discover new things to say, and reach toward new formulations and ideas. If we are not overwhelmed and far beyond our skills (which may leave us worried or even anxious and less able to think), we enjoy the thought and excitement so we do not feel the work — rather we are attempting to relate to others and communicate with them at the limit. As our social networks grow, so do the variety of relations, differences in roles and activities, linguistic needs, and the possibilities of growth and discovery.

Particularly as we interact with specialized groups with unusual activities requiring special knowledge and language skills, we can become engaged at ever higher levels, once we get past the entry barriers of skill, knowledge, and anxiety. This process of entry, particularly in inviting communities of specialized practice and language, has been captured well by communities of practice that provide limited participation roles for newcomers, which Lave and Wenger characterize as LPP (1991). Such situations provide pathways for novices to take on greater roles and responsibilities as their skills and confidence build — a gradient of participation that correlates with engagement and challenge.

Language interactions are particularly well characterized by this LPP model as language use is typically constructed dialogically with interlocutors who are supportive in accommodating and calibrating to the language competence of the less skilled speaker — within material circumstances that themselves provide deictic support. As language skills grow, both participants are able to enter into more articulate, delicate and complex communications. Increased language skills will likely lead to increased interaction with more speakers of the language, as one enters the community of practice. This can also be described in network terms as building more and denser connections with larger groups of people (or nodes), thereby moving one more centrally into the network with all the increased information and practice that is likely to come with that (Breiger, 2004). In these various ways, linguistic immersion provides especially sensitive mechanisms of moving from peripheral participation to centrally engaged skilled communication within large networks of interlocutors.

Immersion in Groups with Barriers of Social Evaluation

Of course, not all groups are inviting and open. Some set up barriers to the uninitiated and stigmatize them in ways that impede participation and growth. The uninitiated may be left at the margins with only the initiated being given access to consequential events. We can see this in sciences that make judgments about the skills and knowledge of people who want to participate, even at the fringe. Pathways to higher levels of participation are usually mediated through educational and mentoring processes, employment in laboratories and academic departments, and meetings and publications — access to all of which are likely to be controlled by gatekeepers (Merton, 1973). Initially, processes of induction may be impersonal in the form courses and exams (though even student activities are mediated by language and writing, both in discussion and in exams). These entry points eliminate many from further engagement, through both formal evaluation and self-selection influenced by formal assessment. As induction continues, the processes become more personal in small seminars and tutorials, working in labs together, attending meetings, and collaboration on papers.

Each of these steps advances one's knowledge of science and the language of science and adds intellectual challenge and emotional commitment as one becomes deeply engaged in problem-solving work with close colleagues. While big rewards may be rare in terms of major discoveries, every time a piece of equipment works, an experiment produces results, a set of equations make sense, or a calculation is correct, one receives an intrinsic reward, pushing one further. Immediate and socially intense rewards come from every successful conversation where scientific information, ideas, and thinking are interchanged. The stories of the pleasures of intense discussion are legion as well as the excitement that comes in collaborative thinking. The possibilities of having smart colleagues one could learn from and share ideas with influence both new and experienced researchers in make choices of where to work and which conferences to attend.

The more elaborate rewards of successful experiments, discoveries and theoretical advances are the consequences of collaboration and communication, and these successes provide access to further opportunities to communicate and work with others in a process labeled the Matthew Effect (Merton, 1973). Citations are outward manifestations of the circulation of one's discoveries and theoretical innovations throughout the network and provide another level of reward (Merton, 1957) and credit for playing the game at a higher level (Latour & Woolgar, 1979). Citation and co-citation networks indicate one's place within various conversations of the field and one's relation to other researchers (Griffith, Small, Stonehill, & Dey, 1974; Small, 1973; Small & Griffith, 1974). That in turn can generate more communication and network density. The adoption of modern practices of citation beginning in the late eighteenth century has been explicit strategy to draw scientists together in social cooperation through intertextual networks (Bazerman, 1991; see also Bazerman, 1993 for how the representation of such networks show rhetorical intention.)

We can think of the process of entering into the engaging communications of science in terms of an emergent and evolving network, where communication, achievement, and recognition are intertwined as one becomes more intensively involved in the work of science. Every successful communication strengthens existing connections and builds new connections, drawing one further into the flow of information and ideas — as well as building skill and confidence (see Nelson, 2008, and Rinck & Boch, this volume, for reviews of research into how students learn to engage with academic intertextual systems.) Psychologically, as one becomes more connected, not only does one feel rewarded, but one's mind becomes more and more engaged by the work of the field being carried out in the network to which one is contributing. Scientists most connected and most central within the networks are most intensively involved in contributing to or communicating with others about the latest work and to have access to the most resources. They are most likely to be described as people who "eat, drink, and breathe science."

One unusual aspect of this network is that it depends on the positive actions of the participants — most specifically their communicative actions. Communicative actions, particularly written communications, often have a thoughtful self-reflexive design and require conscious initiative. Beginning to write is always a conscious choice and effort, even though the words may sometimes flow rapidly as the difficult problem falls in place. Spoken interactions may have more of a sense of spontaneous flow, as thoughts that have been on one's mind resolve and words tumble out. Yet, these are words laden with thought and significant information for the problem, and they are new formulations that extend one's communication potential.

NNES scientists working in a non-English setting, however, frequently have many barriers to being well connected in the network, including the necessity of working though written language without the immediacy and spontaneity of spoken interaction; having fewer and more distant professional connections; feeling stigmatized for language and for being at the periphery; and not being energized by the most current problems. These barriers mitigate the information, energy, focus, and spontaneous cause for action that scientists get from being more central in the network. In sum, NNES scientists' attempts to connect to the network are likely to be through written language, which facilitates precision, reflection, and strategic action because it is visible for careful and repeated examination (Goody, 1977), but which is also conscious, effortful, and anxiety provoking.

These scientists would gain by reflectively understanding the dynamics of networks and their position within them, so they could reach out strategically and act in effective ways. Also, they need to seek all the supports they can get and use them efficiently to make the connections that will give them the practice, motivation, interest, and opportunities to develop as international communicating scientists in English. Because they may have few well-connected sponsors, their writing must be more self-sponsored and self-directed (for the concept of writing sponsorship, see Brandt, 2001).

A Workshop to Support Self-Directed Immersion at a Distance

Traditional language instruction including English for Specific Purposes establishes a precondition to the actual engagement and practice that will build fluency and competence, but then engaged practice is needed within highly motivating situations to develop the fluency and precision needed for full participation. To foster self-monitoring and self-sponsored reaching out, we developed a five-day workshop for about 15 physicists and mathematicians at a major research university in central Mexico who were interested in increasing their English language publication. All of the participants had substantial English language instruction and were able to read articles in their specialty in English. Their oral and written skills in English varied from struggling to near fluent. Several of them as well were multilingual, as immigrants or having had residencies in various European and Asian countries. Yet they all found barriers to their international publication in English. The main goal of the workshop was to increase self-directed immersion and to provide strategic supports, including self-guided tools for specialized language learning and editing. Each day included hands-on composing and editing activities, including peer group processes.

The first day was devoted to the presentation of the concepts of immersion and network engagement (in both Spanish and English, as well as any other languages they may have worked in), which we then explored in relation to their professional experiences. In this day and each subsequent one, we presented our data including quotations from the interviews to foster discussion.

The middle three days considered supports that could be used to develop appropriate contributions to disciplinary communications: the literature, digital language tools, and collegial interaction. One subtheme of all days was that different supports were useful at different points in one's learning, and one should learn when to let go or transform the use of some supports, and when to seek new supports. Day two considered what one could learn from examining other articles in one's field beyond the actual findings or intellectual content. We looked at how to analyze the textual argument structure of varieties of scientific writing, including genre organization and function; the way evidence, theories, and reasoning were presented; and intertextuality in relation both to reference and to use of specialized language.

The third day focused more centrally on digital tools to support language, with a particular focus on precise and appropriate phrasing within the scientific context. Phrasing is a struggle for advanced second language writers, as they may know what is correct and even idiomatic in most circumstances, but they have difficulty in expressing their scientific reasoning in a way that would be understood precisely and accurately and would not leave them with the stigma of awkward second language expression. We considered the strengths and weaknesses of spelling, grammar, and usage checkers and how their suggestions need to be monitored and used heuristically. We also explored the various search engine tricks they used, such as seeing whether certain phrases were used frequently and in what meaning contexts. Following the work of a number of applied and corpus linguists (Charles, 2007; Flowerdew, 2005; Gilquin, Granger, & Paquot, 2007; Hafner & Candlin, 2007;

Krishnamurthy & Kosem, 2007; Lee & Swales, 2006), we then examined specialized corpora, such as PERC (http://www.corpora.jp/~perc04/), and one we assembled from English language articles in the *Revista Mexicana de Fisica*. We then presented procedures to create personalized corpora using texts most relevant to one's specialty and the genres one is working with, using for analysis the open access program ANTCONC (http://www.antlab.sci.waseda.ac.jp/antconc_index.html) (see also Anthony, 2006).

Most controversially, we examined the value and uses of various machine translation programs. We all recognized the often comic inadequacy of current machine translators and the problem of evolving specialized terms and phrasing within research front areas. Yet, we all abashedly admitted our heuristic uses of them, such as to get quick and dirty first pass approximations, to identify possible terminology and phrasing, to catch spelling and morphology of loan words, and to avoid false friends. We also were aware that translation tools were constantly improving, though none was likely to emerge soon with a true understanding of meaning or with the interpretive frame of a specialist in a scientific field. We did double translations of short passages from Spanish to English and back to Spanish to highlight the strengths and weaknesses of current programs. We again discussed reflective use and ultimate responsibility for revision and editing no matter what tools or supports we may use.

The fourth day, to review the practical implications of all we had worked on, we began with a discussion of the revision and editing processes used by the various participants. From there, we discussed the various human and personal supports that were part of an extended composing, revision, and editing process and the different contributions they might make to our writing. From the educational contexts of seminars, faculty mentoring, and writing centers, we moved to the composing dynamics of collaborative groups, in both local labs and large international teams. We considered the problems and benefits of paid editors and translators (whether employed by the laboratory or hired personally) and again how these could be used as opportunities for growth rather than substitutions for individual responsibility. We considered the potential roles of local and international colleagues, discussion groups, and journal review and editorial processes. With respect to each of these, we considered how to build dialogue and networks of communication and support.

On several of the days, we did demonstration consultations with individual authors, working on the revision of manuscripts. Some of these consultations were conducted by the workshop leaders, and others were carried out virtually with science writing tutors in the United States through Skype and e-mail exchange of documents. While more sophisticated software might facilitate the interchanges, we found these tools simple, adequate, and at hand.

The final day we considered two new topics. One was to consider from a Bakhtinian perspective the relationship of the language they use to that of their larger community (Bakhtin, 1981, 1984; Bazerman, 2004a; Vološinov, 1986). Specifically, we discussed the formation of specialized language activities and the language developed for those activities, along with the individual responsibility for originality (Bazerman, 2010). We considered the fraught issue of plagiarism and the subtle, local distinctions in what needed to be cited, what was the received knowledge and phrasing already absorbed into communal practice (or what sociologists of science have called obliteration by incorporation — see Cozzens, 1985; Merton, 1973), and what was the obligation for original contribution and how that could be marked.

Second, as the conceptual payoff for the whole workshop, we considered personal trajectories of language and scientific development within relevant communicative networks. We reflected on what immersive experiences they have had, how current experiences may be made more immersive, and what opportunities were available to engage further in international science discussions. We considered both the experiences available at a distance (such as virtual participation in virtual groups and projects) and the opportunities for spending time in English language environments.

Final Thoughts

While, of course, fluent language use requires learning many language skills and acquiring much linguistic knowledge, formal language instruction only gets one part of the way. Situated practice in significant, immersive, accountable, and consequential activities leads to motivated problem solving and habituated use that advances fluency and accuracy. Thus, as language professionals, we ought to consider providing the means to engage in more regular and more intense language experiences, which will be rewarding, reinforcing, and part of a trajectory of deeper engagement.

There are opportunities for degrees of such immersion, even if participants are not in a face-to-face L2 environment, as long as they can recognize, access, and reach out to these opportunities. Facilitations or supports can be an important part of getting the dynamic of engagement going. As digital communication follows its rapidly expanding course, we will have ever-increasing opportunities to communicate ever intensively with each other at great distances, in ever richer environments. In part, digital gaming is starting to show the way toward the intensity of multi-person interactive experiences, but scientific communication has further advantages of real, motivating stakes, a communal commitment to discovery and critical evaluation, existing networks of communication, and an expanding access to data of the real world, which is represented in the same world of virtual communication.

Immersion at a distance need not be a problem, and in fact is not for those who are already most deeply engaged in scientific work. They live within self-reinforcing and self-nourishing networks. For those who have not yet achieved this level of connection, however, we can provide facilitations for them to increase access and engagement in potentially immersive worlds at a distance. By helping each individual build the reflective and communicative skills to make connections and gain conscious control of the immersion process, we can help them move from the professional margins into the heavily networked center of Matthew Effect rewards.

Acknowledgments

We are grateful for funding from the University of California and *Consejo Nacional de Ciencias y Technologia*, México. We also thank Brendan Barnwell for assistance in corpus construction and John Flowerdew for his helpful comments on an earlier draft.

References

Abasi, A. R., & Graves, B. (2008). Academic literacy and plagiarism: Conversations with international graduate students and disciplinary professors. *Journal of English for Academic Purposes*, 7(4), 221–233.

Ackerman, J. (1995). Postscript: The assimilation and "tactics" of Nate. In C. Berkenkotter & T. N. Huckin (Eds.), *Genre knowledge in disciplinary communication* (pp. 145–150). Hillsdale, NJ: Erlbaum.

Agha, A. (2007). *Language and social relations*. Cambridge University Press.

Ahern, K., & Manathunga, C. (2004). Clutch-starting stalled research students. *Innovative Higher Education*, 28(4), 237–254.

Aitchison, C. (2003). Thesis writing circles. *Hong Kong Journal of Applied Linguistics*, 8(2), 97–115.

Aitchison, C., & Lee, S. (2006). Research writing: Problems and pedagogies. *Teaching in Higher Education*, 11(3), 265–278.

Albertinti, J. (2008). Teaching of writing and diversity: Access, identity, and achievement. In C. Bazerman (Ed.), *Handbook of research on writing, history, society, school, individual, text* (pp. 475–488). New York, NY: Lawrence Erlbaum.

Ammon, U. (2000). Towards more fairness in international English. In R. Philipson (Ed.), *Rights to language, equity, power, and education* (pp. 111–116). Mahwah, NJ: Erlbaum.

Ammon, U. (Ed.) (2001). *The dominance of English as a language of science*. New York, NY: Mouton de Gruyter.

Ammon, U. (2003). The international standing of the German language. In J. Marais & M. Morris (Eds.), *Languages in a globalizing world* (pp. 231–249). Cambridge: Cambridge University Press.

Anscombre, J.-C., & Ducrot, O. (1988). *L'argumentation dans la langue*. Liège: Mardaga.

Anson, C. (2009). The intelligent design of writing programs: Reliance on belief or a future of evidence. *Writing Program Administration*, 32(1), 11–36. Fall/Winter 2008.

Anthony, L. (2006). Developing a freeware, multiplatform corpus analysis toolkit for the technical writing classroom. *IEEE Transactions on Professional Communication*, 49(3), 275–286.

Appel, M., & Dahlgren, L. (2003). Swedish doctoral students' experiences on their journey towards a PhD: Obstacles and opportunities inside and outside the academic building. *Scandinavian Journal of Educational Research*, 47(1), 89–110.

Arnseth, H. C., & Ludvigsen, S. (2006). Approaching institutional contexts: Systemic versus dialogic research in CSCL. *Computer-Supported Collaborative Learning*, (2), 167–185.

Artemeva, N. (2008). Toward a unified social theory of genre learning. *Journal of Business and Technical Communication*, 22(2), 160–185.

250   References

Bakhtin, M. (2002). El problema de los géneros discursivos. In *Estética de la creación verbal*. Buenos Aires: Siglo XXI. Original 1979 Russian edition corresponding to 1953 non-published manuscript (Julio Forcat/César Conroy, Trans.).
Bakhtin, M. M. (1981). *The dialogic imagination: Four essays* (C. Emerson & M. Holquist, Trans.). Austin, TX: University of Texas Press.
Bakhtin, M. M. (1984). *Problems of Dostoevsky's poetics* (C. Emerson, Ed. & Trans.). Minneapolis, MN: University of Minnesota Press.
Bakhtin, M. M. (1986). *Speech genres and other late essays* (V. W. McGee, Trans.). Austin, TX: University of Texas Press.
Bakhtin, M. (Volosinov). (1977). *Le marxisme et la philosophie du langage* [Marxism and the philosophy of language] (M. Yaguello, Trans.). Paris, Les Editions de Minuit, 1ère édition 1929.
Bangert-Drowns, R., Hurley, M., & Wilkinson, B. (2004). The effects of school-based writing-to-learn interventions on academic achievement: A meta-analysis. *Review of Educational Research, 74*(1), 29–58.
Barajas, E. D. (2007). Parallels in academic and nonacademic discursive styles: An analysis of a Mexican woman's narrative performance. *Written Communication, 24*, 140–167.
Barnes, D., Britton, J., & Rosen, H. (1971). *Language, the learner, and the school*. New York,NY: Penguin Books.
Barnett, R., & Griffin, A. (Eds.). (1997). *The end of knowledge in higher education*. London: Institute of Education.
Barré-deMiniac, C. (1996a). L'écriture—vers un projet didactique renouvelé. In C. Barré-de Miniac (Ed.), *Vers une didactique de l'écriture* (pp. 11–18). Paris: DeBroeck.
Barré de Miniac, C. (1996b). *Vers une didactique de l'écriture: Pour une approche pluridisciplinaire*. Bruxelles: De Boeck Université.
Bartholomae, D., & Matway, B. (2010). The Pittsburgh study of writing. *Across the Disciplines, 7*. Retrieved from http://wac.colostate.edu/atd/articles/bartholomae_matway2010/index.cfm. Accessed on August 26, 2011.
Barton, D. (1994). *Literacy: An introduction to the ecology of written language*. London: Blackwell.
Barton, D., & Tusting, K. (2005). *Beyond communities of practice: Language, power, and social context*. Cambridge: Cambridge University Press.
Bawarshi, A., & Reiff, M. (2010). *Genre: An introduction to history, theory, research, and pedagogy*. West Lafayette, IN: Parlor Press and WAC Clearinghouse.
Baynham, M. (1999). Double-voicing and the scholarly "I": On incorporating the words of others in academic discourse. *Text, 19*, 485–504.
Baynham, M. (2000). Academic writing in new and emergent discipline areas. In M. R. Lea & B. Stierer (Eds.), *Student writing in higher education: New contexts* (pp. 17–31). Buckingham: The Society for Research into Higher Education/Open University Press.
Bazerman, C. (1981). What written knowledge does: Three examples of academic discourse. *Philosophy of the Social Sciences, 11*, 361–387.
Bazerman, C. (1988). *Shaping written knowledge: The genre and activity of the experimental article in science*. Madison, WI: University of Wisconsin Press.
Bazerman, C. (1989). *The informed reader: Contemporary issues in the disciplines*. Boston, MA: Houghton Mifflin.
Bazerman, C. (1991). How natural philosophers can cooperate: The rhetorical technology of coordinated research in Joseph Priestley's history and present state of electricity. In

C. Bazerman & J. Paradis (Eds.), *Textual dynamics of the professions* (pp. 13–44). Madison, WI: University of Wisconsin Press.

Bazerman, C. (1993). Intertextual self-fashioning: Gould and Lewontin's representations of the literature. In J. Selzer (Ed.), *Understanding scientific prose* (pp. 361–388). Madison, WI: University of Wisconsin Press.

Bazerman, C. (1994). Systems of genres and the enactment of social intentions. In A. Freedman & P. Medway (Eds.), *Genre and the new rhetoric* (pp. 79–101). London: Taylor & Francis.

Bazerman, C. (1997). Discursively structured activities. *Mind, Culture, and Activity*, *4*, 296–308.

Bazerman, C. (1999). *The languages of Edison's light*. Cambridge: MIT Press.

Bazerman, C. (2001). Anxiety in action: Sullivan's interpersonal psychiatry as a supplement to Vygotskian psychology. *Mind, Culture and Activity*, *8*(2), 174–186.

Bazerman, C. (2003). Social forms as habitats for action. *Journal of the Interdisciplinary Crossroads*, *1*, 123–142.

Bazerman, C. (2004a). Intertextualities: Volosinov, Bakhtin, literary theory, and literacy studies. In A. Ball & S. W. Freedman (Eds.), *Bakhtinian perspectives on languages, literacy, and learning* (pp. 53–65). New York, NY: Cambridge University Press.

Bazerman, C. (2004b). Speech acts, genres, and activity systems: How texts organize activity and people. In C. Bazerman & P. Prior (Eds.), *What writing does and how it does it: An introduction to analyzing texts and textual practices* (pp. 79–101). Mahwah, NJ: Lawrence Erlbaum.

Bazerman, C. (2004c). Intertextuality: How texts rely on other text. In C. Bazerman & P. Prior (Eds.), *What writing does and how it does it. An Introduction to analyzing texts and textual practices* (pp. 83–96). Mahwah, NJ: Lawrence Erlbaum Associates.

Bazerman, C. (2010). Paying the rent: Languaging particularity and novelty. *Revista Brasileira de Lingüística Aplicada*, *10*(2), 459–469.

Bazerman, C., Joseph, L., Bethel, L., Chavkin, T., Fouquette, D., & Garufis, J. (2005). *Reference guide to writing across the curriculum* (Retrieved from http://wac.colostate.edu/books/bazerman_wac/. Accessed on August, 25, 2011). West Lafayette, IN: Parlor Press and The WAC Clearinghouse.

Bazerman, C., & Paradis, J. G. (1991). *Textual dynamics of the professions: Historical and contemporary studies of writing in professional communities*. Madison, WI: University of Wisconsin Press.

Bazerman, C., & Prior, P. (Eds.). (2004). *What writing does and how it does it: An introduction to analyzing texts and textual practices*. Mahwah, NJ: Lawrence Erlbaum.

Beaufort, A. (2007). *College writing and beyond: A new framework for university writing instruction*. Logan, UT: Utah State University Press.

Becher, T. (1989). *Academic tribes and territories: Intellectual enquiry and the cultures of disciplines*. Milton Keynes: The Society for Research into Higher Education and Open University Press.

Beck, I. L., McKeown, M. G., & Worthy, J. (1995). Giving a text voice can improve students' understanding. *Reading Research Quarterly*, *30*, 220–238.

Belcher, D. (1994). The apprenticeship approach to advanced academic literacy: Graduate students and their mentors. *English for Specific Purposes*, *13*, 23–34.

Belcher, D. (2007). Seeking acceptance in and English-only research world. *Journal of Second Language Writing*, *18*(4), 221–234.

Bennati, D., Fanfani, G., Palesi, I. I., & Zunino, C. (2009). *Scrivere tesi e tesine. Breve guida pratica A cura dei tutor della facoltà di Lettere e Filosofia. Facoltà di Lettere e Filosophia Università degli Studi di Siena.* Retrieved from http://web.lett.unisi.it/os/facolta/files/file/Scrivere_tesi_e_tesine.pdf

Bennett, K. (2007). Epistemicide! The tale of a predatory discourse. *The Translator, 13,* 151–169.

Benveniste, E. (1970). L'appareil formel de l'énonciation. *Languages, 5*(17), 12–18.

Benveniste, E. (1966/1974). *Problèmes de linguistique générale* [Problems in general linguistics]. Paris: Gallimard.

Bereiter, C., & Scardamalia, M. (1987). *The psychology of written composition.* Hillsdale, NJ: Erlbaum.

Berkenkotter, C., & Huckin, T. (1995). *Genre knowledge in disciplinary communication.* Hillsdale, NJ: Lawrence Erlbaum.

Berkenkotter, C., Huckin, T. N., & Ackerman, J. (1988). Conventions, conversations, and the writer: Case study of a student in a rhetoric PhD program. *Research in the Teaching of English, 22,* 9–41.

Bernstein, B. (2000). *Pedagogy, symbolic control and identity: Theory, research and critique.* Lanham, MD: Rowman & Littlefield Publishers.

Bhatia, V. K. (1993). *Analysing genre language use in professional settings.* London: Longman.

Bhatia, V. K. (2002). Applied genre analysis: A multi-perspective model. *Ibérica: Revista De La Asociación Europea De Lenguas Para Fines Específicos (AELFE), 4,* 3–19.

Biber, D. (2006). *University language: A corpus-based study of spoken and written registers.* Amsterdam: John Benjamins.

Biber, D., Johansson, S., Leech, G., Conrad, S., & Finegan, E. (1999). *Longman grammar of spoken and written English.* London: Longman.

Björk, L., Bräuer, G., Rienecker, L., & Jørgensen, P. S. (Eds.). (2003). *Teaching academic writing in European higher education.* Amsterdam: Kluwer Academic Publishers.

Björk, L., & Räisänen, C. (1996). *Academic writing. A university writing course.* Lund: Studentlitteratur.

Black, P. J., & Wiliam, D. (1998). Assessment and classroom learning. *Assessment in Education, 5,* 7–77.

Blakeslee, A. (2001). *Interacting with audiences: Social influences on the production of scientific writing.* Mahwah, NJ: Lawrence Erlbaum.

Bloom, L. (1981). Why graduate students can't write. Implications of research on writing anxiety for graduate education. *Journal of Advanced Composition, 2*(1–2), 103–117.

Boch, F., & Frier, C. (forthcoming). L'enseignement de l'écrit dans les universités françaises: Une problématique récente [Teaching writing in French universities: A recent question]. In C. Thaiss, G. Bräuer, P. Carlino, & G.-W. L. (Eds.), *Writing programs worldwide: Profiles of academic writing in many places.* Parlor Press and WAC Clearinghouse, http://wac.colostate.edu/books/

Boch, F., & Grossmann, F. (Eds.). (2001a). *Apprendre à citer le discours d'autrui* [Learning to cite others' discourse]. *LIDIL, 24.* Grenoble: Université Stendhal.

Boch, F., & Grossmann, F. (2001b). De l'usage des citations dans le discours théorique. Des constats aux propositions didactiques [Using citations in theoretical discourse. Observations and didactic proposals]. *LIDIL, 24,* 91–111.

Boch, F., & Grossmann, F. (2002). Se référer au discours d'autrui: Comparaison entre néophytes et experts [Referring to others' discourse: Comparisons between beginners and experts]. *Enjeux, 54,* 41–51.

Boch, F., & Grossmann, F. (2007). L'énonciation dans les manuels scolaires de troisième [Enunciation in junior high school students' textbooks]. *LIDIL*, *35*, 25–40.

Boch, F., & Reuter, Y. (Eds.) (2004). *Les écrits universitaires* [University writing]. *Pratiques, 121–122*, Metz: Cresef.

Boch, F., & Rinck, F. (Eds.) (2010). *Enonciation et rhétorique dans les écrits scientifiques* [Enunciation and rhetoric in scientific writing]. *LIDIL*, *41*. Grenoble: ELLUG.

Boch, F., Rinck, F., & Grossmann, F. (2009). Le cadrage théorique dans l'article scientifique, un lieu propice à la circulation des discours [Theoretical framing in scientific articles, an appropriate location for discourse circulation]. In J.-M. Lopez Munoz, S. Marnette, L. Rosier, & D. Vincent (Eds.), *La circulation des discours* [Discourse circulation] (pp. 1–12). Québec, QC: Nota Bene.

Boice, R. (1993). Writing blocks and tacit knowledge. *Journal of Higher Education*, *64*(1), 54.

Booth, W. C. (1963). The rhetorical stance. *College Composition and Communication*, *14*, 139–145.

Bosch, B., Scheuer, N., & Mateos, M. (2006). Cuando resumir se parece a ... Concepciones de estudiantes universitarios sobre la actividad de resumir [When summarizing looks like ... University students' conceptions about the activity of summarize]. *Espacios en Blanco*, *16*, 71–96.

Boscolo, P., Arfé, B., & Quarisa, M. (2007). Improving the quality of students' academic writing: An intervention study. *Studies in Higher Education*, *32*(4), 419–438.

Boscolo, P., & Carotti, L. (2003). Does writing contribute to improving high school students' approach to literature? *L1 – Educational Studies in Language and Literature*, *3*, 197–224.

Bourdieu, P., & Passeron, J. C. (1977). *Reproduction in education, society and culture*. London: Sage.

Bracewell, R. J., Frederiksen, C. H., & Frederiksen, J. E. (1982). Cognitive processes in composing and comprehending. *Educational Psychologist*, *17*, 146–174.

Brandt, D. (2001). *Literacy in American lives*. New York, NY: Cambridge University Press.

Breiger, R. (2004). The analysis of social networks. In M. Hardy & A. Bryman (Eds.), *Handbook of data analysis* (pp. 505–526). London: Sage Publications.

Britton, R. (1994). Publication anxiety: Conflict between communication and affiliation. *International Journal of Psychoanalysis*, *75*, 1213–1224.

Bronckart, J. P. (1985). *Le fonctionnement des discours. Un modèle psychologique et une méthode d'analyse* [Discursive functioning. A psychological model and an analytic method]. Paris: Delachaux et Niestlé.

Brown, E., & Cairns, P. (2004). A grounded investigation of game immersion. In *Proceedings from CHI' 04: The SIGCHI conference on human factors in computing systems*. ACM Press, NY (pp. 1297–1300).

Buckingham, L. (2008). Development of English academic writing competence by Turkish scholars. *International Journal of Doctoral Studies*, *3*, 1–18.

Burbules, N. C. (1993). *Dialogue in teaching: Theory and practice*. New York: Teachers College Press.

Burrough-Boenisch, J. (1999). International reading strategies for IMRD articles. *Written Communication*, *16*(3), 296–316.

Burrough-Boenisch, J. (2003). Shapers of published NNS research articles. *Journal of Second Language Writing*, *12*, 223–243.

Caffarella, R., & Barnet, B. (2000). Teaching doctoral students to become scholarly writers: The importance of giving and receiving critiques. *Studies in Higher Education*, *25*(1), 39–52.

Campbell, J., Smith, D., & Brooker, R. (1998). From conception to performance: How undergraduate students conceptualise and construct essays. *Higher Education, 36,* 449–469.

Campbell, P. N. (1975). The personae of scientific discourse. *Quarterly Journal of Speech, 61,* 391–405.

Camps, A. (1992). Algunas observaciones sobre la capacidad de revisión de los adolescentes [Some observations about the teenagers' revision skills]. *Infancia Y Aprendizaje, 58,* 65–82.

Camps, A. (2003). Miradas diversas a la enseñanza y el aprendizaje de la composición escrita [Diverse ways to look at teaching and learning writing]. *Lectura Y Vida, 24*(4), 14–23.

Camps, A., & Milian, M. (2000). Metalinguistic activity in learning to write: An introduction. In G. Rijlaarsdam, & E. Espéret (Series Eds.), A. Camps, & M. Milian (Vol. Eds.), *Studies in writing: Vol. 6. Metalinguistic activity in learning to write* (pp. 1–29). Amsterdam: Amsterdam University Press.

Canagarajah, A. S. (2002). *A geopolitics of academic writing.* Pittsburgh, PA: University of Pittsburgh Press.

Canagarajah, A. S. (2004). Multilingual writers and the struggle for voice in academic discourse. In A. Pavlenko & A. Blackledge (Eds.), *Negotiation of identities in multilingual contexts* (pp. 266–288). Tonowanda, NY: Multilingual Matters.

Cargill, M. (2004). Transferable skills within research degrees: A collaborative genre-based approach to developing publication skills and its implications for research education. *Teaching in Higher Education, 9*(1), 84–98.

Carlino, P. (2003). La experiencia de escribir una tesis: Contextos que la vuelven más difícil [The experience of writing a thesis: Contexts that make it more difficult]. *Anales Del Instituto de Lingüística, xxiv-xxv-xxvi,* 41–62. Retrieved from http://www.escrituraylectura.com.ar/posgrado/articulos/Carlino_La experiencia de escribir una tesis.pdf

Carlino, P. (2005a). *Escribir, leer y aprender en la universidad: Una introducción a la alfabetización académica* [Writing, Reading and learning at the university: An introduction to academic literacy]. Buenos Aires: Fondo de Cultura Económica.

Carlino, P. (2005b). Por qué no se completan las tesis en los posgrados? Obstáculos percibidos por maestrandos en curso y *magistri* exitosos [Why theses are not completed in postgraduate courses? Perceived obstacles by successful and unsuccessful postgraduate students. *Educere, Revista Venezolana de Educación, 9*(30), 415–420. Retrieved from http://www.saber.ula.ve/bitstream/123456789/19980/2/articulo19.pdf (last accessed November, 22, 2011).

Carlino, P. (2006). La escritura en la investigación [Writing in researching]. In C. Wainerman (Ed.), *Documentos de Trabajo.* Buenos Aires: Escuela de Educación de la Universidad de San Andrés. Retrieved from http://www.udesa.edu.ar/files/EscEdu/DT/DT19-CARLINO.PDF (last accessed November, 22, 2011).

Carlino, P. (2010). Reading and writing in the social sciences in Argentine universities. In C. Bazerman, R. Krut, S. E. Null, P. Rogers & A. Stansell (Eds.), *Traditions of writing research* (pp. 283–296). Oxford: Routledge.

Carlino, P. (in press). Who takes care of the teaching of writing in Latin America and Spain? In C. Thaiss, G. Bräuer, P. Carlino, & L. Ganobcsik-Williams (Eds.), *Writing programs worldwide: Profiles of academic writing in many places.* Parlor Press and WAC Clearing-house, http://wac.colostate.edu/books/

Carter, M. (2007). Ways of knowing, doing and writing in the disciplines. *College Composition and Communication, 58*(3), 385–418.

Carter, M., Miller, C., & Penrose, A. (1998). *Effective composition instruction: What does the research show?* Center for Communication in Science, Technology and Management, Publication Series, No. 3, April, North Carolina State University. Retrieved from http://

www4.ncsu.edu/~crmiller/Etcetera/Effective_Comp_Instr.pdf (last accessed November, 22, 2011).

Casanave, C. (2002). *Writing games: Multicultural case studies of academic literacy practices in higher education*. Mahwah, NJ: Lawrence Erlbaum.

Castelló, M. (1997). Els textos acadèmics des de la perspectiva dels estudiants: Quan, com i per què cal escriure [Academic texts from the students' perspective: When, how and why writing is needed]. *Articles De Didàctica De La Llengua i De La Literatura*, *13*, 32–45.

Castelló, M. (1999). El conocimiento que tienen los alumnos sobre la escritura [Students' knowledge about writing]. In J. I. Pozo & C. Monereo (Eds.), *El aprendizaje estratégico* (pp. 197–217). Madrid: Santillana.

Castelló, M. (2000). Students' conceptions on academic writing. In A. Camps & M. Milian (Eds.), *Metalinguistic activity in writing* (pp. 49–78). Amsterdam: University Press.

Castelló, M. (2007). Los efectos de los afectos en la comunicación académica [The effects of affects in academic communication]. In M. Castelló (Ed.), *Escribir y comunicarse en contextos científicos y académicos* [Writing and communicating in scientific and academic contexts: Knowledge and strategies] (pp. 137–161). Barcelona: Graó.

Castelló, M. (2008). Escribir trabajos de investigación con alumnos de grado [Writing research papers with undergraduate students]. *Textos: Didáctica De La Lengua Y De La Literatura*, *50*, 21–29.

Castelló, M., Bañales, G., & Vega, N. (2010). Research approaches to regulation of academic writing: State of the art. *Electronic Journal of Research in Educational Psychology*, *8*(3), 1253–1282. No. 22.

Castelló, M., Corcelles, M., Iñesta, A., Bañales, G., & Vega, N. (2011a). La voz del autor en la escritura académica: Una propuesta para su análisis [Authorial voice in academic writing: A methodological proposal for its analysis]. *Signos*, *44*(76), 105–117.

Castelló, M., González, L., & Iñesta, A. (2010). La regulación de la escritura académica en el doctorado: El impacto de la revisión colaborativa en los textos [Academic writing regulation in doctoral studies: The impact of collaborative revision in texts]. *Revista Española de Pedagogía*, *247*, 521–537.

Castelló, M., Iñesta, A., Miras, M., Solé, I., Teberosky, A., & Zanotto, M. (2007). *Escribir y comunicarse en contextos científicos y académicos. Conocimientos y estrategias* [Writing and communicating in scientific and academic contexts: Knowledge and strategies]. Barcelona: Graó.

Castelló, M., Iñesta, A., & Monereo, C. (2009). Towards self-regulated academic writing: An exploratory study with graduate students in a situated learning environment. *Electronic Journal of Research in Educational Psychology*, *22.7*(3), 1107–1130.

Castelló, M., Iñesta, A., Pardo, M., Liesa, E., & Martinez-Fernández, R. (2011b). Tutoring the end-of-studies dissertation: Helping psychology students find their academic voice. *Higher Education* (On-line first; published April 1, 2011). doi: 10.1007/s10734-011-9428-9.

Castelló, M., & Monereo, C. (2005). Students' note-taking as a knowledge construction tool. *L1-Educational Studies in Language and Literature*, *5*(3), 265–285.

Cazden, C. (2009). Writing a narrative of multiple voices. In A. Carter, T. Lillis & S. Parkin (Eds.), *Why writing matters. Issues of access and identity in writing research and pedagogy*. Amsterdam: John Benjamins Publishing Company.

Chanock, K. (2007). Helping thesis writers to think about genre: What is prescribed, what may be possible. *WAC Journal*, *18*, 31–41.

Charaudeau, P., & Maingueneau, D. (2002). *Dictionnaire d'analyse dudDiscours*. Paris: Seuil.

Charles, M. (2007). Reconciling top-down and bottom-up approaches too graduate writing: Using a corpus to teach rhetorical functions. *Journal of English for Academic Purposes*, *6*, 289–302.

Charney, D., Newman, J. H., & Palmquist, M. (1995). "I'm just no good at writing": Epistemological style and attitudes toward writing. *Written Communication, 12*, 298–329.

Chartier, A. M., & Hébrard, J. (1994). *Discursos sobre la lectura (1880–1980)* [Discourses about Reading (1880–1980)]. Barcelona: Gedisa.

Chavez, I. (2008). *La démarcation dans les écrits scientifiques-Les collocations transdisciplinaires comme aide à l'écrit universitaire auprès des étudiants étrangers* [The dissertation in scientific writing: Transdisciplinary collocations as a way to support foreign students' university writing], Mémoire de Master Français Langue Etrangère Recherche, ss.dir. Cristelle Cavalla, Université Stendhal Grenoble3.

Cherry, R. D. (1988). Ethos versus persona: Self-representation in written discourse. *Written Communication, 15*, 384–410.

Chevallard, Y. (1991). *La transposition didactique: Du savoir savant au savoir enseigné* [Didactic transposition: From advanced knowledge to taught knowledge]. Grenoble: La Pensée Sauvage.

Chiseri-Strater, E. (1991). *Academic literacies: The public and private discourse of university students*. Portsmouth: Boynton/Cook.

Cho, D. W. (2009). Science journal paper writing in an EFL context: The case of Korea. *English for Specific Purposes, 28*, 230–239.

Cho, K., & Mac Arthur, C. (2010). Student revision with peer and expert reviewing. *Learning & Instruction, 20*(4), 328–338.

Christie, F. (1991). First and second order registers in education. In E. Ventola (Ed.), *Functional and systemic linguistics: Approaches and uses (Trends in linguistic studies and monographs 55)* (pp. 235–256). Berlin: Walter de Gruyter.

Christie, F. (2000). Pedagogic discourse in the post-compulsory years: Pedagogic subject positioning. *Linguistics and Education, 11*, 313–331.

Clark, W. (2006). *Academic charisma and the origins of the research university*. Chicago, IL: University of Chicago Press.

Clyne, M. G. (1987). Cultural differences in the organization of academic texts: English and German. *Journal of Pragmatics, 11*, 211–241.

Coleman, L. (2012). Possibilities for recontextualisation in academic literacies research: The case of a South African vocational web design and development course. *Higher Education Research and Development, 30*(3) (forthcoming).

Collins, L., Halter, R., Lightbown, P., & Spada, N. (1999). Time and the distribution of time in L2 instruction. *TESOL Quarterly, 33*(4), 655–680.

Connor, U. (1996). *Contrastive rhetoric: Cross-cultural aspects of second language writing*. Cambridge: Cambridge University Press.

Connor, U. (1999). Learning to write academic prose in a second language: A literacy autobiography. In G. Braine (Ed.), *Non-native educators in English-language teaching* (pp. 29–42). Mahwah, NJ: Erlbaum.

Connor, U. (2002). New directions in contrastive rhetoric. *TESOL Quarterly, 36*(4), 493–510.

Conrad, S. (1996). *Academic discourse in two disciplines: Professional writing and student development in biology and history*. Unpublished doctoral dissertation. Northern Arizona University, Arizona.

Cooke, R. (2002). Helping scientists to write scientific English: challenges and issues, *ASp: La Revue Du GERAS* [En ligne], 37–38, http://asp.revues.org/1429 (last retrieved August, 25, 2011).

Cortes, V. (2004). Lexical bundles in published and student disciplinary writing: Examples from history and biology. *English for Specific Purposes, 23*, 397–423.

Council of Graduate Schools. (2007). *Ph.D. completion and attrition: Analysis of baseline program data from the Ph.D. Completion Project.* Retrieved from http://www. phdcompletion.org/quantitative/PhDC_Program_Completion_Data_Demographic.pdf (last accessed November, 22, 2011).

Cozzens, S. (1985). Comparing the sciences: Citation context analysis of papers from neuropharmacology and the sociology of science. *Social Studies of Science, 15*(1), 127–153.

Creme, P., & Hunt, C. (2002). Creative Participation in the essay writing process. *Arts and Humanities in Higher Education, 1*(2), 145–166.

Cribb, A., & Gewirtz, S. (2006). Doctoral supervision in a managerial climate. *International Studies in Sociology of Education, 16*(3), 223–236.

Crinon J., & Guigue M. (2006). *Écriture et professionnalisation* [Writing and professionalization]. Revue française de pédagogie [En ligne], 156. Retrieved from http:// rfp.revues.org/621

Crismore, A. (1983). Mind your footing: The metadiscourse factor in learning from texts. In H. Singer & T. Bean (Eds.), *Learning from text: Explanations and strategies: Proceedings of preconvention institute* (pp. 15–30). Anaheim, CA: International Reading Association.

Crismore, A., Markkanen, R., & Steffensen, M. S. (1993). Metadiscourse in persuasive writing: A study of texts written by American and Finnish university students. *Written Communication, 10*, 39–71.

Crookes, G. (1986). Towards a validated approach to genre analysis: An exploratory study. *Applied Linguistics, 7*(1), 57–70.

Csikszentmihalyi, M. (1975). *Beyond boredom and anxiety: Experiencing flow in work and play.* San Francisco, CA: Jossey-Bass.

Csikzsentmihalyi, M. (1990). *Flow: The psychology of optimal experience.* New York, NY: Harper and Row.

Cummins, J. (1998). Immersion education for the millennium: What have we learned from 30 years of research on second language immersion? In M. R. Childs & R. M. Bostwick (Eds.), *Learning through two languages* (pp. 34–47). Japan: KatohGakuen.

Curry, M. J., & Lillis, T. (2004). Multilingual scholars and the imperative to publish in English: Negotiating interests, demands, and rewards. *TESOL Quarterly, 38*(4), 663–688.

Curry, M. J., & Lillis, T. (2009). *Academic writing in a global context.* Abingdon: Routledge.

Dabène, M. (1987). *L'adulte et l'écriture: Contribution à une didactique de l'écrit en langue maternelle* [The adult and writing: Contributions to a didactics of writing in preschool]. Bruxelles: De Boeck-Université.

Dai, D. Y., & Wang, X. (2007). The role of need for cognition and reader beliefs in text comprehension and interest development. *Contemporary Educational Psychology, 32*, 332–347.

Dalmas, M., Foschi Albert, M., & Neuland, E. (Eds.) (2009). *Wissenschaftliche textsorten im Germanistikstudium Deutsch-Italienischfranzösisch kontrastiv* [Academic text types in Germanic Studies: German-Italian-French contrasts]. *Trilaterales Forschungsprojekt in Der Villa Vigoni (2007–2008).* Loveno di Menaggio: Villa Vigoni. Retrieved from http://www.villavigoni.it/ fileadmin/user_upload/pdfs/WissenschaftlicheTextsortenGermanistikstudium.pdf (last retrieved April 1, 2011).

Daunay, B., Delcambre, I., Dufays, J. L., & Thyrion, F. (2007). Didactique de l'écriture-lecture et formation des enseignants, Villeneuve d'Ascq, CEGES – Université Charles de Gaulle – Lille 3.

Daunay, B., Hassan, R., Lepez, B., & Morisse, M. (2006). *Les écrits professionnels des enseignants: Approche didactique* [The professional writing of teachers: A didactics approach]. Rapport de recherche BQR – Université de Lille 3.

Delamont, S., & Atkinson, P. (2001). Doctoring uncertainty: Mastering craft knowledge. *Social Studies of Science, 31*(1), 87–107.

Delamont, S., Atkinson, P., & Parry, O. (1997). Critical mass and doctoral research: Reflections on the Harris report. *Studies in Higher Education, 22*(3), 319–331.

Delcambre, I. (2001). Formes diverses d'articulation entre discours d'autrui et discours propre. Analyse de commentaires de textes théoriques [Diverse forms of articulation between the discourse of others and one's own. Analysis of commentary on theoretical texts]. *LIDIL, 24*, 135–166.

Delcambre, I. (2010). Genres du discours [Genres of discourse]. In Y. Reuter (Ed.), *Dictionnaire des concepts fondamentaux des didactiques* [Dictionary of fundamental didactic concepts] (pp. 117–122). Bruxelles: De Boeck.

Delcambre, I., & Boch, F. (2006). *Les écrits à l'université. Inventaires, pratiques, modeles* [University writing: Inventories, practices, models]. Grant proposal approved by l'Agence National de Recherches, France.

Delcambre, I., Donahue, C., & Lahanier-Reuter, D. (2010). Ruptures et continuités dans l'écriture à l'université [Ruptures and continuities in university writing]. *Scripta, 13*(24), 227–244.

Delcambre, I., & Jovenet, A.-M. (Eds.) (2002). *Lire-écrire dans le supérieur* [Reading and writing in higher education]. *Spirale, 29*, 3–264.

Delcambre, I., & Laborde-Milaa, I. (2002). Diversité des modes d'investissement du scripteur dans l'introduction du mémoire professionnel [Diversity of modes of the writer's investment in professional report introductions]. *Enjeux, 53*, 11–22.

Delcambre, I., & Reuter, Y. (2002). Images du scripteur et rapports à l'écriture [Images of the writer and relationship to writing]. *Pratiques, 113–114*, 7–28.

Delcambre, I., & Reuter, Y. (2010). The French didactics approach to writing, from elementary school to university. In C. Bazerman, R. Krut, K. Lunsford, S. McLeod, S. Null & P. Rogers (Eds.), *Traditions of writing research* (pp. 17–30). New York: Routledge.

Dell'Aversano, C. (2006). Textbook design for academic writing: The PISA writing program. In C. Dell'Aversano, G. Hexadaktilos, J. Harbord, & O. Kruse (Eds.), *Teaching writing online and face to face* (Vol. 1, pp. 138–157). *Proceedings from the third conference of the European association for the teaching of academic writing*, June 2005, Athens.

Dell'Aversano, C., & Grilli, A. (2005). *La scrittura argomentativa. Dal saggio breve alla tesi di dottorato* [Argumentative writing. From the short essay to the doctoral thesis]. Le Monnier 2005 (pp. 904). Retrieved from http://www.isicast.org/varie/tesina/guidatesina.html (last retrieved April 28, 2011).

Dell'Aversano, C., & Grilli, A. (2009). Das akademische Schreiben im italienischen Hochschulsystem: Traditionen, lehrpraxis, perspektiven [Academic writing in the Italian university system: Traditions, teaching practice, perspectives]. In M. Dalmas, M. Foschi & E. Neuland (Eds.), *Wissenschaftliche textsorten im Germanistikstudium deutsch-italienisch-französisch kontrastiv. Trilaterales forschungsprojekt in der Villa Vigoni 2007–2008* (pp. 283–286). Loveno di menaggio: Villa Vigoni. Retrieved from http://www.villavigoni.it/fileadmin/user_upload/pdfs/Wissenschaf tlicheTextsortenGermanistikstudium.pdf (last retrieved April 1, 2011).

Dérive, M. J., & Fintz, C. (1998). Quelles pratiques implicites de l'écrit à l'université? [What are the implicit practices in university writing?] In C. Fintz (Ed.), *La didactique du français dans l'enseignement supérieur. Bricolage ou rénovation?* [French didactics in higher education: Fixing it up or renovation?] Paris: L'Harmattan.

Devitt, A. (2004). *Writing genres.* Carbondale, IL: Southern Illinois University Press.
Deyrich, M. (2004). Exploration didactique de la langue du milieu professionnel à l'université: Quel apport pour la définition de tâches d'enseignement- apprentissage? [Didactic exploration of professional language at the university: What contributions from the definition of teaching-learning tasks?]. *ASP: La revue du GERAS, 43–44,* 125–134.
Dias, P., Pare, A., Freedman, A., & Medway, P. (1999). *Worlds apart: Acting and writing in academic and workplace contexts.* Mahwah, NJ: Lawrence Erlbaum.
Dillon, C., Keogh, E., Freeman, J., & Davidoff, J. (2000). Aroused and immersed: The psychophysiology of presence. *Studies in Second Language Acquisition, 22*(4), 499–533.
Dirckinck-Holmfeld, L., Jones, C., & Lindström, B. (Eds.). (2009). *Analysing networked learning practices in higher education and continuing professional development.* Rotterdam, NL: Sense Publishers.
Dittmann, J., Geneuss, K. A., Nennstiel, C., & Quast, N. A. (2003). Scheibprobleme im Studium – Eine empirische Untersuchung [Student writing problems – An empirical study]. In K. Ehlich & A. Steets (Eds.), *Wissenschaftlich schreiben – lehren und lernen* (pp. 155–185). Berlin: Walter de Gruyter.
Dochy, J., Seegers, M., & Sluijsmans, D. (1999). The use of self-, peer- and co-assessment in higher education: A review. *Studies in Higher Education, 24*(3), 332–350.
Donahue, C. (2002a). Effets de l'écrit sur la construction du sujet textuel à l'université [Effects of writing on the construction of the textual subject at the university]. *Spirale, 29,* 75–99.
Donahue, C. (2002b). Quelles stratégies pour aider l'étudiant écrivain à gérer la polyphonie énonciative? [What strategies for helping student writers to manage enunciative polyphony?]. *Enjeux, 54,* 67–83.
Donahue, C. (2004). Student writing as negotiation. Fundamental movements between the common and the specific in French essays. In T. Kostouli (Ed.), *Writing in context(s) textual practices and learning processes in sociocultural settings* (pp. 137–164). Amsterdam: Kluwer Academic Publishers.
Donahue, C. (2007). Le sujet-je dans l'écrit universitaire aux Etats-Unis: Le débat 'expressiviste' [The subject-I in U.S. university writing: The 'expressivist' debate]. *Le Français Aujourd'hui, 157,* 53–61.
Donahue, C. (2008). *Ecrire à l'université: Analyse comparee en France et aux Etats-Unis* [Writing at the university: Comparative analysis, France-United States]. Villeneuve d'Ascq: Presses Universitaires du Septentrion.
Donahue, C. (2009). "Internationalization" and composition studies: Re-orienting the discourse. *College Composition and Communication, 61*(2), 212–243.
Donahue, C. (2010). L'écrit universitaire et la disciplinarité [University writing and disciplinarity]. In C. Blaser, & M. Ch. Pollet (Éds.), *L'appropriation des écrits universitaires* [Appropriation of university writing]. *Diptyque, 18,* 43–60.
Donahue, T. (2008). Cross-cultural analysis of student writing: Beyond discourses of difference. *Written Communication, 25,* 319–352.
Douglas, Y., & Hargadon, A. (2000). The pleasure principle: Immersion, engagement, flow. In *Proceedings from the eleventh ACM,* ACM Press, New York, NY.
Dressen, D. (2002). Identifying textual silence in scientific research articles: Recontextualizations of the field account in Geology. *Hermes, Journal of Linguistics, 28,* 81–108.
Dressen-Hammouda, D. (2008). From novice to disciplinary expert: Disciplinary identity and genre mastery. *English for Specific Purposes, 27,* 233–252.

Dudley-Evans, T. (1995). Common-core and specific approaches to the teaching of academic writing. In D. Belcher & G. Braine (Eds.), *Writing in a second language I* (pp. 293–312). Norwood, NJ: Ablex Publishing Corporation.

Dudley-Evans, T., & St John, M. J. (1998). *Developments in English for specific purposes: A multi-disciplinary approach.* Cambridge: Cambridge University Press.

Dysthe, O. (1996). The multivoiced classroom: Interaction of writing and classroom discourse. *Written Communication, 13*(3), 385–425.

Dysthe, O. (2002). Professors as mediators of academic text cultures: An interview study with advisors and Master's degree students in three disciplines in a Norwegian university. *Written Communication, 19*, 493–544.

Dysthe, O. (2007). How a reform affects writing in higher education. *Studies in Higher Education, 32*(2), 237–252.

Dysthe, O. (2009). What factors influence the improvement of academic writing practices? A study of reform of undergraduate writing in Norwegian higher education. In C. Bazerman, R. Krut, K. Lunsford, S. McLeod, S. Null, P. Rogers & A. Stansell (Eds.), *Traditions of writing research.* New York, NY: Routledge.

Dysthe, O., Lillejord, S., Vines, A., & Wasson, B. (2011). Productive E-feedback in higher education – Some critical issues. In S. Ludvigsen, A. Lund, I. Rasmussen & R. Säljö (Eds.), *Learning across sites: New tools, infrastructures and practices.* Oxford, UK: Pergamon Press.

Dysthe, O., Samara, A., & Westrheim, K. (2006). Multivoiced supervision of Master's students: A case study of alternative supervision practices in higher education. *Studies in Higher Education, 31*(3), 299–319.

Dysthe, O., & Tolo, A. (2007). Digital portfolios and feedback practices in a traditional university course. In M. Kankaanranta & P. Linnakylä (Eds.), *Perspectives on e-portfolios* (pp. 107–133). Jyväskylä, Finland: Agora Center, University of Jyväskylä Press.

Dysthe, O., & Webler, W.-D. (2010). Pedagogical issues from Humboldt to Bologna. The case of Norway and Germany. *Higher Education Policy, 23*, 247–270.

Eco, U. (1977). *Come si fa una tesi di laurea* [How to do a thesis]. Milano, Italy: Bompiani.

Eggins, S. (2004). *An introduction to systemic functional linguistics.* London: Continuum International Publishing Group.

Ehlich, K. (2003). Universitäre Textarten, universitäre Struktur [University genres, university structures]. In K. Ehlich & A. Steets (Eds.), *Wissenschaftlich schreiben – lehren und lernen* (pp. 13–28). Berlin: Walter de Gruyter.

Ehlich, K., & Steel (Eds.) (2003). *Wissenschaftlich Schreiben – lehren und lernen* [Academic writing – teaching and learning]. Berlin: Walter de Gruyter.

Ehrenberg, R., Jakubson, G., Groen, J., So, E., & Price, J. (2007). Inside the black box of doctoral education: What program characteristics influence doctoral students' attrition and graduation probabilities? *Educational Evaluation and Policy Analysis, 29*(2), 134–150.

Elbow, P. (1973). *Writing without teachers.* New York,NY: Oxford University Press.

Ellis, N. C. (2002). Frequency effects in second language processing. *Studies in Second Language Acquisition, 24*, 143–188.

Ellis, R. A., Taylor, C., & Drury, H. (2006). University student conceptions of learning science through writing. *Australian Journal of Education, 50*(1), 6–28.

Engeström, Y. (1993). Developmental studies of work as a testbench of activity theory: The case of primary care medical practice. In S. Chaiklin & J. Lave (Eds.), *Understanding practice: Perspectives on activity and context* (pp. 64–103). Cambridge: Cambridge University Press.

Engeström, Y., & Miettinen, R. (1999). *Perspectives on activity theory*. New York, NY: Cambridge University Press.

Engeström, Y., & Sannino, A. (2010). Studies of expansive learning: Foundations, findings and future challenges. *Educational Research Review*, *5*(1), 1–24.

Englander, K. (Ed.) (2006). Revision of scientific manuscripts by non-native English-speaking scientists in response to journal editors' language critiques. *Journal of Applied Linguistics*, *3*(2), 129–161.

Englander, K. (2009). Transformation of the identities of nonnative English speaking scientists. *Journal of Language, Identity and Education*, *8*(1), 35–53.

Englert, C. S., Mariage, T. V., & Dunsmore, K. (2006). Tenets of sociocultural theory in writing instruction research. In C. A. MacArthur, S. Graham & J. Fitzgerald (Eds.), *Handbook of writing research*. New York: The Guilford Press.

Erling, E. J., & Bartlett, T. (2008). Making English their own: The use of ELF among students of English at the FUB. *Nordic Journal of English Studies*, *5*, 9–40.

Ermi, L., & Mäyrä, F. (2005). Fundamental components of the gameplay experience: Analysing immersion. In S. De Castell & J. Jenson (Eds.), *Worlds in play*. Proceedings from Digital Games Research Association. pp. 14–27.

European Commission. (2008). COM(2008) 566: Multilingualism: An asset for Europe and a shared commitment.

Evans, T. (2002). Part-time research students: The 'Reserve Army' of research students for universities. In M. Kiley & G. Mullins (Eds.), *Quality in postgraduate research: Integrating perspectives* (pp. 138–144). Canberra, Australia: CELTS, University of Canberra.

Fabiani, J. L. (2006). A quoi sert la notion de discipline? In J. Boutier, J. C. Passeron & J. Revel (Eds.), *Qu'est-ce qu'une discipline?* (pp. 11–34). Paris: EHESS.

Fahnestock, J. (1986). Accommodating science: The rhetorical life of scientific facts. *Written Communication*, *3*(3), 275.

Fahnestock, J., & Secor, M. (1991). The rhetoric of literary criticism. In C. Bazerman & J. Paradis (Eds.), *Textual dynamics of the professions: Historical and contemporary studies of writing in professional communities* (pp. 74–96). WAC Clearinghouse Landmark Publications in Writing Studies. Retrieved from http://wac.colostate.edu/books/bazerman_dynamics/. Originally Published in Print, 1991. Madison, WI: University of Wisconsin Press.

Fairclough, N. (1993). *Discourse and social change*. Cambridge, UK: Polity Press.

Fairclough, N. L., & Wodak, R. (1997). Critical discourse analysis. In T. A. van Dijk (Ed.), *Discourse as social interaction* (Vol. 2). Discourse Studies. Multidisciplinary Introduction (pp. 258–84). London: Sage.

Farmer, F. (1995). Voice Reprised: Three etudes for a dialogic understanding. *Rhetoric Review*, *13*(2), 304–320.

Ferguson, G. (2002). If you pop over there: A corpus-based study of conditionals in medical discourse. *English for Specific Purposes*, *20*, 61–82.

Ferris, D. (2003). *Response to student writing: Implications for second language writers*. Mahwah, NJ: Lawrence Erlbaum.

Fishman, J., Lunsford, A., McGregor, B., & Otuteye, M. (2005). Performing writing, performing literacy. *College Composition and Communication*, *57*, 224–252.

Fishman, S. M., & McCarthy, L. P. (2002). *Whose goals? Whose aspirations? Learning to teach underprepared writers across the curriculum*. Logan: Utah State University Press.

Fløttum, K. (2003). Personal English, indefinite French and plural Norwegian scientific authors? Pronominal author manifestation in research articles. *Norsk Lingvistisk Tidsskrift*, *21*, 21–55.

Fløttum, K., Dahl, T., & Kinn, T. (2006). *Academic voices. Across languages and disciplines*. Amsterdam: John Benjamins.

Fløttum, K., & Vold, E. T. (2010). L'éthos auto-attribué d'auteurs-doctorants dans le discours scientifique. *LIDIL*, *41*, 41–58.

Flower, L. (1979). Writer-based prose: A cognitive basis for problems in writing. *College English*, *41*, 19–37.

Flower, L., & Hayes, J. R. (1981). The Cognition of discovery: Defining a rhetorical problem. *College Composition and Communication*, *31*, 21–32.

Flower, L., Stein, V., Ackerman, J., Kantz, M. J., McCormick, K., & Peck, W. C. (1990). *Reading to write: Exploring a cognitive and social process*. New York, NY: Oxford University Press.

Flowerdew, J. (1999a). Writing for scholarly publication in English: The case of Hong Kong. *Journal of Second Language Writing*, *8*(2), 123–145.

Flowerdew, J. (1999b). Problems in writing for scholarly publication in English: The case of Hong Kong. *Journal of Second Language Writing*, *8*(3), 243–264.

Flowerdew, J. (2000). Discourse community, legitimate peripheral participation, and the nonnative-English speaking scholar. *TESOL Quarterly*, *34*(1), 127–150.

Flowerdew, J. (Ed.) (2001). Attitudes of journal editors to nonnative speaker contributions *TESOL Quarterly*, *34*(1), 121–150.

Flowerdew, J. (2008a). Critical discourse analysis and strategies of resistance. In V. Bhatia, J. Flowerdew & R. Jones (Eds.), *Advances in discourse studies* (pp. 115–127). Abingdon: Routledge.

Flowerdew, J. (2008b). The non-Anglophone scholar at the periphery of scientific communication. *AILA Review*, *20*, 14–27.

Flowerdew, J., & Li, Y. (2007). Language re-use among Chinese apprentice scientists writing for publication. *Applied Linguistics*, *28*(3), 440–465.

Flowerdew, J., & Peacock, M. (2001). *Research perspectives on English for academic purposes*. Cambridge: Cambridge University Press.

Flowerdew, L. (2005). An integration of corpus-based and genre-based approaches to text analysis in EAP/ESP. *English for Specific Purposes*, *24*, 321–332.

Foster, D. (2002). Making the transition to university: Student writers in Germany. In D. Foster & D. Russell (Eds.), *Writing and Learning in cross-national perspective. Transitions from secondary to higher education* (pp. 192–241). Mahwah, NJ: Lawrence Erlbaum.

Foster, D. (2006). *Writing with authority: Students' roles as writers in cross-national perspective*. Carbondale, IL: Southern Illinois University Press.

Fowler, R. (1991). Critical linguistics. In K. Malmkjaer (Ed.), *The linguistics encyclopedia* (pp. 89–93). London: Routledge.

Fowler, R. (1996). On critical linguistics. In C. R. Caldas-Coulthard & M. Coulthard (Eds.), *Text and practices: Readings in critical discourse analysis* (pp. 3–14). London: Routledge.

Fowler, R., & Fowler, R. (1996). *Linguistic criticism*. Oxford: Oxford University Press.

Freeman, J., Avons, S. E., Pearson, D. E., & IJsselsteijn, W. A. (1999). Effects of sensory information and prior experience on direct subjective ratings of presence. *Presence: Teleoperators and Virtual Environments*, *8*, 1–13.

Galbraith, D. (1999). Writing as a knowledge-constituting process. In M. Torrance & D. Galbraith (Eds.), *Knowing what to write: Conceptual processes in text production.* Amsterdam: Amsterdam University Press.

Gale, K., Speedy, J., & Wyatt, J. (2010). Gatecrashing the oasis? A joint doctoral dissertation play. *Qualitative Inquiry, 16,* 21–28.

Gale, K., & Wyatt, J. (2008). *Between the two: A nomadic inquiry into collaborative writing* (Unpublished doctoral dissertation). University of Bristol, UK.

Galtung, J. (1981). Structure, culture, and intellectual style: An essay comparing saxonic, teutonic, gallic and nipponic approaches. *Social Science Information, 20,* 817–856.

Garcia, A. M. (Ed.) (1997). *Chicana feminist thought: The basic historical writings.* New York, NY: Psychology Press.

García, J. N., & Fidalgo, R. (2004). El papel del autoconocimiento de los procesos psicológicos de la escritura en la calidad de las composiciones escritas [The role of writing psychological processes knowledge awareness in composition writing quality]. *Revista De Psicología General y Aplicada, 57*(3), 281–297.

Gee, J. (1990). *Social linguistics and literacies: Ideology in discourses.* London: The Falmer Press.

Gee, J., Hull, G., & Lankshear, C. (1996). *The new work order: Behind the language of the new capitalism.* London: Allen & Unwin.

Gee, J. P. (2000). Identity as an analytic lens for research in education. *Review of Research in Education, 25,* 99–125.

Gee, J. P. (2005). *An introduction to discourse analysis. Theory and method.* New York, NY: Routledge.

Gentil, G. (2005). Commitments to academic biliteracy: Case studies of francophone university writers. *Written Communication, 22,* 421–471.

Gere, A. R. (1987). *Writing groups: History, theory, and implications.* Carbondale, IL: Southern Illinois University Press.

Gibbs, G. (Ed.) (1994). *Improving student learning: Theory and practice.* Oxford: Oxford Centre for Staff Development.

Giddens, A. (1984). *The constitution of society: Outline of the theory of structuration.* Berkeley, CA: University of California Press.

Gilquin, G., Granger, S., & Paquot, M. (2007). Learner corpora: The missing link in EAP pedagogy. *Journal of English for Academic Purposes, 6,* 319–335.

Goodwin, C. (1994). Professional vision. *American Anthropologist, 96,* 606–633.

Goodwin, C. (2000). Action and embodiment within situated human interaction. *Journal of Pragmatics, 32,* 1489–1522.

Goodwin, C. (2007). Environmentally coupled gestures. In S. Duncan, J. Cassell & E. Levy (Eds.), *Gesture and the dynamic dimensions of language* (pp. 195–212). Amsterdam: John Benjamins.

Goody, J. (1977). *The domestication of the savage mind.* Cambridge: Cambridge University Press.

Goswami, D., & Odell, L. (1985). *Writing in nonacademic settings.* New York, NY: Guilford Press.

Graham, S. (2006). Strategy instruction and the teaching of writing: A meta-analysis. In C. MacArthur, S. Graham & J. Fitzgerald (Eds.), *Handbook of writing research* (pp. 187–207). New York, NY: Guilford.

Graham, S., Schwartz, S., & MacArthur, A. (1993). Knowledge of writing and the composing process, attitude toward writing, and self-efficacy for students with and without learning disabilities. *Journal of Learning Disabilities, 26*(4), 237–249.

Griffith, B. C., Small, H. G., Stonehill, J. A., & Dey, S. (1974). The structure of scientific literatures (II): Towards a macro- and micro-structure for science. *Science Studies, 4*(4), 339–365.

Grodal, T. (2003). Stories for eye, ear, and muscles: Video games, media, and embodied experiences. In M. J. P. Wolf & B. Perron (Eds.), *The video game theory reader* (pp. 129–155). New York, NY: Routledge.

Groom, N. (2000). Attribution and averral revisited: Three perspectives on manifest intertextuality in academic writing. In P. Thompson (Ed.), *Patterns and perspectives: Insights into EAP writing practice* (pp. 14–25). Reading, UK: CALS.

Gross, A. G. (1990). *The rhetoric of science.* Cambridge, MA: Harvard University Press.

Grossmann, F. (2002). Les modes de référence à autrui chez les experts: L'exemple de la revue 'Langages' [Expert modes of reference to others: The example of the journal 'Langages']. *Faits De Langue, 19*, 255–262.

Grossmann, F. (2003). Du discours rapporté au discours autorisé, le maniement des noms d'auteur dans l'article en sciences humaines [From reported to authorized discourse, the use of author names in Humanities articles]. *Estudios de Lengua y Literatura francesas, 14*, 9–26.

Grossmann, F. (2010). L'auteur scientifique [The scientifc author]. Consulté le février 16, 2011, sur *Revue d'anthropologie des connaissances, 4*(3), 410–426. Retrieved from http://www.cairn.info/revue-anthropologie-des-connaissances-2010-3-page-410.htm

Grossmann, F., & Rinck, F. (2004). La surénonciation comme norme du genre. L'exemple de l'article de recherche et du dictionnaire en linguistique [Sur-enunciation as a generic norm. The example of the research article and the linguistics dictionary]. *Langages, 156*, 34–50.

Grossmann, F., Tutin, A., & Garcia da Silva, P. (2009). Filiation et transferts d'objets scientifiques dans les écrits de recherche [Filiation and transfer of scientific objects in research writing]. *Pratiques, 143-144*, 187–202.

Gruber, H., Rheindorf, M., Wetschanow, K., Reisigl, M., Muntigl, P., & Czinglar, C. (2006). *Genre, habitus und wissenschaftliches schreiben.* Wien: Lit Verlag.

Gruel, L., Galland, O., & Houzel, G. (2009). *Les étudiants en France. Histoire et sociologie d'une nouvelle jeunesse [French students. History and sociology of a new youth].* Rennes: Presses universitaires de Rennes.

Gustafsson, M. (2011). Writing centres/centers and English language learners: Research on institutional pressures, programmatic challenges, student expectations, and culturally sensitive strategies (Part II). Writing Research across Borders. Fairfax, VA: George Mason University.

Haas, C. (1994). Learning to read biology: One student's rhetorical development in college. *Written Communication, 11*(1), 43–84.

Hafner, C., & Candlin, C. (2007). Corpus tools as an affordance to learning in professional legal education. *Journal of English for Academic Purposes, 6*, 303–318.

Halliday, M. A. K. (1985). *An introduction to functional grammar.* London: Arnold.

Halliday, M. A. K., & Martin, J. R. (1993). *Writing science: Literacy and discursive power.* Pittsburgh: University of Pittsburgh Press.

Hammann, L. A. (2005). Self-regulation in academic writing tasks. *International Journal of Teaching and Learning in Higher Education, 17*(1), 15–26.

Harbord, J. (2010). *Writing in Central and Eastern Europe: Stakeholders and directions in initiating change.* Across the Disciplines, 7. Retrieved from http://wac.colostate.edu/atd/articles/harbord2010.cfm (last retrieved April 2, 2011).

Hartley, J., Branthwaite, A. J., Ganier, F., & Heurley, L. (Eds.). (2007). Lost in translation: Contributions of editors to the meanings of texts. *Journal of Information Science, 33*(5), 551–565.

Harwood, N. (2005). "Nowhere has anyone attempted…In this article I aim to do just that": A corpus-based study of self-promotional I and we in academic writing across four disciplines. *Journal of Pragmatics, 37*, 1207–1231.

Harwood, N., Austin, L., & Macauley, R. (2007). Proofreading in a UK university. *Journal of Second Language Writing, 18*(3), 166–190.

Hassan, R., Daunay, B., & Fialip, M. (2006). French perspectives on higher education writing research. *Proceedings from WDHE Conference*, May 11–12, Milton Keynes, UK: The Open University.

Haswell, R. (1991). *Gaining ground: Tales of development and interpretation*. Dallas, TX: Southern Methodist University Press.

Haswell, R. H. (2005). NCTE/CCCC's recent war on scholarship. *Written Communication, 22*(2), 198–223.

Hattie, J., & Timperley, H. (2007). The power of feedback. *Review of Educational Research, 77*(1), 81–112.

Hawisher, G., Selfe, C., Kisa, G., & Ahmed, S. (2009). Globalism and multimodality in a digitized world: Computers and composition studies. *Pedagogy: Critical Approaches to Teaching Literature, Language, Composition, and Culture, 10*, 55–68.

Hayes, J., & Flower, L. (1986). Writing research and the writer. *American Psychologist, 41*(10), 1106–1113.

Henderson, A., & Barr, R. (2010). Comparing indicators of authorial stance in psychology students' writing and published research articles. *Journal of Writing Research, 2*, 245–264.

Hepp, M. (2009). Zur Struktur des Bildungssystems in Italien: Das Hochschulwesen. In M. Dalmas, M. Foschi Albert, & E. Neuland (Eds.), *Wissenschaftliche textsorten im Germanistikstudium deutsch-italienisch-französisch kontrastiv. Trilaterales Forschungsprojekt in der Villa Vigoni 2007-2008* (pp. 38–41). [*Academic genres in study programs of German: German-Italian-French contrastive. Trilateral research project in Villa Vigoni. Loveno di Menaggio: Villa Vigoni*]. Loveno di Menaggio: Villa Vigoni. Retrieved from http://www.villavigoni.it/fileadmin/user_upload/pdfs/WissenschaftlicheTextsortenGermanistikstudium.pdf (last retrieved April 1, 2011).

Hermans, T. (1996). The translator's voice in translated narrative. *Target, 8*, 23–48.

Hidden, M. O. (2011). Some writing traditions in use in France: Description of an argumentative genre. *2011 CCCC workshop on international research*. Retrieved from http://compfaqs.org/CompFAQsInternational/2011CCCCWorkshopOnInternationalResearch

Hinton, C., Miyamoto, K., & Della-Chiesa, B. (2008). Brain research, learning and emotions. *European Journal of Education, 43*, 87–103.

Hofer, B. K., & Pintrich, P. R. (1997). The development of epistemological theories: Beliefs about knowledge and knowing and their relation to learning. *Review of Educational Research, 67*(1), 88–140.

Hofer, B. K., & Pintrich, P. R. (Eds.). (2002). *Personal epistemology. The psychology of beliefs about knowledge and knowing*. Mahwah, NJ: Laurence Erlbaum Associates.

Holland, C., Frank, F., & Cooke, T. (1998). *Literacy and the new work order: An international literature review*. Leicester: NIACE.

Horner, B., Necamp, S., & Donahue, C. (in press). Toward a multilingual composition scholarship: From English only to a translingual norm. *CCC*.

Hoskin, K. (1993). Education and the genesis of disciplinarity: The unexpected reversal. In E. Messer-Davidow, D. Shumway & D. Sylvan (Eds.), *Knowledges: Historical and critical studies in disciplinarity* (pp. 271–304). Charlottesville, VA: University of Virginia Press.

Hounsell, D. J. (1984). Learning and essay writing. In F. Marton, D. Hounsell & N. Entwistle (Eds.), *The experience of learning* (pp. 103–123). Edimburgo: Scottish Academic Press.

Howard, R. M. (1993). A plagiarism pentimento. *Journal of Teaching Writing, 11*(2), 233–246.

Hurtado, A., & Gurin, P. (2004). *Chicano/a identity in a changing U.S. society (The Mexican American experience): ¿Quién soy? ¿Quinês somos?* Tucson, AZ: University of Arizona Press.

Hyland, K. (1999). Academic attribution: Citation and the construction of disciplinary knowledge. *Applied Linguistics, 20*(3), 341–367.

Hyland, K. (2000). *Disciplinary discourses: Social interactions in academic writing.* Harlow, England: Pearson Education.

Hyland, K. (2001). Humble servants of the discipline? Self-mention in research articles. *English for Specific Purposes, 20*, 207–226.

Hyland, K. (2002). Authority and invisibility: authorial identity in academic writing. *Journal of Pragmatics, 34*, 1091–1112.

Hyland, K. (2003). Genre-based pedagogies: A social response to process. *Journal of Second Language Writing, 12*, 17–29.

Hyland, K. (2004a). *Disciplinary discourses: Social interactions in academic writing.* New York, NY: Longman.

Hyland, K. (2004b). Disciplinary interactions: Metadiscourse in L2 postgraduate writing. *Journal of Second Language Writing, 13*, 133–151.

Hyland, K. (2005a). *Metadiscourse: Exploring interaction in writing.* London: Continuum.

Hyland, K. (2005b). Stance and engagement: A model of interaction in academic discourse. *Discourse Studies, 7*(2), 173–192.

Hyland, K. (2008a). As can be seen: Lexical bundles and disciplinary variation. *English for Specific Purposes, 27*, 4–21.

Hyland, K. (2008b). Persuasion, interaction and the construction of knowledge: Representing self and others in research writing. *International Journal of English Studies, 8*, 1–23.

Hyland, K., & Tse, P. (2004). Metadiscourse in academic writing: A reappraisal. *Applied Linguistics, 25*, 156–177.

Hyland, K., & Tse, P. (2005). Hooking the reader: A corpus study of evaluative *that* in abstracts. *English for Specific Purposes, 24*, 123–139.

Hymes, D. (1974). *Foundations in sociolinguistics: An ethnographic approach.* Philadelphia, PA: University of Pennsylvania Press.

Hyon, S. (1996). Genre in three traditions: Implications for ESL. *TESOL Quarterly, 30*, 693–722.

Iancu, M., Bălu, I., & Lăzărescu, R. (2009). *Limba şi literatura română.* Manual pentru clasa a Xa. [Romanian Language and Literature. Textbook 10th grade]. Bucureşti: Editura Corint.

Iatcu, T. (2000). Teaching English as a third language to Hungarian-Romanian bilinguals. In J. Cenoz & U. Jessner (Eds.), *English in Europe: The acquisition of a third language* (pp. 236–247). Clevedon: Multilingual Matters.

Iedema, R. A. (2001). 'Analysing film and television: A social semiotic account of 'Hospital: An Unhealthy Business''. In L. van Theo & C. Jewitt (Eds.), *Handbook of visual analysis* (pp. 183–206). London: Sage Publications Ltd.

Iedema, R. A. (2003). *The discourses of post-bureaucratic organization.* Amsterdam: John Benjamins.

Igland, M.-A., & Ongstad, S. (2003a). Introducing Norwegian research on writing. *Written Communication, 19*(3), 339–344.

Igland, M.-A., & Ongstad, S. (2003b). Introducing Norwegian research on writing. *Written Communication, 19*(4), 452–457.

Ijsselsteijn, W., de Kort, Y., Poels, K., Jurgelionis, A., & Bellotti, F. (2007). Characterising and measuring user experiences in digital games. *Proceedings from Advances in Computer Engineering Conference'07*. Salzbourg, Austria, 12-15 June.

Iñesta, A. (2009). *The regulation of research article writing. Strategies of expert writers in Spanish as their first language (L1) and in English as an international language (EIL)*. Retrieved from http://www.tesisenxarxa.net/TDX-1019110-103855/index.html

Ivanič, R. (1998). *Writing and identity. The discoursal construction of identity in academic writing.* Amsterdam: John Benjamins.

Ivanič, R. (2005). The discoursal construction of writer identity. In R. Beach, J. Green, M. Kamil & T. Shanahan (Eds.), *Multidisciplinary perspectives on literacy research* (pp. 391–416). Cresskill, NJ: Hampton Press.

Ivanič, R. (2006). Language, learning and identification. In R. Kiely, P. Read-Dickins, H. Woodfield & G. Clibbons (Eds.), *Language, culture and identity in applied linguistics* (pp. 7–30). London: British Association for Applied Linguistics/Equinox.

Ivanič, R., Edwards, R., & Barton, D. (2009). *Improving learning in college: Rethinking literacies across the curriculum.* New York, NY: Taylor & Francis.

Jakobs, E.-M. (2005). Writing at work. In E.-M. Jakobs, K. Lehnen & K. Schindler (Eds.), *Schreiben am Arbeitsplatz* (pp. 13–40). Frankfurt am Main: Verlag für Sozialwissenschaften.

Jarausch, K. H. (1991). Universität und Hochschule. In C. Berg (Ed.), *Handbuch Der Deutschen Bildungsgeschichte, 4, 1870,1918 [University and College. Handbook of German educational history]* (pp. 313–344). München: CH. Beck.

Järvelä, S., Hurme, T.-R., & Järvenoja, H. (2007). Self-regulation and motivation in computer supported collaborative learning environments. In S. Ludvigsen, A. Lund & R. Säljö (Eds.), *Learning in social practices. ICT and new artifacts-transformation of social and cultural practices. EARLI series: Advances in Learning.* Oxford: Pergamon Press.

Jensen, H. (2010). *The organisation of the university.* Working Papers on University Reform. Danish School of Education, University of Aarhus, April 2010.

Jeppesen, C., Nelson, A., & Guerrini, V. (2004). *Diagnóstico y perspectiva de los estudios de posgrado en Argentina. Informe del Estudio Nacional Realizado por IESALC – UNESCO.*

Johns, A. (2002). *Genre in the classroom: Multiple perspectives.* Mahwah, NJ.: Lawrence Erlbaum.

Johns, A. M. (2007). Genre awareness for the novice academic student. An ongoing quest. *Language Teaching, 41*(2), 237–252.

Johns, T. (1981). Some problems of a world-wide profession. In J. McDonough, & T. French (Eds.), *The ESP teacher: Role, development and prospects. ELT Documents 112.*

Johnson, R. K., & Swain, M. (1997). *Immersion education: International perspectives.* Cambridge, UK: Cambridge University Press.

Jones, C., Turner, J., & Street, B. (2000). *Student writing in higher education: Theory and practice.* Amsterdam: John Benjamins.

Jones, J. (2004). Learning to write in the disciplines: The application of systemic functional linguistic theory to the teaching and research of student writing. In L. Ravelli & R. Ellis (Eds.), *Analysing academic writing* (pp. 254–274). London: Continuum.

Jones, J., Holder, G., Robinson, R., & Kraus, L. (2000). Selcting pharmacy students with appropriate communication skills. *American Journal of Pharmaceutical Education, 64,* 68–73.

Jones, J., Holder, G. M., & Robinson, R. A. (2000). School subjects and academic literacy skills at university. *Australian Journal of Career Development, 9*(2), 27–31.

Kaiser, D. (2002). *Wege zum wissenschaftlichen Schreiben: Eine kontrastive untersuchung zu studentischen texten aus Venezuela und Deutschland. [Roads to academic writing: A contrastive study of student texts from Venezuala and Germany.].* Tübingen: Stauffenburg.

Kaiser, D. (2003). Nachprüfbarkeit versus originalität. Fremdes un eigenes in studentischen texten aus Venezuela und Deutschland. [Verifiability and originality. Others' and own ideas in student texts from Venezuala and Germany.]. In K. Ehlich & A. Steets (Eds.), *Wissenschaftlich schreiben – lehren und lernen* (pp. 305–325). Berlin: Walter de Gruyter.

Kamler, B., & Thomson, P. (2004). Driven to abstraction: Doctoral supervision and writing pedagogies. *Teaching in Higher Education, 9*(2), 195–209.

Kandlbinder, P., & Peseta, T. (2009). Key concepts in postgraduate certificates in higher education teaching and learning in Australasia and the United Kingdom. *International Journal for Academic Development, 14*(1), 19–31.

Kanoksilapatham, B. (2005). Rhetorical structure of biochemistry research articles. *English for Specific Purposes, 24,* 262–296.

Kaplan, R. B. (1966). Cultural thought patterns in inter-cultural education. *Language Learning, 16,* 1–20.

Kara, M. (2004). Pratiques de la citation dans les mémoires de maîtrise [Citation practices in Masters theses]. *Pratiques, 121-122,* 111–142.

Kardash, C. M., & Scholes, R. J. (1996). Effects of pre-existing beliefs, epistemological beliefs, and need for cognition on interpretation of controversial issues. *Journal of Educational Psychology, 88,* 260–271.

Kent, T. (Ed.) (1999). *Post-process theory. Beyond the writing-process paradigm.* Carbondale, IL: Southern Illinois University Press.

Keranen, N., Encinas, F., & Bazerman, C. (2012). Immersed in the game of science: Beliefs, emotions, and strategies of NNES scientists who regularly publish in English. In C. Bazerman, C. Dean, J. Early, K. Lunsford, S. Null, P. Rogers & A. Stansel (Eds.), *International advances in writing research: Cultures, places and measures.* Fort Collins Co: Writing Across the Curriculum Clearinghouse.

Kerbrat-Orecchioni, C. (1980). *L'énonciation. De la subjectivité dans le langage [Enunciation: About subjectivity in language].* Paris: ArmandColin.

Keseling, G. (1993). *Schreibprozess und textstruktur: Empirische untersuchungen zur produktion von zusammenfassungen. [Writing process and text structure: Empirical study on the production of summaries].* Tübingen: Niemeyer.

Keseling, G. (1997). Schreibstörungen. [Writing disorders]. In E. Jakobs & D. Knorr (Eds.), *Schreiben in den Wissenschaften* (pp. 223–237). Frankfurt am Main: Peter Lang.

Kiley, M., & Wisker, G. (2009). Threshold concepts in research education and evidence of threshold crossing. *Higher Education Research & Development, 28*(4), 431–441.

Kim, H.-C., & Eklundh, K. S. (2001). Reviewing practice in collaborative writing. *Computer Supported Cooperative Work, 10,* 247–259.

Knorr-Cetina, K. (1981). *The manufacture of knowledge.* Oxford: Pergamon Press.

Knudson, R. (1995). Writing experiences, attitudes and achievement of first to sixth graders. *Journal of Educational Research, 89,* 90–97.

Koutsantoni, D. (2006). Rhetorical strategies in engineering research articles and research theses: Advanced academic literacy and relations of power. *Journal of English for Academic Purposes*, 5, 19–36.

Kozulin, A. (2000). *Instrumentos psicológicos: La educación desde una perspectiva sociocultural [Psychological instruments: Education from a sociocultural perspective]*. Barcelona: Paidós.

Krashen, S. (1981). *Second language acquisition and second language learning*. New York, NY: Pergamon Press.

Kress, G., & Van Leeuwen, T. (1996). *Reading images: The grammar of visual design*. London: Routledge.

Krishnamurthy, R., & Kosem, I. (2007). Issues in creating a corpus for EAP pedagogy and research. *Journal of English for Academic Purposes*, 6, 356–373.

Kruse, O. (1997). Wissenschaftliche textproduktion und schreibdidaktik. Schreibprobleme sind nicht einfach probleme der studierenden; sie sind auch die probleme der wissenschaft selbst. [Academic text production and the teaching of writing. Writing problems are not simply problems of students but also problems of the sciences.]. In E. Jakobs & D. Knorr (Eds.), *Schreiben in den Wissenschaften* (pp. 141–158). Frankfurt am Main: Peter Lang.

Kruse, O. (2003). Getting started: Academic education in the first year of a university education. In L. Björk, G. Brauer, L. Rienecker & P. S. Jorgensen (Eds.), *Teaching academic writing in European higher education* (pp. 19–28). Dordrecht: Kluwer Academic Publishers.

Kruse, O. (2005a). Zur geschichte des wissenschaftlichen schreibens: Teil 2: Rolle des schreibens und der schreibdidaktik in der seminarpädagogik seit der Humboldtschen universitätsreform. [On the history of academic writing, part 2: The role of writing and the teaching of writing in the seminar pedagogy since Humboldt's university reforms]. Das Hochschulwesen: Forum Für Hochschulforschung. *Praxis Und -Politik*, 53, 214–218.

Kruse, O. (2005b). Zur geschichte des wissenschaftlichen schreibens: Teil 1: Entstehung der seminarpädagogik vor und in der Humboldtschen universitätsreform. Das hochschulwesen: Forum für hochschulforschung. [On the history of academic writing, part 1: Development of seminar pedagogy before and during Humboldt's university reforms]. *Praxis Und -Politik*, 53, 170–174.

Kruse, O. (2006a). The origins of writing in the discipline. Traditions of seminar writing and the Humboldtian ideal of the research university. *Written Communication*, 23(3), 331–352.

Kruse, O. (2006b). *Prozessorientierte schreibdidaktik schreibtraining für schule, studium und beruf. [Process-oriented teaching of writing. Teaching writing at high school, university and work]*. Bern: Haupt.

Kruse, O. (2007). *Keine angst vor dem leeren blatt ohne schreibblockaden durchs studium. [Don't be afraid of the empty space. Studying without writer's block]*. Frankfurt am Main: Campus Verlag.

Kruse, O. (2010). Old and new literacies: Literale praktiken in wissenschaftlichen kontexten. [Old and new literacies. Literacy practices in academic contexts]. Medienimpulse, 4/2010, Retrieved from http://www.medienimpulse.at/articles/view/273 (last retrieved April 12, 2011).

Kruse, O., & Jakobs, E. (1999). Schreiben lehren an der Hochschule: Ein Überblick. In O. Kruse, E. Jakobs & G. Ruhmann (Eds.), *Schlüsselkompetenz schreiben. Konzepte, methoden, projekte für schreibberatung und schreibdidaktik an der hochschule [Writing as a key competence. Concepts, methods, projects for the tutoring and teaching of writing at university level]* (pp. 19–36). Neuwied: Luchterhand.

Kruse, O., Jakobs, E., & Ruhmann, G. (1999). *Schlüsselkompetenz schreiben. Konzepte, methoden, projekte für schreibberatung und schreibdidaktik an der hochschule.* Neuwied: Luchterhand.

Kuhi, D., & Behnam, B. (2011). Generic variations and metadiscourse use in the writing of applied linguists: A comparative study and preliminary framework. *Written Communication, 28*, 97–141.

Kvernbekk, T. (2010). Revisiting dialogues and monologues. *Educational Philosophy and Theory.* doi:11/11/j.1469-5812.2010.00695.x.

Laborde-Milaa, I. (2004). Auto-reformulation et investissement du scripteur: Abstracts et quatrièmes de couvertures de mémoires de maîtrise [Auto-reformulation and the writer's investment: Abstracts and back cover summaries of Masters theses]. *Pratiques, 121-122,* 183–198.

Laffont, H. (2006). Un ingénieur est-il bien an engineer? [Is an engineer really 'an engineer'?]. *ASP: La revue du GERAS, 49-50,* 9–21.

Lahire, B. (1993). *Culture écrite et inégalités scolaires [Written culture and school inequality].* Lyon: Presses Universitaires de Lyon.

Land, R. (2004). *Educational development: Discourse, identity and practice.* Maidenhead: Society for Research into Higher Education/Open University Press/Mc Graw Hill New York.

Langer, J. (1986). Learning through writing: Study skills in the content areas. *Journal of Reading, 29*(5), 400–406.

Langer, J. A., & Appelbee, A. N. (1987). *How writing shapes thinking: A study of teaching and learning.* Urbana, IL: NCTE.

Latour, B. (1999). *Pandora's hope: Essays on the reality of science studies.* Cambridge: Harvard University Press.

Latour, B. (2005). *Reassembling the social: An introduction to actor-network theory.* Oxford: Oxford University Press.

Latour, B., & Fabbri, P. (1977). La rhétorique de la science: Pouvoir et devoir dans un article scientifique [The rhetoric of science: "Can" and 'must' in a scientific article]. *Actes De La Recherche en Science Sociales, 13,* 81–95.

Latour, B., & Woolgar, S. (1979). *Laboratory life: The construction of scientific facts.* Princeton, NJ: Princeton University Press.

Lave, J., & Wenger, E. (1991). *Situated learning: Legitimate peripheral participation.* Cambridge: Cambridge University Press.

Lavelle, E. (1993). Development and validation of an inventory to assess processes in college composition. *British Journal Educational Psychology, 63*(3), 489–499.

Lavelle, E., & Bushrow, K. (2007). Writing approaches of graduate students. *Educational Psychology, 27*(6), 807–822.

Lavelle, E., & Guarino, A. J. (2003). A multidimensional approach to understanding college writing processes. *Educational Phychology, 23*(3), 295–305.

Lavelle, E., Smith, J., & O'Ryan, L. (2002). The writing approaches of secondary students. *British Journal of Educational Psychology, 72*(3), 399–418.

Lavelle, E., & Zuercher, N. (2001). The writing approaches of university students. *Higher Education, 42*(3), 373–391.

Lea, M. (2008). Academic literacies in theory and practice. In B.V. Street, & N.H. Hornberger (Eds.), *Encyclopedia of language and education* (2nd ed.). *Volume 2: Literacy* (pp. 227–238). New York, NY: Springer.

Lea, M. (2009). Writing and meaning making in the context of online learning. In A. Carter, T. Lillis & S. Parkin (Eds.), *Why writing matters: Issues of access and identity in writing research and pedagogy* (pp. 7–26). Amsterdam: Johns Benjamins.

Lea, M., & Street, B. (1997). Student writing and faculty feedback in higher education: An academic literacies approach. *Studies in Higher Education, 23*(2), 157–172.

Lea, M. R. (2004). Academic Literacies: A pedagogy for course design. *Studies in Higher Education, 29*(6), 739–756.

Lea, M. R. (2007). Emerging literacies in online learning. *Journal of Applied Linguistics, 4*(1), 5–32.

Lea, M. R., & Jones, S. (2011). Digital literacies in higher education: Exploring textual and technological practice. *Studies in Higher Education, 36*(3), 377–394.

Lea, M. R., & Stierer, B. (2009). Lecturers' everyday writing as professional practice in the university as workplace: New insights into academic identities. *Studies in Higher Education, 34*(4), 417–428.

Lea, M. R., & Stierer, B. (2011). Changing academic identities in changing academic workplaces: Learning from academics' everyday professional writing practices. *Teaching in Higher Education, 16*(6), 605–616.

Lea, M. R., & Street, B. (2006). The 'Academic Literacies' model: Theory and applications. *Theory into Practice, 45*(4), 368–377.

Lea, M. R., & Street, B. V. (1998). Student writing in higher education: An academic literacies approach. *Studies in Higher Education, 23*(2), 157–172.

Lee, A., & Boud, D. (2003). Writing groups, change and academic identity: Research development as local practice. *Studies in Higher Education, 28*(2), 187–200.

Lee, D., & Swales, J. (2006). A corpus-based EAP course for NNS doctoral students: Moving from available specialized corpora to self-compiled corpora. *English for Specific Purposes, 25*, 56–75.

Leki, I. (1995). Coping strategies of ESL students in writing tasks across the curriculum. *TESOL Quarterly, 27*(4), 235–260.

Leki, I. (2002). Second language writing. In R. Kaplan (Ed.), *Oxford handbook of applied linguistics* (pp. 60–69). Oxford: Oxford University Press.

Leontjew, A. N. (1979). *Tätigkeit, bewusstsein, persönlichkeit*. Berlin: Volk und Wissen.

Lesne, M. (1994). *Travail pédagogique et formation d'adultes*. Paris: L'Harmattan.

Levin, T., & Wagner, T. (2006). In their own words: Understanding student conceptions of writing through their spontaneous metaphors in the science classroom. *Instructional Science, 34*(3), 227–278.

Li, Y., & Flowerdew, J. (2007). Shaping Chinese novice scientists' manuscripts for publication. *Journal of Second Language Writing, 16*(2), 100–117.

Light, G. (2002). From the personal to the public: Conceptions of creative writing in higher education. *Higher Education, 43*, 257–276.

Lillis, T. (1997). New voices in academia? The regulative nature of academic writing conventions. *Language and Education, 11*(2), 182–199.

Lillis, T. (2006). Moving towards an academic literacies pedagogy: Dialogues of participation. In L. Ganobcsik-Williams (Ed.), *Teaching academic writing in UK higher education: Theories, practices and models* (pp. 30–45). Palgrave: MacMillan.

Lillis, T., & Curry, M. J. (2006). Professional academic writing by multilingual scholars: Interactions with literacy brokers in the production of English-medium texts. *Written Communication, 23*, 3–35.

Lillis, T., & Curry, M. J. (2010). *Academic writing in a global context: The politics and practices of publishing in English*. London: Routledge.

Lillis, T. M. (2001). *Student writing: Access, regulation, desire.* London: Routledge.

Lindeman, N. (2007). Creating knowledge for advocacy: The discourse of research at a conservation organization. *Technical Communication Quarterly, 16*(4), 431–451.

Linell, P. (2009). *Rethinking language, mind, and the world dialogically.* Charlotte, NC: Information Age Publishing.

Long, M. (1996). The role of the linguistic environment in second language acquisition. In W. Ritchie & T. Bhatia (Eds.), *Handbook of second language acquisition* (pp. 413–468). San Diego, CA: Academic Press.

Lonka, K. (2003). Helping doctoral students finish their theses. In L. Bjørk, G. Brauer, L. Rienecker & S. P. Jørgensen (Eds.), *Teaching academic writing in European higher education* (pp. 113–131). Dordrecht, NL: Kluver Academic Press.

Lovitts, B. (2005). Being a good course-taker is not enough: A theoretical perspective on the transition to independent research. *Studies in Higher Education, 30*(2), 137–154.

Lovitts, B., & Nelson, C. (2000). The hidden crisis in graduate education: Attrition from Ph.D. programs. *Academe, 86*(6). Retrieved from http://www.aaup.org/AAUP/pubsres/academe/2000/ND/Feat/lovi.htm (last accessed November, 22, 2011).

Lundell, D. B., & Beach, R. (2002). Dissertation writer's negotiations with competing activity systems. In C. Bazerman, & D. Russell (Eds.), *Writing selves/writing societies: Research from activity perspectives.* Fort Collins, CO: The WAC Clearinghouse and Mind, Culture & Activity. Retrieved from http://wac.colostate.edu/books/selves_societies (last accessed November, 22, 2011).

MacDonald, S. (1994). *Professional academic writing in the humanities and social sciences.* Carbondale, IL: Southern Illinois University Press.

Maimon, L. (2002). The relationship between self-efficacy and the functions of writing. *Journal of College Reading and Learning, 33*, 32–45.

Maingueneau, D. (2002). Analysis of an academic genre. *Discourse Studies, 4*(3), 319–341.

Manathunga, C. (2005). Early warning signs in postgraduate research education: A different approach to ensuring timely completions. *Teaching in Higher Education, 10*(2), 219–233.

Mao, L. R. (1993). "I conclude not": Toward a pragmatic account of metadiscourse. *Rhetoric Review, 11*, 265–289.

Marilyn, K. F., & Larry, D. Y. (2004). Learning to write like a scientist: Coauthoring as an enculturation task. *Journal of Research in Science Teaching, 41*(6), 637–668.

Martin, J. R. (1984). Language, register, and genre. In F. Christie (Ed.), *Children writing: Reader* (pp. 21–29). Geelong, Vic: Deakin University Press.

Martin, J. R. (1989). *Factual writing: Exploring and challenging social reality.* Oxford: Oxford University Press.

Martin, Y., Maclachlan, M., & Karmel, T. (2001). *Postgraduate completion rates.* Occasional paper series, department of education, training and youth affairs, Canberra: Commonwealth of Australia.

Marton, F., & Booth, S. (1997). *Learning and awareness.* Hillsdale, NJ: Erlbaum.

Marton, F., & Saljö, R. (1976). On qualitative differences in learning: I, outcome and process. *British Journal of Educational Psychology, 46*, 4–11.

Marton, F., & Saljö, R. (1997). Approaches to learning. In F. Marton, D. Hounsell & N. J. Entwistle (Eds.), *The experience of learning* (pp. 39–58). Edinburgh: Scottish Academic Press.

Marton, F., & Svensson, L. (1979). Conceptions of research in student learning. *Higher Education, 8*(4), 471–486.

Mason, L., & Boscolo, P. (2004). Role of epistemological understanding and interest in interpreting a controversy and in topic-specific belief change. *Contemporary Educational Psychology, 29*(2), 103–128.

Mason, L., & Scirica, F. (2006). Prediction of students' argumentation skills about controversial topics by epistemological understanding. *Learning and Instruction, 16*, 492–509.

Mateos, M. (2001). *Metacognición y educación [Metacognition and Education]*. Buenos Aires: Aique.

Mateos, M., Cuevas, I., Martín, E., Martín, A., Echeíta, G., & Luna, M. (2011). Reading to write an argumentation: The role of epistemological, reading and writing beliefs. *Journal of Research in Reading, 34*, 281–297.

Mateos, M., & Solé, I. (2009). Synthesizing information from various texts: A study of procedures and products at different educational levels. *European Journal of Psychology of Education, 24*(4), 435–451.

Mateos, M., Villalón, R., De Dios, M. J., & Martín, E. (2007). Reading and writing tasks on different university degree courses: What do the students say they do? *Studies in Higher Education, 32*, 489–510.

Matsuda, P. K. (2001). Voice in Japanese written discourse: Implications for second language writing. *Journal of Second Language Writing, 10*, 35–53.

Matsuda, P. K., & Tardy, C. M. (2007). Voice in academic writing: The rhetorical construction of author identity in blind manuscript review. *English for Specific Purposes, 26*, 235–249.

Matusov, E. (2007). Applying Bakhtin scholarship on discourse in education: A critical review essay. *Educational Theory, 57*(2), 215–237.

Matusov, E. (2009). *Journey into dialogic pedagogy*. New York, NY: Nova Science Publishers.

Maxwell, J. (1996). *Qualitative research design. An interactive approach*. Thousand Oaks, CA: Sage.

McAlpine, L., & Amundsen, C. (2008). Academic communities and developing identity: The doctoral student journey. In P. Richards (Ed.), *Global Issues in Higher Education* (pp. 57–83). New York: Nova Publishing.

McCarthy, L. P. (1987). A stranger in strange lands: A college student writing across the curriculum. *Research in the Teaching of English*, 233–265.

McCune, V. (2004). Development of first-year students' conceptions of essay writing. *Higher Education, 47*, 257–282.

McLeod, S. (1997). *Notes on the heart: Affective issues in the writing classroom*. Carbondale, IL: Southern Illinois University Press.

McMahan, A. (2003). Immersion, engagement, and presence: A method for analyzing 3-D video games. In M. J. P. Wolf & B. Perron (Eds.), *The video game theory reader* (pp. 67–86). New York, NY: Routledge.

Meneghini, R., & Packer, A. (2007). Is there science beyond English? Initiatives to increase the quality and visibility of non-English publications might help to break down language barriers in scientific communication. *EMBO Reports, 8*(2), 112–116.

Mercer, N., & Littleton, K. (2007). *Dialogue and the development of children's thinking*. London, UK: Routledge.

Merton, R. K. (1957). Priorities in scientific discovery. *American Sociological Review, 22*(6), 635–659.

Merton, R. K. (1973). *The sociology of science: Theoretical and empirical investigations*. Chicago, IL: University of Chicago Press.

Miller, C. (1984). Genre as social action. *Quarterly Journal of Speech, 70*, 151–167.

Miller, C. R. (1994). Rhetorical community: The cultural basis of genre. *Genre and The New Rhetoric*, 67–78.

Miller, N., & Brimicombe, A. (2004). Mapping research journeys across complex terrain with heavy baggage. *Studies in Continuing Education, 26*(3), 405–417.

Miras, M. (2000). La escritura reflexiva. Aprender a escribir y aprender acerca de lo que se escribe [Reflective writing: learning to write and learning about you write]. *Infancia y Aprendizaje, 89,* 65–80.

Misak, A., Marusic, M., & Marusic, A. (2005). Manuscript editing as a way of teaching academic writing: Experience from a small scientific journal. *Journal of Second Language Writing, 14,* 122–131.

Mitchell, S., & Andrews, R. (Eds.). (2001). *Essays in argument.* London: Middlesex University Press.

Moje, E. B., & Luke, A. (2009). Review of research: Literacy and identity: Examining the metaphors in history and contemporary research. *Reading Research Quarterly, 44*(4), 415–437.

Moll, M. (2002). "Exzerpieren statt fotokopieren"-Das Exzerpt als zusammenfassende Verschriftlichung eines wissenschaftlichen Textes. [Summarizing instead of copying-The excerpt as a summarizing reproduction of academic texts]. In A. Redder (Ed.), *Effektiv studieren. Texte und Diskurse in der Universität* (pp. 104–126). Dilles & Francke.

Moll, M. (2003). "Für mich ist es sehr schwer!" oder: Wie ein protokoll entsteht. [For me this is very difficult!" or: Writing minutes]. In K. Ehlich & A. Steets (Eds.), *Wissenschaftlich schreiben – lehren und lernen* (pp. 29–50). Berlin: Walter de Gruyter.

Molle, D., & Prior, P. (2008). Multimodal genre systems in EAP writing pedagogy: Reflecting on a needs analysis. *TESOL Quarterly, 42,* 541–566.

Morrison-Saunders, A., Moore, S., Newsome, D., & Newsome, J. (2005). Reflecting on the role of emotions in the PhD process. In *The reflective practitioner.* Proceedings from the 14th annual teaching learning forum, February 3–4, 2005. Perth: Murdoch University. Retrieved from http://lsn.curtin.edu.au/tlf/tlf2005/refereed/morrison-saunders.html (last accessed November, 22, 2011).

Morton, J. (2009). Genre and disciplinary competence: A case study of contextualization in an academic speech genre. *English for Specific Purposes, 28,* 217–229.

Motta-Roth, D. (1998). Discourse analysis and academic book reviews: A study of text and disciplinary cultures. In I. Fortanet, S. Posteguillo, J. C. Palmet & J. F. Coll (Eds.), *Genre studies for English Academic Purposes* (pp. 29–58). Castelló, Spain: Universitat Jaume I.

Myers, G. (1990). *Writing biology.* Madison, WI: University of Wisconsin Press.

Myers, G. (1991). Stories and styles in two molecular biology review articles. In C. Bazerman & J. Paradis (Eds.), *Textual dynamics of the professions* (pp. 45–75). Madison, WI: University of Wisconsin Press.

Negroni, M., & Humbley, J. (2004). Termes techniques et marqueurs d'argumentation: Pour débusquer l'argumentation cachée dans les articles de recherché. *ASP: La Revue Du GERAS, 45-46,* 97–109.

Nelson, N. (2001a). Discourse synthesis: Process and product. In R. G. McInnis (Ed.), *Discourse synthesis: Studies in historical and contemporary social epistemology* (pp. 379–396). Westport, CT: Praeger.

Nelson, N. (2001b). Writing to learn: One theory, two rationales. In P. Tynjala, L. Mason & K. Lonka (Eds.), *Writing as a learning tool: Integrating theory and practice* (pp. 23–36). Boston: Kluwer.

Nelson, N. (2008). The reading-writing nexus in discourse research. In C. Bazerman (Ed.), *Handbook of research on writing* (pp. 435–450). New York, NY: Erlbaum.

Nesi, H., Gardner, S., Thompson, P., Wickens, P., Forsyth, R., Heuboeck, ... Alsop, S. (2008). An investigation of genres of assessed writing in British higher education: Full research report. *ESRC End of Award Report* (RES-000-23-0800). Swindon: ESRC.

Newell, G. (2006). Writing to learn: How alternative theories of school writing account for student performance. In C. A. MacArthur, S. Graham & J. Fitzgerald (Eds.), *Handbook of writing research* (pp. 235–247). New York, NY: Gilford.

Ngcongo, R. (2000, April). Self-esteem enhancement and capacity building in the supervision of Masters' students. In M. Kiley y & G. Mullins (Eds.), *Quality in postgraduate research: Making ends meet* (pp. 248–249). Advisory Centre for University Education, University of Adelaide.

Nihalani, P. K., & Mayrath, M. C. (Eds.). (2008). Educational psychology journal editors' comments on publishing. *Educational Research Review*, *20*(1), 29–39.

Noguchi, J. (2001). *The science review article: An opportune genre in the construction of science.* (Unpublished doctoral dissertation). The University of Birmingham, UK.

Norris, S., & Jones, R. (2005). *Discourse in action: Introducing mediated discourse analysis.* New York, NY: Routledge.

Nystrand, M., & Brandt, D. (1989). Response to writing as a context for learning to write. In C. Anson (Ed.), *Writing and response: Models, methods, and curricular.* Urbana, IL: NCTE.

Ochs, E., Taylor, C., Rudolph, D., & Smith, R. (1992). Storytelling as a theory-building activity. *Discourse Processes*, *15*, 37–72.

Okamura, A. (2004). How do British and Japanese scientists publish their academic papers in English. *The Economic Journal of Takasaki City University of Economics*, *46*(4), 39–61.

Okamura, A. (2006). Two types of strategies used by Japanese scientists when writing research articles in English. *System*, *34*, 68–79.

Olesko, K. (1988). *Physics as a calling: Discipline and practice in the Königsberg seminar for Physics.* Ithca, NY: Cornell University Press.

Oliva, M., & Pollastrini, Y. (1995). Internet resources and second language acquisition: An evaluation of virtual immersion. *Foreign Language Annals*, *28*(4), 551–563.

Olson, D. (1994). *The world on paper.* Cambridge: Cambridge University Press.

Olson, D. (2009). Education and literacy. *Infancia y Aprendizaje*, *32*(2), 141–151.

Olson, D., & Torrance, N. (Eds.). (2009). *The Cambridge handbook of literacy.* Cambridge, UK: Cambridge University Press.

Ong, W. (1982). *Orality and literacy: The technologizing of the world.* London: Methuen.

Onwuegbuzie, A. J. (1998). The relationship between writing anxiety and learning styles among graduate students. *Journal of College Student Development*, *39*(6), 589–598.

Opariuc-Dan, C. (2010). *Norme şi procedee de desfăşurare a cercetărilor şi de redactare a articolelor ştiintifice (1). [Norms and methodology of research and scientific article writing].* The Black Sea Journal of Psychology, 1. *Retrieved August, 26, 2011 from http://www.bspsychology.ro/index.php/bspsychology/article/view/8*

Pajares, F. (2003). Self-efficacy beliefs, motivation and achievement in writing: A review of the literature. *Reading & Writing Quarterly*, *19*(2), 139–158.

Paltridge, B. (2006). *Discourse analysis.* London and New York: Continuum.

Paulsen, F. (1921). *Geschichte des gelehrten Unterrichts auf den deutschen Schulen und Universitäten vom Ausgang des Mittelalter bis zur Gegenwart. [The history of academic teaching at German schools and universities from the end oft he Middle Ages to the presence].* Berlin: Walter de Gruyter.

Pecorari, D. (2003). Good and original: Plagiarism and patchwriting in academic second-language writing. *Journal of Second Language Writing*, *12*(4), 317–345.

Perrin, D., Böttcher, I., Kruse, O., & Wrobel, A. (Eds.). (2002). *Schreiben. Von intuitiven zu professionellen Schreibstrategien* [Writing. From Intuitive to Professional Writing Strategies.], Wiesbaden: Westdeutscher Verlag.

Peseta, T. (2007). Troubling our desires for research and writing within the academic development project. *International Journal for Academic Development, 12*(1), 15–23.

Peterson, S. (2003). Peer response and students' revisions of their narrative writing. *Educational Studies in Language and Literature, 3*, 239–272.

Petrucci, R. (2002). Writing-to-learn approach to writing in the discipline in the introductory linguistics classroom. *The WAC Journal, 13*, 133–143.

Philippe, G. (2002). L'appareil formel de l'effacement énonciatif et la pragmatique des textes sans locuteur [Formal apparatus of enunciative erasure and the pragmatics of texts without speakers]. In R. Amossy (Ed.), *Pragmatique et analyse des textes [Pragmatics and text analysis]* (pp. 17–34). Tel-Aviv: Université de Tel-Aviv.

Pichon-Rivière, E. (1971). Técnica de los grupos operativos [Operant groups technique]. In *Del psicoanálisis a la Psicología Social [From psicoanalysis to Social Psychology]. Tomo II* (pp. 259–275). Buenos Aires: Galerna.

Pine, B. J., & Gilmore, J. H. (1999). *The experience economy.* Cambridge, MA: Harvard Business School Press.

Piolat, A., & Pélissier, A. (Eds.). (1998). *La rédaction de textes: Approche cognitive [Writing texts: A cognitive approach].* Lausanne: Delachaux et Niestlé.

Poe, M , Lerner, N., & Craig, J. (2010). *Learning to communicate in science and engineering.* Cambridge, MA: The MIT Press.

Pohl, T. (2009). *Die studentische Hausarbeit. Rekonstruktion ihrer ideen- und institutionsgeschichtlichen Entstehung* [The seminar paper. Reconstruction of the history of ideas and the institutional history underlying its development]. Heidelberg: Synchron.

Pollet, M. C., & Boch, F. (Eds.). (2002). L'écrit dans l'enseignement supérieur [Writing in higher education]. *Enjeux,* 53–54.

Pollet, M. C., & Piette, V. (2002). Citation, reformulation du discours d'autrui. Une clé pour enseigner l'écriture de recherche? [Citation, reformulation of the discourse of others: A key for teaching research writing?]. *Spirale, 29*, 165–179.

Popper, K. (1934). *Logik der forschung. Tübingen: Mohr. English translation The logic of scientific discovery* (5th ed.). New York, NY: Basic Books.

Pozo, J. I., Scheuer, N., Pérez Echeverría, M. P., Mateos, M., Martín, E., & de la Cruz, M. (Eds.). (2006). *Nuevas formas de pensar el aprendizaje y la enseñanza. Concepciones de profesores y alumnos [New ways to think teaching and learning. Teachers' and students' conceptions].* Barcelona: Graó.

Prain, V., & Hand, B. (1999). Students perceptions of writing for learning in secondary school science. *Science Education, 83*, 151–162.

Prior, P. (1995). Tracing authoritative and internally persuasive discourses: A case study of response, revision, and disciplinary enculturation. *Research in the Teaching of English, 29*, 288–325.

Prior, P. (2001). Voices in text, mind, and society. Sociohistoric accounts of discourse acquisition and use. *Journal of Second Language Writing, 10*, 55–81.

Prior, P. (2006). A sociocultural theory of writing. In C. A. MacArthur, S. Graham & F. Fitzgerald (Eds.), *Handbook of writing research* (pp. 54–65). New York, NY: The Guilford Press.

Prior, P., & Hengst, J. (Eds.). (2010). *Exploring semiotic remediation as discourse practice.* Houndsmill: Palgrave MacMillan.

Prior, P., Hengst, J., Roozen, K., & Shipka, J. (2006). "I'll be the Sun": From reported speech to semiotic remediation practices. *Text and Talk, 26*, 733–766.

Prior, P., & Shipka, J. (2003). Chronotopic lamination: Tracing the contours of literate activity. In C. Bazerman, & D. Russell (Eds.), *Writing selves, writing societies: Research from activity perspectives* (pp. 180–238). Fort Collins, CO: WAC Clearinghouse and Mind, Culture, and Activity. Accessed 27 February 2011. Retrieved from http://wac.colostate.edu/books/selves_societies/

Prior, P., Solberg, J., Berry, P., Bellwoar, H., Chewning, B, Lunsford, K., ... Walker, J. (2007). Re-situating and re-mediating the canons: A cultural-historical remapping of rhetorical activity, a collaborative webtext. *Kairos: A Journal of Rhetoric, Technology, and Pedagogy*, *11*(3). Retrieved from http://kairos.technorhetoric.net/11.3/topoi/prior-et-al/index.html

Prior, P. A. (1998). *Writing/disciplinarity: A sociohistoric account of literate activity in the academy*. Mawah, NJ: Lawrence Erlbaum.

Purser, E., Skillen, J., Donohue, J., & Peake, K. (2008). Developing academic literacy in context. *Zeitschrift Schreiben*, (26 June). Retrieved from http://www.zeitschrift-schreiben.eu

Rabatel, A. (2002). Le sous-énonciateur dans les montages citationnels [The sub-speaker in citational montages]. *Enjeux*, *54*, 52–66.

Rabatel, A. (Ed.) (2004). *Effacement énonciatif et discours rapportés, Langages [Enunciative erasure and reported discourse. Languages]* (p. 156). Paris: Larousse.

Rai, L. (2004). Exploring literacy in social work education: A social practices approach to student writing. *Journal of Social Work Education*, *40*(2), 149–162.

Rai, L. (2010). Reflections on writing in social work education and practice. In S. Matthews, M. McCormick, A. Morden & J. Seden (Eds.), *Professional development in social work: Complex issues in practice* (pp. 163–170). London: Routledge.

Raphael, T. E., Englert, C. S., & Kirschner, B. W. (1989). Students' metacognitive knowledge and writing. *Research in the Teaching of English*, *23*(4), 343–379.

Read, B., & Francis, B. (2001). 'Playing Safe': Undergraduate essay writing and the presentation of the student 'voice'. *British Journal of Sociology of Education*, *22*(3), 389–399.

Reddy, M. (1979). The conduit metaphor-a case of frame conflict in our language about language. In A. Ortony (Ed.), *Metaphor and thought*. Cambridge: Cambridge.

Reither, J. A., & Vipond, D. (1989). Writing as collaboration. *College English*, *51*, 855–867.

Reuter, Y. (1996). *Enseigner et apprendre à écrire [Teaching and learning to write]*. Paris: ESF.

Reuter, Y. (1998). De quelques obstacles à l'écriture de recherché [About a few obstacles to research writing]. *LIDIL*, *17*, 11–24.

Reuter, Y. (2004). Analyser les problèmes de l'écriture de recherche en formation [Analysis of problems with research writing in formation]. *Pratiques*, *121-122*, 9–27.

Reuter, Y. (Ed.), (2007). Récits et disciplines scolaires [Stories and school disciplines]. *Pratiques*, pp. 133–134.

Reuter, Y. (2010). Littéracies universitaires et didactiques. Intérêts et limites d'une rencontre possible. Conférence invitée au Colloque international Littéracies universitaires: Savoirs, écrits, disciplines, Villeneuve d'Ascq, 2–4 Septembre.

Reuter, Y., & Donahue, C. (2007). Disciplines, language activities, cultures: Perspectives on teaching and learning in higher education from France and the United States. *L1 Educational Studies in Language and Literature*, *8*, 1–11.

Reynolds, N. (1993). Ethos as location: New sites for understanding discursive authority. *Rhetoric Review*, *11*, 325–338.

Rienecker, L. (2003). Thesis writer's block: Textwork that works. *Proceedings from the Second Conference of the European Association for the teaching of academic writing "teaching and tutorial academic writing"*, Budapest, 23–25 June.

Rinck, F. (2004). Les difficultés d'étudiants dans la construction d'une problématique [Student difficulties in constructing research questions]. *Pratiques, 121/122,* 93–110.

Rinck, F. (2006a). *L'article de recherche en Sciences du Langage et en Lettres, Figure de l'auteur et approche disciplinaire du genre [The research article in Linguistics and Literature.* The figure of the author and disciplinary approaches to genre]. Doctoral thesis. Université Grenoble 3.

Rinck, F. (2006b). Ecrire au nom de la science et de sa discipline: La figure de l'auteur dans l'article en sciences humaines [Writing in the name of Science and one's discipline: The figure of the author in humanities articles]. *Sciences De La Société, 67,* 95–112.

Rinck, F. (2006c). Gestion de la polyphonie et figure de l'auteur dans les parties théoriques de rapports de stage [Managing polyphony and the figure of the author in the theoretical sections of internship reports]. *LIDIL, 34,* 85–103.

Rinck, F. (2010a). Les 'nouveaux entrants' dans le champ scientifique: Analyse des spécificités des articles de doctorants ["New arrivals" in the scientific field: Analysis of the specificities of doctoral students' articles]. *Actes du colloque International Les discours universitaires.* Paris, L'Harmattan.

Rinck, F. (2010b). L'analyse linguistique des enjeux de connaissance dans le discours scientifique [Linguistic analysis of the stakes of knowledge in scientific discourse]. *Revue d'anthropologie des connaissances, 4*(3), 427–450.

Rinck, F., Boch, F., & Grossmann, F. (2007). Quelques lieux de variation du positionnement énonciatif dans l'article de recherche [Some locations of variation in enunciative positioning in research articles]. In P. Lambert, A. Millet, M. Rispail & C. Trimaille (Eds.), *Variations au cœur et aux marges de la sociolinguistique. Mélanges offerts à Jacqueline Billiez [Variations at the heart and on the margins of sociolinguistics. In honor of Jacqueline Billiez]* (pp. 285–296). Paris: L'Harmattan.

Rinck, F., & Pouvreau, L. (2010). La mise en scène de soi dans un écrit d'initiation à la recherche en didactique du français [Setting the I on stage in writing designed to initiate students into French didactics research]. *Revista Scripta, 13*(24), 157–172.

Rivard, L. (1994). A review of writing to learn in science: Implications for practice and research. *Journal of Research in Science Teaching, 31*(9), 969–983.

Robinson-Pant, A. (2005). Research ethics. In A. Robinson-Pant (Ed.), *Cross-cultural perspectives on educational research.* Buckingham: Open University Press. (Chap. 4).

Roca, J., Manchon, R. M., & Murphy, L. (2006). Generating text in native and foreign language writing: A temporal analysis of problem-solving formulation processes. *Modern Language Journal, 90*(1), 100–114.

Rogers, R. (2004). An introduction to critical discourse analysis in education. In R. Rogers (Ed.), *An introduction to critical discourse analysis in education* (pp. 1–18). Mahwah, NJ: Laurence Erlbaum.

Rommetveit, R. (1974). *On message structure: A framework for the study of language and communication.* London: Wiley.

Roozen, K. (2009). "Fan fic-ing" English studies: A case study exploring the interplay of vernacular literacies and disciplinary engagement. *Research in the Teaching of English, 44,* 136–169.

Ropé, F. (1994). *Savoirs universitaires, savoirs scolaires [University knowledges, school knowledges].* Paris: L'Harmattan.

Rose, M., & McClafferty, K. (2001). A call for the teaching of writing in graduate education. *Educational Researcher, 30*(2), 27–33.

Rourke, L., & Kanuka, H. (2007). Barriers to online critical discourse. *International Journal of Computer-Supported Collaborative Learning, 1*(2), 105–126.

Rowley-Jolivet, E., & Carter-Thomas, S. (2005). The rhetoric of conference presentation introductions: Context, argument, and interaction. *International Journal of Applied Linguistics, 15*, 45–70.

Rubdy, R. (2005). A multi-thrust approach to fostering a research culture. *ELT Journal: English Language Teachers Journal, 59*(4), 277–286.

Rüegg, W. (2004). Themes. In W. Rüegg (Ed.), *A history of the university in Europe. Universities In the nineteenth and early twentieth centuries* (Vol. 3, pp. 3–31). New York, NY: Cambridge University Press.

Russell, D. (1997). Rethinking genre in school and society: An activity theory analysis. *Written Communication, 14*(4), 504–554.

Russell, D. (2002). *Writing in the academic disciplines: A curricular history*. Carbondale, IL: Southern Illinois University Press.

Russell, D., Lea, M., Parker, J., Street, B., Donahue, T. (2009). Exploring notions of genre in "Academic Literacies" and "Writing Across the Curriculum": Approaches across countries and contexts. In C. Bazerman, A. Bonini, & D. Figueiredo (Eds.), *Genre in a changing world: Perspectives on writing* (pp. 395–423). Fort Collins, CO: The WAC Clearinghouse and Parlor Press. Retrieved July 28, 2011 from http://wac.colostate.edu/books/genre/

Russell, D. & Yañez, A. (2003). *'Big Picture People Rarely Become Historians': Genre Systems and the Contradictions of General Education. In writing selves/writing societies: Research from activity perspectives, perspectives on writing*. Fort Collins, CO: WAC Clearinghouse. Retrieved from http://wac.colostate.edu/books/selves_societies

Russell, D. R., & Foster, D. (2002). Re-articulating articulation. In D. Foster & D. R. Russell (Eds.), *Writing and learning in cross-national perspective: Transitions from secondary to higher education* (pp. 1–47). Urbana, IL: National Council of Teachers of English.

Salen, K., & Zimmerman, E. (2004). *Rules of play: Game design fundamentals*. Cambridge, MA: MIT Press.

Samara, A. (2006). Group supervision in graduate education: A process of supervision skill development and text improvement. *Higher Education Research and Development Journal, 25*(2), 115–129.

Samraj, B. (2004). Discourse features of the student-produced academic research paper: Variations across disciplinary courses. *Journal of English for Academic Purposes, 3*, 5–22.

Scardamalia, M., & Bereiter, C. (1985). Development of dialectical processes in composition. In D. Olson, N. Torrance & A. Hildyard (Eds.), *Literacy, language and learning* (pp. 307–329). Cambridge: Cambridge University Press.

Schleiermacher, F. (2004/1813). On the different methods of translating (S. Bernofsky, Trans.). In L. Venuti (Ed.), *The translation studies reader* (2nd ed.), (pp. 113–119). New York, NY: Routledge (Original work published 1813).

Schmidt, R. (1983). Interaction, acculturation and the acquisition of communicative competence. In N. Wolfson & E. Judd (Eds.), *Sociolinguistics and language acquisition* (pp. 137–174). Rowley, MA: Newbury House.

Schmidt, R., & Frota, S. (1986). Developing basic conversational ability in a second language: A case study of an adult learner of Portuguese. In R. R. Day (Ed.), *Talking to learn: Conversation in second language acquisition* (pp. 237–326). Rowley, MA: Newbury House.

Schommer, M. (1990). Effects of beliefs about the nature of knowledge on comprehension. *Journal of Educational Psychology, 82*, 498–504.

Schraw, G. (2000). Reader beliefs and meaning construction in narrative text. *Journal of Educational Psychology, 92*, 96–106.

Schraw, G., & Bruning, R. (1996). Readers' implicit models of reading. *Reading Research Quarterly*, *31*, 290–305.

Schryer, C. F. (1993). Records as genre. *Written Communication*, *10*(2), 200.

Schutz, A., & Luckmann, T. (1989). *The Structures of the Life-World*. (R. Zaner & T. Englehardt, Trans.) Evanston, IL: Northwestern University Press.

Scollon, R. (2001). *Mediated discourse: The nexus of practice*. London: Routledge.

Scollon & Scollon. (2003). Intercultural communication: A discourse approach By Ronald Scollon, Suzanne BK Scollon.

Scollon, R., & Scollon, S. (1981). *Narrative, literacy, and face in interethnic communication*. Norwood: Ablex.

Scollon, R., & Wong Scollon, S. (2004). *Nexus analysis: Discourse and the emerging internet*. London: Routledge.

Scott, M., & Lillis, T. (2008). Defining academic literacies research: Issues of epistemology, ideology and strategy. *Journal of Applied Linguistics*, *4*, 5–32.

Sharples, M., Goodlet, J. S., Beck, E. E., Wood, C. C., Easterbrook, S. M., & Plowman, L. (1993). Research issues in the study of computer supported collaborative writing. In M. Sharples (Ed.), *Computer supported collaborative writing* (pp. 9–28). London: Springer-Verlag.

Shipka, J. (2011). *Toward a composition made whole*. Pittsburgh, PA: University of Pittsburgh Press.

Shute, V. J. (2008). Focus on formative feedback. *Review of Educational Research*, *78*(1), 153–189.

Sidorkin, A. M. (1999). *Beyond Discourse: Education, the self, and dialogue*. Albany, NY: Sate University of New York Press.

Siepmann, D. (2006). Academic writing and culture: An overview of differences between English, French and German. *Meta*, *51*, 131–150.

Silva, T., & Nicholls, J. G. (1993). College students as writing theorists: Goals and beliefs about the causes of success. *Contemporary Educational Psychology*, *18*, 281–293.

Silverstein, M. (2005). Languages/cultures are dead! Long live the linguistic-cultural! In D. Segal & S. Yanagisako (Eds.), *Unwrapping the sacred bundle: Reflections on the disciplining of anthropology* (pp. 99–125). Durham: Duke University Press.

Simonin Grumbach, J. (1975). Pour une typologie des discours [For a discourse typology]. In J. Kristeva, J. C. Milner & N. Ruwet (Eds.), *Langue, discours, société: Pour Émile Benveniste* (pp. 85–121). Paris: Editions du Seuil.

Skillen, J., Merten, M., Trivett, N., & Percy, A. (1998). *The IDEALL approach to Learning Development: A model for fostering improved literacy and learning outcomes for students*. Proceedings of the 1998 AARE conference. Retrieved August, 25, 2011 from http://www.swin.edu.au/aare/conf98.htm

Slembrouck, S. (2005). Discourse, critique and ethnography: Class-oriented coding in accounts of child protection. *Language Sciences*, *27*, 619–650.

Small, H. G. (1973). Co-citation in the scientific literature: A new measure of the relationship between two documents. *Journal of the American Society for Information Science*, *24*, 265–269.

Small, H. G., & Griffith, B. C. (1974). The structure of scientific literatures (I): Identifying and graphing specialties. *Science Studies*, *4*(1), 17–40.

Solé, I., Mateos, M., Miras, M., Martín, E., Cuevas, I., Castells, N., & Gràcia, M. (2005). Lectura, escritura y adquisición de conocimientos en Educación Secundaria y Educación Universitaria [Reading, writing and knowledge acquisition in Secondary and Higher Education]. *Infancia y Aprendizaje*, *28*(3), 329–347.

Sommers, N., & Saltz, L. (2004). The novice as expert: Writing the freshman year. *College Composition and Communication*, *56*, 124–149.

Sorrentino, D. (2009). Wissenschaftliche schreibanleitungen in italienischer sprache: Kommentierte bibliographie. [Instructions to academic writing in Italian: A commented bibliography.] In M. Dalmas, M. Foschi Albert, & E. Neuland (Eds.), *Wissenschaftliche Textsorten im Germanistikstudium deutsch-italienisch-französisch kontrastiv. Trilaterales forschungsprojekt in der Villa Vigoni 2007-2008* (pp. 88–94). [Academic genres in study programs of German: German-Italian-French contrastive. Trilateral research project in Villa Vigoni. Loveno di Menaggio: Villa Vigoni]. Loveno di Menaggio: Villa Vigoni.

Spivey, N. N. (1990). Transforming texts: Constructive processes in reading and writing. *Written Communication, 7*, 256–287.

Spivey, N. N. (1997). *The constructivist metaphor: Reading, writing, and the making of meaning.* San Diego, CA: Academic Press.

St. John, M. J. (1987). Writing processes of Spanish scientists publishing in English. *English for Specific Purposes, 6*, 113–120.

Steets, A. (2003). Die Mitschrift als universitäre Textart – schwieriger als gedacht, wichtiger als vermutet. [Notes as a genre – more difficult than believed, more important than assumed]. In K. Ehlich & A. Steets (Eds.), *Wissenschaftlich schreiben – lehren und lernen* (pp. 51–64). Berlin: Walter de Gruyter.

Steinhoff, T. (2007). *Wissenschaftliche textkompetenz. Sprachgebrauch und schreibentwicklung in wissenschaftlichen texten von studenten und experten. [Academic text competence. Language use and writing development in academic texts of students and experts].* Tübingen: Niemeyer.

Stierer, B. (2008). Learning to write about teaching: Understanding the writing demands of lecturer development programmes in higher education. In R. Murray (Ed.), *The scholarship of teaching and learning* (pp. 34–45). Berkshire, UK: McGraw Hill.

Street, B. (1984). *Literacy in theory and practice.* Cambridge: Cambridge University Press.

Street, B. (1996). Academic literacies. In D. Baker, J. Clay & C. Fox (Eds.), *Alternative ways of knowing: Literacies, numeracies, sciences* (pp. 101–134). New York, NY: Falmer Press.

Street, B. V. (2004). Academic literacies and the 'new orders': Implications for research and practice in student writing in HE. *Learning and Teaching in the Social Sciences, 1*(1), 9–32.

Street, B. (Ed.) (2005). *Literacies across educational contexts; mediating, learning and teaching.* Philadelphia, PA: Caslon Press.

Street, B. (2009). Hidden' features of academic paper writing. *Working Papers in Educational Linguistics, 24*(1), 1–17.

Styles, I., & Radloff, A. (2000). Affective reflections: Postgraduate students' feelings about their theses. In M. Kiley & G. Mullins (Eds.), *Quality in postgraduate research: Making ends meet* (pp. 203–214). Advisory Centre for University Education. University of Adelaide.

Swales, J. (1981). *Aspects of article introductions.* Birmingham, UK: The University of Aston, Language Studies Unit.

Swales, J. (1990). *Genre analysis. English in academic and research settings.* Cambridge: Cambridge University Press.

Swales, J. (1996). Occluded genres in the academy: The case of the submission letter. In E. Ventola & A. Mauranen (Eds.), *Academic writing: Intercultural and textual issues.* Amsterdam: John Benjamins.

Swales, J. (1998). *Other floors, other voices: A textography of a small university building.* Mahwah, NJ: Erlbaum.

Swales, J. (2004). *Research genres: Explorations and applications.* Cambridge: Cambridge University Press.

Tadros, A. (1993). The pragmatics of text averral and attribution in academic texts. In M. Hoey (Ed.), *Data, description, discourse* (pp. 98–114). London: Harper.

Tannacito, T. (2004). The literacy of electronic peer response. In B. Huot, B. Stroble & C. Bazerman (Eds.), *Multiple literacies for the 21st century*. Cresskill, NJ: Hampton Press.

Tardy, C. (2009). *Building genre knowledge*. West Lafayette, IN: Parlor Press.

Tardy, C. M., & Matsuda, P. K. (Eds.). (2009). The construction of author voice by editorial board members. *Written Communication, 26*, 32–52.

Thaiss, C., & Zawacki, T. (2006). *Engaged writers and dynamic disciplines: Research on the academic writing life*. Portsmouth, NH: Boynton.

Thompson, D. K. (1993). Arguing for experimental "facts" in science: A study of research article results sections in biochemistry. *Written Communication, 8*, 106–128.

Thomson, P., & Walker, M. (2010). Doctoral education in context; the changing nature of the doctorate and doctoral students. In M. Walker & P. Thomson (Eds.), *The Routledge doctoral supervisor's companion*. London: Routledge.

Tinto, V. (1993). Toward a theory of doctoral persistence. In *Leaving college. Rethinking the causes and cures of student attrition* (pp. 230–256). Chicago, IL: The University of Chicago Press.

Toolan, M. (2002). *Critical discourse analysis*. London: Routledge.

Topping, K. T. (2010). Methodological quandaries in studying process and outcomes in peer assessment. *Learning and Instruction, 20*(4), 339–343.

Tuck, J. (2011). Feedback-giving as social practice: Teachers' perspectives on feedback as institutional requirement, work and dialogue. *Teaching in Higher Education*. Available at http://www.tandfonline.com/doi/abs/10.1080/13562517.2011.611870. Accessed 24th November 2011.

Tusón, J. (1997). *La escritura. Una introducción a la cultura alfabética [Writing. An introduction to the literacy culture]*. Barcelona: Octaedro.

Tutin, A. (2010). Dans cet article, nous souhaitons montrer que … Lexique verbal et positionnement de l'auteur dans les articles en sciences humaines [In this article, we wish to show that… Verbal lexicón and autor positioning in humanities articles]. *LIDIL, 41*, 15–40.

Tynjälä, P. (1998). Traditional study for examination versus constructivist learning tasks: do learning outcomes differ? *Studies in Higher Education, 23*(2), 173–189.

Tynjälä, P., Mason, L., & Lonka, K. (2001). Writing as a learning tool: An introduction. In P. Tynjälä, L. Mason & K. Lonka (Eds.), *Writing as a learning tool. Integrating theory and practice* (pp. 7–22). Dordrecht: Kluwer Academic Publishers.

Valdes, G. (1997). Dual-Language immersion programs: A cautionary note concerning the education of language-minority students. *Harvard Educational Review, 67*(3), 391–430.

Valsiner, J., & Rosa, A. (Eds.). (2007). *The Cambridge handbook of sociocultural psychology*. Cambridge: Cambridge University Press.

Van Dijk, T. (2001). Critical discourse analysis. In D. Schiffrin, D. Tannen & H. Hamilton (Eds.), *The handbook of discourse analysis* (pp. 352–371). Malden, MA: Blackwell Publishing.

Vande Kopple, W. (1985). Some exploratory discourse on metadiscourse. *College Composition and Communication, 36*, 82–93.

Vargolici, N. (2004). *Redactare și corespondență*. Bucuresti: Univ. București.

Vazquez, A., Pelizza, L. Jakob, I., & Rosales, P. (2007). *Enseñanza de estrategias de autorregulación para la escritura de textos académicos en el nivel universitario [Teaching self-regulation strategies for writing academic texts in university education]*. Retrieved July 27,

2011 from http://www.educ.ar/educar/lm/1189101056178/kbee:/educar/content/portal-content/ taxonomia-recursos/recurso/153c38e7-8036-43e3-ac11-46826003321a.recurso/a043ffb4-f044-4a72-9514-c057c5b9fdf2/estrategias_de_autorregulacion.pdf

Venuti, L. (1993). Translation as cultural politics: Regimes of domestication in English. *Textual Practice*, *7*, 208–223.

Vergaro, C. (2011). Shades of impersonality: Rhetorical positioning in the academic setting. *Linguistics and Education*, *22*, 118–132.

Villalón, R., & Mateos, M. (2009). Concepciones del alumnado de secundaria y universidad sobre la escritura académica [Secondary and university students' conceptions about academic writing]. *Infancia y Aprendizaje*, *32*(2), 219–232.

Vincent, G. (Ed.) (1994). *L'éducation prisonnière de la forme scolaire? Scolarisation et socialisation dans les sociétés industrielles [Education, prisoner of the school form? Schooling and socialization in industrial societies]*. Lyon: Presses Universitaires de Lyon.

Vines, A. (2009). Multivoiced e-feedback in the study of law: Enhancing learning opportunities? In R. Krumsvik (Ed.), *Learning in the network society and the digitized school* (pp. 75–201). New York, NY: Nova Science.

Vines, A., & Dysthe, O. (2009). Productive learning in the study of law: The role of technology in the learning ecology of a law faculty. In L. Dirckinck-Holmfeld, C. Jones & B. Lindström (Eds.), *Analysing networked learning practices. Technology-enhanced learning series*. Rotterdam, NL: Sense publishers.

Volet, S., Summers, M., & y Thurman, J. (2009). High-level co-regulation in collaborative learning: How does it emerge and how is it sustained? *Learning and Instruction*, *19*, 128–143.

Vološinov, V. N. (1986). *Marxism and the philosophy of language*. (L. Matejka & I. R. Titunik, Trans.). Cambridge, MA: Harvard University Press.

Vygotsky, L. S. (1978). *Mind in society*. Cambridge, MA: Harvard University Press.

Vygotsky, L. S. (1997). The history of the development of higher mental functions. In R. W. Rieber (Ed.), *The collected works of L.S. Vygotsky. The history of the development of higher mental functions* (Vols. 4). New York, NY: Plenum.

Wake, J. D., Dysthe, O., & Mjelstad, S. (2007). New and changing teacher roles in a digital age. *Educational Technology & Society*, *10*(1), 40–51.

Walker, R. (2007). Sociocultural perspectives on academic regulation and identity: Theoretical issues. *Proceedings from the12th biennial conference for research on learning and instruction*. Budapest, Hungary.

Walvoord, B., & McCarthy, L. (1990). *Thinking and writing in college: A naturalistic study of students in four disciplines*. Urbana, IL: NCTE.

Wang, M., & Bakken, L. L. (2004). An academic writing needs assessment of English as-a-second-language clinical investigators. *The Journal of Continuing Education in the Health Professions*, *24*, 181–189.

Webb, C., Dury, H., & English, L. (1995). Collaboration in subject design: Integration of the teaching and assessment of literacy skills into a first year accounting course. *Accounting Education*, *4*, 335–350.

Welch, M. (1992). The please strategy-a metacognitive learning- strategy for improving the paragraph writing of students with mild learning disabilities. *Learning Disability Quarterly*, *15*, 119–128.

Wells, G. (1988). *Aprender a leer y escribir [Learning to read and write]*. Barcelona: Laia.

Wenger, E. (1998). *Communities of practice. Learning, meaning and identity*. Cambridge/New York: Cambridge University Press.

Wertsch, J. V. (1991). *Voices of the mind, sociocultural approach to mediated action*. Cambridge, MA: Harvard University Press.

White, M. J., & Bruning, R. (2005). Implicit writing beliefs and their relation to writing quality. *Contemporary Educational Psychology, 30*, 166–189.

Williams, B. T. (2009). *Shimmering literacies: Popular culture & reading and writing online*. New York, NY: Peter Lang.

Williams, I. A. (1999). Results sections of medial research articles: Analysis of rhetorical categories for pedagogical purposes. *English for Specific Purposes, 18*, 347–366.

Winsor, D. (1996). *Writing like an engineer*. Mahwah, NJ: Lawrence Erlbaum.

Wong, B. Y. L. (1999). Metacognition in writing. In R. Gallimore, C. Bernheimer, D. MacMillan, D. Speece & S. Vaughn (Eds.), *Developmental perspectives on children with high incidence disabilities: Papers in honor of Barbara K. Keogh* (pp. 183–198). Mahwah, NJ: Erlbaum.

Wood, A. (1982). An examination of the rhetorical structures of authentic chemistry texts. *Applied Linguistics, 3*(2), 121–143.

Yañez, A., & Russell, D. R. (2009). "The world is too messy": The challenge of writing in a general-education liberal arts course. In J. Castner Post & J. A. Inman (Eds.), *Composition(s) in the new liberal arts* (pp. 43–75). Cresskill, NJ: Hampton Press.

Zamel, V., & Spack, R. (Eds.). (1998). *Negotiating academic literacies: Teaching and learning across languages and cultures*. Mahwah, NJ: Lawrence Erlbaum.

Zuber-Skerritt, O., & Knight, N. (1986). Problem definition and thesis writing. Workshops for the post-graduate student. *Higher Education, 15*, 89–103.

Author Index

Subject Index

List of Volumes

Volume 1: Theories, Models and Methodology in Writing Research
Gert Rijlaarsdam, Huub van den Bergh, Michel Couzijn (Eds.) 1996
558 pages; Paperback ISBN 90-5356-197-8

Volume 2: Effective Teaching and Learning of Writing. Current Trends in Research
Gert Rijlaarsdam, Huub van den Bergh, Michel Couzijn (Eds.) 1996
pages 388; Paperback ISBN 90-5356-198-6

Volume 3: The Cognitive Demands of Writing. Processing Capacity and Working Memory Effects in Text Production
Mark Torrance, Gaynor Jeffery (Eds.) 1999
pages 113; Paperback ISBN 90-5356-308-3

Volume 4: Knowing What to Write. Conceptual Processes in Text Production
Mark Torrance, David Galbraith (Eds.) 1999
pages 190; Paperback ISBN 90-5356-307-5

Volume 5: Foundations of Argumentative Text Processing
Pierre Coirier, Jerry Andriessen (Eds.) 2000
Pages 273; Paperback 90-5356-340-7

Volume 6: Metalinguistic Activity in Learning to Write
Anna Camps, Marta Milian (Eds.) 2000
pages 228; Paperback 90-5356-341-5

Volume 7: Writing as a Learning Tool
Päivi Tynjälä, Lucia Mason, Kirsti Lonka (Eds.) 2001
Hardbound, ISBN 0-7923-6877-0; Paperback, ISBN 0-7923-6914-9

Volume 8: Developmental Aspects in Learning to Write
Liliana Tolchinsky (Ed.) 2001
Paperback, ISBN 0-7923-7063-5; Hardbound, ISBN 0-7923-6979-3

Volume 9: Through the Models of Writing
Denis Alamargot, Lucile Chanquoy (Eds.) (2001)
Paperback, ISBN 0-7923-7159-3; Hardbound, ISBN 0-7923-6980-7

Volume 22: Voices, Identities, Negotiations, and Conflicts: Writing Academic English Across Cultures
Phan La Ha, Bradley Baurain (Eds.) 2011
233 pp., Hardcover ISBN: 9780857247193

Volume 23: Research on Writing Approaches in Mental Health
Luciano L'Abate, Laura G. Sweeney (Eds.) 2011
250 pp., Hardcover ISBN: 978-0-85724-955-5

Printed in the United States
By Bookmasters